Animal Stories

For Ted, who helped us make this book
Andrew and Michael

ISBN 0-439-40982-9

This selection and introductions copyright © 1999 by Michael Morpurgo. Illustrations copyright © 1993, 1996, 1999 by Andrew Davidson. The acknowledgments on pages 222 and 223 constitute an extension of this copyright page. The moral right of the compiler, authors, and illustrator has been asserted. All rights reserved. Published by Scholastic Inc., 557 Broadway, New York, NY 10012, by arrangement with Larousse Kingfisher Chambers Inc. SCHOLASTIC and associated logos are trademarks and/or registered trademarks of Scholastic Inc.

12 11 10 9 8 7 6 5 4 3 2   2 3 4 5 6 7/0

Printed in the U.S.A.   40

First Scholastic printing, March 2002

Animal Stories

CHOSEN BY
Michael Morpurgo

ILLUSTRATED BY
Andrew Davidson

SCHOLASTIC INC.
New York Toronto London Auckland Sydney
Mexico City New Delhi Hong Kong Buenos Aires

CONTENTS

INTRODUCTION

I T IS A STRANGE PHENOMENON, but the more urban our lives become, the more we seem to be fascinated by the wildlife that surrounds us. For most of us now, the world of nature, of animals, of the outdoors, is brought to us by television. The lives of otters, of elephants, of pelicans, of the badger, and the rat are brought right into our living rooms. They come to us. We see them second hand, through a glass, distantly. In all the history of mankind, we have never been so isolated from the natural world around us, yet at the same time we are still entranced by it. I think I know why.

I think we yearn to feel close to our fellow creatures. We long to feel we are part of their world, not mere observers. Certainly that is true for me. I am lucky enough to live and work in the heart of the countryside. As I write this, sheep are shifting in the field outside my window, policed by foraging crows, a blue tit clings upside down in the thatch searching for insects in the straw, a whirl of starlings unfolds in the wind and is buffeted away over Innocents' Copse. I have only to put on my boots and walk down the high-hedged lane toward the Torridge River to see where the badger passed last night on his way up his alley through the field hedge. My nose tells me a fox has been by even more recently. Down by the river I might see a heron lifting off and lumbering skyward, and I might hear the slap of a leaping salmon and the plop of a water rat. If I'm lucky, I'll spot a kingfisher flashing by, straight as a jeweled arrow—gone before I saw it. And if I'm very silent, still, and patient, I might know that moment again when an otter came up out of the river and saw me sitting there. He did not run away. We just met. And tonight when I go milking under a star-filled sky, the vixen will cry at me and the tawny owl will let me know he's there and watching, and I'll feel part of it all, just one of them.

It has been such a joy to gather together this selection of stories, to discover new voices, and to hear once again voices I had almost forgotten—to me a story on the page is a told thing, a sounding thing. I have just chosen what I love, that's all there is to it. Certainly there is a unifying theme in the collection—the animal world we live in and are part of. But the writers relate to this world in a multiplicity of ways, seeking always to understand it better, to discover or explain the elemental connections between man and beast and planet. There are of course naturalistic stories of animal life, but there are anthropomorphic folk tales, too, scientific recording, stories that concern the emotional ties we have with nature and animals, our interreliance, our shared existence. So look for no coherent pattern, look just for wonderful storytelling and fine writing, inspired in each case by the writer's intense closeness to his subject, by his intense knowledge and love of it. It is that that draws us in, brings us close again to our fellowship with the world around us and the creatures that inhabit it.

Michael Morpurgo
June 1999

THE BIRDS BEGAN TO SING

JANET FRAME

To begin: an exquisite prose poem about seeing, about listening, about being, by a wonderful writer best known for her autobiography, An Angel at My Table. *She felt life keenly, and spent many long years searching for "the name of the song."*

THE BIRDS BEGAN TO SING. There were four and twenty of them singing, and they were blackbirds.

And I said, what are you singing all day and night, in the sun and the dark and the rain, and in the wind that turns the tops of the trees silver?

We are singing, they said. We are singing and we have just begun, and we've a long way to sing, and we can't stop, we've got to go on and on. Singing.

The birds began to sing.

I put on my coat and I walked in the rain over the hills. I walked through swamps full of red water, and down gullies covered in snowberries, and then up gullies again, with snow grass growing there, and speargrass, and over creeks near flax and tussock and manuka.

I saw a pine tree on top of a hill.

I saw a skylark dipping and rising.

I saw it was snowing somewhere over the hills, but not where I was.

I stood on a hill and looked and looked.

I wasn't singing. I tried to sing but I couldn't think of the song.

So I went back home to the boardinghouse where I live, and I sat on the stairs at the front and I listened. I listened with my head and my eyes and my brain and my hands. With my body.

The birds began to sing.

They were blackbirds sitting on the telegraph wires and hopping on the apple trees. There were four and twenty of them singing.

What is the song? I said. Tell me the name of the song.

I am a human being and I read books and I hear music and I like to see things in print. I like to see *vivace andante* words by music by performed by written for. So I said what is the name of the song, tell me and I will write it and you can listen at my window when I get the finest musicians in the country to play it, and you will feel so nice to hear your song so tell me the name.

They stopped singing. It was dark outside although the sun was shining. It was dark and there was no more singing.

THE SNOW GOOSE

PAUL GALLICO

I have always loved this story. Rhayader is a recluse, seen and feared as an ogre by local children, until one of them, Frith, dares to bring a wounded snow goose to the lighthouse where he lives—for he is known to care for all wild things.

ONE NOVEMBER AFTERNOON, three years after Rhayader had come to the Great Marsh, a child approached the lighthouse studio by means of the sea wall. In her arms she carried a burden.

She was no more than twelve, slender, dirty, nervous, and timid as a bird, but beneath the grime as eerily beautiful as a marsh fairy. She was pure Saxon, large-boned, fair, with a head to which her body was yet to grow, and deep-set, violet-colored eyes.

She was desperately frightened of the ugly man she had come to see, for legend had already begun to gather about Rhayader, and the native wild-fowlers hated him for interfering with their sport.

But greater than her fear was the need of that which she bore. For locked in her child's heart was the knowledge, picked up somewhere in the swampland, that this ogre who lived in the lighthouse had magic that could heal injured things.

She had never seen Rhayader before and was close to fleeing in panic at the dark apparition that appeared at the studio door, drawn by her footsteps—the black head and beard, the sinister hump, and the crooked claw.

She stood there staring, poised like a disturbed marsh bird for instant flight.

But his voice was deep and kind when he spoke to her.

"What is it, child?"

She stood her ground, and then edged timidly forward. The thing she carried in her arms was a large white bird, and it was quite still. There were stains of blood on its whiteness and on her kirtle where she had held it to her.

The girl placed it in his arms. "I found it, sir. It's hurted. Is it still alive?"

"Yes. Yes, I think so. Come in, child, come in."

Rhayader went inside, bearing the bird, which he placed upon a table, where it moved feebly. Curiosity overcame fear. The girl followed and found herself in a room warmed by a coal fire, shining with many colored pictures that covered the walls, and full of a strange but pleasant smell.

The bird fluttered. With his good hand Rhayader spread one of its immense white pinions. The end was beautifully tipped with black.

Rhayader looked and marveled, and said: "Child! where did you find it?"

"In t' marsh, sir, where fowlers had been. What—what is it, sir?"

"It's a snow goose from Canada. But how in all heaven came it here?"

The name seemed to mean nothing to the little girl. Her deep violet eyes, shining out of the dirt on her thin face, were fixed with concern on the injured bird.

She said: "Can 'ee heal it, sir?"

"Yes, yes," said Rhayader. "We will try. Come, you shall help me."

There were scissors and bandages and splints on a shelf, and he was marvelously deft, even with the crooked claw that managed to hold things.

He said: "Ah, she has been shot, poor thing. Her leg is broken, and the wing tip! but not badly. See, we will clip her primaries, so that we can bandage it, but in the spring the feathers will grow and she will be able to fly again. We'll bandage it close to her body, so that she cannot move it until it has set, and then make a splint for the poor leg."

Her fears forgotten, the child watched, fascinated, as he worked, and all the more so because while he fixed a fine splint to the shattered leg he told her the most wonderful story.

The bird was a young one, no more than a year old. She was born in a northern land far, far across the seas, a land belonging to England. Flying to the south to escape the snow and ice and bitter cold, a great storm had seized her and whirled and buffeted her about. It was a truly terrible storm, stronger than her great wings, stronger than anything. For days and nights it held her in its grip and there was nothing she could do but fly before it. When finally it had blown itself out and her sure instincts took her south again, she was over different land and surrounded by strange birds that she had never seen before. At last, exhausted by her ordeal, she had sunk to rest in a friendly green marsh, only to be met by the blast from the hunter's gun.

"A bitter reception for a visiting princess," concluded Rhayader. "We will call her '*La Princesse Perdue*,' the Lost Princess. And in a few days she will be feeling much better.

See!" He reached into his pocket and produced a handful of grain. The snow goose opened its round yellow eyes and nibbled at it.

The child laughed with delight, and then suddenly caught her breath with alarm as the full import of where she was pressed in upon her, and without a word she turned and fled out of the door.

"Wait, wait!" cried Rhayader, and went to the entrance, where he stopped so that it framed his dark bulk. The girl was already fleeing down the sea wall, but she paused at his voice and looked back.

"What is your name, child?"

"Frith."

"Eh?" said Rhayader. "Fritha, I suppose. Where do you live?"

"Wi' t' fisherfolk at Wickaeldroth." She gave the name the old Saxon pronunciation.

"Will you come back tomorrow, or the next day, to see how the Princess is getting along?"

She paused, and again Rhayader must have thought of the wild water birds caught motionless in that split second of alarm before they took to flight.

But her thin voice came back to him: "Ay!"

And then she was gone, with her fair hair streaming out behind her.

The snow goose mended rapidly and by midwinter was already limping about the enclosure with the wild pink-footed geese with which it associated, rather than the barnacles, and had learned to come to be fed at Rhayader's call. And the child, Fritha, or Frith, was a frequent visitor. She had overcome her fear of Rhayader. Her imagination was captured by the presence of this strange white princess from a land far over the sea, a land that was all pink, as she knew from the map that Rhayader showed her, and on which they traced the stormy path of the lost bird from its home in Canada to the Great Marsh of Essex.

Then one June morning a group of late pink-feet, fat and well fed from the winter at the lighthouse, answered the stronger call of the breeding grounds and rose lazily, climbing into the sky in ever-widening circles. With them, her white body and black-tipped pinions shining in the spring sun, was the snow goose. It so happened that Frith was at the lighthouse. Her cry brought Rhayader running from the studio.

"Look! Look! The Princess! Be she going away?"

Rhayader stared into the sky at the climbing specks. "Ay," he said, unconsciously dropping into her manner of speech. "The Princess is going home. Listen! she is bidding us farewell."

Out of the clear sky came the mournful barking of the pink-feet, and above it the higher, clearer note of the snow goose. The specks drifted northward, formed into a tiny *v*, diminished, and vanished.

With the departure of the snow goose ended the visits of Frith to the lighthouse. Rhayader learned all over again the meaning of the word "loneliness."

That summer, out of his memory, he painted a picture of a slender, grime-covered child, her fair hair blown by a November storm, who bore in her arms a wounded white bird.

In mid-October the miracle occurred. Rhayader was in his enclosure, feeding his birds. A gray northeast wind was blowing and the land was sighing beneath the incoming tide. Above the sea and the wind noises he heard a clear, high note. He turned his eyes upward to the evening sky in time to see first an infinite speck, then a black-and-white pinioned dream that circled the lighthouse once, and

finally a reality that dropped to earth in the pen and came waddling forward importantly to be fed, as though she had never been away. It was the snow goose. There was no mistaking her. Tears of joy came to Rhayader's eyes. Where had she been? Surely not home to Canada. No, she must have summered in Greenland or Spitzbergen with the pink-feet. She had remembered and had returned.

When next Rhayader went into Chelmbury for supplies, he left a message with the postmistress—one that must have caused her much bewilderment. He said: "Tell Frith, who lives with the fisherfolk at Wickaeldroth, that the Lost Princess has returned."

Three days later, Frith, taller, still tousled and unkempt, came shyly to the lighthouse to visit *La Princesse Perdue*.

Time passed. On the Great Marsh it was marked by the height of the tides, the slow march of the season, the passage of the birds, and, for Rhayader, by the arrival and departure of the snow goose.

The world outside boiled and seethed and rumbled with the eruption that was soon to break forth and come close to marking its destruction. But not yet did it touch upon Rhayader, or, for that matter, Frith. They had fallen into a curious natural rhythm, even as the child grew older. When the snow goose was at the lighthouse, then she came, too, to visit and learn many things from Rhayader. They sailed together in his speedy boat, that he handled so skillfully. They caught wildfowl for the ever-increasing colony, and built new pens and enclosures for them. From him she learned the lore of every wild bird, from gull to gyrfalcon, that flew the marshes. She cooked for him sometimes, and even learned to mix his paints.

But when the snow goose returned to its summer home it was as though some kind of bar was up between them, and she did not come to the lighthouse. One year the bird did not return, and Rhayader was heartbroken. All things seemed to have ended for him. He painted furiously through the winter and the next summer, and never once saw the child. But in the fall the familiar cry once more rang from the sky, and the huge white bird, now at its full growth, dropped from the skies as mysteriously as it had departed. Joyously, Rhayader sailed his boat into Chelmbury and left his message with the postmistress.

Curiously, it was more than a month after he had left the message before Frith reappeared at the lighthouse, and Rhayader, with a shock, realized that she was a child no longer.

After the year in which the bird had remained away, its periods of absence grew shorter and shorter. It had grown so tame that it followed Rhayader about and even came into the studio while he was working.

In the spring of 1940 the birds migrated early from the Great Marsh. The world was on fire. The whine and roar of the bombers and the thudding explosions frightened them. The first day of May, Frith and Rhayader stood shoulder to shoulder on the sea wall and watched the last of the unpinioned pink-feet and barnacle geese rise from their sanctuary; she, tall, slender, free as air and hauntingly beautiful; he, dark, grotesque, his massive bearded head raised to the sky, his glowing eyes watching the geese form their flight tracery.

"Look, Philip," Frith said.

Rhayader followed her eyes. The snow goose had taken flight, her giant wings spread, but she was flying low, and once came quite close to them, so that for a moment the spreading black-tipped, white pinions seemed to caress them and they felt the rush of the bird's swift passage. Once, twice, she circled the lighthouse, then dropped to earth again in the enclosure with the pinioned geese and commenced to feed.

"She be'ent going," said Frith, with marvel in her voice. The bird in its close passage seemed to have woven a kind of magic about her. "The Princess be goin' t' stay."

"Ay," said Rhayader, and his voice was shaken too. "She'll stay. She will never go away again. The Lost Princess is lost no more. This is her home now—of her own free will."

The spell the bird had girt about her was broken, and Frith was suddenly conscious of the fact that she was frightened, and the things that frightened her were in Rhayader's eyes—the longing and the loneliness and the deep, welling, unspoken things that lay in and behind them as he turned them upon her.

His last words were repeating themselves in her head as though he had said them again: "This is her home now—of her own free will." The delicate tendrils of her instincts reached to him and carried to her the message of the things he could not speak because of what he felt himself to be, misshapen and grotesque. And where his voice might have soothed her, her fright grew greater at his silence and the power of the unspoken things between them. The woman in her bade her take flight from something that she was not yet capable of understanding.

Frith said: "I—I must go. Good-bye. I be glad the—the Princess will stay. You'll not be so alone now."

She turned and walked swiftly away, and his sadly spoken "Good-bye, Frith," was only a half-heard ghost of a sound borne to her ears above the rustling of the marsh grass. She was far away before she dared turn for a backward glance. He was still standing on the sea wall, a dark speck against the sky.

Her fear had stilled now. It had been replaced by

something else, a queer sense of loss that made her stand quite still for a moment, so sharp was it. Then, more slowly, she continued on, away from the skyward-pointing finger of the lighthouse and the man beneath it.

THE HAPPY PRINCE

OSCAR WILDE

Here, in one of my favourite stories, everyone speaks: the townspeople, the statue of the Happy Prince—even the Swallow. Wilde thereby weaves the most tragic and touching of fairy tales, which uses an animal to tell us so much about ourselves.

HIGH ABOVE THE CITY, on a tall column, stood the statue of the Happy Prince. He was gilded all over with thin leaves of fine gold, for eyes he had two bright sapphires, and a large red ruby glowed on his sword hilt.

He was very much admired indeed. "He is as beautiful as a weathercock," remarked one of the Town Councillors who wished to gain a reputation for having artistic tastes; "only not quite so useful," he added, fearing lest people should think him unpractical, which he really was not.

"Why can't you be like the Happy Prince?" asked a sensible mother of her little boy who was crying for the moon. "The Happy Prince never dreams of crying for anything."

"I am glad there is someone in the world who is quite

happy," muttered a disappointed man as he gazed at the wonderful statue.

"He looks just like an angel," said the Charity Children as they came out of the cathedral in their bright scarlet cloaks and their clean white pinafores.

"How do you know?" said the Mathematical Master, "you have never seen one."

"Ah! but we have, in our dreams," answered the children; and the Mathematical Master frowned and looked very severe, for he did not approve of children dreaming.

One night there flew over the city a little Swallow. His friends had gone away to Egypt six weeks before, but he had stayed behind, for he was in love with the most beautiful Reed. He had met her early in the spring as he was flying down the river after a big yellow moth, and had been so attracted by her slender waist that he had stopped to talk to her.

"Shall I love you?" said the Swallow, who liked to come to the point at once, and the Reed made him a low bow. So he flew around and around her, touching the water with his wings, and making silver ripples. This was his courtship, and it lasted all through the summer.

"It is a ridiculous attachment," twittered the other Swallows, "she has no money, and far too many relations"; and indeed the river was quite full of Reeds. Then, when the autumn came they all flew away.

After they had gone he felt lonely, and began to tire of his ladylove. "She has no conversation," he said, "and I am afraid that she is a coquette, for she is always flirting with the wind." And certainly, whenever the wind blew, the Reed made the most graceful curtsies. "I admit that she is domestic," he continued, "but I love traveling, and my wife, consequently, should love traveling also."

"Will you come away with me?" he said finally to her; but the Reed shook her head, she was so attached to her home.

"You have been trifling with me," he cried. "I am off to the Pyramids. Goodbye!" and he flew away.

All day long he flew, and at nighttime he arrived at the city. "Where shall I put up?" he said; "I hope the town has made preparations."

Then he saw the statue on the tall column.

"I will put up there," he cried; "it is a fine position, with plenty of fresh air." So he alighted just between the feet of the Happy Prince.

"I have a golden bedroom," he said softly to himself as he looked around, and he prepared to go to sleep; but just as he was putting his head under his wing a large drop of water fell on him. "What a curious thing!" he cried; "there is not a single cloud in the sky, the stars are quite clear and bright, and yet it is raining. The climate in the north of Europe is really dreadful. The Reed used to like the rain, but that was merely her selfishness."

Then another drop fell.

"What is the use of a statue if it cannot keep the rain off?" he said; "I must look for a good chimney pot," and he determined to fly away.

But before he had opened his wings, a third drop fell, and he looked up, and saw—Ah! what did he see?

The eyes of the Happy Prince were filled with tears, and tears were running down his golden cheeks. His face was so beautiful in the moonlight that the little Swallow was filled with pity.

"Who are you?" he said.

"I am the Happy Prince."

"Why are you weeping then?" asked the Swallow; "you have quite drenched me."

"When I was alive and had a human heart," answered the statue, "I did not know what tears were, for I lived in the Palace of Sans-Souci, where sorrow is not allowed to enter. In the daytime, I played with my companions in the garden, and in the evening I led the dance in the Great Hall. Around the garden ran a very lofty wall, but I never cared to ask what lay beyond it, everything around me was so beautiful. My courtiers called me the Happy Prince, and happy indeed I was, if pleasure be happiness. So I lived, and so I died. And now that I am dead they have set me up here so high that I can see all the ugliness and all the misery of my city, and though my heart is made of lead yet I cannot choose but weep."

"What! Is he not solid gold?" said the Swallow to himself. He was too polite to make any personal remarks out loud.

"Far away," continued the statue in a low musical voice, "far away in a little street there is a poor house. One of the windows is open, and through it I can see a woman seated at a table. Her face is thin and worn, and she has coarse, red hands, all pricked by the needle, for she is a seamstress. She is embroidering passionflowers on a satin gown for the loveliest of the Queen's maids of honor to wear at the next Court ball. In a bed in the corner of the room her little boy is lying ill. He has a fever, and is asking for oranges. His mother has nothing to give him but river water, so he is crying. Swallow, Swallow, little Swallow, will you not bring her the ruby out of my sword-hilt? My feet are fastened to this pedestal and I cannot move."

"I am waited for in Egypt," said the Swallow. "My friends are flying up and down the Nile, and talking to the large lotus flowers. Soon they will go to sleep in the tomb of the great King. The King is there himself in his painted coffin. He is wrapped in yellow linen, and embalmed with spices. Around his neck is a chain of pale green jade, and his hands are like withered leaves."

"Swallow, Swallow, little Swallow," said the Prince, "will you not stay with me for one night, and be my messenger? The boy is so thirsty, and the mother so sad."

"I don't think I like boys," answered the Swallow. "Last summer, when I was staying on the river, there were two rude boys, the miller's sons, who were always throwing stones at me. They never hit me, of course; we swallows fly far too well for that, and besides, I come of a family famous for its agility; but still, it was a mark of disrespect."

But the Happy Prince looked so sad that the little Swallow was sorry. "It is very cold here," he said; "but I will stay with you for one night, and be your messenger."

"Thank you, little Swallow," said the Prince.

So the Swallow picked out the great ruby from the Prince's sword, and flew away with it in his beak over the roofs of the town.

He passed by the cathedral tower, where the white marble angels were sculptured. He passed by the palace and heard the sound of dancing. A beautiful girl came out on the balcony with her lover. "How wonderful the stars are," he said to her, "and how wonderful is the power of love!"

"I hope my dress will be ready in time for the State ball," she answered; "I have ordered passionflowers to be embroidered on it; but the seamstresses are so lazy."

He passed over the river, and saw the lanterns hanging to the masts of the ships. He passed over the Ghetto, and saw the old Jews bargaining with each other, and weighing out money in copper scales. At last he came to the poor house and looked in. The boy was tossing feverishly on his bed, and the mother had fallen asleep, she was so tired. In he hopped, and laid the great ruby on the table beside the woman's thimble. Then he flew gently round the bed, fanning the boy's forehead with his wings. "How cool I feel," said the boy, "I must be getting better"; and he sank into a delicious slumber.

Then the Swallow flew back to the Happy Prince, and told him what he had done. "It is curious," he remarked, "but I feel quite warm now, although it is so cold."

"That is because you have done a good action," said the Prince. And the little swallow began to think, and then he fell asleep. Thinking always made him sleepy.

When day broke he flew down to the river and had a bath. "What a remarkable phenomenon," said the Professor of Ornithology as he was passing over the bridge. "A swallow in winter!" And he wrote a long letter about it to the local newspaper. Everyone quoted it, it was full of so many words that they could not understand.

"Tonight I go to Egypt," said the Swallow, and he was in high spirits at the prospect. He visited all the public monuments, and sat a long time on top of the church steeple. Wherever he went the Sparrows chirruped, and said to each other, "What a distinguished stranger!" so he enjoyed himself very much.

When the moon rose he flew back to the Happy Prince. "Have you any commissions for Egypt?" he cried; "I am just starting."

"Swallow, Swallow, little Swallow," said the Prince, "will you not stay with me one night longer?"

"I am waited for in Egypt," answered the Swallow." Tomorrow my friends will fly up to the Second Cataract. The river horse couches there among the bulrushes, and on a great granite throne sits the God Memnon. All night long he watches the stars, and when the morning star shines he utters one cry of joy, and then he is silent. At noon the yellow lions come down to the water's edge to drink. They have eyes like green beryls, and their roar is louder than the roar of the cataract."

"Swallow, Swallow, little Swallow," said the Prince, "far

away across the city I see a young man in a garret. He is leaning over a desk covered with papers, and in a tumbler by his side there is a bunch of withered violets. His hair is brown and crisp, and his lips are red as a pomegranate, and he has large and dreamy eyes. He is trying to finish a play for the Director of the Theater, but he is too cold to write any more. There is no fire in the grate, and hunger has made him faint."

"I will wait with you one night longer," said the Swallow, who really had a good heart. "Shall I take him another ruby?"

"Alas! I have no ruby now," said the Prince; "my eyes are all that I have left. They are made of rare sapphires, which were brought out of India a thousand years ago. Pluck out one of them and take it to him. He will sell it to the jeweler, and buy food and firewood, and finish his play."

"Dear Prince," said the Swallow, "I cannot do that"; and he began to weep.

"Swallow, Swallow, little Swallow," said the Prince, "do as I command you."

So the Swallow plucked out the Prince's eye, and flew away to the student's garret. It was easy enough to get in, as there was a hole in the roof. Through this he darted, and came into the room. The young man had his head buried in his hands, so he did not hear the flutter of the bird's wings, and when he looked up he found the beautiful sapphire lying on the withered violets.

"I am beginning to be appreciated," he cried; "this is from some great admirer. Now I can finish my play," and he looked quite happy.

The next day the Swallow flew down to the harbor. He sat on the mast of a large vessel and watched the sailors hauling big chests out of the hold with ropes. "Heave a-hoy!" they shouted as each chest came up. "I am going to

Egypt!" cried the Swallow, but nobody minded, and when the moon rose he flew back to the Happy Prince.

"I am come to bid you goodbye," he cried.

"Swallow, Swallow, little Swallow," said the Prince, "will you not stay with me one night longer?"

"It is winter," answered the Swallow, "and the chill snow will soon be here. In Egypt the sun is warm on the green palm trees, and the crocodiles lie in the mud and look lazily about them. My companions are building a nest in the Temple of Baalbec, and the pink and white doves are watching them, and cooing to each other. Dear Prince, I must leave you, but I will never forget you, and next spring I will bring you back two beautiful jewels in place of those you have given away. The ruby shall be redder than a red rose, and the sapphire shall be as blue as the great sea."

"In the square below," said the Happy Prince, "there stands a little matchgirl. She has let her matches fall in the gutter, and they are all spoiled. Her father will beat her if she does not bring home some money, and she is crying. She has no shoes or stockings, and her little head is bare. Pluck out my other eye, and give it to her, and her father will not beat her."

"I will stay with you one night longer," said the Swallow, "but I cannot pluck out your eye. You would be quite blind then."

"Swallow, Swallow, little Swallow," said the Prince, "do as I command you."

So he plucked out the Prince's other eye, and darted down with it. He swooped past the matchgirl, and slipped the jewel into the palm of her hand. "What a lovely bit of glass," cried the little girl; and she ran home, laughing.

Then the Swallow came back to the Prince. "You are blind now," he said, "so I will stay with you always."

"No, little Swallow," said the poor Prince, "you must go

away to Egypt."

"I will stay with you always," said the Swallow, and he slept at the Prince's feet.

All the next day he sat on the Prince's shoulder, and told him stories of what he had seen in strange lands. He told him of the red ibises, who stand in long rows on the banks of the Nile, and catch goldfish in their beaks; of the Sphinx, who is as old as the world itself, and lives in the desert, and knows everything; of the merchants, who walk slowly by the side of their camels and carry amber beads in their hands; of the King of the Mountains of the Moon, who is as black as ebony, and worships a large crystal; of the great green snake that sleeps in a palm tree, and has twenty priests to feed it with honey cakes; and of the pygmies who sail over a big lake on large flat leaves, and are always at war with the butterflies.

"Dear little Swallow," said the Prince, "you tell me of marvelous things, but more marvelous than anything is the suffering of men and of women. There is no Mystery so great as Misery. Fly over my city, little Swallow, and tell me what you see there."

So the Swallow flew over the great city, and saw the rich making merry in their beautiful houses, while the beggars were sitting at the gates. He flew into dark lanes, and saw the white faces of starving children looking out listlessly at the black streets. Under the archway of a bridge two little boys were lying in one another's arms to try and keep themselves warm. "How hungry we are!" they said. "You must not lie here," shouted the Watchman, and they wandered out into the rain.

Then he flew back and told the Prince what he had seen.

"I am covered with fine gold," said the Prince, "you must take it off, leaf by leaf, and give it to my poor; the living always think that gold can make them happy."

Leaf after leaf of the fine gold the Swallow picked off, till the Happy Prince looked quite dull and gray. Leaf after leaf of the fine gold he brought to the poor, and the children's faces grew rosier, and they laughed and played games in the street. "We have bread now!" they cried.

Then the snow came, and after the snow came the frost. The streets looked as if they were made of silver, they were so bright and glistening; long icicles like crystal daggers hung down from the eaves of the houses, everybody went about in furs, and the little boys wore scarlet caps and skated on the ice.

The poor little Swallow grew colder and colder, but he would not leave the Prince, he loved him too well. He picked up crumbs outside the baker's door when the baker was not looking, and tried to keep himself warm by flapping his wings.

But at last he knew that he was going to die. He had just strength to fly up to the Prince's shoulder once more. "Goodbye, dear Prince!" he murmured, "will you let me kiss your hand?"

"I am glad that you are going to Egypt at last, little Swallow," said the Prince, "you have stayed too long here; but you must kiss me on the lips, for I love you."

"It is not to Egypt that I am going," said the Swallow, "I am going to the House of Death. Death is the brother of Sleep, is he not?"

And he kissed the Happy Prince on the lips, and fell down dead at his feet.

At that moment a curious crack sounded inside the statue, as if something had broken. The fact is that the leaden heart had snapped right in two. It certainly was a dreadfully hard frost.

Early the next morning the Mayor was walking in the square below in company with the Town Councillors. As they passed the column he looked up at the statue: "Dear me! how shabby the Happy Prince looks!" he said.

"How shabby indeed!" cried the Town Councillors, who always agreed with the Mayor; and they went up to look at it.

"The ruby has fallen out of his sword, his eyes are gone, and he is golden no longer," said the Mayor; "in fact, he is little better than a beggar!"

"Little better than a beggar," said the Town Councillors.

"And here is actually a dead bird at his feet!" continued the Mayor. "We must really issue a proclamation that birds are not to be allowed to die here." And the Town Clerk made a note of the suggestion.

So they pulled down the statue of the Happy Prince. "As he is no longer beautiful he is no longer useful," said the Art Professor at the University.

Then they melted the statue in a furnace, and the Mayor held a meeting of the Corporation to decide what was to be done with the metal. "We must have another statue, of course," he said, "and it shall be a statue of myself."

"Of myself," said each of the Town Councillors, and they quarrelled. When I last heard of them they were quarrelling still.

"What a strange thing!" said the overseer of the workmen at the foundry. "This broken lead heart will not melt in the furnace. We must throw it away." So they threw it on a dustheap where the dead Swallow was also lying.

"Bring me the two most precious things in the city," said God to one of His Angels; and the Angel brought Him the leaden heart and the dead bird.

"You have rightly chosen," said God, "for in my garden of Paradise this little bird shall sing for evermore, and in my city of gold the Happy Prince shall praise me."

KES

BARRY HINES

In the harsh, urban world of northern industrial England, Billy finds an unexpected ally in life. Kes is the pride of his eye. When Billy sees her fly, he soars with her. He and his teacher, usually a remote authority figure, are brought to a closer understanding of each other. For here the roles are reversed—Billy is doing the teaching.

THE HAWK WAS WAITING FOR HIM. As he unlocked the door she screamed and pressed her face to the bars. He selected the largest piece of beef, then, holding it firmly between finger and thumb with most of it concealed in his palm, he eased the door open and shoved his glove through the space. The hawk jumped on to his glove and attacked the meat. Billy swiftly followed his fist into the hut, secured the door behind him, and while the hawk was tearing at the fringe of beef, he attached her swivel and leash.

As soon as they got outside she looked up and tensed, feathers flat, eyes threatening. Billy stood still, whistling softly, waiting for her to relax and resume her feeding.

Then he walked around the back of the hut and held her high over his head as he climbed carefully over the fence. A tall hawthorn hedge bordered one side of the field, and the wind was strong and constant in the branches, but in the field it had been strained to a whisper. He reached the center and unwound the leash from his glove, pulled it free of the swivel, then removed the swivel from the jesses and raised his fist. The hawk flapped her wings and fanned her tail, her claws still gripping the glove. Billy cast her off by nudging his glove upward, and she banked away, completed a wide circuit then gained height rapidly, while he took the lure from his bag and unwound the line from the stick.

"Come on, Kes! Come on, then!"

He whistled and swung the lure shortlined on a vertical plane. The hawk turned, saw it, and stooped . . . .

"Casper!"

He glanced involuntarily across the field. Mr. Farthing was climbing the fence and waving to him. The hawk grabbed the lure and Billy allowed her to take it to the ground.

"Bloody hellfire."

He pegged the stick into the soil and stood up. Mr. Farthing was tiptoeing toward him, concentrating on his passage through the grass. With his overcoat on, and his trousers pinched up, he looked like a day-tripper paddling at the seaside. Billy allowed him to get within thirty yards, then stopped him by raising one hand.

"You'll have to stop there, sir."

"I hope I'm not too late."

"No, sir, but you'll have to watch from there."

"That's all right. If you think I'm too near I can go back to the fence."

"No, you'll be all right there, as long as you stand still."

"I won't breathe."

He smiled and put his hands in his overcoat pockets. Billy crouched down and made in toward the hawk along the lure line. He offered her a scrap of beef, and she stepped off the lure onto his glove. He allowed her to take the beef, then he stood up and cast her off again. She wheeled away, high around the field. Billy plucked the stick from the ground and began to swing the lure. The hawk turned and stooped at it. Billy watched her as she descended, waiting for the right moment as she accelerated rapidly toward him. Now. He straightened his arm and lengthened the line, throwing the lure into her path and sweeping it before her in a downward arc, then twitching it up too steep for her attack, making her throw up, her impetus carrying her high into the air. She turned and stooped again. Billy presented the lure again. And again. Each time smoothly before her, an inch before her so that the next wing beat must catch it, or the next. Working the lure like a top matador his cape. Encouraging the hawk, making her stoop faster and harder, making Mr. Farthing hold his breath at each stoop and near miss. Each time she made off Billy called her continually, then stopped in concentration as he timed his throw and leaned into the long drawing of the lure and the hawk in its wake, her eyes fixed, beak open, angling her body and adjusting her flight to any slight shift in speed or direction.

She tried a new tactic, and came in low, seeming to flit within a pocket of silence close to the ground. Billy flexed at the knees and flattened the plane of the swing, allowing the lengthening line to pay out before her.

"Come on, this time, Kes! This time!"

She shortened her stoop, and counterstoop, which increased the frequency of her attacks, and made Billy pivot, and whirl, and watch, but never lose control of the lure or its pursuer. Until finally the hawk sheered away

and began to ring up high over the hawthorn hedge.

"Come on, then, Kes! Once more! Last time!"

And she came, headfirst, wings closed, swooping down, hurtling down toward Billy, who waited, then lured her—WHOOSH—up, throwing up, ringing up, turning; and as she stooped again Billy twirled the lure and threw it high into her path. She caught it, and clutched it down to the ground.

He allowed her to take the remaining beef scrap from the lure, then took her up and attached the swivel and leash. She looked up sharply at a series of claps. Mr. Farthing was applauding softly. Billy started toward him and they met halfway, the hawk fixing the stranger every second of their approach.

"Marvelous, Casper! Brilliant! That's one of the most exciting things I've ever seen!"

Billy blushed, and there was silence while they both looked at the hawk. The hawk looked back, her breast still heaving from her exertions.

"It's beautiful, isn't it? Do you know, this is the first time I've ever been really close to a hawk?"

He raised a hand toward it. The hawk pecked and clawed at it. He withdrew his hand quickly.

"Goodness! . . . It's not very friendly, is it?"

Billy smiled and stroked her breast, ruttling under her wings with his fingers.

"Seems all right with you, though."

"Only 'cos she thinks I'm not bothered."

"What do you mean?"

"Well, when she used to peck me, I kept my finger there as though it didn't hurt. So after a bit she just packed it in."

"That's good. I'd never have thought of that."

"You'll notice I always keep my hands away from her claws, though. You don't get used to them striking you."

Mr. Farthing looked at the yellow scaled shins, the four spanned toes, the steely claws gripping the gauntlet.

"No, I'll bet you don't."

Billy produced the sparrow from his bag and pushed it up between the finger and thumb of his glove. The hawk immediately pinned it with one foot and with her beak began to pluck the feathers from its head. Plucking and tossing in bunches, left and right, sowing them to the wind. Baring a spot, then a patch of puckered pink skin. She nipped this skin and pulled, ripping a hole in it and revealing the pale shine of the skull, as fragile and delicately curved as one of the sparrow's own eggs. Scrunch. The shell crumpled, and the whole crown was torn away and swallowed at one gulp. Another bite and the head was gone; even the beak was swallowed, being first finely crushed into fragments. Billy eased the sparrow up between his fingers, revealing most of its body. The hawk lowered her head and began to pluck the breast and wings. The breast fluff puffed away like fairy clocks; the wing quills twirled to the ground like ash keys. Occasionally the hawk shook her head, trying to dislodge feathers which had stuck to the blood on her beak. If this failed she scratched at them with her claws, the flickering points passing within fractions of her eyes, wincing as though half in enjoyment, half in pain, like someone having a good scratch at a nettle rash.

She cleared most of the breast, then pierced the skin with her beak and tore it open, exposing beneath the wafer of breast meat the minute organs, coiled and compact, packed perfectly into the tiny frame. The hawk disturbed their composition by reaching inside and dragging the intestines out. They swung from her beak, with the stomach attached like a watch on a chain. Then she snuffled and gobbled them down in a slithering putty-colored pile.

"Uh!"

"Full o' vitamins them, sir."

The liver, a purply-brown pad; the heart, a slippery pebble; leaving only the carcass, a mess of skin and bone and feathers, which the hawk pulled apart and devoured in pieces. Any bones which were too big to crush and swallow comfortably were flicked away; clean white fragments, precise miniatures, knobbled and hollowed and lost in the grass. Until only the legs remained. The hawk nibbled delicately at the thighs, stripping them of their last shred of meat, leaving only the tarsi and the feet, which she spat aside. All gone. She stood up and shook her head.

Mr. Farthing followed Billy over the fence, around to the front of the shed, and watched through the bars while the hawk was being released inside. She flew straight to her perch, lowered her head and began to feake, using the wood as a strop for her beak. Then she stood up and roused herself. Billy opened the door and stepped aside for Mr. Farthing to enter. He squeezed quickly inside and they stood side by side looking at the hawk, which had settled down on one foot, her other foot bunched up in her feathers.

"Keep lookin' away from her, sir, they don't like being stared at, hawks."

"Right."

Mr. Farthing glanced around at the whitewashed walls and ceiling, the fresh mutes on the clean shelves, the clean dry sand on the floor.

"You keep it nice and clean in here."

"You have to. There's less chance of her gettin' sick then."

"You think a lot about that bird, don't you?"

Billy looked up at him, all the way up to his eyes.

"Course I do. Wouldn't you if it wa' yours?"

Mr. Farthing laughed quietly, once.

"Yes I suppose I would. You like wildlife, don't you, Billy?"

"Yes, sir."

"Have you ever kept any more birds before this one?"

"Stacks. Animals an' all. I had a young fox cub once, reared it and let it go. It wa' a little blinder."

"What birds have you kept?"

"All sorts, magpies, jackdaws; I had a young jay once; that wa' murder though, they're right hard to feed, an' it nearly died. I wouldn't have one again, they're best left to their mothers."

"And which has been your favorite?"

Billy looked at Mr. Farthing as though his mentality had suddenly deteriorated to that of an idiot.

"You what, sir?"

"You mean the hawk?"

"T'others weren't in t'same street."

"Why not? What's so special about this one?"

Billy bent down and scooped up a fistful of sand.

"I don't know right. It just is, that's all."

"What about magpies? They're handsome birds. And jays, they've got beautiful colors."

"It's not only t'colors though, that's nowt."

"What is it, then?"

Billy allowed a trickle of sand out of his fist onto his left pump. The grains bounced off the rubber toe cap like a column of tap water exploding in the sink. He shook his head and shrugged his shoulder. Mr. Farthing stepped forward and raised one hand.

"What I like about it is its shape; it's so beautifully proportioned. The neat head, the way the wings fold over on its back. Its tail, just the right length, and that down on the thighs, just like a pair of plus fours."

He modeled the hawk in the air, emphasizing each point of description with corresponding sweeps and curves of his hands.

"It's the sort of thing you want to paint, or model in clay. Painting would be best I should think, you'd be able to get all those lovely brown markings in then."

"It's when it's flying, though, sir, that's when it's got it over other birds, that's when it's at its best."

"Yes, I agree with you. Do you know, you can tell it's a good flyer just by looking at it sitting there."

"It's 'cos it looks streamlined."

"It's what I was saying about proportion, I think that's got something to do with it. There's a saying about racehorses that if they look good, they probably are good. I think the same applies here."

"It does."

"And yet there's something weird about it when it's flying."

"You what, sir?" Hawks are t'best flyers there are."

"I don't mean . . . ."

"I'm not sayin' there isn't other good uns; look at swallows an' swifts, an' peewits when they're tumblin' about in t'air. An' there's gulls an' all. I used to watch 'em for hours when we used to go away. It wa' t'best at Scarborough, where you could get on t'clifftop an' watch 'em. They're still not t'same though. Not to me anyroad."

"I don't mean anything to do with the beauty of its flight, that's marvelous. I mean . . . well, when it flies there's something about it that makes you feel strange."

"I think I know what you mean, sir, you mean everything seems to go dead quiet."

"That's it!"

His exclamation made the hawk jerk up and tense.

"Steady on, sir, you'll frighten her to death."

42

Mr. Farthing pointed two fingers at his temple and triggered his thumb.

"Sorry, I forgot."

The hawk roused and settled again.

"It was just that you got it so right about the silence."

"Other folks have noticed that an' all. I know a farmer, an' he says it's the same wi' owls. He says that he's seen 'em catchin' mice in his yard at night, an' that when they swoop down, you feel like poking your ears to make 'em pop because it goes that quiet."

"Yes, that's right. That's how I felt, it's as though it was flying in a, . . . in a, . . . in a pocket of silence, that's it, a pocket of silence. That's strange, isn't it?"

"They're strange birds."

"And this feeling, this silence, it must carry over. Have you noticed how quietly we're speaking? And how strange it sounded when I raised my voice. It was almost like shouting in a church."

"It's 'cos they're nervous, sir. You have to keep your voice down."

"No, it's more than that. It's instinctive. It's a kind of respect."

"I know, sir. That's why it makes me mad when I take her out and I'll hear somebody say, 'Look there's Billy Casper there wi' his pet hawk.' I could shout at 'em; it's not a pet, sir, hawks are not pets. Or when folks stop me and say, 'Is it tame?' Is it heck tame, it's trained, that's all. It's fierce, an' it's wild, an' it's not bothered about anybody, not even about me, right. And that's why it's great."

"A lot of people wouldn't understand that sentiment though, they like pets they can make friends with; make a fuss of, cuddle a bit, boss a bit; don't you agree?"

"Ye', I suppose so. I'm not bothered about that, though. I'd sooner have her, just to look at her, an' fly her. That's enough for me. They can keep their rabbits an' their cats an' their talkin' budgies, they're rubbish compared wi' her."

Mr. Farthing glanced down at Billy, who was staring at the hawk, breathing rapidly.

"Yes, I think you're right; they probably are."

"Do you know, sir, I feel as though she's doing me a favor just lettin' me stand here."

"Yes, I know what you mean. It's funny though, when you try to analyse it, exactly what it is about it. For example, it's not its size is it?"

"No, sir."

"And it doesn't look terribly fearsome; in fact there are moments when it looks positively babyish. So what is it, then?"

"I don't know."

Mr. Farthing molded a fender of sand with the toe of one shoe, then slowly looked up at the hawk.

"I think it's a kind of pride, and as you say, independence. It's like an awareness, a satisfaction with its own beauty and prowess. It seems to look you straight in the eye and say, 'Who the hell are you, anyway?' It reminds me of that poem by Lawrence, 'If men were as much men as lizards are lizards they'd be worth looking at.' It just seems proud to be itself."

"Yes, sir."

They stood silent for a minute, then Mr. Farthing pushed his overcoat and jacket sleeves up to look at the time. The watch face was concealed under his shirt cuff. He revealed the face by lifting the cuff and sliding the strap down his wrist.

"Good lord! Look at the time, it's twenty past one. We'd better be off."

He fumbled for the door fastener and backed out of the shed.

"I'll give you a lift if you like. I'm here in the car."

Billy blushed and shook his head. Mr. Farthing smiled in at him through the bars.

"What's the matter, wouldn't do your reputation any good to be seen traveling with a teacher?"

"It's not that, sir . . . I've one or two things to do first."

"Please yourself, then. But you're going to have to look sharp, or you'll be late."

"I know, I'll not be long."

"Right. I'll be off then."

His face disappeared from the bars, and reappeared a few seconds later.

"And thanks for the display, I really enjoyed it. You're an expert, lad."

His face disappeared again, and for a few moments his barred charcoal back blocked the whole square. Then light, and other shapes like jigsaw pieces, grew around his receding silhouette, the house, the garage, the garden.

A car engine bleated. Bleated again and caught. BRUM-BRUMMED to a climax, then hummed away on a rising pitch.

Billy looked down and began to guide an oblong furry pellet through the sand with one toe. There was a kink in the fading car sound, a pause like a missed heartbeat as it changed up to a softer tone, and the final fade.

Billy picked the pellet up and inspected it in his palm. It was the size of a blackbird's egg, charcoal-colored, and shining faintly as though lacquered. He rolled it around his hand awhile, sniffed it, then carefully crumbled it with his fingertips. Inside the lacquered crust the fur was a lighter shade of grey, snuff dry, and wrapped inside the fur were tiny bones, and a tiny skull, with sets of dot-sized teeth dotted to its tiny jaws. Billy rubbed the fur to ash, and gently blew it away like chaff from grain, leaving only the bones and skull in his palm. He placed the skull on the shelf behind the door, then began to push the bones around with his forefinger; aimlessly at first, then linking them into a triangle, which he immediately destroyed, and reformed as an angular C. He studied this letter, then tried to remould it, but he could only make a D, so he shuffled the bones until their formation was meaningless.

Selecting the longest bone, he pincered it, pin thin, between his forefinger and thumb. The pressure drained two small patches of his skin white; then the points punctured, and a spot of blood formed on his fingertip; followed by a second on his thumb. He frowned and squeezed. This made him close one eye and bite his lips. The bone remained intact. Billy opened the pincers, and it stuck up out of the skin of his thumb like a little standard. He turned his thumb over, nail upwards. The bone still stuck, so he pulled it out and snapped it. The crack made the hawk open its eyes. Billy dropped the bones and carefully ground them into the sand with his pumps. Only the skull remained. He turned it to face the bars, then quietly left the hut, locked up, and with a final glance at the hawk, walked away up the path.

THE WEDGE-TAILED EAGLE

GEOFFREY DUTTON

The collision between man and the natural world, brought about by man's madness, man's vanity, is perfectly illustrated here.

THROUGH THE HOT, cloudless days in the back of New South Wales, there is always something beside the sun watching you from the sky. Over the line of the hills, or above the long stretches of plains, a black dot swings around and around; and its circles rise slowly or fall slowly, or simply remain at the same height, swinging in endless indolent curves, while the eyes watch the miles of earth below, and the six- or maybe nine-foot wingspan remains motionless in the air. You know that there is nothing you can do that will not be observed, that the circling eagle, however small the distance may make it, however aloof its flight may seem, has always fixed upon the earth an attention as fierce as its claws.

But the eagles watch the sky as well as the earth, and not only for other birds; when an Air Force Station was established in their country in 1941, they were not alarmed by the noisy yellow airplanes. Occasionally they would

47

even float in circles across the aerodrome itself, and then disappear again behind the hills; the pilots had little fear of colliding with one of these circling, watchful birds. The vast, brown-black shape of the eagle would appear before the little Tiger Moth biplane and then be gone. There was nothing more to it. No question of haste or flapping of wings, simply a flick over and down and then the eagle would resume its circling. Sometimes a pilot would chase the bird and would find, unexpectedly, no response; the eagle would seem not to notice the airplane and hold the course of its circling until the very moment when collision seemed inevitable. Then there would be the quick turn over, under, or away from the plane, with the great span of wings unstirred. The delay and the quick maneuver would be done with a princely detachment and consciousness of superiority, the eagle in the silence of its wings scorning the roar and fuss of the aircraft and its engine.

Two pilots from the station were drinking one day in the local town with one of the farmers over whose land they used to fly.

"Two of us, you know, could do it," one of them said. "By yourself it's hopeless. The eagle can outfly you without moving his wings. But with two of you, one could chase him around while the other climbed above and dived at him. That way you'd at least get him flustered."

The farmer was not at all hopeful.

"Maybe it'd take more than a couple of planes to fluster an eaglehawk. There's a big one around my place, just about twelve feet across. I wish you could get him. Though if you did hit him, there mightn't be much left of your little airplane."

"It always beats me why you call them eaglehawks," said one of the pilots. "The wedge-tailed eagle is the biggest eagle in the world. You ought to pay him more respect, the most magnificent, majestic bird there is."

The farmer was hostile to this idea of majesty.

"Have you ever seen them close-up? Or ever seen them feeding? The king of birds landing on a lolly-legged lamb and tearing him to bits. Or an old, dead, flyblown ewe that's been fool enough to lie down with her legs uphill. Watch him hacking his way into their guts, with the vermin dancing all over his stinking brown feathers. Then all you've got to do is to let him see you five hundred yards off and up he flaps, slow and awkward, to a myall where he sits all bunched-up, looking as if he's going to overbalance the little tree. Still, go ahead with your scheme. I'd like to see you beat one at his own game."

He left, and the two others continued discussing their plans. A pilot in a small, aerobatic aircraft is like a child. He longs for something to play with. He can be happy enough, rolling and looping by himself in the sky, but happiness changes to a kind of ecstasy when there is someone against whom to match his skill, or someone to applaud him when he low-flies through the unforeseeable complications of tree and rock, hill and river. The contest becomes more wonderful the nearer it approaches death, when all else is forgotten in the concentration of the minute. The pilot who fights with bullets and shells is ecstatically involved in his action. This fight with the wedge-tailed eagle was to be to the death, not a battle of bullets or shells, but of skill against inborn mastery. The risk of death would be there, just the same, both for the bird and for the pilot supported by the fragile wood and fabric of the airplane.

One cloudless morning the pilots flew off together, in close formation, toward the valley of the farmer's house. The sky was as clean as a gun barrel and the sun hit them both in the back of the neck as they flew westward toward the scrubby range and the valley beyond. The pilot of the leading aircraft loosened his helmet and let the wind, like a cool rushing sense of elation and freedom, blow around his neck and hair. Like the eagle, he was a watcher, one from whom no secrets could hide on the earth below. The country matched the element in which he moved: both hard and unforgiving of mistakes, yet endlessly stretching, magnificent in freedom. Neither the air nor this land would bring anything for the asking; but they would offer all manner of their peculiar riches to anyone who could conquer them by work and vigilance and love. The foolish and the weak perished like the sheep stuck in the wet mud of the drying dams, in sight of water for the lack of which they died.

As he approached the hills, the earth below him and the creeks were brown and dry as a walnut, with a strip of green along the river and a few bright squares where a farmer had sunk a bore and put in a few acres of lucerne. A mob of sheep stirred along in a cloud of dust through a few scattered myalls and gum trees. He finally bounced over the hills through air rough from the hot rocks, and turning away from the other airplane, moved up the broad valley, searching the sky for the black dot of an eagle wheeling and wheeling like a windmill on its side. There was no sign of anything, not even of a cloud or a high whirly of dust, which in an empty sky looks like a patch of rust in a gun barrel. Everything seemed to him shiny and empty, yet somehow waiting to go off.

He made a long leisurely run up the valley, a few feet above the ground, lifting his wing over a fence or two, turning around a gum tree or away from a mob of sheep. The only other sign of life was the farmer standing near his truck by the gate of a paddock. He answered his wave, turned and flew over him, and then continued up the valley. Above him, in the other airplane, his friend waited for something to happen.

He ran his wheels almost along the ground and turned another fence. Suddenly the whole top of a tree flapped off in front of him and the eagle disappeared behind him before he could turn. Another bird rose from a dead sheep a few hundred yards away, but the pilot's whole attention was concentrated on the bird that had risen from the myall tree. It was undoubtedly the big eagle of which the farmer had told them.

By the time he had turned and come back in a climb the eagle was five hundred feet above him. He opened the throttle wide and pulled the strap of his helmet tight. He looked for the other plane and saw that his friend was moving toward them and climbing also, so that with the added height he could dive as they had planned.

The pilot was astonished to find that he was being out-climbed without the bird even moving a feather of its wings. On the hot, unseen currents it swung lazily around and around, its motionless wings always above the quivering, roaring aircraft. To make things worse, the pilot, in order to climb as quickly as possible, had to move in a straight line and then turn back, whereas the eagle sailed up in a close spiral. His hand pushed harder on the small knob of the throttle already wide open against the stop. Perhaps the battle would come to no more than this, the noisy pursuit of an enemy who could never be reached.

Yet the eagle, its mastery already established, now deliberately ceased climbing and waited for the airplane to struggle up to its level. The pilot, wondering if the farmer below had seen his humiliation, pressed on above the bird, where at about three thousand feet he leveled off and waved to his friend above that the battle was about to begin.

He came around in a curve at the bird, the airplane on the edge of stalling, juddering all over, the control stick suddenly going limp in his hand as a pump handle when a tank is dry, the slots on the end of the wings clattering above him; and then, just as he ducked his head to avoid the shining curved beak, the braced black and brown feathers, the sky amazingly was empty in front of him. The eagle had flicked over as lightly as a swallow, with no sign of panic or haste. He looked over and saw it below him, circling as quietly as if nothing in the whole morning, in the sky or on the land, had disturbed its watchful mastery of the air.

As the pilot dived toward it and followed it around again, he saw his friend drop his wing and come down, steep and straight, to make the attack they had planned. He could see that the eagle, under its apparent negligence, was watching him and not the diving plane. This was the moment for which they had waited, when the eagle would break away as usual, but to find another airplane coming at it before it had time to move. The pilot's heart lunged inside him like the needle of the revolution counter on the instrument panel. Waiting until his friend had only another few hundred feet of his dive left, he jerked the controls hard over toward the shining feathers of the bird. It turned and fell below him, exactly as they had hoped it would. The pilot pulled himself up against his straps to watch its flight. The other airplane was on it just as it began its circling again. But the collision did not happen. The plane shot on and began to pull up out of its dive; the eagle recovered again into its slow swinging, a few hundred feet lower.

Yet it had shown a little concern. For the first time a fraction of dignity had been lost: momentarily the great wings had been disturbed a little from their full stretch. It

52

had been startled into a quick defensive action. The pilot's excitement now blotted out everything but the battle in progress, leaving him poised between earth and sky, forgetful of both except as a blur of blue, a rush of brown. The last thing he saw on land had been the farmer's truck coming across the paddocks to a point somewhere below. Then all the vanity and pride in him had responded to the fact that there was someone to watch him. Now, no response existed except to the detail of the black, polished brownness of the eagle's plumage, the glistening beak, the wedge-shaped tail. His excitement was at that intensity which is part of hope, his first sight of achievement. Previously, the insolent negligence of the bird had destroyed his confidence, and had almost made the air feel the alien element it really was. In contrast with all his noisy maneuvering, his juggling with engine and controls, the eagle had scorned him with its silence, with its refusal to flap its wings, its mastery of the motionless sweep, the quick flick to safety and then the motionless circling again. The pilot had begun to wonder who was playing with whom. Perhaps the bird would suddenly turn, dive, rip him with a talon, and slide sideways down the vast slope to earth.

Yet now the eagle had been forced to move its wings, and he had seen the first sign of victory. Sweat poured around his helmet and down his neck and chest. His shirt clung wetly first to his flesh and then to the parachute harness. He looked at his altimeter and saw that they were down to seven hundred feet. Above him his friend was ready.

He turned in again toward the eagle. The airplane shivered and clung to height, on the last fraction of speed before the spin. Feeling the stiffness of his hands and feet on the controls, he told himself to relax like the eagle in front of him. He looked quickly upward and saw his

friend begin to dive. This was the second stage of their plan. The eagle, however little sign of it appeared, knew now that both airplanes were attacking. It circled, still on unmoving wings, but subtler and harder to follow, and shifted height slightly as it swung around.

The other plane was almost past him in its dive when he completed his turn in a vicious swing toward the eagle; he missed, spun, corrected, looked up to see the other airplane, which had dived this time far below the eagle, coming almost vertically up below the just-leveled bird.

The eagle heard and saw, and flicked over to where, before, safety had always been emptily waiting for it. It flashed, wings still gloriously outstretched, straight into the right-hand end of the upper mainplane of the aircraft, exactly where the metal slot curves across the wood and fabric. Its right wing, at the point where the hard, long feathers give way to the soft, curved feathers of the body, snapped away and fluttered down to earth. The left wing folded into the body, stretched and folded again, as the heavy box of bone, beak, and claw plunged and slewed to the ground. The pilot could not watch the last few feet of its descent. For the first time he was grateful to the roar of the motor that obscured the thud of the body striking earth.

The two pilots landed in the paddock, and, leaving the engines running, walked over to the dark mass of feathers. One of them turned off to the side and came back holding the severed wing. It was almost as big as the man himself.

The two of them stood in silence. The moment of skill and danger was past, and the dead body before them proclaimed their victory. Frowning with the glare of the sun and the misery of their achievement they both looked down at the piteous, one-winged eagle. Not a mark of blood was on it, the beak glistening and uncrushed, the

ribbed feet and talons clenched together. It was not the fact
of death that kept them in silence; the watcher could not
always keep his station in the air. What both of them could
still see was the one-winged heap of bone and feathers,
slewing and jerking uncontrolled to earth.

In the distance they heard the noise of the farmer's truck
approaching, and saw it stop at a gate and the farmer wave
as he got out to open it. They quickly picked up the bird
and its wing, and ran with them to the little hillock covered
in rocks at the corner of the paddock. Between two large
rocks they folded both wings across the bird and piled
stones above it; and then, each lifting, carried a large flat
stone and placed it above the others.

As they ran back toward the airplanes a black dot broke
from the hills and swung out above them, circling around
and around, watching the truck accelerate and then stop as
the two airplanes turned, taxied, and slid into the air before
it could reach them.

GODHANGER

DICK KING-SMITH

The wild birds of Godhanger Wood against the gamekeeper and his gun. An uneven contest, until the Skymaster (or is it God?) takes a hand. A tale of birds, yes, but a tale too of good and evil, a timeless tale.

THREE HUNDRED METERS BELOW, Godhanger Wood lay still in evening sunshine. Gliding silently across the darkening sky, his flight feathers spread like fingertips, Loftus the raven looked down at the massed treetops, the green of their myriad leaves now changing to the reds, golds, and browns of autumn.

The shape of the wood was plain to him, lying along the slope of a valley or combe. In outline it resembled the head and neck of a horse. There was even a clearing at just the place to give an impression of an eye.

In the shelter of the hill, the hardwood trees—oak, beech, ash, sycamore, and chestnut—grew for the most part straight and skyward, but at the ridge, along the horse's neck, only a hogmane of thorn and hedge maple survived, bent crookback by the fierce sea winds.

The breeze on which Loftus rode came also from the west, a light air, a breath only, and his all-seeing eyes marked how motionless was the canopy of Godhanger Wood. The only movement below him was that of another bird, almost as large as himself but dark brown instead of his glossy sable, that wheeled endlessly above the valley bottom on broad unmoving wings. Buzzard-baiting appealed to Loftus' sense of humor, and he tipped off his pitch and fell like a black arrow toward the big hawk.

"Whee-oo!" cried the bird in distress at the sound of the raven's coming, and threw himself sideways in frantic flapping haste. Again, "Whee-oo!" mewed the buzzard, as Loftus shot past him, and his plaintive cries were echoed by his mate, hunting behind the hill.

"Pee-oo! Pee-oo!" called the hen bird in reply, and they said to each other, "It's that damned raven again." "I suppose he thinks it's amusing."

At that moment they saw Loftus come swooping up over the top of the hill, and, still complaining, they made their heavy way off in search of more peaceful hunting grounds.

Chuckling in his deep voice, the raven climbed above the wood, circling as he gained height, and watching the treetops darkening as the daylight died.

Now his old familiar nesting place beckoned, high on a sheltered ledge on the Atlantic cliffs, with his old familiar mate, mother in her time to his many children; the gruff-spoken, hairy-chinned, comfortable roosting partner at the end of so many thousands of days. He was just about to turn for home when he saw a solitary black and white bird flying silently along the wood's edge. As he watched, it perched for a moment in the top of a single outlying skeleton elm, long tail dipping up and down, and then flew suddenly and rapidly away with loud calls of alarm.

"Chakka-chakka-chakka-chak!" cried Myles the magpie,

and Loftus circled higher still. He knew Myles for a thief and a double-dyed villain, but he also knew better than to doubt the 'pie's warning.

And at that precise moment the evening's peace was shattered by the blast of a gunshot. After a heartbeat's pause came the noise of a second shot, followed by a thin agonized screaming that ceased as suddenly as it had arisen. Silence fell again on Godhanger Wood as the raven beat away toward the west.

The two spent cartridges spun away as the gamekeeper broke open his gun. He reloaded and stood still, eyes narrowed, watching his dog working a bramble patch. Very soon she came running to the man, a squealing rabbit in her mouth, and laid it, broken-legged and bulging-eyed, before him. The noise stopped abruptly as the gamekeeper took the rabbit and broke its neck.

One glance at the limp body told him that it was a milky doe, its belly plucked of the soft fur in which now, somewhere, its kittens were warmly snuggled and would soon lie cold and stiff.

Gun in the crook of his left arm, he pulled from his right-hand coat pocket a bone-handled knife and opened its ten-centimeter blade. Neatly he slashed the middle of the doe's upturned belly between the two rows of swollen teats, closed and replaced the knife, then reached in and twisted out guts and paunch, which he tossed away into the undergrowth.

The dog made no move but sat watching, hoping, on this occasion rightly, that the carcass would be hers at the end of the day. The gamekeeper slipped the rabbit into his game-bag and wiped his red hand on the silky hair of the spaniel's back. Then he straightened up and set off again, dog at heel, with long strides through the tall trees of Godhanger.

All was quiet as before his coming, all was as it had been, save for two orange-colored cartridge cases on the ground, and, caught upon a bramble, a little festoon of warm innards whose coils still wriggled and slid uneasily.

A meat fly landed upon the guts, and stood, moving its feet in pleased anticipation until it was dislodged by a final spasmodic motion of the glazing intestines. They slipped from the briar and fell to the ground.

After a gap of time the stillness of the darkening wood was broken. At intervals, among the great oaks and beeches, there were a few small stands of larches, and into these, homecoming pigeons began to crash. Nearer, a pair of little owls started up their shrill, plaintive cries. Above the bramble patch, on a low bough of a big horse chestnut, a robin sang with that heartcatching wistfulness that tells of summer gone and hard cold nights to come. The breeze had dropped to nothing. Nothing moved.

Suddenly, quite silently, a head appeared, poking out beneath the tangle of blackberry bushes. It was a blackish head with white marks around the sharp muzzle and between eye and ear.

For a moment the head moved to and fro, quick, questing nostrils dilated to suck in the gut scent—and then, out of the briar patch slid the low, dark, humpbacked shape of Rippin the polecat, foul-smelling killer of any creature that might come his way. Unlike other animals, it was the nature of his kind to kill and keep on killing. He was programmed to do so. Mice, rats, ground-nesting birds, frogs, snakes—all were fair game to Rippin, as indeed was far larger prey when chance offered: in his time he had put paid to many chickens, and once, one glorious, never-to-be-forgotten winter's night, sixteen turkeys had died to satisfy his bloodlust. Such monsters, of course, he had not been able to drag away, but they had provided a feast of his favorite delicacy: the brains.

However, Rippin was not fussy. Rabbit guts would do for starters. He had begun to tug and gulp at them, growling softly in his throat, when suddenly, from out of nowhere, a broad-winged shape came swooping noiselessly upon him with talons hanging ready to grasp, only to sheer away at the last moment as the polecat rose up on his hind legs to his full height, all forty-five centimeters of it, his mouth agape, his coarse fur on end, and chattered in fearless fury.

"Damn you! Damn you!" he raved, dancing in his rage. "If I could only catch hold of you, I'd have the feathers off you, I'd tear your throat out, suck your blood, chew up your great staring eyeballs, I'd kill you, kill you, kill you!" And the air about grew thick with his choking, acrid stink.

Circling, the tawny owl flew back and pitched on a branch of the chestnut to stare silently down, till at last the polecat ceased his cursing and made off, towing a rope of guts with him and grumbling all the while. "Bloody owls, I hate 'em, I hate 'em," the bird could hear, until finally the sound passed beyond even his acute earshot.

"Horrible beast," said the tawny owl softly to himself. He straightened a feather or two on his streaky breast, and swiveled his round head to look all about him.

"That's the nastiest-natured creature in Godhanger, bar none," he said. "Sure as my name is Glyde."

"Glyde."

The word was instantly repeated, like an echo. But it was not an echo. The name was spoken in a different voice, a voice whose authority was instantly recognizable, even in the uttering of that monosyllable.

Glyde looked up into the branches high above. "Master?" he said. "Is it you?"

From somewhere high within the still-leafy crown of the

horse chestnut, a great shape dropped on silent wings, and pitched upon the tawny owl's branch, almost half a meter below him. Even so, their heads were on a level. This was the mighty bird who had come to Godhanger Wood, known to those that lived there as the Skymaster.

Some of the birds of the wood had come together as followers of the Skymaster, and all these carried different pictures of him in their minds. Because all found themselves unable to meet his gaze directly, each tended to think of him in the image of his own kind, as some sort of hawk or falcon or crow or owl. Only once in their lives were they able to look directly at him, and then it was too late.

Glyde looked away as usual, saying, "You called, Master?"

Had he been able to see the other's eyes, he would have noticed a twinkle in them. "'The nastiest-natured creature in Godhanger' I think you remarked?" said the Skymaster. His tone was not of rebuke but of amusement. "Why so, my friend?"

"He is evil-tempered," said Glyde.

"He was angry, yes, certainly. But there are times when anger rouses each and every one of us."

"Not you, Master."

"That you have not known me angered does not mean, Glyde, that I have never been so, or that you will never so see me. Anger may be healthy, cleansing, a relief to the spirit at certain times, just as a violent thunderstorm clears the air and cools the overheated land."

The tawny owl scratched the side of his round face with a claw. "At certain times, maybe," he said reasonably. "But Rippin the foumart is always angry." He used the old name for a polecat, the marten that is foul-scented, though the word itself was meaningless to him, since like almost all the birds, he had little or no sense of smell.

"And," he went on, "he is always hungry for the taste of blood."

"Do you not kill?" asked the Skymaster.

"Yes, but for food, not for fun, Master. To feed myself, my mate, our owlets. To this end the roosting bird must die, the rat, the mouse, the cockchafer. I cannot live by berries alone. It is not in my nature."

"Yet your nature—for this is what you are saying—is less nasty than the polecat's? You are a nicer creature (remembering that just now it was you who dived upon him), you are more to be esteemed, of greater value, more likeable?"

"Yes, Master," said Glyde stubbornly. "I think I am."

"Perhaps, then," said the Skymaster, "you had better try to think better of Rippin the polecat, lest you, too, become nasty-natured, as you say he is," and he spread his great wings and sailed away into the darkness.

The tawny owl sat for some minutes and bent his head to peer at the ground below. The moonlight glinted upon the brass ends of two cartridge cases that lay in the short grass of the floor of the wood, and Glyde put his head on one side to consider better this unusual pair of shining eyes.

His was not the only curious gaze, for in a moment there came the tiniest scratching noise to tense his muscles, and a woodmouse appeared from its hole between the tree roots and began a series of little darting runs toward the strange objects. Instantly Glyde dropped like a stone from his branch to take the mouse in one foot. The four curved talons crushed out its life, and into Glyde's beak it went headfirst, the tail sticking out just for a second, waving a little as though the woodmouse were still alive.

Then, from deeper in the wood there came the noise of grunting, and the tawny owl gulped down his meal and flew silently away.

Now the grunting sounds grew louder, and presently there emerged into a moonlit clearing a low, heavy animal that walked flat-footed with the slow rolling shuffle of a bear, stopping often for a scratch or to nose about for food.

Baldwin the badger was the least fussy of feeders. Anything that was edible he ate—fledgling birds fallen from the nest, mice, voles, hedgehogs even, plus insects, especially the larvae of wasp and bumblebee, and quantities of earthworms.

"Snakes," he would say, "are very tasty. I'm very partial to a nice grass snake. But what I really relish is a nest of young rabbits. Delicious, they are."

Never a fast mover, even as a young boar, Baldwin in old age took life very steadily. Let the junior badgers go galloping about Godhanger, burning up their energy in play, or mating, or fighting. He was past all that, he told himself. A solitary badger now, he told himself everything, finding comfort in this, as the old often do.

"Always look after Number One, Baldwin, my boy," he would say. "You're not so sprack as you were, and the old bones ache a bit when the wind's in the north. So long as you can keep the old belly full, that's what matters. Still got your teeth, praise be. And your nose."

Now, as Baldwin reached the bramble patch beneath the horse chestnut, that nose brought him a sudden clear message.

"Hello, hello!" he said. "I smell rabbit," and he poked his white-striped head into the undergrowth and sniffed deeply.

The doe whose guts Rippin had eaten had been a stub-rabbit, a rabbit that contrives to live its life not in tunnels

below ground but in runs beneath heather or furze bushes or, as here, within a tangle of briars.

Nothing had remained of the doe but her pelt, flung on the midden behind the gamekeeper's cottage, for his spaniel had gone to her kennel full-fed. But her five kittens still stirred feebly in the shallow scrape which she had dug for this late and last litter under the blackberry bushes.

Baldwin pushed his twenty-kilo frame into the briar fortress, his thick silvery coat armoring him against the spears and lances of the defending thorns, and dug out and ate the five babies in less than half that number of minutes. Then, clucking with pleasure, he made his rolling way to the horse chestnut's nearest neighbor, a giant gray-skinned beech tree, one of several within the wood that he used to clean and sharpen his claws upon. Its smooth bark was scored vertically to a height of a meter or more by the marks of his many visits, and he stood against the trunk and added to their number.

"That's better, Baldwin, my dear," said Baldwin, dropping back on all fours and giving himself a good shake. "That's a good start. And the night's still young so stir your stumps and let's be off again," and he trundled away through the trees.

Above him, in those trees, many of the animals of Godhanger Wood perched or sat or lay. Some were creatures of the night as he was, and heard or watched his passing as he rustled through the first-fallen leaves. Some were of the daytime and paid no heed to the badger, but slept sound and waited for the dawn.

There were birds in plenty, but there were beasts aloft, too. There were bats in those trees that age or disease had hollowed, squirrels snug in their bulky dreys, and in his nest in the low crown of an ancient, thickset oak there crouched a fearsome figure that peered down with eyes of coldest green at Baldwin as he snuffled noisily among the roots below, and showed its fangs in a soundless snarl. This was Gilbert the cat.

Everything about Gilbert was twisted: his corkscrew tail (caught and broken in a gin trap), his beat-up ears, his nature. Chance survivor of a litter of farm kittens murdered by a roving cannibal tom, he viewed the world through a haze of bitterness. He had no friends among the woodlanders, from the smallest to the largest, from the pygmy shrew who weighed five grams to the thirty-kilo roebuck. He especially hated any invasion of his territory. Mateless, childless, friendless, Gilbert's home was all in all to him. No matter that it was only a rough hollow four meters up in the ruined oak, it was his den, and so, to his way of thinking, the tree was his and he cursed all who came near it.

Now he began to growl deep in his throat at the badger rootling below.

"Temper, temper!" cried a cheerful voice above him, and, peering up, the wild cat saw a small tubby shape perched on a branch directly over his head. It was a little owl, and at sight of this second intruder, Gilbert positively spat with anger. His green eyes glowed, and his unsheathed claws rasped on the bark at the rim of his hole in impotent fury.

"One of these nights," he hissed, "I shall kill you. Slowly."

The small squat bird, whose name was Eustace, gave a sharp bark of amusement.

"First catch your owl," he said, and then by way of comment opened wide his gape and brought up a pellet composed of mouse skin, bones and beetle fragments. The pellet narrowly missed Gilbert's head and fell to earth in front of Baldwin, who swallowed it absently before lumbering away in search of more appetizing food.

"That's more like it!" said Eustace comfortably. "I bet you wish you could do that, old moggy. It must be very unpleasant having to digest all the rubbish you eat. Probably what makes you so bad-tempered."

"I hate you," said Gilbert softly.

"That's your trouble, old moggy," said Eustace. "You hate everybody. You should try listening to someone I know."

"Who might that be?"

"He is known as the Skymaster. He is the greatest of birds."

"A bird! I should listen to a bird!"

"He is not like other birds," said Eustace.

All the time that they had been talking, Gilbert, infinitely slowly, was altering his position, inching forward from the mouth of his hole, setting his hind feet and gradually twisting his body, ready for a sudden upward pounce that would carry him the short distance to the little owl's perch, but a split second before he sprang, Eustace jumped nimbly off his branch. Striking and missing, Gilbert lost his footing and tumbled and slid all anyhow down the trunk of the oak, spitting and snarling with rage.

"Love your enemies!" shouted Eustace. "Do good to those that hate you, old moggy!" and he swooped away, quick and low, with a final burst of laughter.

CHARLOTTE'S WEB

E. B. WHITE

It is sometimes said that to give animals thoughts and feelings is absurd. Is it? Are they not sentient creatures? Do they not, like us, respond to affection, protect their young, struggle to survive? Here, Wilbur the pig is feeling sad and lonely (I've seen pigs like that, and I know a happy pig when I see one!). He is longing for a friend—and friends come in all shapes and sizes, as he's about to find out.

THE NEXT DAY WAS RAINY AND DARK. Rain fell on the roof of the barn and dripped steadily from the eaves. Rain fell in the barnyard and ran in crooked courses down into the lane where thistles and pigweed grew. Rain spattered against Mrs. Zuckerman's kitchen windows and came gushing out of the downspouts. Rain fell on the backs of the sheep as they grazed in the meadow. When the sheep tired of standing in the rain, they walked slowly up the lane and into the fold.

Rain upset Wilbur's plans. Wilbur had planned to go out, this day, and dig a new hole in his yard. He had other plans, too. His plans for the day went something like this:

Breakfast at six thirty. Skim milk, crusts, middlings, bits

of doughnuts, wheat cakes with drops of maple syrup sticking to them, potato skins, leftover custard pudding with raisins, and bits of Shredded Wheat.

Breakfast would be finished at seven.

From seven to eight, Wilbur planned to have a talk with Templeton, the rat that lived under his trough. Talking with Templeton was not the most interesting occupation in the world but it was better than nothing.

From eight to nine, Wilbur planned to take a nap outdoors in the sun.

From nine to eleven, he planned to dig a hole, or trench, and possibly find something good to eat buried in the dirt.

From eleven to twelve, he planned to stand still and watch flies on the boards, watch bees in the clover, and watch swallows in the air.

Twelve o'clock—lunchtime. Middlings, warm water, apple parings, meat gravy, carrot scrapings, meat scraps, stale hominy, and the wrapper off a package of cheese. Lunch would be over at one.

From one to two, Wilbur planned to sleep.

From two to three, he planned to scratch itchy places by rubbing against the fence.

From three to four, he planned to stand perfectly still and think of what it was like to be alive, and to wait for Fern.

At four would come supper. Skim milk, provender, leftover sandwich from Lurvy's lunchbox, prune skins, a morsel of this, a bit of that, fried potatoes, marmalade drippings, a little more of this, a little more of that, a piece of baked apple, a scrap of upside-down cake.

Wilbur had gone to sleep thinking about these plans. He awoke at six and saw the rain, and it seemed as though he couldn't bear it.

"I get everything all beautifully planned out and it has to go and rain," he said.

For a while he stood gloomily indoors. Then he walked to the door and looked out. Drops of rain struck his face. His yard was cold and wet. His trough had an inch of rainwater in it. Templeton was nowhere to be seen.

"Are you out there, Templeton?" called Wilbur. There was no answer. Suddenly Wilbur felt lonely and friendless.

"One day just like another," he groaned. "I'm very young, I have no real friends here in the barn, it's going to rain all morning and all afternoon, and Fern won't come in such bad weather. Oh, honestly!" And Wilbur was crying again, for the second time in two days.

At six thirty Wilbur heard the banging of a pail. Lurvy was standing outside in the rain, stirring up breakfast.

"C'mon, pig!" said Lurvy.

Wilbur did not budge. Lurvy dumped the slops, scraped the pail, and walked away. He noticed that something was wrong with the pig.

Wilbur didn't want food, he wanted love. He wanted a friend—someone who would play with him. He mentioned this to the goose, who was sitting quietly in a corner of the sheepfold.

"Will you come over and play with me?" he asked.

"Sorry, sonny, sorry," said the goose. "I'm sitting-sitting on my eggs. Eight of them. Got to keep them toasty-oasty-oasty warm. I have to stay right here, I'm no flibberty-ibberty-gibbet. I do not play when there are eggs to hatch. I'm expecting goslings."

"Well, I didn't think you were expecting woodpeckers," said Wilbur bitterly.

Wilbur next tried one of the lambs.

"Will you please play with me?" he asked.

"Certainly not," said the lamb. "In the first place, I cannot get into your pen, as I am not old enough to jump over the fence. In the second place, I am not interested in

71

pigs. Pigs mean less than nothing to me."

"What do you mean, *less* than nothing?" replied Wilbur. "I don't think there is any such thing as *less* than nothing. Nothing is absolutely the limit of nothingness. It's the lowest you can go. It's the end of the line. How can something be less than nothing? If there were something that was less than nothing, then nothing would not be nothing, it would be something—even though it's just a very little bit of something. But if nothing is *nothing*, then nothing has nothing that is less than *it* is."

"Oh, be quiet!" said the lamb. "Go play by yourself! I don't play with pigs."

Sadly, Wilbur lay down and listened to the rain. Soon he saw the rat climbing down a slanting board that he used as a stairway.

"Will you play with me, Templeton?" asked Wilbur.

"Play?" said Templeton, twirling his whiskers. "Play? I hardly know the meaning of the word."

"Well," said Wilbur, "it means to have fun, to frolic, to run and skip and make merry."

"I never do those things if I can avoid them," replied the rat, sourly. "I prefer to spend my time eating, gnawing, spying, and hiding. I am a glutton but not a merrymaker. Right now I am on my way to your trough to eat your breakfast, since you haven't got sense enough to eat it yourself." And Templeton, the rat, crept stealthily along the wall and disappeared into a private tunnel that he had dug between the door and the trough in Wilbur's yard. Templeton was a crafty rat, and he had things pretty much his own way. The tunnel was an example of his skill and cunning. The tunnel enabled him to get from the barn to his hiding place under the pig trough without coming out into the open. He had tunnels and runways all over Mr. Zuckerman's farm and could get from one place to another without being seen. Usually he slept during the daytime and was abroad only after dark.

Wilbur watched him disappear into his tunnel. In a moment he saw the rat's sharp nose poke out from underneath the wooden trough. Cautiously Templeton pulled himself up over the edge of the trough. This was almost more than Wilbur could stand: on this dreary, rainy day to see his breakfast being eaten by somebody else. He knew Templeton was getting soaked, out there in the pouring rain, but even that didn't comfort him. Friendless, dejected, and hungry, he threw himself down in the manure and sobbed.

Late that afternoon, Lurvy went to Mr. Zuckerman. "I think there's something wrong with that pig of yours. He hasn't touched his food."

"Give him two spoonfuls of sulphur and a little molasses," said Mr. Zuckerman.

Wilbur couldn't believe what was happening to him when Lurvy caught him and forced the medicine down his throat. This was certainly the worst day of his life. He didn't know whether he could endure the awful loneliness any more.

Darkness settled over everything. Soon there were only shadows and the noises of the sheep chewing their cuds, and occasionally the rattle of a cowchain up overhead. You can imagine Wilbur's surprise when, out of the darkness, came a small voice he had never heard before. It sounded rather thin, but pleasant. "Do you want a friend, Wilbur?" it said. "I'll be a friend to you. I've watched you all day and I like you."

"But I can't see you," said Wilbur, jumping to his feet. "Where are you? And *who* are you?"

"I'm right up here," said the voice. "Go to sleep. You'll see me in the morning."

* * *

The night seemed long. Wilbur's stomach was empty and his mind was full. And when your stomach is empty and your mind is full, it's always hard to sleep.

A dozen times during the night Wilbur woke and stared into the blackness, listening to the sounds and trying to figure out what time it was. A barn is never perfectly quiet. Even at midnight there is usually something stirring.

The first time he woke, he heard Templeton gnawing a hole in the grain bin. Templeton's teeth scraped loudly against the wood and made quite a racket. "That crazy rat!" thought Wilbur. "Why does he have to stay up all night, grinding his clashers and destroying people's property? Why can't he go to sleep, like any decent animal?"

The second time Wilbur woke, he heard the goose turning on her nest and chuckling to herself.

"What time is it?" whispered Wilbur to the goose.

"Probably-obably-obably about half past eleven," said the goose. "Why aren't you asleep, Wilbur?"

"Too many things on my mind," said Wilbur.

"Well," said the goose, "that's not *my* trouble. I have nothing at all on my mind, but I've too many things under my behind. Have you ever tried to sleep while sitting on eight eggs?"

"No," replied Wilbur. "I suppose it *is* uncomfortable. How long does it take a goose egg to hatch?"

"Approximately-oximately thirty days, all told," answered the goose. "But I cheat a little. On warm afternoons, I just pull a little straw over the eggs and go out for a walk."

Wilbur yawned and went back to sleep. In his dreams he heard again the voice saying, "I'll be a friend to you. Go to sleep—you'll see me in the morning."

About half an hour before dawn, Wilbur woke and listened. The barn was still dark. The sheep lay motionless.

Even the goose was quiet. Overhead, on the main floor, nothing stirred: the cows were resting, the horses dozed. Templeton had quit work and gone off somewhere on an errand. The only sound was a slight scraping noise from the rooftop, where the weathervane swung back and forth. Wilbur loved the barn when it was like this—calm and quiet, waiting for light.

"Day is almost here," he thought.

Through a small window, a faint gleam appeared. One by one the stars went out. Wilbur could see the goose a few feet away. She sat with head tucked under a wing. Then he could see the sheep and the lambs. The sky lightened.

"Oh, beautiful day, it is here at last! Today I shall find my friend."

Wilbur looked everywhere. He searched his pen thoroughly. He examined the window ledge, stared up at the ceiling. But he saw nothing new. Finally he decided he would have to speak up. He hated to break the lovely stillness of dawn by using his voice; but he couldn't think of any other way to locate the mysterious new friend who was nowhere to be seen. So Wilbur cleared his throat.

"Attention, please!" he said in a loud, firm voice. "Will the party who addressed me at bedtime last night kindly make himself or herself known by giving an appropriate sign or signal!"

Wilbur paused and listened. All the other animals lifted their heads and stared at him. Wilbur blushed. But he was determined to get in touch with his unknown friend.

"Attention, please!" he said. "I will repeat the message. Will the party who addressed me at bedtime last night kindly speak up. Please tell me where you are, if you are my friend!"

The sheep looked at each other in disgust.

"Stop your nonsense, Wilbur!" said the oldest sheep. "If

you have a new friend here, you are probably disturbing his rest; and the quickest way to spoil a friendship is to wake somebody up in the morning before he is ready. How can you be sure your friend is an early riser?"

"I beg everyone's pardon," whispered Wilbur. "I didn't mean to be objectionable."

He lay down meekly in the manure, facing the door. He did not know it, but his friend was very near. And the old sheep was right—the friend was still asleep.

Soon Lurvy appeared with slops for breakfast. Wilbur rushed out, ate everything in a hurry, and licked the trough. The sheep moved off down the lane, the gander waddled along behind them, pulling grass. And then, just as Wilbur was settling down for his morning nap, he heard again the thin voice that had addressed him the night before.

"Salutations!" said the voice.

Wilbur jumped to his feet. "Salu-*what*?" he cried.

"Salutations!" repeated the voice.

"What are *they*, and where are *you*?" screamed Wilbur. "Please, *please*, tell me where you are. And what are salutations?"

"Salutations are greetings," said the voice, "When I say 'salutations,' it's just my fancy way of saying hello or good morning. Actually, it's a silly expression, and I am surprised that I used it at all. As for my whereabouts, that's easy. Look up here in the corner of the doorway! Here I am. Look, I'm waving!"

At last Wilbur saw the creature that had spoken to him in such a kindly way. Stretched across the upper part of the doorway was a big spider's web and hanging from the top of the web, head down, was a large gray spider. She was about the size of a gumdrop. She had eight legs, and she was waving one of them at Wilbur in friendly greeting. "See me now?" she asked.

"Oh, yes indeed," said Wilbur. "Yes indeed! How are you? Good morning! Salutations! Very pleased to meet you. What is your name, please? May I have your name?"

"My name," said the spider, "is Charlotte."

"Charlotte what?" asked Wilbur, eagerly.

"Charlotte A. Cavatica. But just call me Charlotte."

"I think you're beautiful," said Wilbur.

"Well, I *am* pretty," replied Charlotte. "There's no denying that. Almost all spiders are rather nice-looking. I'm not as flashy as some, but I'll do. I wish I could see you, Wilbur, as clearly as you can see me."

"Why can't you?" asked the pig. "I'm right here."

"Yes, but I'm nearsighted," replied Charlotte. "I've always been dreadfully nearsighted. It's good in some ways, not so good in others. Watch me wrap up this fly."

A fly that had been crawling along Wilbur's trough had flown up and blundered into the lower part of Charlotte's web and was tangled in the sticky threads. The fly was beating its wings furiously trying to break loose and free itself.

"First," said Charlotte, "I dive at him." She plunged headfirst toward the fly. As she dropped, a tiny silken thread unwound from her rear end.

"Next, I wrap him up." She grabbed the fly, threw a few jets of silk round it, and rolled it over and over, wrapping it so that it couldn't move. Wilbur watched in horror. He could hardly believe what he was seeing, and although he detested flies he was sorry for this one.

"There!" said Charlotte. "Now I knock him out, so he'll be more comfortable." She bit the fly. "He can't feel a thing now," she remarked. "He'll make a perfect breakfast for me."

"You mean you *eat* flies?" gasped Wilbur.

"Certainly. Flies, bugs, grasshoppers, choice beetles,

moths, butterflies, tasty cockroaches, gnats, midgets, daddy longlegs, centipedes, mosquitoes, crickets—anything that is careless enough to get caught in my web. I have to live, don't I?"

"Why, yes, of course," said Wilbur. "Do they taste good?"

"Delicious. Of course, I don't really eat them. I drink them—drink their blood. I love blood," said Charlotte, and her pleasant, thin voice grew even thinner and more pleasant.

"Don't say that!" groaned Wilbur. "Please don't say things like that!"

"Why not? It's true, and I have to say what is true. I am not entirely happy about my diet of flies and bugs, but it's the way I'm made. A spider has to pick up a living somehow or other, and I happen to be a trapper. I just naturally build a web and trap flies and other insects. My mother was a trapper before me. Her mother was a trapper before her. All our family have been trappers. Way back for thousands and thousands of years we spiders have been laying for flies and bugs."

"It's a miserable inheritance," said Wilbur, gloomily. He was sad because his new friend was so bloodthirsty.

"Yes, it is," agreed Charlotte. "But I can't help it. I don't know how the first spider in the early days of the world happened to think up this fancy idea of spinning a web, but she did, and it was clever of her, too. And since then, all of us spiders have had to work the same trick. It's not a bad pitch, on the whole."

"It's cruel," replied Wilbur, who did not intend to be argued out of his position.

"Well, *you* can't talk," said Charlotte. "You have your meals brought to you in a pail. Nobody feeds me. I have to get my own living. I live by my wits. I have to be sharp and clever, lest I go hungry. I have to think things out, catch what I can, take what comes. And it just so happens, my friend, that what comes is flies and insects and bugs. And *further*more," said Charlotte, shaking one of her legs, "do you realize that if I didn't catch bugs and eat them, bugs would increase and multiply and get so numerous that they'd destroy the earth, wipe out everything?"

"Really?" said Wilbur. "I wouldn't want *that* to happen. Perhaps your web is a good thing after all."

The goose had been listening to this conversation and chuckling to herself. "There are a lot of things Wilbur doesn't know about life," she thought. "He's really a very innocent little pig. He doesn't even know what's going to happen to him around Christmastime; he has no idea that Mr. Zuckerman and Lurvy are plotting to kill him." And the goose raised herself a bit and poked her eggs a little farther under her so that they would receive the full heat from her warm body and soft feathers.

Charlotte stood quietly over the fly, preparing to eat it. Wilbur lay down and closed his eyes. He was tired from his wakeful night and from the excitement of meeting someone for the first time. A breeze brought him the smell of clover— the sweet-smelling world beyond his fence. "Well," he thought, "I've got a new friend, all right. But what a gamble friendship is! Charlotte is fierce, brutal, scheming, bloodthirsty—everything I don't like. How can I learn to like her, even though she is pretty and, of course, clever?"

Wilbur was merely suffering the doubts and fears that often go with finding a new friend. In good time he was to discover that he was mistaken about Charlotte. Underneath her rather bold and cruel exterior, she had a kind heart, and she was to prove loyal and true to the very end.

TARKA THE OTTER

HENRY WILLIAMSON

Henry Williamson lived very near where I live in Devon in England. He walked the same rivers, saw the herons, the barn owls, the kingfishers that I see. So close is he to the creatures he writes about that we feel we are swimming alongside Tarka in the Torridge. We feel his terror as Deadlock comes hunting.

HE WAS AWAKENED by the tremendous baying of hounds. He saw feet splashing in the shallow water, a row of noses, and many flacking tongues. The entrance was too small for any head to enter. He crouched a yard away, against the cold rock. The noise hurt the fine drums of his ears.

Hobnailed boots scraped on the brown shillets of the waterbed, and iron-tipped hunting poles tapped the rocks.

Go'r'n leave it! Leave it! Go'r'n leave it! Deadlock! Harper! Go'r'n leave it!

Tarka heard the horn and the low opening became lighter.

Go'r'n leave it! Captain! Deadlock! Go'r'n leave it!

The horn twanged fainter as the pack was taken away.

Then a pole was thrust into the holt and prodded about blindly. It slid out again. Tarka saw boots and hands and the face of a terrier. A voice whispered, *Leu in there, Sammy, leu in there!* The small, ragged brown animal crept out of the hands. Sammy smelled Tarka, saw him and began to sidle toward him. *Waugh-waugh-waugh-wa-waugh.* As the otter did not move, the terrier crept nearer to him, yapping with head stretched forward.

After a minute, Tarka could bear the irritating noises no more. Tissing, with open mouth, he moved past the terrier, whose snarly yapping changed to a high-pitched yelping. The men on the opposite bank stood silent and still. They saw Tarka's head in sunlight, which came through the trees behind them and turned the brown shillets a warm yellow. The water ran clear and cold. Tarka saw three men in blue coats; they did not move and he slipped into the water. It did not cover his back, and he returned to the bankside roots. He moved in the shadows and under the ferns at his ordinary traveling pace. One of three watching men declared that an otter had no sense of fear.

No hound spoke, but the reason of the silence was not considered by Tarka, who could not reason such things. He had been awakened with a shock, he had been tormented by a noise, he had left a dangerous place, and he was escaping from human enemies. As he walked upstream, with raised head, his senses of smell, sight, and hearing were alert for his greatest enemies, the hounds.

The stream being narrow and shallow, the otter was given four minutes' law. Four minutes after Tarka had left he heard behind him the short and long notes of the horn, and the huntsman crying amid the tongues of hounds *Ol-ol-ol-ol-ol-ol-over! Get on to 'm! Ol-ol-ol-ol-ol-over!* as the pack returned in full cry to the water. Hounds splashed into the water around the rock, wedging themselves at its opening and breaking into couples and half-couples, leaping through the water after the wet and shivering terrier, throwing their tongues and dipping their noses to the wash of scent coming down.

Deadlock plunged at the lead, with Coraline, Sailoress, Captain, and Playboy. They passed the terrier, and Deadlock was so eager that he knocked him down. Sammy picked up his shivery body and followed.

Tarka sank all but his nostrils in a pool and waited. He lay in the sunlit water like a brown log slanting to the stones on which his rudder rested. The huntsman saw him. Tarka lifted his whiskered head out of the water, and stared at the huntsman. Hounds were speaking just below. From the pool the stream flowed for six feet down the smooth slide up which he had crept. When Deadlock jumped into the pool and lapped the scent lying on the water, Tarka put down his head with hardly a ripple, and like a skin of brown oil moved under the hound's belly. Soundlessly he emerged, and the sun glistened on his water-sleeked coat as he walked down on the algae-smeared rock. He seemed to walk under their muzzles slowly, and to be treading on their feet.

Let hounds hunt him! Don't help hounds or they'll chop him!

The pack was confused. Every hound owned the scent, which was like a tangled line, the end of which was sought for unraveling. But soon Deadlock pushed through the pack and told the way the otter had gone.

As Tarka was running over shillets with water scarcely deep enough to cover his rudder, Deadlock saw him and with stiff stern ran straight at him. Tarka quit the water. The dead twigs and leaves at the hedge bottom crackled and rustled as he pushed through to the meadow. While he was running over the grass, he could hear the voice of Deadlock raging as the bigger black-and-white hound

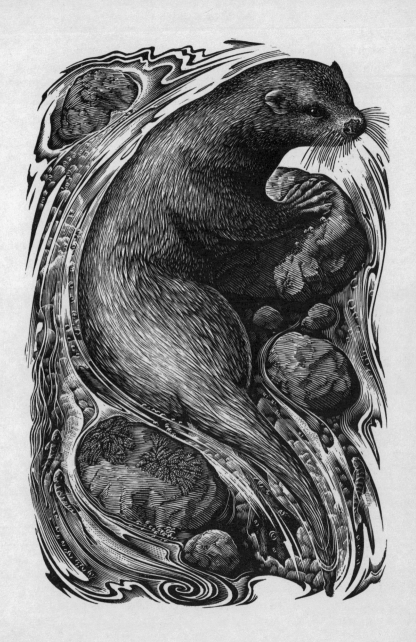

struggled though the hazel twigs and brambles and honeysuckle bines. He crossed fifty yards of meadow, climbed the bank, and ran down again onto a tarred road. The surface burned his pads, but he ran on, and even when an immense crimson creature bore down upon him he did not go back into the meadow across which hounds were streaming. With a series of shudders the crimson creature slowed to a standstill, while human figures rose out of it, and pointed. He ran under the motor coach, and came out into brown sunshine, hearing above the shouts of men the clamor of hounds trying to scramble up the high bank and pulling each other down in their eagerness.

He ran in the shade of the ditch, among bits of newspaper, banana and orange skins, cigarette ends, and crushed chocolate boxes. A long yellow creature grew bigger and bigger before him, and women rose out of it and peered down at him as he passed it. With smarting eyes he ran two hundred yards of the road, which for him was a place of choking stinks and hurtful noises. Pausing in the ditch, he harkened to the clamor changing its tone as hounds leaped down into the road. He ran on for another two hundred yards, then climbed the bank, pushed through dusty leaves and grasses and briars that would hold him, and down the sloping meadow to the stream. He splashed into the water and swam until rocks and boulders rose before him. He climbed and walked over them. His rudder drawn on mosses and lichen left a strong scent behind him. Deadlock, racing over the green-shadowed grassland, threw his tongue before the pack.

In the water, through shallow and pool, his pace was steady, but not hurried; he moved faster than the stream; he insinuated himself from slide to pool, from pool to boulder, leaving his scent in the wet marks of his pads and rudder.

People were running through the meadow, and in the near distance arose the notes of the horn and hoarse cries. Hounds' tongues broke out united and firm, and Tarka knew that they had reached the stream. The sun-laden water of the pools was spun into eddies by the thrusts of his webbed hindlegs. He passed through shadow and dapple, through runnel and plash. The water sparkled amber in the sunbeams, and his brown sleek pelt glistened whenever his back made ripples. His movements in water were unhurried, like an eel's. The hounds came nearer.

The stream after a bend flowed near the roadway, where more motorcars were drawn up. Some men and women, holding notched poles, were watching from the cars—sportsmen on wheels.

Beggars' Roost Bridge was below. With hounds so near, Tarka was heedless of the men that leaned over the stone parapet, watching for him. They shouted, waved hats, and cheered the hounds. There were ducks above the bridge, quacking loudly as they left the stream and waddled to the yard, and when Tarka came to where they had been, he left the water and ran after them. They beat their wings as they tried to fly from him, but he reached the file and scattered them, running through them and disappearing. Nearer and nearer came Deadlock, with Captain and Waterwitch leading the pack. Huntsman, whippers-in, and field were left behind, struggling through hedges and over banks.

Hounds were bewildered when they reached the yard. They ran with noses to ground in puzzled excitement. Captain's shrill voice told that Tarka had gone under a gate. Waterwitch followed the wet seals in the dust, but turned off along a track of larger webs. The line was tangled again. Deadlock threw his belving tongue. Other hounds followed, but the scent led only to a duck that beat its wings and quacked in terror before them. A man with a rake drove them off, shouting and threatening to strike them. Dewdrop spoke across the yard and the hounds galloped to her, but the line led to a gate which they tried to leap, hurling themselves up and falling from the top bar. A duck had gone under the gate, but not Tarka.

All scent was gone. Hounds rolled in the dust or trotted up to men and women, sniffing their pockets for food. Rufus found a rabbit skin and ate it; Render fought with Sandboy—but not seriously, as they feared each other; Deadlock went off alone. And hounds were waiting for a lead when the sweating huntsman, "white" pothat pushed back from his red brow, ran up with the two whippers-in and called them into a pack again. The thick scent of Muscovy ducks had checked the hunt.

Tarka had run through a drain back to the stream, and now he rested in the water that carried him every moment nearer to the murderous glooms of the glen below. He saw the colored blur of a kingfisher perching on a twig as it eyed the water for beetle or loach. The kingfisher saw him moving under the surface, as his shadow broke the net of ripple shadows that drifted in meshes of pale gold on the stony bed beneath him.

While he was walking past the roots of a willow under the bank, he heard the yapping of the terrier. Sammy had crept through the drain, and was looking out at the end, covered with black filth, and eagerly telling his big friends to follow him downstream. As he yapped, Deadlock threw his tongue. The stallion hound was below the drain, and had re-found the line where Tarka had last touched the shillets. Tarka saw him ten yards away, and slipping back into the water, swam with all webs down the current, pushing from his nose a ream whose shadow beneath was an arrow of gold pointing down to the sea.

Again he quit the water and ran on land to wear away

his scent. He had gone twenty yards when Deadlock scrambled up the bank with Render and Sandboy, breathing the scent that was as high as their muzzles. Tarka reached the waterside trees again a length ahead of Deadlock, and fell into the water like a sodden log. Deadlock leaped after him and snapped at his head; but the water was friendly to the otter, who rolled in smooth and graceful movement away from the jaws, a straight bite of which would have crushed his skull.

Here sunlight was shut out by the oaks, and the roar of the first fall was beating back from the leaves. The current ran faster, narrowing into a race with twirls and hollows marking the sunken rocks. The roar grew louder in a drifting spray. Tarka and Deadlock were carried to where a broad sunbeam came down through a break in the foliage and lit the mist above the fall. Tarka went over in the heavy white folds of the torrent and Deadlock was hurled over after him. They were lost in the churn and pressure of the pool until a small brown head appeared and gazed for its enemy in the broken honeycomb of foam. A black and white body uprolled beside it, and the head of the hound was thrust up as he tried to tread away from the current that would draw him under. Tarka was master of whirlpools; they were his playthings. He rocked in the surge with delight; then high above he heard the note of the horn. He yielded himself to the water and let it take him away down the gorge into a pool where rocks were piled above. He searched under the dripping ferny clitter for a hiding place.

Under water he saw two legs, joined to two wavering and inverted images of legs, and above them the blurred shapes of a man's head and shoulders. He turned away from the fisherman into the current again, and as he breathed he heard the horn again. On the road above the glen the pack was trotting between huntsman and whippers-in, and before them men were running with poles at the trail, hurrying down the hill to the bridge, to make a stickle to stop Tarka reaching the sea.

Tarka left Deadlock far behind. The hound was feeble and bruised and breathing harshly, his head battered and his sight dazed, but still following. Tarka passed another fisherman, and by chance the tiny feathered hook lodged in his ear. The reel spun against the check, *re-re-re* continuously, until all the silken line had run through the snake rings of the rod, which bent into a circle, and whipped back straight again as the gut trace snapped.

Tarka saw the bridge, the figure of a man below it, and a row of faces above. He heard shouts. The man standing on a rock took off his hat, scooped the air, and holla'd to the huntsman, who was running and slipping with the pack on the loose stones of the steep red road. Tarka walked out of the last pool above the bridge, ran over a mossy rock merged with the water again, and pushed through the legs of the man.

Tally Ho!

Tarka had gone under the bridge when Harper splashed into the water. The pack poured through the gap between the end of the parapet and the hillside earth, and their tongues rang under the bridge and down the walls of the houses built on the rock above the river.

Among rotting motor tires, broken bottles, tins, pails, shoes, and other castaway rubbish lying in the bright water, hounds made their plunging leaps. Once Tarka turned back; often he was splashed and trodden on. The stream was seldom deep enough to cover him, and always shallow enough for the hounds to move at double his speed. Sometimes he was under the pack, and then, while hounds were massing for the worry, his small head would look out beside a rock ten yards below them.

Between boulders and rocks crusted with shellfish and shaggy with seaweed, past worm-channered posts that marked the fairway for fishing boats at high water, the pack hunted the otter. Off each post a gull launched itself, cackling angrily as it looked down at the animals. Tarka reached the sea. He walked slowly into the surge of a wavelet, and sank away from the chop of old Harper's jaws, just as Deadlock ran through the pack. Hounds swam beyond the line of waves, while people stood at the sea lap and watched the huntsman wading to his waist. It was said that the otter was dead beat, and probably floating stiffly in the shallow water. After a few minutes the huntsman shook his head, and withdrew the horn from his waistcoat. He filled his lungs and stopped his breath and was tightening his lips for the four long notes of the call-off, when a brown head with hard dark eyes, was thrust out of the water a yard from Deadlock. Tarka stared into the hound's face and cried *Ic-yang!*

The head sank. Swimming under Deadlock, Tarka bit on to the loose skin of the flews and pulled the hound's head under water. Deadlock tried to twist around and crush the otter's skull in his jaws, but he struggled vainly. Bubbles blew out of his mouth. Soon he was choking. The hounds did not know what was happening. Deadlock's hindlegs kicked the air weakly. The huntsman waded out and pulled him inshore, but Tarka loosened his bite only when he needed new air in his lungs; and then he swam under and gripped Deadlock again. Only when hounds were upon him did Tarka let go. He vanished in a wave.

Long after the water had been emptied out of Deadlock's lungs, and the pack had trotted off for the long uphill climb to the railway station, the gulls were flying over something in the sea beyond the mouth of the little estuary.

Sometimes one dropped its yellow webs to alight on the water; always it flew up again into the restless, wailing throng, startled by the snaps of white teeth. A cargo steamer was passing up the Severn Sea, leaving a long smudge of smoke on the horizon, where a low line of clouds billowed over the coast of Wales. The regular thumps of its screws in the windless blue calm were borne to where Tarka lay, drowsy and content, but watching the pale yellow eyes of the nearest bird. At last the gulls grew tired of seeing only his eyes, and flew back to their posts; and turning on his back, Tarka yawned and stretched himself, and floated at his ease.

THE OLD MAN AND THE SEA

ERNEST HEMINGWAY

This is the most extraordinary evocation of the respect of the hunter for the hunted, of a man's closeness to the world about him. To me there is no cruelty here, only empathy.

WHEN THE SUN HAD RISEN FURTHER the old man realized that the fish was not tiring. There was only one favorable sign. The slant of the line showed he was swimming at a lesser depth. That did not necessarily mean that he would jump. But he might.

"God, let him jump," the old man said. "I have enough line to handle him."

Maybe if I can increase the tension just a little it will hurt him and he will jump, he thought. Now that it is daylight let him jump so that he'll fill the sacs along his backbone with air and then he cannot go deep to die.

He tried to increase the tension, but the line had been taut up to the very edge of the breaking point since he had hooked the fish and he felt the harshness as he leaned back to pull and knew he could put no more strain on it. I must not jerk it ever, he thought. Each jerk widens the cut the hook makes and then when he does jump he might throw it. Anyway, I feel better with the sun and for once I do not have to look into it.

There was yellow weed on the line but the old man knew that only made an added drag and he was pleased. It was the yellow Gulf weed that had made so much phosphorescence in the night.

"Fish," he said, "I love you and respect you very much. But I will kill you dead before this day ends."

Let us hope so, he thought.

A small bird came toward the skiff from the north. He was a warbler and flying very low over the water. The old man could see that he was very tired.

The bird made the stern of the boat and rested there. Then he flew around the old man's head and rested on the line where he was more comfortable.

"How old are you?" the old man asked the bird. "Is this your first trip?"

The bird looked at him when he spoke. He was too tired even to examine the line and he teetered on it as his delicate feet gripped it fast.

"It's steady," the old man told him. "It's too steady. You shouldn't be that tired after a windless night. What are birds coming to?"

The hawks, he thought, that come out to sea to meet them. But he said nothing of this to the bird who could not understand him anyway and who would learn about the hawks soon enough.

"Take a good rest, small bird," he said. "Then go in and take your chance like any man or bird or fish."

It encouraged him to talk because his back had stiffened in the night and it hurt truly now.

"Stay at my house if you like, bird," he said. "I am sorry I cannot hoist the sail and take you in with the small breeze that is rising. But I am with a friend."

Just then the fish gave a sudden lurch that pulled the old man down onto the bow and would have pulled him overboard if he had not braced himself and given some line.

The bird had flown up when the line jerked and the old man had not even seen him go. He felt the line carefully with his right hand and noticed his hand was bleeding.

"Something hurt him then," he said aloud and pulled back on the line to see if he could turn the fish. But when he was touching the breaking point he held steady and settled back against the strain of the line.

"You're feeling it now, fish," he said. "And so, God knows, am I."

He looked around for the bird now because he would have liked him for company. The bird was gone.

You did not stay long, the man thought. But it is rougher where you are going until you make the shore. How did I let the fish cut me with that one quick pull he made? I must be getting very stupid. Or perhaps I was looking at the small bird and thinking of him. Now I will pay attention to my work and then I must eat the tuna so that I will not have a failure of strength.

"I wish the boy were here and that I had some salt," he said aloud.

Shifting the weight of the line to his left shoulder and kneeling carefully he washed his hand in the ocean and held it there, submerged, for more than a minute watching the blood trail away and the steady movement of the water against his hand as the boat moved.

"He has slowed much," he said.

The old man would have liked to keep his hand in the saltwater longer, but he was afraid of another sudden lurch by the fish and he stood up and braced himself and held his hand up against the sun. It was only a line burn that had cut his flesh. But it was in the working part of his hand. He knew he would need his hands before this was over and he did not like to be cut before it started.

"Now," he said, when his hand had dried, "I must eat the small tuna. I can reach him with the gaff and eat him here in comfort."

He knelt down and found the tuna under the stern with the gaff and drew it toward him keeping it clear of the coiled lines. Holding the line with his left shoulder again, and bracing on his left hand and arm, he took the tuna off the gaff hook and put the gaff back in place. He put one knee on the fish and cut strips of dark red meat longitudinally from the back of the head to the tail. They were wedge-shaped strips and he cut them from next to the backbone down to the edge of the belly. When he had cut six strips he spread them out on the wood of the bow, wiped his knife on his trousers, and lifted the carcass of the bonito by the tail and dropped it overboard.

"I don't think I can eat an entire one," he said and drew his knife across one of the strips. He could feel the steady hard pull of the line and his left hand was cramped. It drew up tight on the heavy cord and he looked at it in disgust.

"What kind of a hand is that," he said. "Cramp then if you want. Make yourself into a claw. It will do you no good."

Come on, he thought and looked down into the dark water at the slant of the line. Eat it now and it will strengthen the hand. It is not the hand's fault and you have been many hours with the fish. But you can stay with him for ever. Eat the bonito now.

He picked up a piece and put it in his mouth and chewed it slowly. It was not unpleasant.

Chew it well, he thought, and get all the juices. It would not be bad to eat with a little lime or with lemon or with salt.

"How do you feel, hand?" he asked the cramped hand that was almost as stiff as rigor mortis. "I'll eat some more for you."

He ate the other part of the piece that he had cut in two. He chewed it carefully and then spat out the skin.

"How does it go, hand? Or is it too early to know?"

He took another full piece and chewed it.

"It is a strong full-blooded fish," he thought. "I was lucky to get him instead of dolphin. Dolphin is too sweet. This is hardly sweet at all and all the strength is still in it."

There is no sense in being anything but practical though, he thought. I wish I had some salt. And I do not know whether the sun will rot or dry what is left, so I had better eat it all although I am not hungry. The fish is calm and steady. I will eat it all and then I will be ready.

"Be patient, hand," he said. "I do this for you."

I wish I could feed the fish, he thought. He is my brother. But I must kill him and keep strong to do it. Slowly and conscientiously he ate all of the wedge-shaped strips of fish.

He straightened up, wiping his hand on his trousers.

"Now," he said. "You can let the cord go, hand, and I will handle him with the right arm alone until you stop that nonsense." He put his left foot on the heavy line that the left hand had held and lay back against the pull against his back.

"God help me to have the cramp go," he said. "Because I do not know what the fish is going to do."

But he seems calm, he thought, and following his plan. But what is his plan, he thought. And what is mine? Mine I must improvise to his because of his great size. If he will jump I can kill him. But he stays down forever. Then I will stay down with him forever.

He rubbed the cramped hand against his trousers and

tried to gentle the fingers. But it would not open. Maybe it will open with the sun, he thought. Maybe it will open when the strong raw tuna is digested. If I have to have it, I will open it, cost whatever it costs. But I do not want to open it now by force. Let it open by itself and come back of its own accord. After all, I abused it much in the night when it was necessary to free and unite the various lines.

He looked across the sea and knew how alone he was now. But he could see the prisms in the deep dark water and the line stretching ahead and the strange undulation of the calm. The clouds were building up now for the trade wind and he looked ahead and saw a flight of wild ducks etching themselves against the sky over the water, then blurring, then etching again, and he knew no man was ever alone on the sea.

He thought of how some men feared being out of sight of land in a small boat and knew they were right in the months of sudden bad weather. But now they were in hurricane months and, when there are no hurricanes, the weather of hurricane months is the best of all the year.

If there is a hurricane you always see the signs of it in the sky for days ahead, if you are at sea. They do not see it ashore because they do not know what to look for, he thought. The land must make a difference too, in the shape of the clouds. But we have no hurricane coming now.

He looked at the sky and saw the white cumulus built like friendly piles of ice cream and high above were the thin feathers of the cirrus against the high September sky.

"Light *brisa*," he said. "Better weather for me than for you, fish."

His left hand was still cramped, but he was unknotting it slowly.

I hate a cramp, he thought. It is a treachery of one's own body. It is humiliating before others to have a diarrhea from ptomaine poisoning or to vomit from it. But a cramp, he thought of it as a *calambre*, humiliates oneself especially when one is alone.

If the boy were here he could rub it for me and loosen it down from the forearm, he thought. But it will loosen up.

Then, with his right hand he felt the difference in the pull of the line before he saw the slant change in the water. Then, as he leaned against the line and slapped his left hand hard and fast against his thigh he saw the line slanting slowly upward.

"He's coming up," he said. "Come on hand. Please come on."

The line rose slowly and steadily and then the surface of the ocean bulged ahead of the boat and the fish came out. He came out unendingly and water poured from his sides. He was bright in the sun and his head and back were dark purple and in the sun the stripes on his sides showed wide and a light lavender. His sword was as long as a baseball bat and tapered like a rapier and he rose his full length from the water and then reentered it, smoothly, like a diver and the old man saw the great scythe blade of his tail go under and the line commenced to race out.

"He is two feet longer than the skiff," the old man said. The line was going out fast but steadily and the fish was not panicked. The old man was trying with both hands to keep the line just inside of breaking strength. He knew that if he could not slow the fish with a steady pressure the fish could take out all the line and break it.

He is a great fish and I must convince him, he thought. I must never let him learn his strength nor what he could do if he made his run. If I were him, I would put in everything now and go until something broke. But, thank God, they are not as intelligent as we who kill them; although they are more noble and more able.

The old man had seen many great fish. He had seen many that weighed more than a thousand pounds and he had caught two of that size in his life, but never alone. Now alone, and out of sight of land, he was fast to the biggest fish that he had ever seen, and bigger than he had ever heard of, and his left hand was still as tight as the gripped claws of an eagle.

It will uncramp though, he thought. Surely it will uncramp to help my right hand. There are three things that are brothers: the fish and my two hands. It must uncramp. It is unworthy of it to be cramped. The fish had slowed again and was going at his usual pace.

I wonder why he jumped, the old man thought. He jumped almost as though to show me how big he was. I know now, anyway, he thought. I wish I could show him what sort of man I am. But then he would see the cramped hand. Let him think I am more man than I am, and I will be so. I wish I was the fish, he thought, with everything he has against only my will and my intelligence.

He settled comfortably against the wood and took his suffering as it came and the fish swam steadily and the boat moved slowly through the dark water. There was a small sea rising with the wind coming up from the east, and at noon the old man's left hand was uncramped.

"Bad news for you, fish," he said and shifted the line over the sacks that covered his shoulders.

He was comfortable but suffering, although he did not admit the suffering at all.

"I am not religious," he said. "But I will say ten Our Fathers and ten Hail Marys that I should catch this fish, and I promise to make a pilgrimage to the Virgin de Cobre if I catch him. That is a promise."

He commenced to say his prayers mechanically. Sometimes he would be so tired that he could not remember the prayer and then he would say them fast so that they would come automatically. Hail Marys are easier to say then Our Fathers, he thought.

"Hail Mary, full of Grace, the Lord is with thee. Blessed art thou among women and blessed is the fruit of thy womb, Jesus. Holy Mary, Mother of God, pray for us sinners now and at the hour of our death. Amen." Then he added, "Blessed Virgin, pray for the death of this fish. Wonderful though he is."

With his prayers said, and feeling much better, but suffering exactly as much, and perhaps a little more, he leaned against the wood of the bow and began, mechanically, to work the fingers of his left hand.

The sun was hot now although the breeze was rising gently.

"I had better rebait that little line out over the stern," he said. "If the fish decides to stay another night I will need to eat again and the water is low in the bottle. I don't think I can get anything but a dolphin here. But if I eat him fresh enough he won't be too bad. I wish a flying fish would come on board tonight. But I have no light to attract them. A flying fish is excellent to eat raw and I would not have to cut him up. I must save all my strength now. Christ, I did not know he was so big."

"I'll kill him though," he said. "In all his greatness and his glory."

Although it is unjust, he thought. But I will show him what a man can do and what a man endures.

THE IRON WOMAN

TED HUGHES

*Now a piece from Ted Hughes's powerful ecological tale: a dread
warning that we despoil, destroy, and pollute the world about us at
our peril, for we are an integral part of it.*

*The Iron Woman is the harbinger of this message—and Lucy is
about to meet her. Lucy has just woken from a terrible nightmare,
the latch rattling at her door, a seal-like face peering down at her,
begging her to wake up. Outside, "she could see a gigantic shape
towering there in the darkness," a shape that seems to be beckoning
her outside.*

LUCY EASED OPEN THE FRONT DOOR and looked out. Her
heart was pounding. What was she going to see? A
person on top of a vehicle? Or on top of one of those
cranes they use for repairing streetlights? Or simply a
colossal person with those immense fingers? Whatever it
was, the three snowdrops had been real enough. But the
street was empty.

Now she was outside, the world seemed not quite so
dark. Already, behind the roofs to the east, the inky sky had
paled a little. She closed the door behind her and stood a
moment, listening. She realized she was hearing a skylark,

far up. Somewhere on the other side of the village a thrush sang a first few notes. But the great shape had vanished.

Then something brushed her face lightly and fell to the ground. She picked it up. A foxglove.

At the same moment, she smelled a dreadful, half-rotten smell. She knew it straightaway: the smell of the mud of the marsh. She thought it came from the foxglove. But no, it filled the whole air, and she looked upward.

An immense dark head with two huge eyes was looking down at her, around the end of the house. It must be standing in the driveway, she thought, in front of the garage.

Lucy walked slowly around the end of the house, gazing up. And there it was. Not standing, but sitting—its back to the house wall. And here was the smell all right. This immense creature seemed to be made entirely of black slime, with reeds and tendrils of roots clinging all over. Lucy simply stared up at the face that stared down at her. She felt a wild excitement, as if she were traveling at the most tremendous speed. Had this thing come from the sea, and waded through the marsh? She remembered the face like a seal's in her nightmare, the girl's face with eyes like a seal, and then very sharp and clear that voice crying: "Clean me." Had it said: "Clean me"? Was this what the snowdrops meant?

Lucy knew exactly what to do. She unrolled her father's hosepipe, which was already fitted to an outside tap, turned the tap full on, and pressed her finger half over the nozzle to make a stiff jet.

It was then she thought she heard another voice, a soft, rumbling voice. Like far-off thunder. She could not be sure where it came from. A strange voice. At least, it had a strange effect on Lucy. It made her feel safe and bold. And she seemed to hear:

"Waste no time."

The moment the jet hit the nearest leg she saw the bright gloss beneath. It looked like metal—polished black metal. The mud sluiced off easily. But it was a big job. And Lucy was thinking: What are people going to think when it gets light and they see this? She washed the nearest leg, the giant foot, the peculiar toes. She hosed between the toes. This first leg took about as much hosing as an entire car.

The voice came again, so low it seemed to vibrate inside her:

"Hurry!"

A faint tinge of pink outlined the chimneys to the east. Already it seemed that every single bird in the village must be singing. A van went past.

Lucy switched the jet to the face. It was an awesome face, like a great, black, wet mudpack. Then the giant hand opened palm upwards, flat on the driveway. Lucy saw what was wanted. She stepped on to the hand, which lifted her close to the face.

The jet sizzled into the deep crevices around the tightly closed eyes and over the strange curves of the cheeks. As she angled the jet to the massively folded shape of the lips, the eyes opened, brilliantly black, and beamed at her. Then Lucy saw that this huge being was a woman. It was exactly as if the rigid jet of water were carving this gleaming, black, giant woman out of a cliff of black clay. Last, she drove the slicing water into the hair—huge coils of wires in a complicated arrangement. And the great face closed its eyes and opened its mouth and laughed softly.

Lucy could see the muddy water splashing onto the white, pebble-dashed wall of the house and realized it was almost daylight. She turned, and saw a red-hot cinder of sun between two houses. A lorry thumped past. She knew then that she wasn't going to get this job finished.

At the same moment, still holding Lucy in her hand, the giant figure heaved upright. Lucy knew that the voice had rumbled, somewhere: "More water." She dropped the hose, which writhed itself into a comfortable position and went on squirting over the driveway.

"There's the canal," she said.

The other great hand pushed her gently, till she lay in the crook of the huge arm, like a very small doll. This was no time to bother about the mud or the smell of it. She saw the light of her own bedroom go past, slightly below her, the window still open, as the giant woman turned up the street.

When they reached the canal, and stood on the bridge looking down, Lucy suddenly felt guilty. For some reason, it was almost empty of water, as she had never seen it before. A long, black, oily puddle lay between slopes of drying gray mud. And embedded in the mud were rusty bicycle wheels, supermarket trolleys, bedsteads, prams, old refrigerators, washing machines, car batteries, even two or three old cars, along with hundreds of rusty, twisted odds and ends, tangles of wire, cans and bottles and plastic bags. They both stared for a while. Lucy felt she was seeing this place for the first time. It looked like a canal only when it was full of water. Now it was nearly empty, it was obviously a rubbish dump.

"The river," came the low, rumbling voice, vibrating Lucy's whole body where she lay.

The river ran behind a strip of woodland, a mile away across the fields. That was a strange ride for Lucy. The sun had risen and hung clear, a red ball. She could see a light on in a farmhouse. A flock of sheep and lambs poured wildly into a far corner. Any second she expected to hear a shout.

But they reached the strip of trees. And there was the

104

river. It swirled past, cold and unfriendly in the early light. The hand set Lucy down among the weeds of the bank, and she watched amazed as the gigantic figure waded out into midstream, till the water bulged and bubbled past those thighs that were like the pillars of a bridge. There, in the middle of the river, the giant woman kneeled, bowed, and plunged under the surface. For a moment, a great mound of foaming water heaved up. Then the head and shoulders hoisted clear, glistening black, and plunged under again, like the launching of a ship. Waves slopped over the bank and soaked Lucy to the knees. For a few minutes, it was like a giant sea beast out there, rearing up and plunging back under, in a boiling of muddy water.

Then abruptly the huge woman levered herself upright and came ashore. All the mud had been washed from her body. She shone like black glass. But her great face seemed to writhe. As if in pain. She spat out water and a groan came rumbling from her.

"It's washed you," cried Lucy. "You're clean!"

But the face went on trying to spit out water, even though it had no more water to spit.

"It burns!" Lucy heard. "It burns!" And the enormous jointed fingers, bunched into fists, rubbed and squeezed at her eyes.

Lucy could now see her clearly in full daylight. She gazed at the giant tubes of the limbs, the millions of rivets, the funny concertinas at the joints. It was hard to believe what she was seeing.

"Are you a robot?" she cried.

Perhaps, she thought, somebody far off is controlling this creature, from a panel of dials. Perhaps she's a sort of human-shaped submarine. Perhaps . . .

But the rumbling voice came up out of the ground, through Lucy's legs:

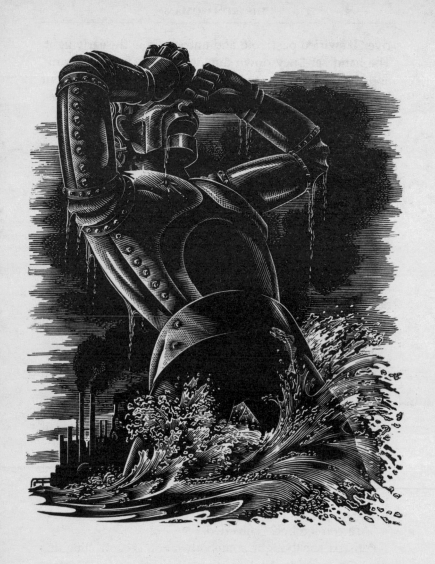

"I am not a robot," it said. "I am the real thing."

And now the face was looking at her. The huge eyes, huge black pupils, seemed to enclose Lucy—like the gentle grasp of a warm hand. The whole body was like a robot, but the face was somehow different. It was like some colossal metal statue's face, made of parts that slid over each other as they moved. Now the lips opened again, and Lucy almost closed her eyes, she almost shivered, in the peculiar vibration of the voice:

"I am Iron Woman."

"Iron Woman!" whispered Lucy, staring at her again.

"And you are wondering why I have come," the voice went on.

Lucy nodded.

"Because of this!" The voice was suddenly louder, and angry. Lucy winced, as the eyes opened even wider, larger, glaring at her.

"What? Because of what?" Lucy had no idea.

"Listen," rumbled the voice.

Lucy listened. By now, the whole land, inside the circle of the horizon, was simmering and bubbling with birdsong, like a great pan.

The birds?" she asked. "I can hear—"

"No!" And the black eyes flashed. A red light pulsed in their depths. Lucy felt suddenly afraid. What did she mean?

"Listen—listen—" The rumbling voice almost cracked into a kind of yell. A great hand had come out now and folded around Lucy's shoulders, just as her father would put his arm around her, while the other hand, with that colossal finger and thumb, just as daintily as it had held the snowdrops, took hold of her hand and gripped it, softly but firmly.

Lucy's fright lasted only for a second. Then she was

overwhelmed by what she heard. A weird, horrible sound. A roar of cries. Thousands, millions of cries—wailings, groans, screams. She closed her eyes and put her free hand over her ear. But it made no difference. The dreadful sound seemed to pound her body, as if she were standing under a waterfall of it, as if it might batter her off her feet. Or as if she were standing in a railway tunnel, and the express train was rushing toward her, an express of screaming voices—

Finally, she could stand it no longer and she actually screamed herself. She opened her eyes, trying to drag her hand free and to twist free of the hand enclosing her shoulders. But the thumb and finger held her too tightly, and the enfolding hand gripped her too firmly. And all the time the immense black eyes, so round and so fixed, stared at her. And even though her own eyes were wide open that horrible mass of screams, yells, wails, groans came hurtling closer and closer, louder and louder—till she knew that in the next moment it would hit her like that express train and sweep her away.

But at that moment, the fingers and the hand let her go, and the sound stopped. As if a switch had switched it off.

Lucy stood panting with fear. She almost started to run—anywhere away from where she had been standing. But the great eyes, now half-closed, had become gentle again.

"Oh, what was it?" cried Lucy. "Oh, how awful!" She felt herself trembling and knew she might burst into tears. Her ears were still ringing.

"What you heard," said the voice, "is what I am hearing all the time."

"But what is it?" cried Lucy again.

"That," said the voice, "is the cry of the marsh. It is the cry of the insects, the leeches, the worms, the shrimp, the water skeeters, the beetles, the bream, the perch, the carp, the pike, the eels."

"They're crying." whispered Lucy.

"The cry of the ditches and the ponds," the voice went on. "Of the frogs, the toads, the newts. The cry of the rivers and the lakes. Of all the creatures under the water, on top of the water, and all that go between. The waterbirds, the water voles, the water shrews, the otters. Did you hear what they were crying?"

Lucy was utterly amazed. She saw, in her mind's eye, all those millions of creatures, all the creepy-crawlies, clinging to stones and weeds under the water, with their mouths wide, all screeching. And the fish—she could see the dense processions of shuddering, flashing buckles and brooches, the millions of gold-ringed eyes, with their pouting lips stretched wide—screeching. And the frogs that have no lips—screaming. She suddenly remembered how the giant woman had rubbed her eyes in pain, and she thought of the wet frogs, just as wet and naked as eyeballs, burning— rubbing their eyes with their rubbery almost human fingers. And the eels—that eel. Now she knew. That eel's silent writhings had been a screaming

"What's happening?" she cried.

The Iron Woman raised her right arm and pointed at the river with her index finger. The ringing in Lucy's ears now seemed to be coming out of the end of that finger. She looked toward where the finger was pointing. The river rolled and swirled, just as before. But now it seemed that a hole had appeared in it, a fiery hole, and she could see something moving far down in the hole.

It was the eel again. Just as she had seen it before, there it was, writhing, and knotting and unknotting itself. But it was coming toward her, just as if the fiery hole were a tunnel. It came dancing and contorting itself up the bright, fiery tunnel. Now it was very close to them, in the mouth of the strange hole. She heard a crying, and knew it was the eel. And there were words in the crying. She could almost make them out, but not quite. She strained to hear the words coming from the eel that seemed to be twisting and burning in a kind of fiery furnace. And it did seem to be burning. In front of her eyes it blazed and charred, becoming a smoky, dim shape, a spinning wisp. Then the hole was empty.

But already another form had appeared far down in the fiery hole, coming toward them in a writhing dance.

It was a barbel. It danced as if it walked the water on its vibrating tail, swaying and twisting to keep its balance. Lucy could see the little tentacles of its beard lashing around its mouth as it jerked and spun in the fiery hole. And the barbel, too, was crying. It seemed to be shouting, or rather yelling, the same thing over and over. But still Lucy could not make out the words. And again, as she strained to catch the words, the barbel writhed into a twist of smoke and vanished, just as the eel had done. But already, far down inside the hole, she could see the next creature. And this time it was an otter.

Just like the others, the otter came twisting and tumbling toward them, up the fiery tunnel, in a writhing sort of dance, as if it were trying to escape from itself. And as it came it was crying something, just like the eel and the barbel. Again, Lucy could almost hear the words, louder and louder as it danced nearer and nearer, till it spun into a blot of smoke at the hole mouth and vanished.

After that came a kingfisher. This dazzling little bird came whirling and crying till it fluttered itself into a blaze of smoke like a firework spinning on a nail.

After that came a frog. The frog's dance was simply a leaping up and a falling down on its back. Then it scrambled to its feet, leaped up and fell on its back, over and over, as if it were inside some kind of spinning fiery bubble, inside the fiery hole. But its voice came loud and clear, a wailing cry like the same words shouted again and again. But Lucy still could not make out what words those were, till the frog, too, whirled into smoke.

Then came a squirming thing that Lucy could not make out. Then with a shock she recognized it. It was a human baby. It looked like a fat pink newt, jerking and flailing inside a fiery bubble. But just like those other creatures it came up the fiery tunnel, doing its dance, which was like a fighting to kick, and claw its way out of the fiery bubble. This time the crying was not like words. It was simply crying—the wailing, desperate cry of a human baby when it cries as if the world had ended.

Lucy could not bear to see any more. She knew this baby, too, would suddenly burst into flames, blaze into a whirl of smoke and vanish. She dropped her face into her hands. Her shoulders shook as she sobbed.

As she got control of herself, she suddenly thought: This is my nightmare. I'm back in it. If I make a big effort, I'll wake up and everything will be all right. And she looked up.

But if she hoped to see her attic bedroom with the case of five stuffed owls, it was no good. There in front of her eyes were the black columns of the legs of the Iron Woman. And there was the cold river. And she could feel that strangeness in her ears, that ringing, but fainter now, with the singing of the birds breaking through.

The Iron Woman was gazing out through the trees. "What's happened?" cried Lucy. "Oh, what's wrong with everything?"

The rumbling voice shook the air softly all around her. "Them," she heard, in a low thunder. "Them. Them.

They have done it. And I have come to destroy them."

The great black eyes stared at Lucy—black and yet also red, with a dull glow. Then the voice came again, louder, like a distant explosion: "Destroy them!"

And again, still louder, so the air or her ears or her whole head seemed to split. Her whole body cringed, as if a jet fighter had suddenly roared down out of nowhere ten feet above the treetops:

"Destroy them!"

Who? Lucy was wondering wildly. Who does she mean? Who are "them"? And she would have asked, but the Iron Woman had lifted a foot high above the ground and for a frightful moment Lucy thought this huge, terrible being had gone mad, like a mad elephant, and was going to stamp her flat. Then the foot came down hard, and the river bank jumped. The Iron Woman raised her other foot. She raised her arms. Her giant fists clenched and unclenched. Her foot came down and the ground leaped. Her eyes now glared bright red, like traffic lights at danger.

Slowly, the vast shape began to dance, there on the river bank. Lifting one great foot and slamming it down. Lifting the other great foot. She began to circle slowly. Her stamping sounded like deep slow drumbeats, echoing through her iron body. But as she danced, she sang, in that awful voice, as if Lucy were dangling from the tail of a jet fighter just behind the jets:

"DESTROY THE POISONERS.
THE IGNORANT ONES.
DESTROY THE POISONERS.
THE IGNORANT ONES.
THE RUBBISHERS.
DESTROY.
THE RUBBISHERS.
DESTROY."

She wasn't singing so much as roaring and groaning. She seemed to have forgotten Lucy. It was an incredible sight. The size of several big elephants rolled into one, and now working herself up, every second more and more enraged. And Lucy was thinking: She must mean the Waste Factory. People are always worrying about how the Waste Factory poisons everything. She'll trample the whole thing flat. Nothing can stop her.

Lucy's father worked at the Waste Factory. Everybody worked at the Waste Factory. Only the month before, the Waste Factory had doubled its size. It was importing waste now from all over the world. It was booming. Her father had just had another raise in wages.

At the same time, she thought of the million screams of all the water creatures, and even that human baby, inside the Iron Woman's body. No wonder she was roaring and writhing in that awful dance. All the creatures were screaming inside her, and the sound came out of her mouth as this terrible roar. Everybody within miles must be hearing it. And maybe the Iron Woman truly was going mad in front of her eyes, with the torments of all those burning, twisting, screaming water creatures inside her.

Then Lucy swayed on her feet, the darkness came rushing in from all sides, and she dropped in a faint. And she lay there unconscious, as the earth beneath her jolted and quivered.

NOAH'S ARK

THE KING JAMES BIBLE, GENESIS 6–8

A very early conservation tale, and the most famous of all. Echoes here of the global destruction we bring upon ourselves if we do not live in harmony with the world around us.

AND IT CAME TO PASS, when men began to multiply on the face of the earth, and daughters were born unto them, that the sons of God saw the daughters of men that they were fair; and they took them wives of all which they chose.

And the Lord said, My spirit shall not always strive with man, for that he also is flesh: yet his days shall be an hundred and twenty years.

There were giants in the earth in those days; and also after that, when the sons of God came in unto the daughters of men, and they bare children to them, the same became mighty men that were of old, men of renown.

And God saw that the wickedness of man was great in the earth, and that every imagination of the thoughts of his heart was only evil continually.

And it repented the Lord that he had made man on the

earth, and it grieved him at his heart.

And the Lord said, I will destroy man whom I have created from the face of the earth; both man, and beast, and the creeping thing, and the fowls of the air; for it repenteth me that I have made them.

But Noah found grace in the eyes of the Lord.

These are the generations of Noah: Noah was a just man and perfect in his generations, and Noah walked with God.

And Noah begat three sons, Shem, Ham, and Japheth.

The earth also was corrupt before God, and the earth was filled with violence.

And God looked upon the earth, and, behold, it was corrupt; for all flesh had corrupted his way upon the earth.

And God said unto Noah, The end of all flesh is come before me; for the earth is filled with violence through them; and, behold, I will destroy them with the earth.

Make thee an ark of gopher wood; rooms shalt thou make in the ark, and shalt pitch it within and without with pitch.

And this is the fashion which thou shalt make it of: The length of the ark shall be three hundred cubits, the breadth of it fifty cubits, and the height of it thirty cubits.

A window shalt thou make to the ark, and in a cubit shalt thou finish it above; and the door of the ark shalt thou set in the side thereof; with lower, second, and third stories shalt thou make it.

And, behold, I, even I, do bring a flood of waters upon the earth, to destroy all flesh, wherein is the breath of life, from under heaven; and every thing that is in the earth shall die.

But with thee I will establish my covenant; and thou shalt come into the ark, thou, and thy sons, and thy wife, and thy sons' wives with thee.

And of every living thing of all flesh, two of every sort

shalt thou bring into the ark, to keep them alive with thee; they shall be male and female.

Of fowls after their kind, and of cattle after their kind, of every creeping thing of the earth after his kind, two of every sort shall come unto thee, to keep them alive.

And take thou unto thee of all food that is eaten, and thou shalt gather it to thee; and it shall be for food for thee, and for them.

Thus did Noah; according to all that God commanded him, so did he.

And the Lord said unto Noah, Come thou and all thy house into the ark: for thee have I seen righteous before me in this generation.

Of every clean beast thou shalt take to thee by sevens, the male and his female: and of beasts that are not clean by two, the male and his female.

Of fowls also of the air by sevens, the male and the female; to keep seed alive upon the face of all the earth.

For yet seven days, and I will cause it to rain upon the earth forty days and forty nights; and every living substance that I have made will I destroy from off the face of the earth.

And Noah did according unto all that the Lord commanded him.

And Noah was six hundred years old when the flood of waters was upon the earth.

And Noah went in, and his sons, and his wife, and his sons' wives with him, into the ark, because of the waters of the flood.

Of clean beasts, and of beasts that are not clean, and of fowls, and of every thing that creepeth upon the earth, there went in two and two unto Noah into the ark, the male and the female, as God had commanded Noah.

And it came to pass after seven days, that the waters of the flood were upon the earth.

In the six hundredth year of Noah's life, in the second month, the seventeenth day of the month, the same day were all the fountains of the great deep broken up, and the windows of heaven were opened.

And the rain was upon the earth forty days and forty nights.

In the selfsame day entered Noah, and Shem, and Ham, and Japheth, the sons of Noah, and Noah's wife, and the three wives of his sons with them, into the ark; they, and every beast after his kind, and all the cattle after their kind, and every creeping thing that creepeth upon the earth after his kind, and every fowl after his kind, every bird of every sort.

And they went in unto Noah into the ark, two and two of all flesh, wherein is the breath of life.

And they that went in, went in male and female of all flesh, as God had commanded him: and the Lord shut him in.

And the flood was forty days upon the earth; and the waters increased, and bare up the ark, and it was lift up above the earth.

And the waters prevailed, and were increased greatly upon the earth; and the ark went upon the face of the waters.

And the waters prevailed exceedingly upon the earth; and all the high hills that were under the whole heaven were covered.

Fifteen cubits upward did the waters prevail; and the mountains were covered.

And all flesh died that moved upon the earth, both of fowl, and of cattle, and of beast, and of every creeping thing that creepeth upon the earth, and every man: all in whose nostrils was the breath of life, of all that was in the dry land, died.

And every living substance was destroyed which was upon the face of the ground, both man, and cattle, and the creeping things, and the fowl of the heaven; and they were destroyed from the earth: and Noah only remained alive, and they that were with him in the ark.

And the waters prevailed upon the earth an hundred and fifty days.

And God remembered Noah and every living thing, and all the cattle that was with him in the ark: and God made a wind to pass over the earth, and the waters asswaged; the fountains also of the deep and the windows of heaven were stopped, and the rain from heaven was restrained; and the waters returned from off the earth continually: and after the end of the hundred and fifty days the waters were abated.

And the ark rested in the seventh month, on the seventeenth day of the month, upon the mountains of Ararat.

And the waters decreased continually until the tenth month: in the tenth month, on the first day of the month, were the tops of the mountains seen.

And it came to pass at the end of forty days, that Noah opened the window of the ark which he had made: and he sent forth a raven, which went forth to and fro, until the waters were dried up from off the earth.

Also he sent forth a dove from him, to see if the waters were abated from off the face of the ground; but the dove found no rest for the sole of her foot, and she returned unto him into the ark, for the waters were on the face of the whole earth: then he put forth his hand, and took her, and pulled her in unto him into the ark.

And he stayed yet other seven days; and again he sent forth the dove out of the ark; and the dove came in to him in the evening; and, lo, in her mouth was an olive leaf pluckt off: so Noah knew that the waters were abated from off the earth.

And he stayed yet other seven days; and sent forth the dove; which returned not again unto him any more.

And it came to pass in the six hundredth and first year, in the first month, the first day of the month, the waters were dried up from off the earth: and Noah removed the covering of the ark, and looked, and, behold, the face of the ground was dry.

And in the second month, on the seven and twentieth of the month, was the earth dried.

And God spake unto Noah, saying, Go forth of the ark, thou, and thy wife, and thy sons, and thy sons' wives with thee.

Bring forth with thee every living thing that is with thee, of all flesh, both of fowl, and of cattle, and of every creeping thing that creepeth upon the earth; that they may breed abundantly in the earth, and be fruitful, and multiply upon the earth.

And Noah went forth, and his sons, and his wife, and his sons' wives with him: every beast, every creeping thing, and every fowl, and whatsoever creepeth on the earth, after their kinds, went forth out of the ark.

And Noah builded an altar unto the Lord; and took of every clean beast, and took of every clean fowl, and offered burnt offerings on the altar.

And the Lord smelled a sweet savor; and the Lord said in his heart, I will not again curse the ground anymore for man's sake; for the imagination of man's heart is evil from his youth; neither will I again smite anymore everything living, as I have done.

While the earth remaineth, seedtime and harvest, and cold and heat, and summer and winter, and day and night shall not cease.

THE VOYAGE OF THE *BEAGLE*

CHARLES DARWIN

Darwin's five-year scientific survey of the coasts and interiors from South America to the South Sea Islands on H.M.S. Beagle began in 1831. His observations as a naturalist were to change entirely the way we think of ourselves and our origins. Published in 1839, and written as a journal, this is a true tale of never-to-be-forgotten adventures, of wonderful encounters with animals of all kinds—but written always as a scientist, closely observed and meticulously recorded.

OCTOBER 8TH—We arrived at James Island; this island, as well as Charles Island, were long since thus named after our kings of the Stuart line. Mr. Bynoe, myself, and our servants were left here for a week, with provisions and a tent, while the *Beagle* went for water. We found here a party of Spaniards, who had been sent from Charles Island to dry fish, and to salt tortoise meat. About six miles inland, and at the height of nearly 2000 feet, a hovel had been built in which two men lived, who were employed in catching tortoises, while the others were fishing on the coast. I paid this party two visits, and slept there one night. As on the other islands, the lower region was covered by nearly leafless bushes, but the trees were here of a larger growth than elsewhere, several being two feet and some even two feet, nine inches in diameter. The upper region being kept damp by the clouds, supports a green and flourishing vegetation. So damp was the ground, that there were large beds of a coarse cyperus, in which great numbers of a very small water rail lived and bred. While staying in this upper region, we lived entirely on tortoise meat: the breastplate roasted (as the gauchos do *carne con cuero*), with the flesh on it, is very good; and the young tortoises make excellent soup; but otherwise the meat to my taste is indifferent.

One day we accompanied a party of the Spaniards in their whaleboat to a *salina*, or lake from which salt is procured. After landing, we had a very rough walk over a rugged field of recent lava, which has almost surrounded a tuff crater, at the bottom of which the salt lake lies. The water is only three or four inches deep, and rests on a layer of beautifully crystallized, white salt. The lake is quite circular, and is fringed with a border of bright green succulent plants; the almost precipitous walls of the crater are clothed with wood, so that the scene was altogether both picturesque and curious. A few years since, the sailors belonging to a sealing vessel murdered their captain in this quiet spot; and we saw his skull lying among the bushes.

During the greater part of our stay of a week, the sky was cloudless, and if the trade wind failed for an hour, the heat became very oppressive. On two days, the thermometer within the tent stood for some hours at 93°; but in the open air, in the wind and sun, at only 85°. The sand was extremely hot; the thermometer placed in some of a brown color immediately rose to 137°, and how much above that it would have risen, I do not know, for it was not graduated any higher. The black sand felt much hotter, so that even in thick boots it was quite disagreeable to walk over it.

The natural history of these islands is eminently curious, and well deserves attention. Most of the organic productions are aboriginal creations, found nowhere else; there is even a difference between the inhabitants of the different islands; yet all show a marked relationship with those of America, though separated from that continent by an open space of ocean, between 500 and 600 miles in width. The archipelago is a little world within itself, or rather a satellite attached to America, whence it has derived a few stray colonists, and has received the general character of its indigenous productions. Considering the small size of these islands, we feel the more astonished at the number of their aboriginal beings, and at their confined range. Seeing every height crowned with its crater, and the boundaries of most of the lava streams still distinct, we are led to believe that within a period, geologically recent, the unbroken ocean was here spread out. Hence, both in space and time, we seem to be brought somewhat near to that great fact—that mystery of mysteries—the first appearance of new beings on this earth.

Of terrestrial mammals, there is only one that must be considered as indigenous, namely, a mouse (*Mus galapagoensis*), and this is confined, as far as I could ascertain, to Chatham Island, the most easterly island of the group. It belongs, as I am informed by Mr. Waterhouse, to a division of the family of mice characteristic of America. At James Island, there is a rat sufficiently distinct from the common kind to have been named and described by Mr. Waterhouse; but as it belongs to the old world division of the family, and as this island has been frequented by ships for the last hundred and fifty years, I can hardly doubt that this rat is merely a variety, produced by the new and peculiar climate, food, and soil, to which it has been subjected. Although no one has a right to speculate without distinct facts, yet even with respect to the Chatham Island mouse, it should be borne in mind, that it may possibly be an American species imported here; for I have seen, in a most unfrequented part of the pampas, a native mouse living in the roof of a newly-built hovel, and therefore its transportation in a vessel is not improbable: analogous facts have been observed by Dr. Richardson in North America.

We will now turn to the order of reptiles, which gives the most striking character to the zoology of these islands. The species are not numerous, but the numbers of individuals of each species are extraordinarily great. There is one small lizard belonging to a South American genus, and two species (and probably more) of the *Amblyrhynchus*—a genus confined to the Galapagos islands. There is one snake which is numerous; it is identical, as I am informed by M. Bibron, with the *Psammophis temminckii* from Chile. Of sea turtle I believe there is more than one species; and of tortoises there are, as we shall presently show, two or three species or races. Of toads and frogs there are none: I was surprised at this, considering how well suited for them the temperate and damp upper woods appeared to be. It recalled to my mind the remark made by Bory St. Vincent, namely, that none of this family are found on any of the volcanic islands in the great oceans. As far as I can ascertain from various works, this seems to hold good throughout the Pacific, and even in the large islands of the Sandwich Archipelago. Mauritius offers an apparent exception, where I saw the *Rana mascariensis* in abundance: this frog is said now to inhabit the Seychelles, Madagascar, and Bourbon; but on the other hand, Du Bois, in his voyage of 1669, states that there were no reptiles in Bourbon except tortoises; and the Officier du Roi asserts that before 1768 it had been attempted, without success, to introduce frogs into Mauritius—I presume, for the purpose of eating: hence it may be well doubted whether this frog is an aboriginal of these islands. The absence of the frog family in the oceanic islands is the more remarkable, when contrasted with the case of lizards, which swarm on most of the smallest islands. May this difference not be caused, by the greater facility with which the eggs of lizards, protected by calcareous shells, might be transported through saltwater, than could the slimy spawn of frog?

I will first describe the habits of the tortoise (*Testudo nigra*, formerly called *indica*), which has been so frequently alluded to. These animals are found, I believe, on all the islands of the archipelago; certainly on the greater number. They frequent in preference the high damp parts, but they likewise live in the lower and arid districts. I have already shown, from the numbers that have been caught in a single day, how very numerous they must be. Some grow to an immense size: Mr. Lawson, an Englishman, and vice governor of the colony, told us that he had seen several so large, that it required six or eight men to lift them from the ground; and that some had afforded as much as 200 pounds of meat. The old males are the largest, the females rarely growing to so great a size: the male can readily be distinguished from the female by the greater length of its tail. The tortoises which live on those islands where there is no water, or in the lower and arid parts of the others, feed chiefly on the succulent cactus. Those which frequent the higher and damp regions, eat the leaves of various trees, a kind of berry (called *guayavita*), which is acid and austere, and likewise a pale green filamentous lichen (*Usnera plicata*), which hangs in tresses from the boughs of the trees.

The tortoise is very fond of water, drinking large quantities, and wallowing in the mud. The larger islands alone possess springs, and these are always situated towards the central parts, and at a considerable height. The tortoises, therefore, which frequent the lower districts, when thirsty are obliged to travel from a long distance. Hence broad and well-beaten paths branch off in every direction from the wells down to the seacoast; and the Spaniards by following them up, first discovered the watering places. When I landed at Chatham Island, I could not imagine what animal traveled so methodically along well-chosen tracks. Near the springs it was a curious spectacle to behold many of these huge creatures, one set eagerly traveling onward with outstretched necks, and another set returning, after having drunk their fill. When the tortoise arrives at the spring, quite regardless of any spectator, he buries his head in the water above his eyes, and greedily swallows great mouthfuls, at the rate of about ten in a minute. The inhabitants say each animal stays three or four days in the neighborhood of the water, and then returns to the lower country; but they differed respecting the frequency of these visits. The animal probably regulates them according to the nature of the food on which it has lived. It is, however, certain, that tortoises can subsist even on those islands, where there is no other water than what falls during a few rainy days in the year.

I believe it is well ascertained that the bladder of the frog acts as a reservoir for the moisture necessary to its existence: such seems to be the case with the tortoise. For some time after a visit to the springs, their urinary bladders are distended with fluid, which is said gradually to decrease in volume, and to become less pure. The inhabitants, when walking in the lower district, and overcome with thirst, often take advantage of this circumstance, and drink the contents of the bladder if full: in one I saw killed, the fluid was quite limpid, and had only a very slightly bitter taste. The inhabitants, however, always first drink the water in the pericardium, which is described as being best.

The tortoises, when purposely moving toward any point, travel by night and day, and arrive at their journey's end much sooner than would be expected. The inhabitants, from observing marked individuals, consider that they travel a distance of about eight miles in two or three days. One large tortoise, which I watched, walked at the rate of sixty yards in ten minutes, that is 360 yards in the hour, or four miles a day—allowing a little time for it to eat on the road. During the breeding season, when the male and female are together, the male utters a hoarse roar or bellowing, which, it is said, can be heard at the distance of more than a hundred yards. The female never uses her voice, and the male only at these times; so that when the people hear this noise, they know that the two are together. They were at this time (October) laying their eggs. The female, where the soil is sandy, deposits them together, and covers them up with sand; but where the ground is rocky she drops them indiscriminately in any hole: Mr. Bynoe found seven placed in a fissure. The egg is white and spherical; one which I measured was seven inches and three eighths in circumference, and therefore larger than a hen's egg. The young tortoises, as soon as they are hatched, fall a prey in great numbers to the carrion-feeding buzzard. The old ones seem generally to die from accidents, as from falling down precipices: at least, several of the inhabitants told

me that they had never found one dead without some evident cause.

The inhabitants believe that these animals are absolutely deaf; certainly they do not overhear a person walking close behind them. I was always amused when overtaking one of these great monsters, as it was quietly pacing along, to see how suddenly, the instant I passed, it would draw in its head and legs, and uttering a deep hiss fall to the ground with a heavy sound, as if struck dead. I frequently got on their backs, and then giving a few raps on the hinder part of their shells, they would rise up and walk away—but I found it very difficult to keep my balance. The flesh of this animal is largely employed, both fresh and salted; and a beautiful clear oil is prepared from the fat. When a tortoise is caught, the man makes a slit in the skin near its tail, so as to see inside its body, whether the fat under the dorsal plate is thick. If it is not, the animal is liberated; and it is said to recover soon from this strange operation. In order to secure the tortoises, it is not sufficient to turn them like turtles, for they are often able to get on their legs again.

There can be little doubt that this tortoise is an aboriginal inhabitant of the Galapagos; for it is found on all, or nearly all, the islands, even on some of the smaller ones where there is no water; had it been an imported species, this would hardly have been the case in a group which has been so little frequented. Moreover, the old buccaneers found this tortoise in greater numbers even than at present: Wood and Rogers also, in 1708, say that it is the opinion of the Spaniards that it is found nowhere else in this quarter of the world. It is now widely distributed; but it may be questioned whether it is in any other place aboriginal. The bones of a tortoise at Mauritius, associated with those of the extinct dodo, have generally been considered as belonging to this tortoise: if this had been so, undoubtedly it must have been there indigenous; but M. Bibron informs me that he believes that it was distinct, as the species now living there certainly is.

* * *

From just such observations, Darwin went on to develop his theory of evolution by natural selection, which he put forward in The Origin of Species, *published in 1859.*

WOLF BROTHER

CHIEF BUFFALO CHILD LONG LANCE

Chief Buffalo Child Long Lance was born in the early 1880s. He was a boxer, a wrestler, a soldier in World War I, and a writer. Here he provides an insight into how it was when men lived close to the animal world—so close they felt as one with their fellow creatures. There have been moments in the countryside when I have genuinely felt that closeness. They are moments of the purest pleasure.

FOLLOWING THIS TERRIBLE BATTLE with the Crees, our chiefs decided that we should pick some quiet place in the Rockies and spend the remainder of the winter there. There were large herds of Wild Horses running the ranges of the big plateau between the Cascades and the Rocky Mountains—Northern British Columbia—and our fathers decided that we should stay here until spring came, and then go west to this plateau and capture a herd of good Horses, before venturing out onto the plains again.

We traveled northwestward through the mountains until we came to the western foothills of the Rockies, and here, in a deep snow-covered pocket of the Rockies, we settled down for the remainder of the winter.

In our band at that time we had a very noted warrior and hunter named Eagle Plume. It was the custom in those days, when the men were being killed so often and the women were growing to outnumber them, for one warrior to have from three to five wives. It was the only way that we could make sure that all of our women would be taken care of when they should reach old age.

But this warrior, Eagle Plume, had only one wife. He was a tall, handsome warrior of vigorous middle age, and but for one thing he was well contented with his pretty wife. She had served him well. She was always busy preparing his meals and waiting upon him; and tanning the hides of the furry denizens of the wilderness, which were killed in large numbers by this famous hunter of the Blackfeet. But she had no children.

Indians are extremely fond of children, and to have no offspring is regarded as a calamity, a curse. Boy children were always preferred; as they could grow up to be hunters and warriors, while girl children could be of little economic use to the family or the tribe.

Eagle Plume thought of adding another wife to his camp, one who might bear him a child; but he loved his faithful young woman and he was reluctant to put this idea into execution. He was unlike many men; he could love but one woman.

However, children were wanted, and Eagle Plume's wife had spent many hours crying alone in her tepee, because the Great Spirit had not given her the power to present him with a baby with which to make their life complete. We heard our old people discuss this, and many times they would send us over to Eagle Plume's camp to play and to keep them company. They would treat us like their own children and give us attentions that we would not receive even from our own parents.

Like all great Indian hunters, Eagle Plume liked most to hunt alone. As we camped in the Northern Rockies that winter, he would go out by himself and remain for days. He would return heavily laden with the pelts of Otter, Mink, Black Wolf, Marten, and Lynx.

It was well through the winter toward spring, and the snow was still very deep, when early one morning he set out on one of his periodic hunting trips into the wild country to the north of where we were camping. That evening as he was making his way down a mountain draw to seek out a campsite, a Wolf came out of the bush and howled at him in the bitter white twilight.

It was a big Wolf, not a Coyote, but one of the largest specimens of the huge black Timber Wolf. With the true curiosity of the Wolf, it watched Eagle Plume make camp, then it went quietly away.

"Go now, my brother," said Eagle Plume. "Tomorrow, I will follow you for that thick fur on your skin."

And so the next morning, running on his snowshoes, and with a large round ball in his muzzle loader, Eagle Plume went on the trail of the Wolf.

It was easy for an Indian to follow its path, because its tracks were bigger than any Wolf tracks he had ever seen. It led Eagle Plume a far journey across a hanging mountain valley and on through a heavily forested range of low-lying mountains. The Wolf seemed to be bent steadily on a trail that led due north. Nothing, not even the fresh crosstrails of Caribou, had swerved it from this purposeful course. It acted not like a hunted thing evading its pursuer.

Eagle Plume had traveled all day, and the late afternoon sun was making long shadows, when suddenly as he peered ahead, he saw the big Wolf run out on a naked ridge that rolled up from a bushy mountain plain.

It had been snowing for some hours in a quiet, intense

way; and with the descent of the sun, the wind was rising with fitful whines, making little swirling gusts of snowdrift on the white surface of the land, which foretold the approach of a mountain storm. The new snow had made the going heavy for Eagle Plume, and it must have been tiring to the Wolf, too; for it was now sinking to its belly with each step.

Eagle Plume was a tireless hunter, and he knew that if the Wolf kept to the open country, he, with the superiority of his snowshoes, could wear it down. Already the big, shaggy creature was showing signs of fatigue, and the intrepid hunter was remorselessly closing up the distance that his quarry was losing.

After his first view of the Wolf on the ridge, Eagle Plume lost sight of it for a while; then he saw it again, and when the sun, with its sinister attendants of two false suns, touched the rim of the mountains to the west, the Wolf remained in plain view all of the time. The Blackfoot was sweeping forward on the bumpy surface of the great rolling sea of snow at a long, tireless lope, while the Wolf seemed to be floundering along in distress.

The wind continued to rise, and soon the country was enveloped in a stinging, blinding chaos of drifting snow. A blizzard was coming up. And even the Wolf, wild denizen of the region as he was, was now seeking harborage.

The mountain valley lay flat and expressionless under its snowy mantle. The only relief to the landscape was a pine grove which stood like an island straight ahead.

A blizzard had no terrors for a good hunter like Eagle Plume, when there was wood and shelter in sight. He knew that the Wolf was making for cover, and he hurried his footsteps so that he might overtake it and make his kill before it escaped into the pines or became lost in the darkness of the raging blizzard.

But the storm gathered in strength and violence, and Eagle Plume was forced to summon all of his remaining energies to reach the shelter of the trees before darkness and death should overtake him. When, panting and exhausted, he at last made his objective, he had long since lost sight and track of his game.

He rested briefly and then began to skirt the lea side of the pines for a suitable place to make fire and camp. As he was doing this, he suddenly became aware that the Wolf was watching him from a nearby snowbank. Cautiously he turned in his tracks and leveled the long, cold barrel of his gun straight between a pair of furtive gray eyes—wild, slanted eyes, which looked calmly at him like two pieces of gray flint. He paused for a second and then pulled the trigger. There was a flash in the nipple—but no explosion. The priming had been affected by the drifting snow.

With his teeth he pulled the wooden stopper of his powder horn and poured dry powder into the pan, keeping his eyes on the steady gaze of the Wolf, which made no effort to move or escape. As he deftly reloaded and primed his gun, he spoke softly to the Wolf in the manner of the Indian, saying:

"Oh, my brother, I will not keep you waiting in the cold and snow, I am preparing the messenger I will send you. Have patience for just a little while."

As he shook the dry powder onto the pan of his gun, the Wolf, without any previous movement of warning, suddenly made a mighty leap—and vanished.

The swift-gathering darkness and the howling blizzard made useless any further effort to capture this remarkable pelt, and realizing for the first time the futility of his quest, Eagle Plume now laid aside his gun and unloosened an ax that hung at his belt, and made hurried preparations to shield himself from the blizzard. He cut down some dead spruce for a fire, and then made himself a shelter of mountain bushes.

During a slight pause in his labor, his ear, keenly attuned to the voices of the wilderness, caught a strange sound. When he listened intently and caught it a second time there was no mistaking what it was. It was the wail of a child.

Throwing down his ax and wrapping his blanket about his head and body, he stumbled out into the darkness and hurried blindly into the direction whence the wail had come. As he jogged along through the swirling snow, his ears alert to hold the wailing sound above that of the screeching wind, one of his snowshoes caught in something and he fell face-forward into the snow. As he got up and reached down to pick up his blanket, his hand touched the heavy object that had tripped him. He kneeled down and looked at it—and it was a woman—an Indian woman—a dead Indian woman.

Still the wailing continued. He walked around and around trying to locate it. It seemed to come from the air, not from the ground. From point to point he walked and stopped and listened. Finally he walked up to a tree, and there, hanging high out of the reach of prowling animals, he found a living child in a moss bag—a baby a few months old.

Snug in its native cradle, packed with dry moss and Rabbit skins, it had suffered none from the cold.

He built a great fire and made a camp, and slept that night with the foundling wrapped in his arms.

In the morning he snared some Rabbits, and slitting the throat of one with his hunting knife, he pressed the warm blood into the mouth of the hungry infant.

With his ax and some saplings it did not take him long to knock together a rough sleigh. And so he came back to our camp in the valley, dragging the unknown dead woman behind him; and underneath his capote he carried the child in its moss bag.

When the people of our camp came out to meet this strange company of two living and one dead, he handed the baby to his wife and said:

"Here is our child; we will no longer have need for a strange woman in our lodge."

Eagle Plume's wife cradled the child in her arms and warmed it to her bosom; and our old people said that the fires of maternity kindled in her at the touch of the infant, and that milk for its sustenance flowed in those breasts that for so long had been dry.

That night, as we sat around the campfire and Eagle Plume told his story with all the graphic detail of an Indian recital, a big Wolf cried its deep-throated howl from a high butte that overlooked our camp.

"*Mokuyi!*—It is he, the Wolf!" cried Eagle Plume. Then, raising his hand, he declared: "I shall never kill another; they are my brothers."

And, on the instant he turned to the child and christened him, Mokuyi-Oskon, Wolf Brother, and he was known by this name until he was eighteen.

The child grew and flourished. He became a great chief; and his name is today graven on a stone shaft which commemorates the termination of intertribal Indian wars in the Northwest.

SON-SON FETCHES THE MULE

JAMES BERRY

I have noticed on our farm how animals often seem to empathize with children. The horse, the donkey, the goose, the cow—all know they have nothing to fear from a child. Sometimes though, as in this story set in Jamaica, empathy needs a little encouragement.

ANIMALS HAVE ANOTHER SENSE, it would seem. They know when you are a child, and they love you for being a child. An animal will let a child pet him, boss him, and even handle him upside-down, in any crazy or awkward old way, like he was dead. He would love it and give himself up to it, limply and totally. But there are other times when an animal hates it if a boy gets the better of him. That happened to Son-Son. Just fetching the mule, Son-Son found himself in trouble with him. Not expecting it, the good-good behavior of the work mule was all spite, all vicious teeth and hooves kicked up in the air. And now Son-Son had the mule to fetch as a regular morning job, before school.

Yesterday—first time he started this new job—the mule gave him a really bad time. He played bad man. Could

140

have damaged him! And nobody must ever know—*must ever know*—he couldn't handle Maroontugger, couldn't deal with him. Son-Son knew it and saw it: this job was his job. He must do it himself.

Like yesterday, today was an everyday warm tropical early morning. Son-Son carried a coil of rope over his shoulder. His dad had told him to carry it. He should use the rope to make a halter around Maroontugger's head, before he untethered him.

Son-Son came alone into the field of high grass. Much more excited than worried, he felt good. And he looked good. He wore his long-peaked white cap, short-sleeved floral shirt, short trousers, and his sandals. He walked under one of the coconut palm trees that stood scattered about. Even when his sandals and toes quickly got wet with dew from the grass and weeds he didn't mind. Son-Son took no notice of the morning sunlight or the tree shadows. He took no notice of noisy birds fluttering in trees, doing peep-peeps, squawk-squawks, coo-coos, or just straight singing. Son-Son's job made him walk nippily on, eyes ahead. Everything about him made him look purposeful.

In truth, Son-Son was thinking he liked the business of helping his dad. It made him feel grown-up. But, best, really, it was great to handle and ride the big mule totally on his own. He'd handled Maroontugger before, lots of times, though not by himself, till yesterday. They knew each other well. Yet when he came to take Maroontugger in for work yesterday, the mule treated him like a stranger. The mule put on a bad-bad face. Tried to attack him! He had to jump quick, away from the mule's kicks! And he wouldn't let him get the loop of rope around his long head; he wouldn't let him get on his back to ride him home; then he kicked-up and kicked-up, trying to throw him off.

At one time yesterday he'd gotten worried his job was taking him too long. And he'd figured it out that the mule didn't at all like a ten-year-old taking him in for work. Then he'd also seen that it wasn't anything about *him* that Maroontugger disliked. The mule worked too hard. And, after all, who could blame him trying to get a day off? But a job was a job. He had to show Maroontugger that he had a job to do, just as he, Son-Son, had a job to do as well. And bad and vicious as the mule was, he had to take him in for work.

Son-Son came on into the field lit with morning sunlight. He saw Maroontugger. He was still feeding – head down in the field of high grass and scattered trees. Son-Son stopped. He watched the mule. He saw Maroontugger and yesterday's terrible mule-madness went from him. Evaporated! Son-Son felt good. It was great to be there alone with this big elephant-looking reddish fellow. He listened to the mule's greedy and noisy chewing. The huge jaws with half circles of axlike grabber teeth chewed grass again and again. The working of the big jaws made a noise like a grinding in an empty barrel. Son-Son's eyes widened and shone. "Jees!" he thought. "Terrific! Terrific how the grinding of the strong and loud eating has no good manners! No good manners at all!"

In his friendliest voice, Son-Son said, "Good mornin', Maroontug! Good mornin'!"

The mule lifted his head, tossed his long ears forward and stopped chewing. His steady eyes watched Son-Son. And Son-Son couldn't guess that in the straight look the mule said, "Oh! So that's it! It's you again. The boss sent you again. You the boy to take me in for work! Well, we'll see! We'll see about that, won't we?"

Son-Son grinned. "Ahright, Maroontugger? Between we, you an' me the tops, you know! Ahright?" The mule's long ears, tossed forward over his eyes, reminded him of his own long-peaked cap on his head. He walked forward. "Had a good night, Tugger-boy? Sleeping alone under stars?" Son-Son stopped again, looking around, fascinated as he had been the morning before. The high grass had been eaten or trampled down in a circle, as much as the mule's rope would allow. Son-Son said, "So you eat an' eat all through the night! No sleep, then? You just eat an' eat right through till daylight? Gosh! I couldn't do that. I couldn't eat all night like that, Tugger-boy." He looked at the mule's huge bulge of two-sided belly. "Look at your belly! Jees! Look at you! I bet you the greediest an' strongest mule, ever. I bet you could pull away any great house. And could run away pulling any busload of people! Or any high-up loaded banana truck! Listen, listen, Maroontug! I just get a great new idea."

"Everyday's always so, so sunny an' hot. Suppose one day—one day—when it really raining hard, I take you fo' a wet gallop, an' you take me fo' the wet-wet ride? Eh? How about that? Roun' an' roun' the big pasture land fo' a good wet rainy gallop, when the two of we soak-soak to the skin, dripping? Eh? Naw? Dohn like it? Okay. I think again."

"You always working. An' I always going school. Suppose, one day—one day—I dohn go school an' you dohn go work, an' we just team up? We team up big-big. We go cricket match. You walk beside me. We walk like man an' man. No rope on your head or anything. An' then, we stand together an' watch play-ball. Just watch! An' I explain the whole game to you. Then, then, when I have my best-best favorite thing—which is my barbecue jerk pork an' dry bread—I get you some sugar. Naw? No good? Well—when I have my second best-best favorite thing— which is fried fish and fried dumplin', followed by cool ginger beer—I get you a pint-a stout. Naw? I can see you would-a like rum. Noh. No rum. I cahn buy rum like that. But—all the same—Maroontug, I got to go to school. An' you got-to go work. An' I must take you in. So, I better."

The mule stood there all the time, staring. Son-Son walked up to him, taking the coil of rope from his shoulder. He reached up to put the rope around its head and the mule's rebellion again was on. The meanest, wildest attacking look came over the mule's face. It flattened its ears back against its head. A swift dread in Son-Son's face said, stop it! stop it! as the mule swung around and kicked out at Son-Son. Only swift evasive movement saved him. But mud from the mule's iron shoes had flown up to his cheek and stuck. The mule trotted off, turned its back and stood at the full stretch of its rope, looking away.

Really cross, Son-Son was brisk. Wiping the soft blob of earth and grass from his cheek, he rushed up to the mule's face and shouted. "Maroontugger! What you think you playing at? Eh? What you think you doing? You think you all wild, stupid, bad, and fool-fool! Why you behaving like you have no training? An' no respect? You want a good friend get rough an' careless with you? You wahn me beat you? You wahn feel my whip hand? I tell you—dohn change me. You well know, you a good trained worker. An' I Son-Son," tapping his chest with his fingers, "I the man who must take you in. Take you in fo' work. This very mornin'. Understan'? Ahright? So no more wild foolishness! You hear me? Good. I going put the rope around your head, softly, softly. Know that. So, easy now. Easy . . . Steady now, boy . . . Steady. Easy now . . ."

As Son-Son again was about to slip the wide loop of rope over Maroontugger's head, the mule bared his enormous teeth and clapped his jaws together near Son-Son's face. Horror-struck, "Stop et!" he bawled. His screaming rage echoed through the field and panicked the mule. It tossed its head in the air, backed off, turned around, and walked away. Again it stood with its rear end turned on Son-Son, as if to say, "Go away. I don't want to see you. Don'y want anybody collecting me. Don't want any work. Sweating, sweating, all day, pulling logs uphill, pulling, pulling . . ."

Son-Son felt upset and looked it. It hurt him that Maroontugger didn't take him as a friend. "How can he not take me as a friend?" he whispered. He looked out up and down along the track at the side of the land. He stood still in the grassy field. If his dad came after him there'd be trouble. His dad knew he'd handled Maroontugger before. He might forget it was never by himself—except yesterday. It would be hard to make his dad believe Maroontugger wanted to hurt or scare him off. And—he had other morning jobs to do.

Unexpectedly, Son-Son felt better. He knew—he just knew—it wasn't himself Maroontugger disliked. For sure, it was hard work the mule wanted a rest from. True-true, the mule's job was sweaty, terrible. Two other mules tugged and pulled timber logs up to the sawmill with Maroontugger. Even so, cutting up the hillside was neither fun nor easy game to play. And whether his dad worked Maroontugger himself or not, the mule went uphill-downhill, all day long in the hot-hot sun.

His dad never took things easy himself. His dad gave way to nothing. His dad worked himself as hard as he worked his mule. Partner to another man using the electric saw, he ripped and ripped massive tree trunks into timber. By himself with a handsaw, ax, or machete, he cut and chopped away the tree limbs and branches. He cleared away branches and heaved logs. At sundown, when he and Maroontugger came home each night, his dad's clothes were full of hot-sun smell and sweat and woodsap.

And when he changed clothes, sawdust fell off his shirt and out of his turnups and boots.

Son-Son began to imagine everybody else getting on with their morning jobs at his yard. He imagined his mum at the paraffin stove getting breakfast. His oldest brother had fed the chickens and now fed the pigs. His sister tidied the house. His smaller brother had got the barrel more than half full with water from the standing pipe on the village road. His dad had milked the cow. His dad would soon be sitting on the back steps sharpening his ax and machete. First to have breakfast, his dad could be having it any time now, giving half of it to the dog, Judoboy. All that meant he'd soon be ready to saddle up Maroontugger. He would soon want to wrap and sheath his machete and ax and then fasten them against the saddle, before he rode out of the yard with Judoboy following.

Unexpectedly, Son-Son head a voice, "Havin' a spot a trouble, Son-Son, mi boy?"

Son-Son swung his head around quickly and saw Mister G. He was a short man in straw hat, short sleeves, and sandals, carrying a bag around his shoulder and a machete in his hand. On his way to his plot of land, Mister G. had come down the lane.

"Maroontugger trying play bad-man with me, sir."

Mister G. chuckled. "Yeh, I see that." He stood. He and the mule looked at each other. "Son-Son, do you job. Go right on, Son-Son. Handle him!" Mister G. watched. Then he strolled away.

Son-Son began walking up to the mule. He had a new feeling. He always knew he was the mule's boss. But, now, unexpectedly, that feeling had grown much bigger. A big and bold confidence came more and more into his steps and whole body. It flowed in him like a strange magic light. The mule looked away and stood quietly, peacefully.

The fearless feeling Son-Son had was terrific. He knew he had grown taller, into something almost as muscular and strong and tough as his dad. He knew this new light in him subdued the mule. He knew Maroontugger couldn't move and wouldn't move.

The mule just stood there, calm-calm, letting himself be handled. "Tuggerboy? You see how it easy? See how it easy-easy? Nice an' easy?" Son-Son had put the big loop of rope round Maroontugger's head. He then brought it against each side of the face, all the way down to the corners of the mouth. He tied the dangling rope on one side, took it across above the nose, tied it, drew a long loop for reins and tied it the other side of the mule's jaw. All the time, Son-Son looked like a midget harnessing an elephant. He completed the haltermaking, feeling good. He stroked Maroontugger's neck. "You see, is ahright. Ahright an' easy? Eh? Ahright an' easy? Good boy."

Son-Son led the mule to the post in the ground where he was tethered. He loosed the rope.

Son-Son really thought his battles with Maroontugger were all over. But, Maroontugger knew differently. Maroontugger's head kept a lot more secret spite to force Son-Son to leave him alone. As Son-Son tried to get up on to the mule's back the new tricks started. Every time Son-Son tried to clamber up, Maroontugger gently eased himself away like a sideways dance. And Son-Son came down again, right on his own two legs. Over and over, holding on to the rope-reins against the mule's shoulder, Son-Son heaved himself up; and each time, that smart sideways movement made him miss his mount and come down again. Finally, Son-Son chuckled with a sigh, saying "Tugger-boy—okay. You've had your go. Now I'll have mine."

Son-Son led the mule and tied his head close against a coconut tree. Then, holding the end of the rope, he climbed up the tree trunk and lowered himself down on the mule's back. Son-Son thought at last he'd won; he couldn't believe the mule kept an extra reserve store of badness saved up. The moment Son-Son drew that slippery knot he'd tied around the tree and loosed the mule, that was it! Maroontugger tugged his head, swished his tail, and jumped off, racing away like a wild bull, all crazy and malicious. The mule bolted on, going its own way, without control. Son-Son could not check him. Bobbing his head with a stubborn defiance, Maroontugger raced on, going deeper into the field. He galloped recklessly under trees, trying to knock his rider off. Son-Son ducked under branches, lying down on the mule's bare back, like a North American Indian rider. His cap blew away. All the time now, he pulled and jerked and tugged at the mule's head as hard as he could, shouting, "Whoa! Whoa, now! Whoa, Maroontugger! Whoa, boy!"

At last, pulling and holding him firmly now, Son-Son turned Maroontugger around and held him to a walking pace. Not even allowed to break into a trot, he was ridden right back across the field out onto the track and then the village road.

Son-Son rode home into his yard on the big mule. He dismounted and tethered him, to await saddling up by his dad. The smell of brewed coffee, fried fish, and breadfruit roasting on the woodfire made Son-Son realize how hungry he was.

He went into the kitchen and couldn't believe how everything was normal. And nobody said anything about taking too long fetching the mule. Nobody even mentioned he'd lost his cap. And he certainly would say nothing about it.

Nobody was ever going to say he couldn't manage Maroontugger. Nobody was even going to know the mule gave him a hard time. Yet, as he ate breakfast, Son-Son knew the struggle with Maroontugger wasn't over. But, he was ready. He was ready. Always, he was going to let that mule understand—Son-Son was tall-tall.

HE WAS A GOOD LION

BERYL MARKHAM

Beryl Markham was born in 1902 and grew up on a farm in East Africa. As an adult she was the first pilot to fly solo across the Atlantic, east to west. Her life reads like a novel—but then the best of fiction rings true. This story is true *and reads like the best of fiction: the story of a tame lion whose instincts get the better of him, just once.*

WHEN I WAS A CHILD, I spent all my days with the Nandi Murani, hunting barefooted, in the Rongai Valley, or in the cedar forests of the Mau Escarpment.

At first I was not permitted to carry a spear, but the Murani depended on nothing else.

You cannot hunt an animal with such a weapon unless you know the way of his life. You must know the things he loves, the things he fears, the paths he will follow. You must be sure of the quality of his speed and the measure of his courage. He will know as much about you, and at times make better use of it.

But my Murani friends were patient with me.

"*Amin yut!*" one would say, "what but a dik-dik will run like that? Your eyes are filled with clouds today, Lakweit!"

That day my eyes were filled with clouds, but they were young enough eyes and they soon cleared. There were other days and other dik-dik. There were so many things.

There were dik-dik and leopard, kongoni and warthog, buffalo, lion, and the hare that jumps. There were many thousands of the hare that jumps.

And there were wildebeest and antelope. There was the snake that crawls and the snake that climbs. There were the birds and young men like whips of leather, like rainshafts in the sun, like spears before a singiri.

"*Amin yut!*" the young men would say, "that is no buffalo spoor, Lakweit. Here! Bend down and look. Bend down and look at this mark. See how this leaf is crushed. Feel the wetness of this dung. Bend down and look so that you may learn!"

And so, in time, I learned. But some things I learned alone.

There was a place called Elkington's Farm by Kabete Station. It was near Nairobi on the edge of the Kikuyu Reserve, and my father and I used to ride there from town on horses or in a buggy, and along the way my father would tell me things about Africa.

Sometimes he would tell me stories about the tribal wars—wars between the Masai and the Kikuyu (which the Masai always won), or between the Masai and the Nandi (which neither of them ever won), and about their great leaders and their wild way of life which, to me, seemed much greater fun than our own. He would tell me of Lenana, the brilliant Masai *ol-oiboni*, who prophesied the coming of the White Man, and of Lenana's tricks and stratagems and victories, and about how his people were unconquerable and unconquered—until, in retaliation against the refusal of the Masai warriors to join the King's African Rifles, the British marched upon the Native villages; how, inadvertently, a Masai woman was killed, and how two Hindu shopkeepers were murdered in reprisal by the Murani. And thus, why it was that the thin, red line of Empire had grown slightly redder.

He would tell me old legends sometimes about Mount Kenya, or about the Menegai Crater, called the Mountain of God, or about Kilimanjaro. He would tell me these things and I would ride alongside and ask endless questions, or we would sit together in the jolting buggy and just think about what he had said.

One day, when we were riding to Elkington's, my father spoke about lions.

"Lions are more intelligent than some men," he said, "and more courageous than most. A lion will fight for what he has and for what he needs; he is contemptuous of cowards and wary of his equals. But he is not afraid. You can always trust a lion to be exactly what it is—and never anything else.

"Except," he added, looking more paternally concerned than usual, "that damned lion of Elkington's!"

The Elkington lion was famous within a radius of twelve miles in all directions from the farm, because, if you happened to be anywhere inside that circle, you could hear him roar when he was hungry, when he was sad, or when he just felt like roaring. If, in the night, you lay sleepless on your bed and listened to an intermittent sound that began like the bellow of a banshee trapped in the bowels of Kilimanjaro and ended like the sound of that same banshee suddenly at large and arrived at the foot of your bed, you knew (because you had been told) that this was the song of Paddy.

Two or three of the settlers in East Africa at that time had caught lion cubs and raised them in cages. But Paddy, the Elkington lion, had never seen a cage.

He had grown to full size, tawny, black-maned, and muscular, without a worry or a care. He lived on fresh meat, not of his own killing. He spent his waking hours (which coincided with everybody else's sleeping hours) wandering through Elkington's fields and pastures like an affable, if apostrophic, emperor, a-stroll in the gardens of his court.

He thrived on solitude. He had no mate, but pretended indifference and walked alone, not toying too much with imaginings of the unattainable. There were no physical barriers to his freedom, but the lions of the plains do not accept into their respected fraternity an individual bearing in his coat the smell of men. So Paddy ate, slept, and roared, and perhaps he sometimes dreamed, but he never left Elkington's. He was a tame lion, Paddy was. He was deaf to the call of the wild.

"I'm always careful of that lion," I told my father, "but he's really harmless. I have seen Mrs. Elkington stroke him."

"Which proves nothing," said my father. "A domesticated lion is only an unnatural lion—and whatever is unnatural is untrustworthy."

Whenever my father made an observation as deeply philosophical as that one, and as inclusive, I knew there was nothing more to be said.

I nudged my horse and we broke into a canter covering the remaining distance to Elkington's.

It wasn't a big farm as farms went in Africa before the First World War, but it had a very nice house with a large veranda on which my father, Jim Elkington, Mrs. Elkington, and one or two other settlers sat and talked with what to my mind was always unreasonable solemnity.

There were drinks, but beyond that there was a tea table lavishly spread, as only the English can spread them. I have sometimes thought since of the Elkingtons' tea table—round, capacious, and white, standing with sturdy legs against the green vines of the garden, a thousand miles of Africa receding from its edge.

It was a mark of sanity, I suppose, less than of luxury. It was evidence of the double debt England still owes to ancient China for her two gifts that made expansion possible—tea and gunpowder.

But cakes and muffins were no fit bribery for me. I had pleasures of my own then, or constant expectations. I made what niggardly salutations I could bring forth from a disinterested memory and left the house at a gait rather faster than a trot.

As I scampered past the square hay shed a hundred yards or so behind the Elkington house, I caught sight of Bishon Singh, whom my father had sent ahead to tend our horses.

I think the Sikh must have been less than forty years old then, but his face was never any indication of his age. On some days he looked thirty and on others he looked fifty, depending on the weather, the time of day, his mood, or the tilt of his turban. If he had ever disengaged his beard from his hair and shaved the one and clipped the other, he might have astonished us all by looking like one of Kipling's elephant boys, but he never did either, and so, to me at least, he remained a man of mystery, without age, or youth, but burdened with experience, like the wandering Jew.

He raised his arm and greeted me in Swahili as I ran through the Elkington farmyard and out toward the open country.

Why I ran at all or with what purpose is beyond my answering, but when I had no specific destination I always ran as fast as I could in the hope of finding one—and I always found it.

I was within twenty yards of the Elkington lion before I saw him. He lay sprawled in the morning sun, huge, black-maned, and gleaming with life. His tail moved slowly, stroking the rough grass like a knotted rope end. His body was sleek and easy, making a mold where he lay, a cool mold, that would be there when he had gone. He was not asleep; he was only idle. He was rusty-red, and soft, like a strokable cat. I stopped and he lifted his head with magnificent ease and stared at me out of yellow eyes.

I stood there staring back, scuffling my bare toes in the dust, pursing my lips to make a noiseless whistle—a very small girl who knew nothing about lions.

Paddy raised himself then, emitting a little sigh, and began to contemplate me with a kind of quiet premeditation, like that of a slow-witted man fondling an unaccustomed thought.

I cannot say that there was any menace in his eyes, because there wasn't, or that his "frightful jowls" were drooling, because they were handsome jowls and very tidy. He did sniff the air, though, with what impressed me as being close to audible satisfaction. And he did not lie down again.

I remembered the rules that one remembers. I did not run. I walked very slowly, and I began to sing a defiant song.

"*Kali coma Simba sisi,*" I sang. "*Askari yoti ni udari!*—Fierce like the lion are we, Askari all are brave!"

I went in a straight line past Paddy when I sang it, seeing his eyes shine in the thick grass, watching his tail beat time to the meter of my ditty.

"Twendi, twendi—ku pigana—pigna aduoi—piga sana!— Let us go, let us go—to fight—beat down the enemy! Beat hard, beat hard!"

What lion would not be impressed with the marching song of the King's African Rifles?

Singing it still, I took up my trot toward the rim of the low hill that might, if I were lucky, have Cape gooseberry bushes on its slopes.

The country was gray-green and dry, and the sun lay on it closely, making the ground hot under my bare feet. There was no sound and no wind.

Even Paddy made no sound, coming swiftly behind me.

What I remember most clearly of the moment that followed are three things—a scream that was barely a whisper, a blow that struck me to the ground, and, as I buried my face in my arms and felt Paddy's teeth close on the flesh of my leg, a fantastically bobbing turban, that was Bishon Singh's turban, appear over the edge of the hill.

I remained conscious, but I closed my eyes and tried not to be. It was not so much the pain as it was the sound.

The sound of Paddy's roar in my ears will only be duplicated, I think, when the doors of hell slip their wobbly hinges, one day, and give voice and authenticity to the whole panorama of Dante's poetic nightmares. It was an immense roar that encompassed the world and dissolved me in it.

I shut my eyes very tight, and lay still under the weight of Paddy's paws.

Bishon Singh said afterward that he did nothing. He said he had remained by the hayshed for a few minutes after I ran past him, and then, for no explainable reason had begun to follow me. He admitted, though, that a little while before, he had seen Paddy go in the direction I had taken.

The Sikh called for help, of course, when he saw the lion meant to attack, and a half-dozen of Elkington's syces had come running from the house. Along with them had come Jim Elkington with a rawhide whip.

Jim Elkington, even without a rawhide whip, was very impressive. He was one of those enormous men whose girths alone seem to preclude any possibility of normal movement, much less of speed. But Jim had speed—not to be loosely compared with lightning, but rather like the speed of something spherical and smooth and relatively irresistible, like the cannonballs of the Napoleonic Wars. Jim was, without question, a man of considerable courage, but in the case of my Rescue From the Lion, it was, I am told, his momentum rather than his bravery for which I must forever be grateful.

It happened like this—as Bishon Singh told it:

"I am resting against the walls of the place where hay is kept and first the large lion and then you, Beru, pass me going toward the open field, and a thought comes to me that a lion and a young girl are strange company, so I follow. I follow to the place where the hill that goes up becomes the hill that goes down, and where it goes down deepest I see that you are running without much thought in your head, and the lion is running behind you with many thoughts in his head, and I scream for everybody to come very fast.

"Everybody comes very fast, but the large lion is faster than anybody, and he jumps on your back and I see you scream but I hear no scream. I only hear the lion, and I begin to run with everybody and this included Bwana Elkington, who is saying a great many words I do not know and is carrying a long kiboko which he is holding in his hand and is meant for beating the large lion.

"Bwana Elkington goes past me the way a man with

lighter legs and fewer inches around his stomach might go past me, and he is waving the long kiboko so that it whistles over all our heads like a very sharp wind, but when we get close to the lion it comes to my mind that the lion is not of the mood to accept a kiboko.

"He is standing with the front of himself on your back, Beru, and you are bleeding in three or five places, and he is roaring. I do not believe Bwana Elkington could have thought that that lion at that moment would consent to being beaten, because the lion was not looking the way he had ever looked before when it was necessary for him to be beaten. He was looking as if he did not wish to be disturbed by a kiboko, or the Bwana, or the syces, or Bishon Singh, and he was saying so in a very large voice.

"I believe that Bwana Elkington understood this voice when he was still more than several feet from the lion, and I believe the Bwana considered in his mind that it would be the best thing not to beat the lion just then, but the Bwana when he runs very fast is like the trunk of a great baobab tree rolling down a slope, and it seems that because of this it was not possible for him to explain the thought of his mind to the soles of his feet in a sufficient quickness of time to prevent him from rushing much closer to the lion than in his heart he wished to be.

"And it was in this circumstance, as I am telling it," said Bishon Singh, "which in my considered opinion made it possible for you to be alive, Beru."

"Bwana Elkington rushed at the lion then, Bishon Singh?"

"The lion, as of the contrary, rushed at Bwana Elkington," said Bishon Singh. "The lion deserted you for the Bwana, Beru. The lion was of the opinion that his master was not in any way deserving of a portion of what he, the lion, had accomplished in the matter of fresh meat through no effort by anybody except himself."

Bishon Singh offered this extremely reasonable interpretation with impressive gravity, as if he were expounding the Case For the Lion to a chosen jury of Paddy's peers.

"Fresh meat . . . ," I repeated dreamily, and crossed my fingers.

"So then what happened . . . ?"

The Sikh lifted his shoulders and let them drop again. "What could happen, Beru? The lion rushed for Bwana Elkington, who in his turn rushed from the lion, and in so rushing did not keep in his hand the long kiboko, but allowed it to fall upon the ground, and in accomplishing this the Bwana was free to ascend a very fortunate tree, which he did."

"And you picked me up, Bishon Singh?"

He made a little dip with his massive turban. "I was happy with the duty of carrying you back to this very bed, Beru, and of advising your father, who had gone to observe some of Bwana Elkington's horses, that you had been moderately eaten by the large lion. Your father returned very fast, and Bwana Elkington some time later returned very fast, but the large lion has not returned at all."

The large lion had not returned at all. That night he killed a horse, and the next night he killed a yearling bullock, and after that a cow fresh for milking.

In the end he was caught and finally caged, but brought to no rendezvous with the firing squad at sunrise. He remained for years in his cage, which, had he managed to live in freedom with his inhibitions, he might never have seen at all.

It seems characteristic of the mind of man that the representation of what is natural to humans must be abhorred, but that what is natural to an infinitely more natural animal must be confined within the bounds of a reason peculiar only to men—more peculiar sometimes than seems reasonable at all.

Paddy lived, people stared at him and he stared back, and this went on until he was an old, old lion. Jim Elkington died, and Mrs. Elkington, who really loved Paddy, was forced, because of circumstances beyond her control or Paddy's, to have him shot by Boy Long, the manager of Lord Delamere's estates.

This choice of executioners was, in itself, a tribute to Paddy, for no one loved animals more or understood them better, or could shoot more cleanly than Boy Long.

But the result was the same to Paddy. He had lived and died in ways not of his choosing. He was a good lion. He had done what he could about being a tame lion. Who thinks it just to be judged by a single error?

I still have the scars of his teeth and claws, but they are very small now and almost forgotten, and I cannot begrudge him his moment.

THE CALL OF THE WILD

JACK LONDON

Set in the late 1890s, The Call of the Wild *is the story of Buck, a St. Bernard–collie crossbreed. As a young dog he is captured by dog thieves who eventually sell him to be a sled dog in Alaska during the Klondike gold rush. Only when he meets his new master, Thornton, does he begin to experience any kind of human affection. The bond between man and dog becomes one of absolute trust and respect.*

T HAT WINTER, at Dawson, Buck performed another exploit, not so heroic, perhaps, but one that put his name many notches higher on the totem pole of Alaskan fame. This exploit was particularly gratifying to the three men; for they stood in need of the outfit that it furnished, and were enabled to make a long-desired trip into the virgin East, where miners had not yet appeared. It was brought about by a conversation in the Eldorado Saloon, in which men waxed boastful of their favorite Dogs. Buck, because of his record, was the target for these men, and Thornton was driven stoutly to defend him. At the end of half an hour one man stated that his Dog could start a sled with five hundred pounds and walk off with it;

a second bragged six hundred for his Dog; and a third, seven hundred.

"Pooh! pooh!" said John Thornton; "Buck can start a thousand pounds."

"And break it out? and walk off with it for a hundred yards?" demanded Matthewson, a Bonanza King, he of the seven hundred vaunt.

"And break it out, and walk off with it for a hundred yards," John Thornton said coolly.

"Well," Matthewson said, slowly and deliberately, so that all could hear, "I've got a thousand dollars that says he can't. And there it is." So saying, he slammed a sack of gold dust of the size of a bologna sausage down upon the bar.

Nobody spoke. Thornton's bluff, if bluff it was, had been called. He could feel a flush of warm blood creeping up his face. His tongue had tricked him. He did not know whether Buck could start a thousand pounds. Half a ton! The enormousness of it appalled him. He had great faith in Buck's strength, and had often thought him capable of starting such a load; but never, as now, had he faced the possibility of it, the eyes of a dozen men fixed upon him, silent and waiting. Further, he had no thousand dollars; nor had Hans or Pete.

"I've got a sled standing outside now, with twenty fifty-pound sacks of flour on it," Matthewson went on with brutal directness; "so don't let that hinder you."

Thornton did not reply. He did not know what to say. He glanced from face to face in the absent way of a man who has lost the power of thought and is seeking somewhere to find the thing that will start it going again. The face of Jim O'Brien, a Mastodon King and old-time comrade, caught his eyes. It was as a cue to him, seeming to rouse him to do what he would never have dreamed of doing.

"Can you lend me a thousand?" he asked, almost in a whisper.

"Sure," answered O'Brien, thumping down a plethoric sack by the side of Matthewson's. "Though it's little faith I'm having, John, that the beast can do the trick."

The Eldorado emptied its occupants into the street to see the test. The tables were deserted, and the dealers and gamekeepers came forth to see the outcome of the wager and to lay odds. Several hundred men, furred and mittened, banked around the sled within easy distance. Matthewson's sled, loaded with a thousand pounds of flour, had been standing for a couple of hours, and in the intense cold (it was sixty below zero) the runners had frozen fast to the hard-packed snow. Men offered odds of two to one that Buck could not budge the sled. A quibble arose concerning the phrase "break out." O'Brien contended it was Thornton's privilege to knock the runners loose, leaving Buck to "break it out" from a dead standstill. Matthewson insisted that the phrase included breaking the runners from the frozen grip of the snow. A majority of the men who had witnessed the making of the bet decided in his favor, whereat the odds went up to three to one against Buck.

There were no takers. Not a man believed him capable of the feat. Thornton had been hurried into the wager, heavy with doubt; and now that he looked at the sled itself, the concrete fact, with the regular team of ten Dogs curled up in the snow before it, the more impossible the task appeared. Matthewson waxed jubilant.

"Three to one!" he proclaimed. "I'll lay you another thousand at that figure, Thornton. What d'ye say?"

Thornton's doubt was strong on his face, but his fighting spirit was aroused—the fighting spirit that soars above odds, fails to recognize the impossible, and is deaf to all save the clamor for battle. He called Hans and Pete to him. Their sacks were slim, and with his own the three partners could rake together only two hundred dollars. In the ebb of their fortunes, this sum was their total capital; yet they laid it unhesitatingly against Matthewson's six hundred.

The team of ten Dogs was unhitched; and Buck, with his own harness, was put into the sled. He had caught the contagion of the excitement, and he felt that in some way he must do a great thing for John Thornton. Murmurs of admiration at his splendid appearance went up. He was in perfect condition, without an ounce of superfluous flesh, and the one hundred and fifty pounds that he weighed were so many pounds of grit and virility. His furry coat shone with the sheen of silk. Down the neck and across the shoulders, his mane, in repose as it was, half bristled and seemed to lift with every movement, as though excess of vigor made each particular hair alive and active. The great breast and heavy forelegs were no more than in proportion with the rest of the body, where the muscles showed in tight rolls underneath the skin. Men felt these muscles and proclaimed them hard as iron, and the odds went down to two to one.

"Gad, sir! Gad, sir!" stuttered a member of the latest dynasty, a king of the Skookum Benches. "I offer you eight hundred for him, sir, before the test, sir; eight hundred just as he stands."

Thornton shook his head and stepped to Buck's side

"You must stand off from him," Matthewson protested. "Free play and plenty of room."

The crowd fell silent; only could be heard the voices of the gamblers vainly offering two to one. Everybody acknowledged Buck a magnificent animal, but twenty fifty-pound sacks of flour bulked too large in their eyes for them to loosen their pouchstrings.

Thornton knelt down by Buck's side. He took his head in his two hands and rested cheek on cheek. He did not playfully shake him, as was his wont, or murmur soft love curses; but he whispered in his ear. "As you love me, Buck. As you love me," was what he whispered. Buck whined with suppressed eagerness.

The crowd was watching curiously. The affair was growing mysterious. It seemed like a conjuration. As Thornton got to his feet, Buck seized his mittened hand between his jaws, pressing in with his teeth and releasing loosely, half-reluctantly. It was the answer, in terms, not of speech, but of love. Thornton stepped well back.

"Now, Buck," he said.

Buck tightened the traces, then slacked them for a matter of several inches. It was the way he had learned.

"Gee!" Thornton's voice rang out, sharp in the tense silence.

Buck swung to the right, ending the movement in a plunge that took up the slack and with a sudden jerk arrested his one hundred and fifty pounds. The load quivered, and from under the runners arose a crisp crackling.

"Haw!" Thornton commanded.

Buck duplicated the maneuver, this time to the left. The crackling turned into a snapping, the sled pivoting and the runners slipping and grating several inches to the side. The sled was broken out. Men were holding their breaths, intensely unconscious of the fact.

"Now, MUSH!"

Thornton's command cracked out like a pistol shot. Buck threw himself forward, tightening the traces with a jarring lunge. His whole body was gathered compactly together in

the tremendous effort, the muscles writhing and knotting like live things under the silky fur. His great chest was low to the ground, his head forward and down, while his feet were flying like mad, the claws scarring the hard-packed snow in parallel grooves. The sled swayed and trembled, half-started forward. One of his feet slipped, and one man groaned aloud. Then the sled lurched ahead in what appeared a rapid succession of jerks, though it never really came to a dead stop again . . . half an inch . . . an inch . . . two inches . . . The jerks perceptibly diminished; as the sled gained momentum, he caught them up, till it was moving steadily along.

Men gasped and began to breathe again, unaware that for a moment they had ceased to breathe. Thornton was running behind, encouraging Buck with short, cheery words. The distance measured off, and as he neared the pile of firewood which marked the end of the hundred yards, a cheer began to grow and grow, which burst into a roar as he passed the firewood and halted at command. Every man was tearing himself loose, even Matthewson. Hats and mittens were flying in the air. Men were shaking hands, it did not matter with whom, and bubbling over in a general incoherent babel.

But Thornton fell on his knees beside Buck. Head was against head, and he was shaking him back and forth. Those who hurried up heard him cursing Buck, and he cursed him long and fervently, and softly and lovingly.

"Gad, sir! Gad, sir!" spluttered the Skookum Bench king. "I'll give you a thousand for him, sir, a thousand, sir— twelve hundred, sir."

Thornton rose to his feet. His eyes were wet. The tears were streaming frankly down his cheeks. "Sir," he said to the Skookum Bench king, "no, sir. You can go to hell, sir. It's the best I can do for you, sir."

Buck seized Thornton's hand in his teeth. Thornton shook him back and forth. As though animated by a common impulse, the onlookers drew back to a respectful distance; nor were they again indiscreet enough to interrupt.

THE RED PONY

JOHN STEINBECK

The relationship beween man and horse has often been explored in story form—I did it myself in my book War Horse. *But no one has done it better than Steinbeck in his great masterpiece* The Red Pony, *when he writes of Jody's first meeting with his beloved pony.*

IT WAS FOUR O'CLOCK in the afternoon when Jody topped the hill and looked down on the ranch again. He looked for the saddle horses, but the corral was empty. His father was not back yet. He went slowly, then, toward the afternoon chores. At the ranch house, he found his mother sitting on the porch, mending socks.

"There's two doughnuts in the kitchen for you," she said. Jody slid to the kitchen, and returned with half of one of the doughnuts already eaten and his mouth full. His mother asked him what he had learned in school that day, but she didn't listen to his doughnut-muffled answer. She interrupted: "Jody, tonight see you fill the wood box clear full. Last night you crossed the sticks and it wasn't only about half full. Lay the sticks flat tonight. And Jody, some of the hens are hiding eggs, or else the dogs are eating them.

Look about in the grass and see if you can find any nests."

Jody, still eating, went out and did his chores. He saw the quail come down to eat with the chickens when he threw out the grain. For some reason his father was proud to have them come. He never allowed any shooting near the house for fear the quail might go away.

When the wood box was full, Jody took his twenty-two rifle up to the cold spring at the brush line. He drank again and then aimed the gun at all manner of things, at rocks, at birds on the wing, at the big black pig kettle under the cypress tree, but he didn't shoot for he had no cartridges and wouldn't have until he was twelve. If his father had seen him aim the rifle in the direction of the house he would have put the cartridges off another year. Jody remembered this and did not point the rifle down the hill again. Two years was enough to wait for cartridges. Nearly all of his father's presents were given with reservations which hampered their value somewhat. It was good discipline.

The supper waited until dark for his father to return. When at last he came in with Billy Buck, Jody could smell the delicious brandy on their breaths. Inwardly he rejoiced, for his father sometimes talked to him when he smelled of brandy, sometimes even told things he had done in the wild days when he was a boy.

After supper, Jody sat by the fireplace and his shy polite eyes sought the room corners, and he waited for his father to tell what it was he contained, for Jody knew he had news of some sort. But he was disappointed. His father pointed a stern finger at him.

"You'd better go to bed, Jody. I'm going to need you in the morning."

That wasn't so bad. Jody liked to do the things he had to do as long as they weren't routine things. He looked at the floor and his mouth worked out a question before he spoke it. "What are we going to do in the morning, kill a pig?" he asked softly.

"Never you mind. You better get to bed."

When the door was closed behind him, Jody heard his father and Billy Buck chuckling and he knew it was a joke of some kind. And later, when he lay in bed, trying to make words out of the murmurs in the other room, he heard his father protest, "But, Ruth, I didn't give much for him."

Jody heard the hoot owls hunting the mice down by the barn, and he heard a fruit tree limb tap-tapping against the house. A cow was lowing when he went to sleep.

When the triangle sounded in the morning, Jody dressed more quickly even than usual. In the kitchen, while he washed his face and combed back his hair, his mother addressed him irritably. "Don't you go out until you get a good breakfast in you."

He went to the dining room and sat at the long white table. He took a steaming hotcake from the platter, arranged two fried eggs on it, covered them with another hotcake and squashed the whole thing with his fork.

His father and Billy Buck came in. Jody knew from the sound on the floor that both of them were wearing flat-heeled shoes, but he peered under the table to make sure. His father turned off the oil lamp, for the day had arrived, and he looked stern and disciplinary, but Billy Buck didn't look at Jody at all. He avoided the shy questioning eyes of the boy and soaked a whole piece of toast in his coffee.

Carl Tiflin said crossly, "You come with us after breakfast!"

Jody had trouble with his food then, for he felt a kind of doom in the air. After Billy had tilted his saucer and drained the coffee which had slopped into it, and had wiped his hands on his jeans, the two men stood up from the table and went out into the morning light together, and Jody respectfully followed a little behind them. He tried to keep his mind from running ahead, tried to keep it absolutely motionless.

His mother called, "Carl! Don't you let it keep him from school."

They marched past the cypress, where a singletree hung from a limb to butcher the pigs on, and past the black iron kettle, so it was not a pig killing. The sun shone over the hill and threw long, dark shadows of the trees and buildings. They crossed a stubble field to shortcut to the barn. Jody's father unhooked the door and they went in. They had been walking toward the sun on the way down. The barn was black as night in contrast and warm from the hay and from the beasts. Jody's father moved over toward the one box stall. "Come here!" he ordered. Jody could begin to see things now. He looked into the box stall and then stepped back quickly.

A red pony colt was looking at him out of the stall. Its tense ears were forward and a light of disobedience was in its eyes. Its coat was rough and thick as an airedale's fur and its mane was long and tangled. Jody's throat collapsed in on itself and cut his breath short.

"He needs a good currying," his father said, "and if I ever hear of you not feeding him or leaving his stall dirty, I'll sell him off in a minute."

Jody couldn't bear to look at the pony's eyes any more. He gazed down at his hands for a moment, and he asked very shyly, "Mine?" No one answered him. He put his hand out toward the pony. Its gray nose came close, sniffing loudly, and then the lips drew back and the strong teeth closed on Jody's fingers. The pony shook its head up and down and seemed to laugh with amusement. Jody regarded his bruised fingers. "Well," he said with pride—"well, I guess he can bite all right." The two men laughed, somewhat in relief. Carl Tiflin went out of the barn and walked up a side-hill to be by himself, for he was embarrassed, but Billy Buck stayed. It was easier to talk to Billy Buck. Jody asked again—"Mine?"

Billy became professional in tone. "Sure! That is, if you look out for him and break him right. I'll show you how. He's just a colt. You can't ride him for some time."

Jody put out his bruised hand again, and this time the red pony let his nose be rubbed. "I ought to have a carrot," Jody said. "Where'd we get him, Billy?"

"Bought him at a sheriff's auction," Billy explained. "A show went broke in Salinas and had debts. The sheriff was selling off their stuff."

The pony stretched out his nose and shook the forelock from his wild eyes. Jody stroked the nose a little. He said softly, "There isn't a—saddle?"

Billy Buck laughed. "I'd forgot. Come along."

In the harness room he lifted down a little saddle of red morocco leather. "It's just a show saddle," Billy Buck said disparagingly. "It isn't practical for the brush, but it was cheap at the sale."

Jody couldn't trust himself to look at the saddle either, and he couldn't speak at all. He brushed the shining red leather with his fingertips, and after a long time he said, "It'll look pretty on him though." He thought of the grandest and prettiest things he knew. "If he hasn't a name already, I think I'll call him Gabilan Mountains," he said.

Billy Buck knew how he felt. "It's a pretty long name. Why don't you just call him Gabilan? That means hawk. That would be a fine name for him." Billy felt glad. "If you will collect tail hair, I might be able to make a hair rope for you sometime. You could use it for a hackamore."

Jody wanted to go back to the box stall. "Could I lead him to school, do you think—to show the kids?"

But Billy shook his head. "He's not even halter-broke yet. We had a time getting him here. Had to almost drag him. You better be starting for school though."

"I'll bring the kids to see him here this afternoon," Jody said.

Six boys came over the hill half an hour early that afternoon, running hard, their heads down, their forearms working, their breath whistling. They swept by the house and cut across the stubble-field to the barn. And then they stood self-consciously before the pony, and then they looked at Jody with eyes in which there was a new admiration and a new respect. Before today Jody had been a boy, dressed in overalls and a blue shirt—quieter than most, even suspected of being a little cowardly. And now he was different. Out of a thousand centuries they drew the ancient admiration of the footman for the horseman. They knew instinctively that a man on a horse is spiritually, as well as physically, bigger than a man on foot. They knew that Jody had been miraculously lifted out of equality with them, and had been placed over them. Gabilan put his head out of the stall and sniffed them.

"Why'n't you ride him?" the boys cried. "Why'n't you braid his tail with ribbons like in the fair?" "When you going to ride him?"

Jody's courage was up. He too, felt the superiority of the horseman. "He's not old enough. Nobody can ride him for a long time. I'm going to train him on the long halter. Billy Buck is going to show me how."

"Well, can't we even lead him around a little?"

"He isn't even halter-broke," Jody said. He wanted to be

completely alone when he took the pony out for the first time. "Come and see the saddle."

They were speechless at the red morocco saddle, completely shocked out of comment. "It isn't much use in the brush," Jody explained. "It'll look pretty on him though. Maybe I'll ride bareback when I go into the brush."

"How you going to rope a cow without a saddle horn?"

"Maybe I'll get another saddle for everyday. My father might want me to help him with the stock." He let them feel the red saddle, and showed them the brass chain throatlatch on the bridle and the big brass buttons at each temple where the headstall and brow band crossed. The whole thing was too wonderful. They had to go away after a little while, and each boy, in his mind, searched among his possessions for a bribe worthy of offering in return for a ride on the red pony when the time should come.

Jody was glad when they had gone. He took brush and currycomb from the wall, took down the barrier of the box stall and stepped cautiously in. The pony's eyes glittered, and he edged around into kicking position. But Jody touched him on the shoulder and rubbed his high arched neck as he had always seen Billy Buck do, and he crooned, "So-o-o, boy," in a deep voice. The pony gradually relaxed his tenseness. Jody curried and brushed until a pile of dead hair lay in the stall and until the pony's coat had taken on a deep red shine. Each time he finished he thought it might have been done better. He braided the mane into a dozen little pigtails, and he braided the forelock, and then he undid them and brushed the hair out straight again.

Jody did not hear his mother enter the barn. She was angry when she came, but when she looked in at the pony and at Jody working over him, she felt a curious pride rise up in her. "Have you forgot the wood box?" she asked gently. "It's not far off from dark and there's not a stick of wood in the house, and the chickens aren't fed."

Jody quickly put up his tools. "I forgot, ma'am."

"Well, after this, do your chores first. Then you won't forget. I expect you'll forget lots of things now if I don't keep an eye on you."

"Can I have carrots from the garden for him, ma'am?"

She had to think about that. "Oh—I guess so, if you only take the big tough ones."

"Carrots keep the coat good," he said, and again she felt the curious rush of pride.

Jody never waited for the triangle to get him out of bed after the coming of the pony. It became his habit to creep out of bed even before his mother was awake, to slip into his clothes and to go quietly down to the barn to see Gabilan. In the gray quiet mornings when the land and the brush and the houses and the trees were silver-gray and black like a photograph negative, he stole toward the barn, past the sleeping stones and the sleeping cypress tree. The turkeys, roosting in the tree out of coyotes' reach, clicked drowsily. The fields glowed with a gray frostlike light and in the dew the tracks of rabbits and of field mice stood out sharply. The good dogs came stiffly out of their little houses, hackles up and deep growls in their throats. Then they caught Jody's scent, and their stiff tails rose up and waved a greeting—Doubletree Mutt with the big thick tail, and Smasher, the incipient shepherd—then went lazily back to their warm beds.

It was a strange time and a mysterious journey, to Jody— an extension of a dream. When he first had the pony he liked to torture himself during the trip by thinking Gabilan would not be in his stall, and worse, would never have been there. And he had other delicious little self-induced pains. He thought how the rats had gnawed ragged holes in the red saddle, and how the mice had nibbled Gabilan's tail until it was stringy and thin. He usually ran the last little way to the barn. He unlatched the rusty hasp of the barn door and stepped in, and no matter how quietly he opened the door, Gabilan was always looking at him over the barrier of the box stall and Gabilan whinnied softly and stamped his front foot, and his eyes had big sparks of red fire in them like oakwood embers.

Sometimes, if the workhorses were to be used that day, Jody found Billy Buck in the barn harnessing and currying. Billy stood with him and looked long at Gabilan and he told Jody a great many things about horses. He explained that they were terribly afraid for their feet, so that one must make a practice of lifting the legs and patting the hooves and ankles to remove their terror. He told Jody how horses love conversation. He must talk to the pony all the time, and tell him the reasons for everything. Billy wasn't sure a horse could understand everything that was said to him, but it was impossible to say how much was understood. A horse never kicked up a fuss if someone he liked explained things to him. Billy could give examples, too. He had known, for instance, a horse nearly dead beat with fatigue to perk up when told it was only a little farther to his destination. And he had known a horse paralyzed with fright to come out of it when his rider told him what it was that was frightening him. While he talked in the mornings, Billy Buck cut twenty or thirty straws into neat three-inch lengths and stuck them into his hatband. Then, during the whole day, if he wanted to pick his teeth or merely to chew on something, he had only to reach up for one of them.

Jody listened carefully, for he knew and the whole country knew that Billy Buck was a fine hand with horses. Billy's own horse was a stringy cayuse with a hammer head, but he nearly always won the first prizes at the stock trials. Billy could rope a steer, take a double half hitch about the horn with his riata, and dismount, and his horse would play the steer as an angler plays a fish, keeping a tight rope until the steer was down or beaten.

Every morning, after Jody had curried and brushed the pony, he let down the barrier of the stall, and Gabilan thrust past him and raced down the barn and into the corral. Around and around he galloped, and sometimes he jumped forward and landed on stiff legs. He stood quivering, stiff ears forward, eyes rolling so that the whites showed, pretending to be frightened. At last he walked, snorting, to the water trough and buried his nose in the water up to the nostrils. Jody was proud then, for he knew that was the way to judge a horse. Poor horses only touched their lips to the water, but a fine, spirited beast put his whole nose and mouth under, and only left room to breathe.

Then Jody stood and watched the pony, and he saw things he had never noticed about any other horse, the sleek, sliding flank muscles and the cords of the buttocks, which flexed like a closing fist, and the shine the sun put on the red coat. Having seen horses all his life, Jody had never looked at them very closely before. But now he noticed the moving ears that gave expression and even inflection of expression to the face. The pony talked with his ears. You could tell exactly how he felt about everything by the way his ears pointed. Sometimes they were stiff and upright and sometimes lax and sagging. They went back when he was angry or fearful, and forward when he was anxious and curious and pleased; and their exact position indicated which emotion he had.

Billy Buck kept his word. In the early fall the training began. First there was the halter-breaking, and that was the

hardest because it was the first thing. Jody held a carrot and coaxed and promised and pulled on the rope. The pony set his feet like a burro when he felt the strain. But before long he learned. Jody walked all over the ranch leading him. Gradually he took to dropping the rope until the pony followed him unled wherever he went.

And then came the training on the long halter. That was slower work. Jody stood in the middle of a circle, holding the long halter. He clucked with his tongue and the pony started to walk in a big circle, held in by the long rope. He clucked again to make the pony trot, and again to make him gallop. Around and around Gabilan went thundering and enjoying it immensely. Then he called, "Whoa," and the pony stopped. It was not long until Gabilan was perfect at it. But in many ways he was a bad pony. He bit Jody in the pants and stomped on Jody's feet. Now and then his ears went back and he aimed a tremendous kick at the boy. Every time he did one of these bad things, Gabilan settled back and seemed to laugh to himself.

Billy Buck worked at the hair rope in the evenings before the fireplace. Jody collected tail hair in a bag, and he sat and watched Billy slowly constructing the rope, twisting a few hairs to make a string and rolling two strings together for a cord, and then braiding a number of cords to make the rope. Billy rolled the finished rope on the floor under his foot to make it round and hard.

The long halter work rapidly approached perfection. Jody's father, watching the pony stop and start and trot and gallop, was a little bothered by it.

"He's getting to be almost a trick pony," he complained. "I don't like trick horses. It takes all the—dignity out of a horse to make him do tricks. Why, a trick horse is kind of like an actor—no dignity, no character of his own." And his father said, "I guess you better be getting him used to the saddle pretty soon."

Jody rushed for the harness room. For some time he had been riding the saddle on a sawhorse. He changed the stirrup length over and over, and could never get it just right. Sometimes, mounted on the sawhorse in the harness-room, with collars and hames and tugs hung all about him, Jody rode out beyond the room. He carried his rifle across the pommel. He saw the fields go flying by, and he heard the beat of the galloping hoofs.

WAITING FOR ANYA

MICHAEL MORPURGO

I stayed for a while in Lescun in France where I set this novel. I walked the Pyrenees, encountered angry sheep dogs, saw my first European bear, watched eagles soaring over the peaks. I discovered the village was occupied by German border guards during World War II. Many Jewish people and others escaped over the mountains to neutral Spain. Many French people risked their lives to help them.

In my novel, Jo is drawn into greater and greater danger as he plays his own part in helping dozens of children to safety. It is his terrifying encounter with the bear, in this excerpt, that begins his story.

JO SHOULD HAVE KNOWN BETTER. After all, Papa had told him often enough: "Whittle a stick Jo, pick berries, eat, look for your eagle if you must," he'd said, "but do something. You sit doing nothing on a hillside in the morning sun with the tinkle of sheep bells all about you and you're bound to drop off. You've got to keep your eyes busy, Jo. If your eyes are busy then they won't let your brain go to sleep. And whatever you do, Jo, never lie down. Sit down, but don't lie down." Jo knew all that, but he'd been up since half past five that morning and milked a hundred sheep. He was tired, and anyway the sheep seemed settled enough grazing the pasture below him. Rouf lay beside him, his head on his paws, watching the sheep. Only his eyes moved.

Jo lay back on the rock and considered the lark rising above him and wondered why larks seem to perform when the sun shines. He could hear the church bells of Lescun in the distance but only faintly. Lescun, his village, his valley, where the people lived for their sheep and their cows. And they lived with them, too. Half of each house was given over to the animals, a dairy on the ground floor, a hayloft above; and in front of every house was a walled yard that served as a permanent sheep fold.

For Jo, the village was his whole world. He'd only been out of it a few times in all his twelve years, and one of those was to the railway station just two years before to see his father off to the war. They'd all gone, all the men who weren't too young and who weren't too old. It wouldn't take long to hammer the Boche and they'd be back home again. But when the news had come it had all been bad, so bad you couldn't believe it. There were rumors first of retreat and then of defeat, of French armies disintegrating, of English armies driven into the sea. Jo did not believe any of it at first, nor did anyone; but then one morning outside the Mairie he saw Grandpère crying openly in the street and he had to believe it. Then they heard that Jo's father was a prisoner of war in Germany and so were all the others who had gone from the village; except Jean Marty, cousin Jean, who would never be coming back. Jo lay there and tried to picture Jean's face; he could not. He could remember his dry cough though, and the way he would spring down a mountain like a deer. Only Hubert could run faster than Jean. Hubert Sarthol was the giant of the village. He had the mind of a child and could only speak a few recognizable words. The rest of his talk was a miscellany of grunting and groaning and squeaking but somehow he managed to make himself more or less understood. Jo remembered how Hubert had cried when they told him he couldn't join the army like the others. The bells of Lescun and the bells of the sheep blended in soporific harmony to lull him away into his dreams.

Rouf was the kind of dog that didn't need to bark too often. He was a massive white mountain dog, old and stiff in his legs but still top dog in the village and he knew it. He was barking now though, a gruff roar of a bark that woke Jo instantly. He sat up. The sheep were gone. Rouf roared again from somewhere behind him, from in among the trees. The sheep bells were loud with alarm, their cries shrill and strident. Jo was on his feet and whistling for Rouf to bring them back. They scattered out of the wood and came running and leaping down toward him. Jo thought it was a lone sheep at first that had got itself caught up on the edge of the wood, but then it barked as it backed away and became Rouf—Rouf rampant, hackles up, snarling; and there was blood on his side. Jo ran toward him, calling him back, and it was then that he saw the bear and stopped dead. As the bear came out into the sunlight she stood up, her nose lifted in the air. Rouf stayed his ground, his body shaking with fury as he barked.

The nearest Jo had ever been to a bear before was to the bearskin that hung on the wall in the café. Stood up as she was, she was as tall as a full-grown man, her coat a creamy brown, her snout black. Jo could not find his voice to shout with, he could not find his legs to run with. He stood mesmerized, quite unable to take his eyes off the bear. A terrified ewe blundered into him and knocked him over. Then he was on his feet, and without even a look over his shoulder he was running down toward the village. He careered down the slopes, his arms flailing to keep his

balance. Several times he tumbled and rolled and picked himself up again, but as he gathered speed his legs would run away with him once more. All it needed was a rock or a tussock of grass to send him sprawling once again. Bruised and bloodied he reached the track to the village and ran, legs pumping, head back, and shouting whenever he could find the breath to do it.

By the time he reached the village—and never had it taken so long—he hadn't the breath to say more than one word, but one word was all he needed. "Bear!" he cried and pointed back to the mountains, but he had to repeat it several times before they seemed to understand or perhaps before they would believe him. Then his mother had him by the shoulders and was trying to make herself heard through the hubbub of the crowd about them.

"Are you all right, Jo? Are you hurt?" she said.

"Rouf, Maman," he gasped. "There's blood all over him."

"The sheep," Grandpère shouted. "What about the sheep?"

Jo shook his head. "I don't know," he said. "I don't know."

Monsieur Sarthol, Hubert's father and mayor of the village as long as Jo had been alive, was trying to organize loudly; but no one was paying him much attention. They had gone for their guns and for their dogs. Within minutes they were all gathered in the square, some on horseback but most on foot. Those children that could be caught were shut indoors in the safekeeping of grandmothers, mothers or aunts; but many escaped their clutches and dived unseen into the narrow streets to join up with the hunting party as it left the village. A bear hunt was once in a lifetime and not to be missed. This was the stuff of legends and here was one in the making. Jo pleaded with Grandpère to be allowed to go but Grandpère could do nothing for him, Maman would have none of it. He was bleeding profusely from his nose and his knee, so despite all his objections he was bustled away into the house to have his wounds cleaned and bandaged. Christine, his small sister, gazed up at him with big eyes as Maman wiped away the blood.

"Where's the bear, Jo?" Christine asked. "Where's the bear?"

Maman kept saying he was as pale as a ghost and should go and lie down. He appealed one last time to Grandpère, but Grandpère ruffled his hair proudly, took his hunting rifle from the corner of the room and went out with everyone else to hunt the bear.

"Was it big, Jo?" said Christine tugging at his arm. She was full of questions. You could never ignore Christine or her questions—she wouldn't let you. "Was it as big as Hubert?" And she held up her hands as high as she could.

"Bigger," said Jo.

Bandaged like a wounded soldier he was taken up to his bedroom and tucked under the blankets. He stayed in bed only until Maman left the room, and then he sprang out of bed and ran to the window. He could see nothing but the narrow streets and the gray roofs of the village, and beyond the church tower, just a glimpse of the jagged mountain peaks still white in places with winter snow. The streets were empty of people, all except the priest, Father Lasalle, who was hurrying past, his hand on his hat to stop it blowing away.

All afternoon Jo watched as the clouds came down and began to swallow the valley. It was just after the church clock struck five that he heard a distant baying of dogs and shortly after a volley of shots that echoed through the mountains and left a terrible silence hanging over the village.

He was down in the square half an hour later with

everyone else to watch the triumphant procession as it wound its way through the streets. Grandpère came first, Hubert gamboling alongside him.

"We got her," Grandpère was shouting. "We got her. Give us a hand here, Hubert, give us a hand." And they disappeared together into the café. They brought out two chairs each and set them down in front of the war memorial.

Limp in death, carried on two long poles by four men, the bear rocked into view, blood on her lolling tongue. She was laid out on the chairs, her legs hanging down on either side, her snout pressed up against the back of a chair. Jo was looking everywhere for Rouf but could not find him. He asked Grandpère if he had seen him but, like everyone else, Grandpère was too busy telling the story of the hunt or having his photograph taken. It was the grocer, Armand Jollet, who took pride of place in the photograph; it seemed he was the one who had actually shot the bear. He proclaimed this noisily, his round face red with pride and exhilaration. "Two hundred meters away I was, and I hit him right between the eyes."

"It's a she," said Father Lasalle bending over the bear.

"What's the difference?" said Armand Jollet. "He or she, that skin's worth a fortune."

In the celebrations that followed the photograph, the war was suddenly forgotten. Even Marie, Cousin Jean's widow, was laughing with them, swept along on a tide of communal joy and relief. Hubert clapped and cavorted about the place like a wild thing. He reared up like a bear and roared around the streets chasing screaming children and shouting, "Baar! Baar!" Jo looked down at the bear and stroked her back. The fur was long and close and soft, the body still warm with life. Blood from the bear's nose dropped onto his shoe and he felt suddenly sick. He turned to run away but Monsieur Sarthol had his arm around his shoulders and was calling for silence.

"Here's the lad himself," he said. "Without Jo Lalande there'd be no bear. This is the first bear we have shot in Lescun for over twenty-five years."

"Thirty," said Father Lasalle.

The Mayor ignored him and went on. "Lord knows how many of our sheep she'd have killed. We've a lot to thank him for." Jo saw Maman's eyes smiling back at him in the front of the crowd but he could not smile back. The Mayor lifted his glass—most people seemed to have a glass in their hands by now. "So, here's to Jo, and here's to the bear, and down with the Boche."

"Long live the bear," someone shouted and the laughter that followed echoed in Jo's head. He could stand it no longer. He pulled away and ran, ignoring Maman's call to come back.

Until the Mayor's speech he had not thought about his part in it all. The she-bear was lying there dead, spread out on the chairs in the square and he knew now it was all his doing. And perhaps Rouf was out there in the hills with his throat torn out, and none of it would have happened if he had not fallen asleep.

He ran all the way back along the track to the sheep pastures and up toward the trees. He stood there and called Rouf again and again until his voice cracked, but only the crows answered him. He pushed the tears back out of his eyes and tried to calm himself, to remember the exact spot where he'd last seen Rouf. He called again, he whistled; but the clouds seemed to soak up the echoes. He looked up. There were no longer any mountains to be seen above the tree line, only a pall of thick mist. It was still now, not a whisper of wind. He could see where the sheep had been; there was wool caught on the bark of the trees, there were droppings here, footprints there. And then he saw the blood, Rouf's blood perhaps, a brown smattering on the root of a tree.

He could not be sure what it was that he was hearing, not at first. He thought perhaps it was the mewing of an invisible buzzard flying through the clouds but then he heard the sound again and knew it for what it was, the whining of a dog—high-pitched and distant but now quite unmistakable. He called and he climbed, it was too steep to run. He ducked under low-slung branches, he clambered over fallen trees calling all the while: "I'm coming Rouf, I'm coming."

The whining was punctuated now with a strange, intermittent growling, quite unlike anything he had heard before. He came upon Rouf sooner than he had expected. He spotted him through the trees sitting still as a rock, his head lowered as if he was pointing. He did not even turn around to look as Jo broke through into the clearing behind him. He seemed intent upon something in the mouth of a small cave. It was brown and it was small; and then it moved and became a bear cub. It was sitting in the shadows and waving one of its front paws at Rouf. Jo crouched down and put a hand on Rouf's neck. Rouf looked up at him whining with excitement. He licked his lips and resumed his focus on the bear cub, his body taut. The bear cub rocked back against the side of the cave, legs apart, and growled. Yet it was hardly a growl, more a bleat of hunger, a cry for help, a call for mother. "They'll kill him, Rouf," he whispered. "If they find out about him, they'll hunt him down and kill him, just like his mother." Still looking at the bear he stroked Rouf's neck. It was matted and wet to the touch—like blood—but when he looked down at Rouf there wasn't a mark on him.

Suddenly Rouf was on his feet, he swung around,

hackles up, a rumbling growl in his throat. Jo turned. There was a man standing under the trees at the edge of the clearing. He wore a dirty black coat, a battered hat on his head. They looked at each other. Rouf stopped growling and his tail began to wag.

"Only me again," said the man coming out of the trees toward them. Even with his hat he was a short man and as he came closer, Jo saw that he had the gaunt, gray look of old men, yet his beard was rust red with not a fleck of white in it. There was a wine bottle in one hand and a stick in the other.

"Milk," he said holding out the bottle. Rouf sniffed at it and the man laughed. "Not for you," he said and he patted Rouf on the head. "For the little fellow. Starving he is. Perhaps you'd hold my stick for me," he said. "We don't want to frighten him do we?" He gave his hat to Jo as well and took off his coat. "I saw the whole thing, you know. I saw you running off, too. Your dog, is he?" Jo nodded. "Fights like a tiger, doesn't he? Bears like that can knock your head off, you know. One swipe of the paw that's all it takes. He was lucky. She tore his ear a bit, a lot of blood; but we soon cleaned you up, didn't we, old son? Right as rain he is now." He bent down and poured some milk onto a rock. "Now, let's see if we can get this little fellow to take a drink." He backed away a few paces and knelt down. "He'll smell it soon, you'll see. Give him time and he won't be able to resist it." He sat back on his heels.

The cub ventured out of the shadows of the cave, lifting his nose and sniffing the air as he came. "Come on, come on, little fellow," said the man, "we won't hurt you." And he reached out very slowly and poured out some more milk but closer to the bear cub this time. "She could've got away you know."

"Who?" said Jo.

"The bear, the mother bear. I've been thinking about it. She was leading them away from her cub. Deliberate it was, I'm sure of it. And what's more she led them a fair old dance, I can tell you. Did you see the hunt?" Jo shook his head. "Right away, down the valley she took them. I saw it all—well most of it anyway. Course I couldn't know why she was doing that, not at the time; and then I was on my way back home through the woods and there was this little fellow, and your dog just sitting here watching him. Covered in blood he was. Once I'd cleaned him up I went back home for some milk—the only thing I could think of. There you are, he's coming for it now." The cub came forward tentatively, touched the milk with his paw, smelled it, licked it to taste, and then began to lap noisily. Suddenly, the man's free arm shot out and scooped the cub onto his lap. There was a flurry of paws and a furious scratching and yowling until all the flailing arms and legs were trapped. His whole head was white with milk by now but the end of the bottle was in his mouth and he was sucking in deeply. The man looked up at Jo and smiled. He had milk all over his beard and was licking his lips. "Got him," he said and he chuckled until he laughed. The cub still clung to the bottle when it was empty and would not let go.

"He'll die out here on his own won't he?" said Jo.

"No he won't, not if we don't let him," said the man and he tickled the cub under his chin. "Someone's going to have to look after him."

"I can't," said Jo. "They'd kill him. If I took him home they'd kill him. I know they would." He touched the pad of the cub's paw, it was harder than he'd expected. The man thought for a while nodding slowly.

"Well then, I'll have to do it, won't I?" he said. "Won't be long, only a month or two at the most I should think, and then he'll be able to cope on his own. I've got nothing much else to do with myself, not at the moment." For just a moment as he caught his eye Jo thought he recognized the man from somewhere before but he could not think where. Yet he was sure he knew everyone who lived in the valley—not by name necessarily, but by place or by face. "You don't know who I am, do you?" said the man. It was as if he could read Jo's thoughts. Jo shook his head. "Well that makes us even doesn't it, because I don't know you either. Maybe it's better it stays that way. You've got to promise me never to say a word, you understand?" There was a new urgency in his voice. "There was no cub, you never met me, you never even saw me. None of this ever happened." He reached out and gripped Jo's arm tightly. "You have to promise me. Not a word to anyone—not your father, not your mother, not your best friend, no one, not ever."

"All right," said Jo who was becoming alarmed. He felt the grip on his arm relax.

"Good boy, good boy," he said and patted Jo's arm.

The man looked up. The mist was filtering down through the treetops above them. "I'd better get back," he said. "I don't want to get caught out in this, I'll never find my way home."

Once he was on his feet Jo gave him his hat and his stick. "Now you hang on to that dog of yours," he said. "I don't want him following me home. Where one goes others can follow, if you understand my meaning." Jo wasn't sure he did. The cub clambered up his shoulder and put an arm around his neck. "Seems to like me, doesn't he?" said the man. He turned to go and then stopped. "And don't you go blaming yourself for what happened this afternoon. You had your job to do, and that old mother bear, she had hers to do, and that's all there is to it. Besides," and he smiled broadly as the cub snuffled in his ear, "besides, if none of it had happened, we'd never have met, would we?"

"We haven't met," said Jo catching Rouf by the scruff of his neck as he made to follow them. The man laughed.

"Nor we have," he said. "Nor we have. And if we haven't met we can't say good-bye, can we?" And he turned, waved his stick above his head, and walked away into the trees, the cub's chin resting on his shoulder. The eyes that looked back at Jo were two little moons of milk.

ANDROCLES AND THE LION

Retold by ANDREW LANG

Without sentimentality, this story illustrates that there can exist a great bond of trust and understanding between ourselves and our fellow creatures. It may be legend, it may be fact. Either way it is utterly believable—but that may be the way it is told. It is all in the telling.

MANY HUNDRED YEARS AGO, there lived in the north of Africa a poor Roman slave called Androcles. His master held great power and authority in the country, but he was a hard, cruel man, and his slaves led a very unhappy life. They had little to eat, had to work hard, and were often punished and tortured if they failed to satisfy their master's caprices. For long, Androcles had borne with the hardships of his life; but at last he could bear it no longer, and he made up his mind to run away. He knew that it was a great risk, for he had no friends in that foreign country with whom he could seek safety and protection; and he was aware that if he was overtaken and caught, he would be put to a cruel death.

But even death, he thought, would not be so hard as the

life he now led, and it was possible that he might escape to the seacoast, and somehow someday get back to Rome and find a kinder master.

So he waited till the old moon had waned to a tiny gold thread in the skies, and then, one dark night, he slipped out of his master's house, and, creeping through the deserted forum and along the silent town, he passed out of the city into the vineyards and cornfields lying outside the walls. In the cool night air, he walked rapidly. From time to time he was startled by the sudden barking of a Dog, or the sound of voices coming from some late revelers in the villas that stood beside the road along which he hurried. But as he got farther into the country, these sounds ceased, and there was silence and darkness all around him. When the sun rose, he had already gone many miles away from the town in which he had been so miserable.

But now a new terror oppressed him—the terror of great loneliness. He had got into a wild, barren country, where there was no sign of human habitation. A thick growth of low trees and thorny mimosa bushes spread out before him, and as he tried to thread his way through them, he was severely scratched, and his scant garments torn by the long thorns. Besides, the sun was very hot, and the trees were not high enough to afford him any shade. He was worn out with hunger and fatigue, and he longed to lie down and rest. But to lie down in that fierce sun would have meant death; and he struggled on, hoping to find some wild berries to eat, and some water to quench his thirst.

But when he came out of the scrub wood, he found he was as badly off as before. A long, low line of rocky cliffs rose before him, but there were no houses, and he saw no hope of finding food. He was so tired that he could not wander farther; and seeing a cave which looked cool and dark in the side of the cliffs, he crept into it, and, stretching his tired limbs on the sandy floor, fell fast asleep.

Suddenly he was awakened by a noise that made his blood run cold. The roar of a wild beast sounded in his ears, and as he started trembling and in terror to his feet, he beheld a huge, tawny Lion, with great glistening white teeth, standing in the entrance of the cave. It was impossible to fly, for the Lion barred the way. Immovable with fear, Androcles stood rooted to the spot, waiting for the Lion to spring on him and tear him limb from limb.

But the Lion did not move. Making a low moan as if in great pain, it stood licking its huge paw, from which Androcles now saw that blood was flowing freely. Seeing the poor animal in such pain, and noticing how gentle it seemed, Androcles forgot his own terror, and slowly approached the Lion, who held up its paw as if asking the man to help it. Then Androcles saw that a monster thorn had entered the paw, making a deep cut, and causing great pain and swelling. Swiftly but firmly he drew the thorn out, and pressed the swelling to try to stop the flowing of the blood. Relieved of the pain, the Lion quietly lay down at Androcles' feet, slowly moving his great bushy tail from side to side as a Dog does when it feels happy and comfortable.

From that moment, Androcles and the Lion became devoted friends. After lying for a little while at his feet, licking the poor wounded paw, the Lion got up and limped out of the cave. A few moments later, it returned with a little dead Rabbit in its mouth, which it put down on the floor of the cave beside Androcles. The poor man, who was starving with hunger, cooked the Rabbit somehow, and ate it. In the evening, led by the Lion, he found a place where there was a spring, at which he quenched his dreadful thirst.

And so, for three years, Androcles and the Lion lived

cave; wandering about the woods together
, sleeping together at night. For in summer, the cave
was cooler than the woods, and in winter it was warmer.

At last, the longing in Androcles' heart to live once more
with his fellow man became so great that he felt he could
remain in the woods no longer, but that he must return to
a town, and take his chance of being caught and killed as a
runaway slave. And so, one morning, he left the cave, and
wandered away in the direction where he thought the sea
and the large towns lay. But in a few days, he was captured
by a band of soldiers who were patrolling the country in
search of fugitive slaves, and he was put in chains and sent
as a prisoner to Rome.

Here he was cast into prison and tried for the crime of
having run away from his master. He was condemned as a
punishment to be torn to pieces by wild beasts on the first
public holiday, in the great circus at Rome.

When the day arrived, Androcles was brought out of his
prison, dressed in a simple, short tunic, and with a scarf
around his right arm. He was given a lance with which to
defend himself—a forlorn hope, as he knew that he had to
fight with a powerful Lion that had been kept without food
for some days to make it more savage and bloodthirsty. As
he stepped into the arena of the huge circus, above the roar
of the voices of thousands on thousands of spectators, he
could hear the savage roar of the wild beasts from their
cages below the floor on which he stood.

Of a sudden, the silence of expectation fell on the
spectators, for a signal had been given, and the cage
containing the Lion with which Androcles had to fight had
been shot up into the arena from the floor below. A great
animal had sprung out of its cage into the arena, and with
a bound had rushed at the spot where Androcles had stood
trembling. But suddenly, as he saw Androcles, the Lion

stood still, wondering. Then, quickly but quietly, it approached him, and gently moved its tail and licked the man's hands, and fawned upon him like a great Dog. And Androcles patted the Lion's head, and gave a sob of recognition, for he knew that it was his own Lion, with whom he had lived and lodged all those months and years.

And, seeing this strange and wonderful meeting between the man and the wild beast, all the people marveled; and the emperor, from his high seat above the arena, sent for Androcles, and bade him tell his story and explain this mystery. And the emperor was so delighted with the story that he said Androcles was to be released and to be made a free man from that hour. And he rewarded him with money, and ordered that the Lion was to belong to him, and to accompany him wherever he went.

And when the people in Rome met Androcles walking, followed by his faithful Lion, they used to point at them and say: "That is the Lion, the guest of the man, and that is the man, the doctor of the Lion."

THE TIGER, THE BRAHMAN,
AND THE JACKAL

Retold by JOSEPH JACOBS

Many folk tales use animals and their characterization to illustrate human frailties and moral dilemmas. Joseph Jacobs, in his retelling of this traditional Indian tale, does just this—the storyweaving is deft, and everything is implicit.

O NCE UPON A TIME, a Tiger was caught in a trap. He tried in vain to get out through the bars, and rolled and bit with rage and grief when he failed.

By chance a poor Brahman came by. "Let me out of this cage, oh, pious one!" cried the Tiger.

"Nay, my friend," replied the Brahman mildly; "you would probably eat me if I did."

"Not at all!" swore the Tiger with many oaths; "on the contrary, I should be forever grateful, and serve you as a slave!"

Now, when the Tiger sobbed and sighed and wept and swore, the pious Brahman's heart softened; and at last he consented to open the door of the cage. Out popped the Tiger, and, seizing the poor man, cried, "What a fool you are! What is to prevent my eating you now; for after being cooped up so long, I am just terribly hungry?"

In vain the Brahman pleaded for his life; the most he could gain was a promise to abide by the decision of the first three things he chose to question as to the justice of the Tiger's action.

So the Brahman first asked a pipal tree what it thought of the matter, but the pipal tree relied coldly, "What have you to complain about? Don't I give shade and shelter to everyone who passes by, and don't they in return tear down my branches to feed their Cattle? Don't whimper—be a man!"

Then the Brahman, sad at heart, went farther afield till he saw a Buffalo turning a well wheel; but he fared no better from it, for it answered: "You are a fool to expect gratitude! Look at me! While I gave milk, they fed me on cottonseed and oil cake, but now I am dry they yoke me here, and give me refuse as fodder!"

The Brahman, still more sad, asked the road to give him its opinion. "My dear sir," said the road, "how foolish you are to expect anything else! Here am I, useful to everybody, yet all, rich and poor, great and small, trample on me as they go past, giving me nothing but the ashes of their pipes and the husks of their grain!"

At this the Brahman turned back sorrowfully; and on the way he met a Jackal, who called out, "Why, what's the matter, Mr. Brahman? You look as miserable as a fish out of water!"

The Brahman told him all that had occurred. "How confusing!" said the Jackal, when the recital was ended. "Would you mind telling me over again, for everything was so mixed up?"

The Brahman told it all over again, but the Jackal shook his head in a distracted sort of way, and still could not understand.

"It's very odd," said he sadly, "but it all seems to go in at one ear and out at the other! I will go to the place where it all happened, and then, perhaps, I shall be able to give a judgement."

So they returned to the cage, by which the Tiger was waiting for the Brahman, and sharpening his teeth and claws.

"You've been away a long time!" growled the savage beast, "but now let us begin our dinner."

"*Our* dinner!" thought the wretched Brahman, as his knees knocked together with fright; "what a remarkably delicate way of putting it!"

"Give me five minutes, my lord!" he pleaded, "in order that I may explain matters to the Jackal here, who is somewhat slow in his wits."

The Tiger consented, and the Brahman began the whole story over again, not missing a single detail, and spinning as long a yarn as possible.

"Oh, my poor brain! Oh, my poor brain!" cried the Jackal, wringing its paws. "Let me see! How did it all begin? You were in the cage, and the Tiger came walking by—"

"Pooh!" interrupted the Tiger, "What a fool you are! I was in the cage."

"Of course!" cried the Jackal, pretending to tremble with fright; "Yes! I was in the cage—no, I wasn't—dear! dear! Where are my wits? Let me see—the Tiger was in the Brahman, and the cage came walking by—no, that's not it, either! Well, don't mind me, but begin your dinner, for I shall never understand!"

"Yes, you shall!" returned the Tiger, in a rage at the Jackal's stupidity. "I'll *make* you understand! Look here—I am the Tiger—"

"Yes, my lord!"

"And that is the Brahman—"

"Yes, my lord!"

"And that is the cage—"

"Yes, my lord!"

"And I was in the cage—do you understand?"

"Yes—no—please, my lord—"

"Well?" cried the Tiger impatiently.

"Please, my lord!—how did you get in?"

"How?—why in the usual way, of course!"

"Oh, dear me!—My head is beginning to whirl again! Please don't be angry, my lord, but what is the usual way?"

At this the Tiger lost patience, and, jumping into the cage, cried, "This way! Now do you understand how it was?"

"Perfectly!" grinned the Jackal, as he dexterously shut the door; "And if you will permit me to say so, I think matters will remain as they were!"

THE CAT THAT WALKED BY HIMSELF

RUDYARD KIPLING

Whenever I read this story I hear my mother's voice. I must have been about six when she first read it to me. I used to know it by heart—I still do in part. I milk cows most days of my life, and often think of the Man and the Woman who first milked a cow. I simply adore this story—and I'm getting on for sixty now. I don't throw boots at the cat, honestly; but I do love it when the dog chases him up a tree.

HEAR AND ATTEND AND LISTEN; for this befell and behappened and became and was, O my Best Beloved, when the Tame animals were wild. The Dog was wild, and the Horse was wild, and the Cow was wild, and the Sheep was wild, and the Pig was wild—as wild as wild could be—and they walked in the Wet Wild Woods by their wild lones. But the wildest of all the wild animals was the Cat. He walked by himself, and all places were alike to him.

Of course the Man was wild, too. He was dreadfully wild. He didn't even begin to be tame until he met the

Woman, and she told him that she did not like living in his wild ways. She picked out a nice dry Cave, instead of a heap of wet leaves, to lie down in; and she strewed clean sand on the floor; and she lit a nice fire of wood at the back of the cave; and she hung a dried wild horse skin, tail-down, across the opening of the Cave; and she said, "Wipe your feet, dear, when you come in, and now we'll keep house."

That night, Best Beloved, they ate wild sheep roasted on the hot stones, and flavored with wild garlic and wild pepper; and wild duck stuffed with wild rice and wild fenugreek and wild coriander; and marrowbones of wild oxen; and wild cherries, and wild grenadillas. Then the Man went to sleep in front of the fire ever so happy; but the Woman sat up, combing her hair. She took the bone of the shoulder of mutton—the big flat blade bone—and she looked at the wonderful marks on it, and she threw more wood on the fire, and she made a Magic. She made the First Singing Magic in the world.

Out in the Wet Wild Woods all the wild animals gathered together where they could see the light of the fire a long way off, and they wondered what it meant.

Then Wild Horse stamped with his wild foot and said, "O my Friends and O my Enemies, why have the Man and the Woman made that great light in that great Cave, and what harm will it do us?"

Wild Dog lifted up his wild nose and smelled the smell of the roast mutton, and said, "I will go up and see and look, and say; for I think it is good. Cat, come with me."

"Nenni!" said the Cat. "I am the Cat who walks by himself, and all places are alike to me. I will not come."

"Then we can never be friends again," said Wild Dog, and he trotted off to the Cave. But when he had gone a little way the Cat said to himself, "All places are alike to me.

Why should I not go too, and see and look and come away at my own liking?" So he slipped after Wild Dog softly, very softly, and hid himself where he could hear everything.

When Wild Dog reached the mouth of the Cave he lifted up the dried horse skin with his nose and sniffed the beautiful smell of the roast mutton, and the Woman, looking at the blade bone, heard him, and laughed, and said, "Here comes the first. Wild Thing out of the Wild Woods, what do you want?"

Wild Dog said, "O my Enemy and Wife of my Enemy, what is this that smells so good in the Wild Woods?"

Then the Woman picked up a roasted mutton bone and threw it to Wild Dog, and said, "Wild Thing out of the Wild Woods, taste and try." Wild Dog gnawed the bone, and it was more delicious than anything he had ever tasted, and he said, "O my Enemy and Wife of my Enemy, give me another."

The Woman said, "Wild Thing out of the Wild Woods, help my Man to hunt through the day and guard this Cave at night, and I will give you as many roast bones as you need."

"Ah!" said the Cat, listening. "This is a very wise Woman, but she is not so wise as I am."

Wild Dog crawled into the Cave and laid his head on the Woman's lap, and said, "O my Friend and Wife of my Friend, I will help your Man to hunt through the day, and at night I will guard your Cave."

"Ah!" said the Cat, listening. "That is a very foolish Dog." And he went back through the Wet Wild Woods waving his wild tail, and walking by his wild lone. But he never told anybody.

When the Man waked up he said, "What is Wild Dog doing here?" And the Woman said, "His name is not Wild

Dog any more, but the First Friend, because he will be our friend for always and always and always. Take him with you when you go hunting."

Next night, the Woman cut great green armfuls of fresh grass from the water meadows, and dried it before the fire, so that it smelled like new-mown hay, and she sat at the mouth of the Cave and plaited a halter out of horsehide, and she looked at the shoulder of mutton bone—at the big broad blade bone—and she made a Magic. She made the Second Singing Magic in the world.

Out in the Wild Woods all the wild animals wondered what had happened to Wild Dog, and at last Wild Horse stamped with his foot and said, "I will go and see and say why Wild Dog has not returned. Cat, come with me."

"Nenni!" said the Cat. "I am the Cat who walks by himself, and all places are alike to me. I will not come." But all the same he followed Wild Horse softly, very softly, and hid himself where he could hear everything.

When the Woman heard Wild Horse tripping and stumbling on his long mane, she laughed and said, "Here comes the second. Wild Thing out of the Wild Woods, what do you want?"

Wild Horse said, "O my Enemy and Wife of my Enemy, where is Wild Dog?"

The Woman laughed, and picked up the blade bone and looked at it, and said, "Wild Thing out of the Wild Woods, you did not come here for Wild Dog, but for the sake of this good grass."

And Wild Horse, tripping and stumbling on his long mane, said, "That is true; give it me to eat."

The Woman said, "Wild Thing out of the Wild Woods, bend your wild head and wear what I give you, and you shall eat the wonderful grass three times a day."

"Ah," said the Cat, listening, "this is a very clever

Woman, but she is not so clever as I am."

Wild Horse bent his wild head, and the Woman slipped the plaited hide halter over it, and Wild Horse breathed on the Woman's feet and said, "O my Mistress, and Wife of my Master, I will be your servant for the sake of the wonderful grass."

"Ah," said the Cat, listening, "that is a very foolish Horse." And he went back through the Wet Wild Woods, waving his wild tail and walking by his wild lone. But he never told anybody.

When the Man and the Dog came back from hunting, the Man said, "What is Wild Horse doing here?" And the Woman said, "His name is not Wild Horse any more, but the First Servant, because he will carry us from place to place for always and always and always. Ride on his back when you go hunting."

Next day, holding her wild head high that her wild horns should not catch in the wild trees, Wild Cow came up to the Cave, and the Cat followed, and hid himself just the same as before; and everything happened just the same as before; and the Cat said the same things as before; and when Wild Cow had promised to give her milk to the Woman every day in exchange for the wonderful grass, the Cat went back through the Wet Wild Woods waving his wild tail and walking by his wild lone, just the same as before. But he never told anybody. And when the Man and the Horse and the Dog came home from hunting and asked the same questions same as before, the Woman said, "Her name is not Wild Cow any more, but the Giver of Good Food. She will give us the warm white milk for always and always and always, and I will take care of her while you and the First Friend and the First Servant go hunting."

Next day, the Cat waited to see if any other Wild Thing would go up to the Cave, but no one moved in the Wet

Wild Woods, so the Cat walked there by himself; and he saw the Woman milking the Cow, and he saw the light of the fire in the Cave, and he smelled the smell of the warm white milk.

Cat said, "O my Enemy and Wife of my Enemy, where did Wild Cow go?"

The Woman laughed and said, "Wild Thing out of the Wild Woods, go back to the Woods again, for I have braided up my hair, and I have put away the magic blade bone, and we have no more need of either friends or servants in our Cave."

Cat said, "I am not a friend, and I am not a servant. I am the Cat who walks by himself, and I wish to come into your Cave."

Woman said, "Then why did you not come with First Friend on the first night?"

Cat grew very angry and said, "Has Wild Dog told tales of me?"

Then the Woman laughed and said, "You are the Cat who walks by himself, and all places are alike to you. You are neither a friend nor a servant. You have said it yourself. Go away and walk by yourself in all places alike."

Then Cat pretended to be sorry and said, "Must I never come into the Cave? Must I never sit by the warm fire? Must I never drink the warm white milk? You are very wise and very beautiful. You should not be cruel even to a Cat."

Woman said, "I knew I was wise, but I did not know I was beautiful. So I will make a bargain with you. If ever I say one word in your praise, you may come into the Cave."

"And if you say two words in my praise?" said the Cat.

"I never shall," said the Woman, "but if I say two words in your praise, you may sit by the fire in the Cave."

"And if you say three words?" said the Cat.

"I never shall," said the Woman, "but if I say three words in your praise, you may drink the warm white milk three times a day for always and always and always."

Then the Cat arched his back and said, "Now let the Curtain at the mouth of the Cave, and the Fire at the back of the Cave, and the Milkpots that stand beside the Fire, remember what my Enemy and the Wife of my Enemy has said." And he went away through the Wet Wild Woods waving his wild tail and walking by his wild lone.

That night when the Man and the Horse and the Dog came home from hunting, the Woman did not tell them of the bargain that she had made with the Cat, because she was afraid they might not like it.

Cat went far and far away and hid himself in the Wet Wild Woods by his wild lone for a long time till the Woman forgot all about him. Only the Bat—the little upside-down Bat—that hung inside the Cave knew where Cat hid; and every evening Bat would fly to Cat with news of what was happening.

One evening Bat said, "There is a Baby in the Cave. He is new and pink and fat and small, and the Woman is very fond of him."

"Ah," said the Cat, listening, "but what is the Baby fond of?"

"He is fond of things that are soft and tickle," said the Bat. "He is fond of warm things to hold in his arms when he goes to sleep. He is fond of being played with. He is fond of all those things."

"Ah," said the Cat, listening, "then my time has come."

Next night, Cat walked through the Wet Wild Woods and hid very near the Cave till morningtime, and Man and Dog and Horse went hunting. The Woman was busy cooking that morning, and the Baby cried and interrupted. So she carried him outside the Cave and gave him a

handful of pebbles to play with. But still the Baby cried.

Then the Cat put out his paddy paw and patted the Baby on the cheek, and it cooed; and the Cat rubbed against its fat knees and tickled it under its fat chin with his tail. And the Baby laughed; and the Woman heard him and smiled.

Then the Bat—the little upside-down Bat—that hung in the mouth of the Cave said, "O my Hostess and Wife of my Host and Mother of my Host's Son, a Wild Thing from the Wild Woods is most beautifully playing with your Baby."

"A blessing on that Wild Thing whoever he may be," said the Woman, straightening her back, "for I was a busy woman this morning, and he has done me a service."

That very minute and second, Best Beloved, the dried horse skin Curtain that was stretched tail-down at the mouth of the Cave fell down—*whoosh!*—because it remembered the bargain she had made with the Cat; and when the Woman went to pick it up—lo and behold!—the Cat was sitting quite comfy inside the Cave.

"O my Enemy and Wife of my Enemy and Mother of my Enemy," said the Cat, "it is I: for you have spoken a word in my praise, and now I can sit within the Cave for always and always and always. But still I am still the Cat who walks by himself, and all places are alike to me."

The Woman was very angry, and shut her lips tight and took up her spinning wheel and began to spin.

But the Baby cried because the Cat had gone away, and the Woman could not hush it, for it struggled and kicked and grew black in the face.

"O my Enemy and Wife of my Enemy and Mother of my Enemy," said the Cat, "take a strand of the thread that you are spinning and tie it to your spinning whorl and drag it along the floor, and I will show you a Magic that shall make your Baby laugh as loudly as he is now crying."

"I will do so," said the Woman, "because I am at my

wits' end; but I will not thank you for it."

She tied the thread to the little clay spindle whorl and drew it across the floor, and the Cat ran after it and patted it with his paws and rolled head over heels, and tossed it backward over his shoulder and chased it between his hind legs and pretended to lose it, and pounced down upon it again, till the Baby laughed as loudly as it had been crying, and scrambled after the Cat and frolicked all over the Cave till it grew tired and settled down to sleep with the Cat in its arms.

"Now," said Cat, "I will sing the Baby a song that shall keep him asleep for an hour." And he began to purr, loud and low, low and loud, till the Baby fell fast asleep. The Woman smiled as she looked down upon the two of them, and said, "That was wonderfully done. No question but you are very clever, O Cat."

That very minute and second, Best Beloved, the smoke of the Fire at the back of the Cave came down in clouds from the roof—*puff!*—because it remembered the bargain she had made with the Cat; and when it had cleared away—lo and behold!—the Cat was sitting quite comfy close to the fire.

"O my Enemy and Wife of my Enemy and Mother of my Enemy," said the Cat, "it is I: for you have spoken a second word in my praise, and now I can sit by the warm fire at the back of the Cave for always and always and always. But still I am the Cat who walks by himself, and all places are alike to me."

Then the Woman was very very angry, and let down her hair and put more wood on the fire and brought out the broad blade bone of the shoulder of mutton and began to make a Magic that should prevent her from saying a third word in praise of the Cat. It was not a Singing Magic, Best Beloved, it was a Still Magic; and by and by the Cave grew so still that a little wee-wee mouse crept out of a corner and ran across the floor.

"O my Enemy and Wife of my Enemy and Mother of my Enemy," said the Cat, "is that little mouse part of your magic?"

"Ouh! Chee! No indeed!" said the Woman, and she dropped the blade bone and jumped upon the footstool in front of the fire and braided up her hair very quick for fear that the mouse should run up it.

"Ah," said the Cat, watching, "then the mouse will do me no harm if I eat it?"

"No," said the Woman, braiding her hair, "eat it quickly and I will ever be grateful to you."

Cat made one jump and caught the little mouse, and the Woman said, "A hundred thanks. Even the First Friend is not quick enough to catch little mice as you have done. You must be very wise."

That very moment and second, O Best Beloved, the Milkpot that stood by the fire cracked in two pieces—*ffft!*—because it remembered the bargain she had made with the Cat; and when the Woman jumped down from the footstool—lo and behold!—the Cat was lapping up the warm white milk that lay in one of the broken pieces.

"O my Enemy and Wife of my Enemy and Mother of my Enemy," said the Cat, "it is I: for you have spoken three word in my praise, and now I can drink the warm white milk three times a day for always and always and always. But *still* I am the Cat who walks by himself, and all places are alike to me."

Then the Woman laughed and set the Cat a bowl of the warm white milk and said, "O Cat you are as clever as a man, but remember that your bargain was not made with the Man or the Dog, and I do not know what they will do when they come home."

"What is that to me?" said the Cat. "If I have my place in the Cave by the fire and my warm white milk three times a day I do not care what the Man or the Dog can do."

That evening when the Man and the Dog came into the Cave, the Woman told them all the story of the bargain, while the Cat sat by the fire and smiled. Then the Man said, "Yes, but he has not made a bargain with *me* or with all proper Men after me." Then he took off his two leather boots and he took up his little stone ax (that makes three) and he fetched a piece of wood and a hatchet (that is five altogether), and he set them out in a row and he said, "Now we will make *our* bargain. If you do not catch mice when you are in the Cave for always and always and always, I will throw these five things at you whenever I see you, and so shall all proper Men do after me."

"Ah," said the Woman, listening, "this is a very clever Cat, but he is not so clever as my Man."

The Cat counted the five things (and they looked very knobby) and he said, "I will catch mice when I am in the Cave for always and always and always; but *still* I am the Cat who walks by himself, and all places are alike to me."

"Not when I am near," said the Man. "If you had not said that last I would have put all these things away for always and always and always; but now I am going to throw my two boots and my little stone ax (that makes three) at you whenever I meet you. And so shall all proper Men do after me."

Then the Dog said, "Wait a minute. He has not made a bargain with *me* or with all proper Dogs after me." And he showed his teeth and said, "If you are not kind to the Baby while I am in the Cave for always and always and always, I will hunt you till I catch you, and when I catch you, I will bite you. And so shall all proper Dogs do after me."

"Ah," said the Woman, listening, "this is a very clever

Cat, but he is not so clever as the Dog."

Cat counted the Dog's teeth (and they looked very pointed) and he said, "I will be kind to the Baby while I am in the Cave, as long as he does not pull my tail too hard, for always and always and always. But *still* I am the Cat that walks by himself, and all places are alike to me!"

"Not when I am near," said the Dog. "If you had not said that last I would have shut my mouth for always and always and always; but *now* I am going to hunt you up a tree whenever I meet you. And so shall all proper Dogs do after me."

Then the Man threw his two boots and his little stone ax (that makes three) at the Cat, and the Cat ran out of the Cave and the Dog chased him up a tree; and from that day to this, Best Beloved, three proper Men out of five will always throw things at a Cat whenever they meet him, and all proper Dogs will chase him up a tree. But the Cat keeps his side of the bargain, too. He will kill mice, and he will be kind to Babies when he is in the house, just as long as they do not pull his tail too hard. But when he has done that, and between times, and when the moon gets up and night comes, he is the Cat that walks by himself, and all places are alike to him. Then he goes out to the Wet Wild Woods or up the Wet Wild Trees or on the Wet Wild Roofs, waving his wild tail and walking by his wild lone.

ACKNOWLEDGMENTS

The publisher would like to thank the copyright holders for permission to reproduce the following copyright material:

James Berry: "Son-Son Fetches the Mule" from *The Future-Telling Lady* by James Berry (Hamish Hamilton Ltd., 1991). Text copyright © James Berry 1991. Reprinted by permission of The Peters, Fraser, and Dunlop Group Ltd. on behalf of James Berry. **Geoffrey Dutton**: "The Wedge-Tailed Eagle" by Geoffrey Dutton. Reprinted by permission of the copyright owner, care of Curtis Brown (Aust) Pty Ltd. **Janet Frame**: "The Birds Began to Sing" from The *Lagoon and Other Stories* by Janet Frame. Copyright © Janet Frame 1951, 1991. Reproduced with permission of Curtis Brown Ltd., London, on behalf of Janet Frame. **Paul Gallico**: Excerpt from *The Snow Goose* by Paul Gallico. Copyright © 1940 by The Curtis Publishing Company and renewed 1968 by Paul Gallico. Reprinted by permission of Alfred A. Knopf Inc. **Ernest Hemingway**: Excerpt from *The Old Man and the Sea* by Ernest Hemingway. Copyright © 1952 by Ernest Hemingway. Copyright renewed © 1980 by Mary Hemingway. Reprinted with permission of Scribner, a division of Simon & Schuster, Inc. **Barry Hines**: Excerpt from *A Kestrel for a Knave* (*Kes*) by Barry Hines. First published by Michael Joseph, 1968. Copyright © Barry Hines 1968. Reproduced by permission of The Agency (London) Ltd. All rights reserved and enquiries to The Agency (London) Ltd., 24 Pottery Lane, London, W11 4LZ, U.K. **Ted Hughes**: Excerpt from *The Iron Woman* by Ted Hughes. Copyright © 1993 by Ted Hughes. Used by permission of Dial Books for Young Readers, a division of Penguin Putnam Inc. **Dick King-Smith**: Excerpt from *Godhanger* by Dick King-Smith. Copyright © Fox Busters Ltd. 1996. Reprinted by permission of A. P. Watt Ltd. on behalf of

Fox Busters Ltd. **Rudyard Kipling**: "The Cat That Walked by Himself" from *Just So Stories* by Rudyard Kipling. Reprinted by permission of A. P. Watt Ltd. on behalf of The National Trust for Places of Historic Interest or Natural Beauty. **Beryl Markham**: "He Was a Good Lion" from *West With the Night* by Beryl Markham. Copyright © 1942, 1983 by Beryl Markham. Reprinted by permission of North Point Press, a division of Farrar, Straus & Giroux Inc. **Michael Morpurgo**: Excerpt from *Waiting for Anya* by Michael Morpurgo. Copyright © 1990 by Michael Morpurgo. Used by permission of Viking Penguin, a division of Penguin Putnam Inc. **John Steinbeck**: Excerpt from *The Red Pony* by John Steinbeck. Copyright © 1933, 1937, 1938 © renewed 1961, 1965, 1966 by John Steinbeck. Used by permission of Viking Penguin, a division of Penguin Putnam Inc. **E. B. White**: Excerpt from *Charlotte's Web* by E. B. White. Copyright © 1952 by E. B. White renewed © 1980 by E. B. White. Used by permission of HarperCollins Publishers. **Henry Williamson**: Excerpt from *Tarka the Otter* by Henry Williamson. Copyright © Henry Williamson 1929. Reprinted by permission of A. M. Heath & Co. Ltd. on behalf of the Estate of the Late Henry Williamson.

BILLY GRAHAM
Evangelistic Association

Always Good News.

Dear Friend,

I am pleased to send you this copy of *What in the World Is Going On?* by David Jeremiah. If you've ever wondered about the meaning behind what you see in the daily news, you'll find the answers in this informative and inspirational book.

Interpreting current global events in light of biblical prophecy, Dr. Jeremiah clearly explains what we can expect as the end times approach and reminds us how to live as we *watch*, *work*, and *wait* for the Lord's return. I pray you will be encouraged as you discover how world developments in our time are setting the stage for the return of Jesus Christ.

For nearly 60 years the Billy Graham Evangelistic Association has worked to take the Good News of Jesus Christ throughout the world by every effective means available, and I'm excited about what God will do in the years ahead. If you would like to know more about our ministry, please contact us:

In the U.S.:

Billy Graham Evangelistic Association
1 Billy Graham Parkway
Charlotte, NC 28201-0001
billygraham.org
info@bgea.org
Toll-free: 1-877-2GRAHAM (1-877-247-2426)

In Canada:

Billy Graham Evangelistic Association of Canada
20 Hopewell Way NE
Calgary, Alberta T3J 5H5
billygraham.ca
Toll-free: 1-888-393-0003

We would appreciate knowing how our ministry has touched your life. May God bless you.

Sincerely,

Franklin Graham
President

What in the World Is Going On?

10 Prophetic Clues You Cannot Afford to Ignore

David Jeremiah

This *Billy Graham Library Selection* is published for
the Billy Graham Evangelistic Association
by Thomas Nelson, Inc.

Thomas Nelson
Since 1798

NASHVILLE   DALLAS   MEXICO CITY   RIO DE JANEIRO   BEIJING

Published in Nashville, Tennessee, by Thomas Nelson. Thomas Nelson is a registered trademark of Thomas Nelson, Inc.

Published in association with Yates & Yates, LLP, www.yates2.com.

Thomas Nelson, Inc. titles may be purchased in bulk for educational, business, fund-raising, or sales promotional use. For information, please e-mail SpecialMarkets@ThomasNelson.com.

"Battle of Armageddon" © 1944 Sony/ATV Music Publishing LLC. All rights administered by Sony/ATV Music Publishing LLC, 8 Music Square West, Nashville, TN 37203. All rights reserved. Used by permission.

Unless otherwise noted, Scripture quotations are taken from the New King James Version®. © 1982 by Thomas Nelson, Inc. Used by permission. All rights reserved.

Scripture quotations marked ASV are from the American Standard Version.

Scripture quotations marked KJV are from the King James Version.

Scripture quotations marked NASB are from the New American Standard Bible®, © The Lockman Foundation 1960, 1962, 1963, 1968, 1971, 1972, 1973, 1975, 1977, 1995. Used by permission.

Scripture quotations marked NIV are from the Holy Bible: New International Version®. © 1973, 1978, 1984 by International Bible Society. Used by permission of Zondervan Publishing House. All rights reserved.

Scripture quotations marked NLT are from the Holy Bible, New Living Translation. © 1996. Used by permission of Tyndale House Publishers, Inc., Wheaton, Illinois 60189. All rights reserved.

ISBN 978-0-8499-2147-6 (SE)
ISBN 978-0-7852-8974-6 (BGEA Ed.)

Library of Congress Cataloging-in-Publication Data

Jeremiah, David.
    What in the world is going on? : 10 prophetic clues you cannot afford to ignore / David Jeremiah.
      p. cm.
    ISBN 978-0-7852-2887-5 (hardcover)
    1. Bible—Prophecies. 2. World politics—21st century—Forecasting. 3. International relations—Forecasting. 4. Civilization, Modern—21st century—Forecasting. 5. World politics—21st century. 6. International relations—21st century. 7. Civilization, Modern—21st century. I. Title.
BS647.3.J47 2008
236'.9—dc22   2008029176

Printed in the United States of America

09 10 11 12 13 BTY 5 4 3 2 1

"Blessing and honor and glory and power

Be to Him who sits on the throne,

And to the Lamb, forever and ever!" (Revelation 5:13*b*)

Contents

Acknowledgments

LAST FALL, WHEN I BEGAN TO TEACH THE TRUTHS OF THIS BOOK TO the church I pastor in Southern California, I was taken aback by the number of people who came to me each week and said, "You are going to put this information in a book, aren't you?" Here's my answer! Thanks for your encouragement!

Barbara Boucher is my administrative assistant at Shadow Mountain Community Church. Her servant-hearted willingness to serve where she is needed reflects the spirit of this church family.

I owe a great deal to the team of people who surround me at Turning Point Ministries. Diane Sutherland understands the pressures that descend upon our office when a book is in the making. During those days especially, she guards my time and organizes my life. I dare not think of the chaos of my existence without her dedicated ministry.

Since this book seeks to shine the light of the Scriptures on twenty-first-century world events, the burden of research has been huge. Cathy Lord excels at this task. She never rests until she has found the exact quote, statistic, or source we are looking for. Cathy, your commitment to detail amazes me. Thank you for your hard work!

Paul Joiner is the creative services director at Turning Point. He is an integral part of all that we do around the world through radio, television, and print media. Paul, your creativity is infectious, and your fingerprints are all over this project.

Rob Morgan and William Kruidenier read each chapter and added their suggestions. Rob and William, thank you for your thoughtful contributions. Thanks also to my friend Chuck Emert for his valuable input.

Thomas Nelson editor Joey Paul has been encouraging me to write another book on prophecy for several years. When I sent him the preliminary notes for this book, he called back immediately and said, "David, this is it!" Joey, your friendship is a blessing in my life.

This was my first opportunity to work with writer and editor Tom Williams. He has been a gracious addition to our publication team. Tom, I hope we get to work together again soon.

On the first pages of all my books, you will see the name of Yates and Yates, the literary agency founded by Sealy Yates. Thank you, Sealy, for believing in this book and for coordinating the efforts between the Turning Point team and the Thomas Nelson team.

I want to express my gratitude to my son David, whose leadership at Turning Point makes it possible for me to invest my time in studying and writing.

Finally, I give thanks to Almighty God for my wife, Donna. When I first started talking about *What in the World Is Going On?*, I told her that my plans were to teach this material in our Sunday night services. She looked at me and said, "David, that needs to be taught in the morning services so everyone can hear it." I always do what she tells me to do!

Most of all, I want to express my hope that God will be glorified as we tell the story of His plans for our future!

Knowing the Signs

WHAT IN THE WORLD IS GOING ON? NEVER BEFORE IN MY lifetime have I read such jarring headlines, distressing news analyses, or dire predictions for America and the world. Things are getting so chaotic that many pundits are using the term *perfect storm* to explain the confluence of wide-ranging food shortages, record-high fuel prices, and natural disasters.

In a recent twenty-four-hour period, major newswires carried the following disturbing reports: A cyclone in Myanmar caused upwards of eighty-four thousand deaths, along with the loss of primary rice fields in a time of severe global rice shortages. A powerful volcano that had been considered dormant for nine thousand years erupted in Chile. A virulent new virus infected tens of thousands of China's children, causing mounting fears of a widespread epidemic. Longtime antagonists China and Japan announced a pledge of "peace, friendship and cooperation as neighbors," including a joint venture in oil refining. In resurgent Russia, newly installed president Dmitri Medvedev promptly named Vladimir Putin as prime minister, calling it "the most important position in the executive power."[1]

Within that same time frame, housing defaults and foreclosures continued to fuel America's economic tailspin. As if that weren't enough bad news, oil soared to its highest closing price on the New York Mercantile Exchange since oil trading began twenty-five years ago, and the dollar continued to sputter against most foreign currencies. When stories like these pile one on top of the other, we can't help but wonder . . . what in the world is going on?

As we look out at the world of the early twenty-first century, food shortages are producing widespread hunger in places that have previously known plenty. Outright starvation is replacing hunger in regions that have known want. Among the poorest, it has become a struggle just to survive. In Thailand, the world's leading rice exporter, prices doubled in the first quarter of this year. Food prices have fueled riots in Haiti, Cameroon, Egypt, Mexico, Philippines, Indonesia, Ivory Coast, and several other African nations. Desperation is so high in Thailand, Philippines, and Pakistan that armed personnel have been called in to protect food harvesters, supervise grain sales, and guard warehouses. A UN observer warned, "A hungry man is an angry man, and as food gets more and more difficult to access . . . we can expect to see more incidents of civil unrest."[2]

While natural disasters cannot be prevented, the wise remain alert to signs of their approach so they can take protective measures. This was done when the volcano erupted in Chile. Despite being perceived as benign or even extinct, the Chaitén volcano gave off dozens of warning signs, in the form of earthquakes. Surprised by the first eruption, wise government officials recognized the continuing danger. They ordered mandatory evacuations as the volcano again turned violent and spewed deadly ash and lava into the air. As a result, not one death was directly attributed to the eruption.[3] When signs are recognized and appropriate warnings are issued, disaster can often be avoided.

On the other hand, the disaster in Myanmar shows what happens when the signs are ignored. As early as six days before Cyclone Nargis made landfall, Myanmar officials were notified of the potential for a large-scale storm. Throughout the next several days, as the storm intensified and took direct aim at the country's heavily populated delta, the ruling military junta received regular weather updates and warnings. Even with the increasing urgency of these warnings and the obvious signs in the intensely churning sky, the government issued no warnings and ordered no evacuations. Their failure left the people at the mercy of the 160-mile-per-hour winds and twelve-foot storm surges. The result? Several weeks later, with the number of dead and missing already totaling more than 78,000, and with more than 2.5 million left homeless, global relief teams remained poised to deliver food and supplies but, for political reasons, were denied entry into the country.

Within days, before the world could absorb the events in Myanmar, a 7.9 earthquake decimated southern China. Seven thousand school-children and their teachers were buried beneath the rubble of their schools. Upwards of 70,000 died, and 5 million were left homeless. Scores of powerful aftershocks continued to threaten further destruction and hampered rescue efforts. China tested her new friendship agreement with Japan by requesting that they send their crack rescue teams to supplement the 130,000 military personnel already mobilized by China. One aftershock that no one anticipated was China's request for aid from Taiwan, long considered a renegade, if not an enemy. China also accepted help from Russia and North Korea.

Are we seeing signs today that should warn us of anything? What in the world is going on when enemies of Israel bestow posthumous honors to the headmaster of a UN school in Gaza for his work as chief engineer of the Islamic Jihad's bomb squad?[4] What about that parade of tankers, fighter jets, and missiles in Moscow on May Day, reminiscent of the Cold War era? What about the doubling of millions of dollars of investments in Iraqi stocks, currently traded by scribbles on a dry-erase board? Or what about the largest US embassy complex ever built now ready for occupancy in Baghdad, formerly the infamous ancient Babylon, the city that throughout the Bible stands as the antithesis of everything good? What about the planned restoration of Babylon to its fabled glory? What about the increased use of biometrics, those scans of fingerprints, irises, and faces used for personal identification in Iraq and other "places of global conflict"? Currently such forms of ID are used to bar people from markets or certain neighborhoods, and they are ready to be implemented worldwide in the name of security. When you hear these reports, do you find yourself thinking, *What in the world is going on?*

The events unfolding in today's world are ominously threatening to unsettle institutions, reorder national political alignments, change the balance of world power, and destabilize the equitable distribution of resources. People everywhere are beginning to live in a state of fear and anxiety. Serious people are asking, "If these things are happening today, what will the future be like for my children and grandchildren? Do current headlines give us any signs about what is coming next?"

There is one reliable source of information about the future—one that has an astounding record of accuracy. The Bible! But, strangely, many who purport to preach God's Word shy away from teaching prophecy. A preacher friend tells of "a pastor who once boasted that he didn't preach about prophecy because, in his words, 'Prophecy only distracts people from the present.' An astute colleague deftly retorted, 'Well, then, there's certainly a lot of distraction in the Scripture!' Fulfilling prophecy is one of God's calling cards."[5]

Indeed, one of the most convincing evidences of biblical inspiration is the staggering number of prophecies that have been fulfilled with pinpoint accuracy. Perhaps the most familiar examples are the fulfillments of more than three hundred prophecies relating to Christ's first coming to earth. In his book *The Rapture*, Dr. Tim LaHaye remarked, "No scholar of academic substance denies that Jesus lived almost 2,000 years ago. And we find three times as many prophecies in the Bible relating to His second coming as to His first. Thus, the second advent of our Lord is three times as certain as His first coming, which can be verified as historical fact."[6]

The Bible has proven to be absolutely dependable. Therefore we can trust it as the one source of reliable information about the meaning of the events of our day and what those events tell us about our hope for the future as we look toward the return of Christ. The Lord Jesus Himself spoke of the wisdom of discerning the signs of the times and of taking appropriate action as we wait for His return (Matthew 24, Mark 16). The Bible gives us clues conveying crucial information for interpreting the signs as the days of man's rule on earth wind toward their end. In each of the ten chapters of this book, we will apply these clues and point out these signs, viewing current events from the perspective of God's wonderful Word. We will be warned and challenged, but we will also be encouraged and comforted. Our purpose is not to make you fearful, but to make you aware so you can be prepared.

Popular radio personality Clifton Fadiman was a certifiable book-worm. Not only was he the book editor for a national magazine and a published author, but his love of books and his sense of what made a book good landed him the position of an editor for the Book of the Month Club, a post he held for fifty years. He once explained how he went about deciding what kind of book the reading public wanted: "What do our members, in the depths of their being, hanker for? They want books that explain our terrifying age honestly . . . Our age is so scary and fractionated that we need this kind of help more than people did in the [last] century. We thirst for books that put together pieces of the jigsaw puzzle."[7]

I am sure there have never been any times more "scary and fraction-ated" than these early days of the twenty-first century. In this book, I want to help you find the truth about what is going on. I want to show you that while our age is certainly "fractionated," it need not be scary—not for Christians who trust the Lord and know how to read the signs and understand coming events. As you read this book, I trust you will begin to put together the pieces of the puzzle, that you will recognize the clues that God has given us to find peace in "our terrifying age," and that you will come to an understanding of what in the world is going on. But mostly, I hope this book will help to "Let not your heart be troubled, neither let it be afraid" (John 14:27).

—David Jeremiah
San Diego, California
July 2008

ONE

The Israel Connection

MAY 14, 1948, WAS A PIVOTAL DAY IN HUMAN HISTORY. ON THAT afternoon, a car carrying prominent Jewish leader David Ben-Gurion rushed down Rothschild Boulevard in Tel Aviv and stopped in front of the Tel Aviv Art Museum. Four o'clock was only minutes away, and inside, more than four hundred people—Jewish religious and political leaders and press representatives from all over the world—were assembled in an auditorium, anxiously awaiting his arrival. Ben-Gurion quickly bounded up the steps. Precisely at four o'clock, local time, he stepped to the podium, called the meeting to order, and read these historic words[1]:

> This right is the natural right of the Jewish people to be masters of their own fate, like all other nations, in their own sovereign State. Accordingly, we . . . are here assembled . . . and by virtue of our natural and historic right, and on the strength of the resolution of the General Assembly of the United Nations, hereby declare the establishment of the Jewish State in Eretz-Israel, to be known as the State of Israel.[2]

Six thousand miles away, President Truman sat in the Oval Office, reading a forty-word statement about to be released to the press. He penciled in a few added words, then signed his approval and noted the time. It was 6:10 p.m. One minute later, the White House press secretary read the release to the world. The United States had officially recognized the birth of the modern nation of Israel.

Isaiah's prophecy, written 740 years before the birth of Jesus, declared: "Who has heard such a thing? Who has seen such things? Shall the earth be made to give birth in one day? Or shall a nation be born at once?" (Isaiah 66:8). Secular Israel was born that day.

As I write this chapter, Israel is about to celebrate her sixtieth anniversary as a nation. What amazes many people is that in those six decades, this tiny nation with a population of slightly more than 7 million has become the geopolitical center of the world. Why is this so? Why is a fledgling country with a total land space smaller than New Jersey mentioned in the nightly news more than any other nation except the United States?

To answer these questions, we must understand what happened on that day in 1948, what is happening today in Israel, and how these events affect the entire world. For answers, we must turn not to the evening news or the front page of the newspaper, but to the Bible. As Rabbi Binyamin Elon, a member of the Israeli Knesset, wrote:

> I believe that if you do not know how to read the Bible, you cannot understand the daily newspaper. If you do not know the biblical story of Abraham, Isaac, and Jacob, you cannot possibly understand the miracle of the modern state of Israel.[3]

The story of Israel begins at the very beginning of the Bible, in the book of Genesis. The very proportion of the coverage tells us something about the importance of Israel. Only two chapters are given to the whole story of creation. One chapter records the fall of man. Eight chapters cover the thousands of years from creation to the time of Abram. Then we find that fully thirty-eight chapters deal with the life stories of Abraham, Isaac, and Jacob—the progenitors of the Jewish race. Apparently God finds Abraham and his descendants to be of enormous importance.

The Abrahamic Covenant

The Almighty God of heaven and earth made a binding covenant with Abraham, who was to be the father of the Jewish nation. The provisions of that covenant are recorded in Genesis 12:1–3:

> Now the LORD had said to Abram:
> "Get out of your country,
> From your family
> And from your father's house,
> To a land that I will show you.
> I will make you a great nation;
> I will bless you
> And make your name great;
> And you shall be a blessing.
> I will bless those who bless you,
> And I will curse him who curses you;
> And in you all the families of the earth shall be blessed."

Notice that God's covenant with Abraham consists of four unconditional promises. First, God promised to bless Abraham. That promise has been lavishly kept; Abraham has been blessed in many ways. For thousands of years, the very name of Abraham has been revered by Jews, Christians, and Muslims alike—a significant portion of the world's population. Abraham has also been blessed through the gifts God gave to his descendants, the Jews. Mark Twain once wrote:

> Jews constitute but one percent of the human race. It suggests a nebulous dim puff of star dust in the blaze of the Milky Way. Properly the Jew ought hardly to be heard of; but he is heard of. He is as prominent on this planet as any other people. His commercial importance is extravagantly out of proportion to the smallness of his bulk. His contributions to the world's list of great names in literature, science, art, music, finance, medicine, and abstruse learning are also altogether out of proportion to the weakness of his numbers. He has made a marvelous fight in the world in all ages and he has done it with his hands tied behind him.[4]

One astounding fact that dramatically illustrates Twain's point is the disproportionate number of Nobel Prizes awarded to Jews. From 1901 to 2007, a total of 777 Nobel Prizes have been given to individuals in recognition of significant contributions to mankind. Of that total, 176 have been awarded to Jews. Of the 6 billion inhabitants of the world, only slightly more than 13 million are Jewish—less than two-thirds of 1 percent of the total world population. That miniscule percentage of the population has won 22.6 percent of all the Nobel Prizes awarded to date.[5]

Second, God promised to bring out of Abraham a great nation. Currently, nearly 5.4 million Jews live in Israel alone. Another 5 million live in the United States, and a significant Jewish population remains scattered throughout the world.[6] Add to these present figures all the descendants of Abraham who have lived throughout history and you truly have a population as uncountable as the nighttime stars (see appendix A for a chart of Jewish population statistics).

Third, God promised to make Abraham a blessing to many. That promise has been spectacularly kept. Just think what the world would be missing had it not been for the Jews. Without the Jews, we would have no Bible. Without the Jews, there would have been no Jesus. Without the Jewish Jesus, there would be no Christianity. Without the Jews, there would be no Ten Commandments, the Law that has largely been the basis of jurisprudence and statutory proceedings among most of the civilized nations of the world.

Fourth, God promised to bless those who blessed Israel and curse those who cursed her. He has kept that promise faithfully. No nation has blessed Israel like the United States of America, and no nation has been as blessed as the United States. In one of my previous books, I elaborated on this fact:

> I believe one of the reasons America has been blessed as a nation is that she has become a homeland for the Jewish people. Here the Jews can retain their religion. Here they have economic, social, and educational opportunities. Today the Christian church in America stands firmly between the Jew and the repetition of any further anti-Semitism.[7]

Throughout history, the judgments of God have fallen heavily upon Israel's oppressors—Egypt, Assyria, Babylon, Rome, and in more modern times, Spain, Germany, and Russia. Today, as forces less friendly to Israel gain influence in the United States, there are many who believe that America is dangerously close to being added to this hit list. Hal Lindsey wrote:

Although America continues to be Israel's principal protector, and continues to enjoy the concomitant blessings that come with it, America's good fortunes began to wane about the time the White House forced Israel into the Oslo Agreement. The "land for peace" formula called for Israel to give up some of the land of Promise in exchange for peace. In other words, it was a form of blackmail whose terms were drawn up in Washington and forced upon Israel for the express purpose of undoing what God had already done, including dividing Jerusalem and taking part of it from the Jews.[8]

God has certainly kept his promise to Abraham. He has blessed him and the nation that has come from him; He has multiplied his seed as the sands of the earth and stars of the sky; He has made him a blessing to the whole world; those who have blessed him have been blessed, and those who have cursed him have been cursed.

Of all God's covenant promises to Abraham, I believe the most amazing is His promise concerning the land. God told Abraham to leave his country, his family, and his father's house and go "to a land that I will show you" (Genesis 12:1). God then led Abraham to the land that would belong to his descendants forever. You can feel the awe and sense the meaning this promise has to Jews in this passage from Rabbi Binyamin Elon's book, *God's Covenant with Israel*:

I travel to my home in Beth El from Jerusalem on the same route that Abraham and others traveled in Biblical times, from Shechem to Hebron and places in between. Today we pass many other beautiful flourishing Jewish communities along the way . . . When I reach the Givat Assaf intersection, I am always inspired by the large sign posted there, sponsored by our local grocer: "Here, in Beth El, 3800 years ago, the Creator of the World promised the Land of Israel to the people of Israel. It is by virtue of this promise that we dwell today in Haifa, Tel Aviv, Shilo, and Hebron."⁹

The Record of Israel's Land

To this very day, the issue of who controls the Promised Land is the most volatile in international politics. But we need not worry; the right to the Promised Land has already been determined by the only One who has the authority to determine it. The land is called holy because it belongs to God. The Bible tells us that the earth is the Lord's to do with as He wills (Psalm 24:1; Exodus 19:5). In His covenant with Abraham, God designated who would control this land: He gave it to Abraham and his descendants, the people of Israel.

We read of God's choice of the Jews in Deuteronomy 7:6, where He declared the people of Israel holy, chosen to be "a people for Himself, a special treasure above all the peoples on the face of the earth." When I first began studying prophecy, I remember reading an offbeat little rhyme about Israel by British journalist William Norman Ewer: "How odd of God to choose the Jews." And when you think about it, this poetic quip expresses a valid observation. Doesn't it seem a little odd that of all the people on earth, God selected these particular people to be His chosen nation? Why would God choose the Jews?

The Bible tells us that His choice of Israel had nothing to do with merit. It was not because she was more numerous than other people in the world; she was the least (Deuteronomy 7:7). It was not because Israel was more sensitive to God than other nations. Although God called her by name, Israel did not know Him (Isaiah 45:4). It was not because Israel was more righteous than other nations. When God later confirmed His promise of land to the Jews, He reminded them that they were a rebellious, stiff-necked people (Deuteronomy 9:6–7).

If God chose to bless the nation of Israel not because she was more populous or spiritually responsive or righteous than other nations, just why did He choose the Jews? The answer: because *it was His sovereign purpose to do so*. His sovereign purpose means He cares what happens to His people and their land. He is not merely a passive observer to all that is taking place in Israel. As He told the people through Moses, theirs was "a land for which the LORD your God cares; the eyes of the LORD your God are always on it, from the beginning of the year to the very end of the year" (Deuteronomy 11:12).

God's Covenant and the Land of Israel

The people of Israel today are the beneficiaries of God's covenant with Abraham. And to those who are sensitive to the historical nature of the covenant, their possession of the land God promised to Abraham thousands of years ago has great meaning. The deep feeling Jews have for their land is powerfully expressed in this passage by Rabbi Binyamin Elon:

> I walk the streets of the Promised Land where Abram walked. I drive through the roads and plains where Isaac tended his flocks. I hike to the hilltops from where Jacob peered expectantly in all directions . . . I see these things and remember clearly the biblical truth. God gave the Promised Land, all of it, to our Patriarchs: Abraham, Isaac, and Jacob.[10]

Another rabbi, Abraham Joshua Heschel, attributes the Jews' strong connection with their land to the power of God's covenant with

Abraham to hold the Jewish people together throughout the ages with a common, bonding love for the land:

> The love of this land was due to an imperative, not an instinct, not to a sentiment. There is a covenant, an engagement of the people to the land. We live by covenants. We could not betray our pledge or discard the promise. When Israel was driven into exile, the pledge became a prayer; the prayer a dream; the dream a passion, a duty, a dedication . . . It is a commitment we must not betray . . . To abandon the land would make a mockery of all our longings, prayers, and commitments. To abandon the land would be to repudiate the Bible.[11]

An Exact Covenant

Some have suggested that the promise of land to Abraham's descendants is not to be taken literally. They say it is merely a symbol that indicates a general blessing, or perhaps the promise of heaven. But the Bible is too specific to let us get by with such ephemeral vagueness. It describes the land in definite terms and outlines it with clear geographical boundaries. Dr. John Walvoord stressed this point when he wrote:

> The term *land* . . . used in the Bible, means exactly what it says. It is not talking about heaven. It is talking about a piece of real estate in the Middle East. After all, if all God was promising Abraham was heaven, he could have stayed in Ur of the Chaldees. Why go on the long journey? Why be a pilgrim and a wanderer? No, God meant *land*.[12]

The land promised to Abraham takes in much more area than what the present nation of Israel occupies. Genesis 15:18 tells us that it stretches all the way from the Mediterranean Sea on the west to the

Euphrates River on the east. Ezekiel fixes the northern boundary of Palestine at Hamath, one hundred miles north of Damascus (Ezekiel 48:1), and the southern boundary at Kadesh, about one hundred miles south of Jerusalem (Ezekiel 48:28).

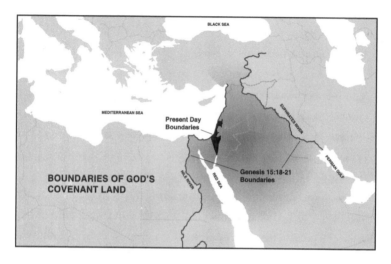

An Everlasting Covenant

And I will establish My covenant between Me and you and your descendants after you . . . Also I give to you and your descendants after you the land in which you are a stranger, all the land of Canaan, as an everlasting possession; and I will be their God. (Genesis 17:7–8)

In this remarkable prophecy God promised Abraham and his descendants the land of Canaan as their possession in perpetuity. When you look at a map and locate that tiny strip of land Israel now claims as hers, you can see that she does not now, nor has she ever fully occupied the land that was described to Abraham in God's covenant promise. If Israel were currently occupying all the land promised to her, she would control all the holdings of present day Israel, Lebanon, the West Bank of Jordan, and substantial portions of Syria, Iraq, and Saudi Arabia. Not until the Millennium will Israel occupy all the land the Lord gave her in His promise to Abraham.

The Relocation of the People of Israel

The Scattering of the Jews

Just as the people of Israel were about to enter the land of promise, Moses told them that a time was coming when their idolatry would cause them to be driven from the land: "And the LORD will scatter you among the peoples, and you will be left few in number among the nations where the LORD will drive you" (Deuteronomy 4:27). God reiterated this prophecy through Ezekiel and Hosea (Ezekiel 12:15; Hosea 9:17). Israel had no excuse. Her people had been warned again and again that God was a jealous God and would not tolerate His people worshipping false gods (Exodus 34:14).

Centuries before the Roman emperor Titus destroyed Jerusalem in AD 70, Jews had been scattered into the world by the Assyrians and Babylonians. Describing the prevalence of Jews throughout the known world, the historian and philosopher Strabo wrote:

> This people has already made its way into every city, and it is not easy to find any place in the habitable world which has not received this nation and in which it has not made its power felt.[13]

After the fall of Jerusalem to the Romans, this dispersion intensified, and Jews were scattered like chaff in the wind to the four corners of the earth.

The Suffering of the Exiled Jews

No doubt you remember the poor Jewish milkman Tevye in the classic movie *Fiddler on the Roof*. Burdened with poverty and trying to maintain traditions while coping with oppression from the Jew-hating Russians, he cries out to God, "I know, I know, we are Your chosen people. But, once in a while, can't You choose someone else?"[14] Tevye is a picture of the quintessential displaced Jew. What he experienced was exactly what Moses prophesied:

> And among those nations you shall find no rest, nor shall the sole of your foot have a resting place; but there the LORD will give you a trembling heart, failing eyes, and anguish of soul. (Deuteronomy 28:65)

Tevye illustrated this prophecy by providing a vivid picture of what scattered Jews have endured throughout the centuries since their dispersions from their promised land. Like Tevye, Jews in many lands have faced persecution in the form of pogroms, discrimination, exclusion from certain occupations, isolation in ghettos, and forced evacuation when the space they occupied was wanted for other purposes.

To appreciate the broad scope and magnitude of Jewish dispersion and persecution, consider the following historical facts:

> Before and during World War II, Jews throughout Europe were the target of merciless state-sponsored persecution. In 1933, nine million Jews lived in twenty-one European countries. By 1945, two out of three European Jews had been murdered. When the smoke finally cleared, the terrible truth came out. The Holocaust brought about the extermination of one-third of the worldwide Jewish population

at the time. Following the German invasion of the Soviet Union in 1941, mobile killing units following the German army began shooting massive numbers of Jews on the outskirts of conquered cities and towns. Seeking more efficient means to accomplish their obsession, the Nazis created a private and organized method of killing huge numbers of Jewish civilians. Extermination centers were established in Poland. Millions died in the ghettos and concentration camps through starvation, execution, brutality and disease. Of the six million Jews murdered during the Second World War, more than half were exterminated in the Nazi death camps. And the names Treblinka, Auschwitz, and Dachau became synonymous with the horrors of the Holocaust.[15]

Yes, God chose the Jews. He singled them out to be the recipients of His great and unique covenant blessings. But the greater the blessing, the greater the burden they bore for failing God. So the question is, was it worth it? How should Tevye's question be answered—would the Jews have been better off if God had chosen someone else? Rabbi Leo Baeck (1873–1956) weighed the sufferings of the Jewish people against their covenant blessings and drew a helpful conclusion:

> No people is heir to such a revelation as the Jew possesses; no people has had such a weight of divine commandment laid upon it; and for this reason no people has been so exposed to difficult and exacting times. The inheritance has not always been realized, but it is one that will endure, awaiting its hour.[16]

Baeck tells us that the story of the Jews is not over yet. It may seem that their sufferings outstrip their blessings, but that's because the fullness of their inheritance is yet to come. It is *awaiting its hour*. In other words, if you think the Jews have not yet been sufficiently blessed, just wait; you ain't seen nothing yet. God's promise in its fullness is yet to be kept.

The Rebirth of the Nation of Israel

Do we have reason to believe that God's promise to Israel will be kept? Will the Jews ever realize the fulfillment of the covenant to possess that particular tract of land with clear geographic boundaries promised as an everlasting possession? The prophet Isaiah asserted that it would happen in the Millennium. He prophesied that the Lord would "set His hand again the second time to recover the remnant of His people who are left" (Isaiah 11:11). God also addressed the issue through Ezekiel when He said, "I will take you from among the nations, gather you out of all countries, and bring you into your own land" (Ezekiel 36:24).

The fulfillment of those prophecies was set in motion on that day in 1948 when the United States recognized the new state of Israel. On the evening of that announcement, popular radio commentator Lowell Thomas said in his evening broadcast that Americans in every part of the country would be turning to their Bibles for historical background, enabling them to understand "this day in history."[17] And indeed, as the prophecies found in Isaiah, Ezekiel, Matthew, and Revelation show, both the Old Testament and the New Testament pointed to this day when the Jews would return to the land promised them and initiate fulfillment of the ancient prophecies.

To comprehend what an incredible act of God it is to preserve the beleaguered Jews throughout history and then return them to their land, consider this observation by Gary Frazier:

You cannot find the ancient neighbors of the Jews anywhere. Have you ever met a Moabite? Do you know any Hittites? Are there any tours to visit the Ammonites? Can you find the postal code of a single Edomite? No! These ancient peoples disappeared from history and from the face of the earth. Yet the Jews, just as God promised, returned to their land.[18]

While the complete fulfillment is yet to come, the return of the Jews to Israel in 1948 was an astounding event unprecedented in world history. Never had a decimated ancient people managed to retain their individual identity through almost twenty centuries and reestablish their nation in their original homeland. The event was specifically prophesied, and it happened exactly as foretold. It was clearly a miraculous act of God.

Many events had to dovetail perfectly to bring about the fulfillment of God's promise to Israel, but I want to point out two events in particular that serve to illustrate the miraculous nature of the rebirth of the nation of Israel. You will be amazed at the mysterious workings of God's providence.

The single most influential event that triggered the return of the scattered Jews to their homeland began with Chaim Weizmann. Weizmann was a Russian Jew, a brilliant chemist and a leader in the Zionist movement, who immigrated to England in 1904. During World War I, English armies used gunpowder made of cordite, which produced little smoke and thus did not blind gunners to their targets or reveal their positions. But since the manufacture of cordite required acetone made from a compound imported from their enemy, Germany, the English government was desperate to find another source. Prime Minister Lloyd George and Winston Churchill turned to Weizmann and set him up in a gin distillery, where he quickly developed a biochemical process for producing synthetic acetone.

The success of his ingenious process for creating acetone contributed to the ultimate Allied victory. The minimal salary and token reward that Weizmann received from the government earned him significant leverage when he pressed his persistent petitions for a Jewish homeland in Israel.[19]

As it happened, by the war's end, England gained possession of the land of Palestine—the very land promised in God's covenant with Abraham—from the defeated Ottoman Empire. As an act of a grateful nation and through Weizmann's influence within the government, England officially issued the Balfour Declaration of 1917, which declared:

> His Majesty's Government views with favor the establishment in Palestine of a national home for the Jewish people, and will use their best endeavors to facilitate the achievement of this object . . .[20]

The second influential event that brought the scattered Jews back to Palestine was the liberation of Jewish prisoners from Auschwitz, Dachau, and other Nazi concentration camps. When Germany collapsed at the end of World War II, the liberation of these Jewish prisoners caused worldwide shock at the grossly inhumane treatment inflicted by the Nazis. This generated sympathy that drew Jewish wealth from around the world and enabled the relocation of more than a million displaced Jews to Palestine.

That brings us all the way back to May 14, 1948. On this day, the United Nations officially recognized the State of Israel, with US president Harry Truman determining the deciding vote. The Israeli government established the State of Israel, thus fulfilling the twenty-five-hundred-year-old prophecy recorded in the Bible. Great Britain ended its mandate in Palestine and removed its troops, leaving more than 650,000 Jews to govern themselves in their own land.

The Return to the God of Israel

I am often asked if Israel's presence in her own land today is the final fulfillment of God's promise to regather His people. Many assume that it is, but I have to tell them that the answer is no! What is happening in Israel today is primarily the result of a secular Zionist movement, whereas Ezekiel wrote about a spiritual return of God's people to Him when he said:

> For I will take you from the nations, gather you from all the lands and bring you into your own land . . . Moreover, I will give you a new heart and put a new spirit within you . . . I will put My Spirit within you and cause you to walk in My statutes, and you will be careful to observe My ordinances. You will live in the land that I gave to your forefathers; so you will be My people, and I will be your God. (Ezekiel 36:24–28 NASB)

The return of Jews to the refounded nation of Israel is the first stage of that regathering, but it certainly does not fulfill the requirements of a spiritual return to the Lord. Secularist Israeli Yossi Beilin makes this point abundantly clear. Beilin is an agnostic and proponent of "secular conversion to Judaism," who has served in many roles in Israel's government. He speaks for many Israelis when he says that "secular Jews are not a marginal group in Jewish life. We are the mainstream. We are people in the government, we are people in the Parliament."[21] To him,

Judaism is "a people, a culture, an existence" as well as a religion; there-fore, the Jewishness of its atheists and agnostics goes unquestioned.[22]

From the moment of God's promise to Abraham to this present hour, the prophecies concerning Israel's total possession and blessing in the land remain unfulfilled. The most dramatic events lie ahead of us. Israel today is an island of a few million immigrants surrounded by a sea of three hundred million enemies, many of them militant and eager to wipe the tiny nation off the map. From a purely human point of view, it would seem inevitable that, sooner or later, Israel will be destroyed.

Indeed, Israel has been attacked over and over since its founding, sometimes in all-out wars and incessantly by terrorists. The Jewish people have survived by remaining vigilant, but they long for peace. According to the Bible, a future leader will fulfill this longing by bro-kering a seven-year peace deal with Israel's enemies. But Scripture also tells us that this peace plan will be broken, and Israel will be attacked once again, this time as never before. Countless armies will amass against the boxed-in nation, leaving it with no human hope of victory. Only Christ's return, His judgment, and His reign will finally bring true peace to Israel.

It is then that God's covenant with Abraham will reach its ultimate fulfillment. The Jews will return to the Lord, and as Ezekiel and Jeremiah prophesied, they will be His people, and He will be their God. The bor-ders of the land will expand to the dimensions described in Genesis 15 and Ezekiel 48. Christ's return will also fulfill the prophecy of Jeremiah that God would gather the Jews. "Behold, I will gather them out of all countries where I have driven them . . . I will bring them back to this place, and I will cause them to dwell safely. They shall be My people, and I will be their God" (Jeremiah 32:37–38).

Ezekiel makes it clear that this gathering means He will return every single living Jew back to the land. For he wrote that the Lord said He would gather them again to their own land "and . . . none of them [will be] captive any longer" (Ezekiel 39:28).

Today we see this prophecy being fulfilled right before our eyes. In 2006, for the first time in nineteen hundred years, Israel became home to the largest Jewish community in the world, surpassing the Jewish population in the United States. From the 650,000 who returned when the Jewish state was founded in 1948, the population of Israel has swelled to approximately 5.4 million, and it is expected to exceed 6 million by 2020.[23]

The significance of Israel's reemergence in her ancient homeland is that this had to occur in order to set the stage for the final fulfillment of biblical prophecies. Israel had to be a nation in her own land before the predictions previously noted could come about. The return of the Jews to their homeland is also significant in another way: it pinpoints where we are on history's timeline. As author Milton B. Lindberg pointed out:

> Without the existence of the nation of Israel, we would not be able to say with certainty that we are in the last days. That single event, more than any other, is the most prominent sign that we are living in the final moments before the coming of Jesus! The Hebrew People have been called God's timepiece of the ages.[24]

God's Providence in Action: The Story Behind the Story

Clark Clifford (1906–1998), an influential Washington lawyer, became a political advisor to President Harry Truman. He also became one of Truman's most trusted personal counselors and friends. Clifford opened his memoirs, *Counsel to the President,* by describing a meeting in the president's office on a Wednesday afternoon in the spring of 1948.

"Of all the meetings I ever had with the Presidents," wrote Clifford, "this one remains the most vivid." President Truman was meeting with Secretary of State General George C. Marshall, whom Truman regarded as "the greatest living American," about whether or not to recognize the state of Israel. British control of Palestine would run out in two days, and when it did, the Jewish Agency intended to announce the creation of a new state, still unnamed at that time. Most observers thought it would be named Judea.[25]

Marshall, mastermind of America's victory in World War II and author of the Marshall Plan, inspired a respect bordering on awe. He was adamantly opposed to recognizing Israel and not at all hesitant to express his opinion forcefully. His view was shared by almost every member of Truman's White House—except Clifford—and by virtually everyone in the State Department and Defense Department.

Several months before that meeting, James Forrestal, Truman's secretary of defense, had bluntly told Clifford, "You fellows over at the White House are just not facing up to the realities in the Middle East. There are thirty million Arabs on one side and about six hundred thousand Jews on the other. It is clear that in any contest, the Arabs are going to overwhelm the Jews. Why don't you face up to the realities? Just look at the numbers!"[26]

Clifford, however, knew that Truman had strong reasons for wanting to help the Jews, reasons that would not register on the scale of values at the departments of State or Defense. Truman detested intolerance and discrimination and had been deeply moved by the plight of the Jews during World War II. More to the point, Clifford wrote, Truman was "a student and believer in the Bible from his youth. From his reading of the Old Testament he felt the Jews derived a legitimate historical right to Palestine, and he sometimes cited such biblical lines as Deuteronomy 1:8, 'Behold, I have given up the land before you; go in and take possession of the land which the Lord hath sworn unto your fathers, to Abraham, to Isaac, and to Jacob.'"[27]

So at 4:00 p.m. on that Wednesday, May 12, the president met with his advisors in the Oval Office. Truman sat at his desk facing his famous plaque that read, *The Buck Stops Here*. Around the desk sat General Marshall and his deputy, officials from the State Department, and a handful of Truman's counselors, including Clark Clifford. They were exactly fifty hours away from the birth of the new, unnamed nation.

One by one, the president's advisors gave reasons for deferring any decision on the recognition of Israel. Finally it was Clifford's turn. Bucking the overwhelming consensus in the room, he boldly presented reasons for recognizing the new state. He barely finished before General Marshall erupted in a torrent of anger, and the officials from the State Department backed his opposition unanimously and vigorously. After the heated discussion, Marshall glared icily at the president and said, "If you follow Clifford's advice and if I were to vote in the election, I would vote against you!"[28]

Everyone in the room was stunned. The meeting came to an abrupt end with the question unresolved. Truman himself was greatly shaken by the fierceness of the general's opposition. The president, running for reelection, was on thin ice politically, and he could not afford to lose the support of such a towering figure as Marshall. Clifford left the meeting thinking the case was lost.

But over the next two days, Clifford, Truman, and a handful of others worked toward reaching a compromise within the administration. They succeeded when General Marshall finally said bitterly that while he could not support the president's position, he would not oppose it. So at 6:11 p.m. on May 14, 1948, Truman's press secretary, Charlie Ross, stepped out to meet an awaiting press and read these words:

> The government has been informed that a Jewish state has been proclaimed in Palestine . . . The United States recognizes the provisional government as de facto authority of the new State of Israel.[29]

Another biographer wrote that "he [Truman] felt great satisfaction in what he had been able to do for the Jewish people, and was deeply moved by their expressions of gratitude, then and for years to come. When the Chief Rabbi of Israel, Isaac Halevi Herzog, called at the White House, he told Truman, 'God put you in your mother's womb so that you would be the instrument to bring about the rebirth of Israel after two thousand years.'" Another witness to the scene, Truman's administrative assistant David Niles, reported the president's reaction to Herzog's generous assertion: "I thought he was overdoing things," remembered Niles, "but when I looked over at the President, tears were running down his cheeks."[30]

What Does All this Mean to Me?

Let's return to the questions we posed at the beginning of this chapter. Why has this tiny nation with a population of less than six million become the geopolitical center of the world? Why is a fledgling country with a total land space hardly larger than New Jersey mentioned in the nightly news more than any other nation except the United States? Or, to sum it up, why is Israel so important? I hope this chapter has helped you answer that question. Israel is important because the fulfillment of

God's covenant with its founder, Abraham, greatly affects every one of us. We have shown why it's important for our nation to continue to support and protect Israel. Nations who befriend Israel will be blessed; those that do not will be cursed.

We have shown how the playing out of prophetic events concerning Israel places us in the last days of history's timeline. We have shown how the miraculous survival of God's covenant people, the Jews, demonstrates God's providence and His ability to accomplish His purpose in the face of what seems to human minds impossible odds. The existence of Israel today is exhibit A in the lineup of convincing evidences that the Bible's prophecies concerning the future ahead of us will be fulfilled. This means the future not only of Israel, but also of our world, our nation, as well as your future and mine. This, perhaps, is the most important blessing we can receive from the astounding history of the Jews. It reveals the reality of God—His overwhelming power, the authenticity of His promises, the certainty of His existence, the urgency of His call to us, and His claim on our very being.

When we consider all this, perhaps we can see that it's not so odd of God to choose the Jews.

TWO

The Crude Awakening

WHO DOESN'T KNOW THE WORDS TO THE THEME SONG OF *The Beverly Hillbillies* by heart? If you're not old enough to have heard this ditty in the original episodes of the popular sixties sitcom, you've no doubt seen reruns. The series features a dirt-poor hillbilly family that strikes it rich in oil and moves to the upscale Hollywood neighborhood of Beverly Hills. The sitcom plays on the fact that discovering oil on one's property means becoming instantly wealthy, a phenomenon that occurs because oil has become vital to running our highly industrialized society.

America's quest for oil began forty years before Spindletop ever spouted its first Texas oil, when "the most important oil well ever drilled was [bored] in the middle of quiet farm country in northwestern Pennsylvania in 1859." Oil had actually been found and used on our continent much earlier: centuries before, Native Americans had noticed oil seeping out of the rocks and had used it for medicine and in trade with neighboring tribes. Almost thirty years before the signing of the American Declaration of Independence, a map had already been printed showing known oil springs in Pennsylvania.[1]

But on August 27, 1859, Edwin Drake launched the modern petroleum industry by drilling a 69.5-foot well near Titusville, Pennsylvania. It was the first well purposely drilled to find oil, and thus began a search for petroleum that quickly became international and changed the way we live . . . *forever*!

Now, fast-forward to the twenty-first century and observe what has happened in the decades since the drilling of Edwin Drake's little well:

- Mankind's thirst for oil has passed 86 million barrels per day and is expected to rise to 98.5 million barrels a day in 2015.[2]

- The psychological barrier of one hundred dollars a barrel was finally breached in early 2008.

- Oil prices have quintupled in the past six years.[3]

- As I write this, surplus oil production has doubled over recent years, and demand is somewhat reduced,[4] but new, unsettling record highs have been registered so far this year in all gasoline products: home heating fuels, automobile fuel, and, especially, diesel fuel.[5]

Oil is the new gold in the world economy, and more than any factor other than the nation of Israel, oil holds the key to the prophetic events of the future. Oil explains why the Bible focuses its end-time attention on the Middle East. The demand for oil in America has outstripped its capacity to produce the black gold, and the same holds true for much of the rest of the world. Therefore, since the discovery of huge supplies of oil in the Middle Eastern countries, world attention has focused on that area. In an article entitled "The Power of Oil," Dilip Hiro wrote:

> The overarching fact is that political leaders all over the world are committed to raising living standards through economic growth, heavily dependent on energy in the form of gas and oil. That includes the United States. Ever since 1932, when American oil companies acquired a stake in the oil resources of Saudi Arabia, Washington's policies have been geared to securing Middle East oil at the expense of all else.[6]

Few would question the fact that oil has become the new basis for our world economy. It is now the stuff of life, the resource most highly valued by the industrialized and emerging nations of the world, the blood that flows through their economic veins and gives life to prosperity in today's global economy. The greatest source of that lifeblood is now in the Middle East, so that is where the eyes of the world are focused.

What does this tell us about coming events? In Luke's gospel, Jesus contrasts our ability to discern weather signs with our inability to understand the more important signs of the time: "You can discern the face of the sky and of the earth, but how is it you do not discern this time?" (Luke 12:56). Surely the world's fascination with oil—a hot commodity with a source in lands hostile or borderline hostile to Israel and to us—qualifies as a "sign."

The Control of the World's Oil Supply

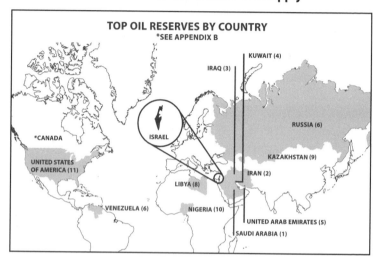

To get a clear picture of the primary sources for oil, here is a 2007 list of the world's greatest conventional oil reserves by country:[7]

Rank	Country	Billions of Barrels
1	Saudi Arabia	264.3
2	Iran	137.5
3	Iraq	115.0
4	Kuwait	101.5
5	United Arab Emirates	97.8
6	Venezuela	80.0
6	Russia	79.5
8	Libya	41.5

The United States is ranked eleventh with a mere 29.9 billion barrels!

The five top countries with the greatest known oil reserves are Arab nations, and the reserves in those countries total almost *716 billion barrels.* The Middle East/Persian Gulf area has about 60 percent of the world's known oil reserves lying beneath its desert sands. The sophisticated handling and processing facilities developed in those countries by the major Western oil companies have been nationalized. They are now controlled by a few Arab leaders.

Furthermore, Arab control of oil goes beyond the realities of supply and demand. Historically, all of the world's oil has been traded in US dollars, which has assured stability for the dollar and the US economy. The dollar had always been backed by the gold standard until President Nixon took it off in 1971. But then in 1973, oil prices rose sharply, threatening to throw the dollar into free fall around the world. In order to stabilize the dollar, the US government entered into a relationship with Saudi Arabia, the world's largest oil supplier. According to the agreement, the United States would back the Saudi government as an ally if the Saudis would demand that all purchases of its oil be in US dollars. This would ensure the primacy of the dollar in the world economy. The net effect of this agreement was that the US dollar was, in effect, backed by oil instead of gold. Then on February 17, 2008, Iran opened its own trading exchange in which oil is brokered in euros instead of dollars, further threatening the stability of the US dollar.

The Middle Eastern countries are not the only ones giving the United States trouble in the global oil market. You probably noticed that Venezuela, tied for number six on the oil reserve list, is another primary source of America's oil. But Hugo Chavez, the president of Venezuela, is no friend of America. During the 2006 United Nations sessions in New York City, Chavez verbally assaulted the American government and called our president a devil. Chavez has met several times with Iranian president Mahmoud Ahmadinejad and has vowed to "unite the Persian Gulf and the Caribbean, giving Iran entrée into Latin America."[8] This could bring even more insecurity to United States oil sources, giving powerful influence over South American oil to a Middle Eastern country. So as you can see, control of the lion's share of the world's oil is centralized in the Middle East.

No doubt you've heard preachers assert that civilization as we know it will face a gargantuan, final showdown in the Middle East. In the not-too-distant past you may have wondered, *Why the Middle East? Why would this handful of relatively small countries become so important to world powers?* Perhaps you figured the showdown would more likely be brought on by the population masses in China, the wealth and global power of the United States, the ingenuity of Japan, or the rising up of poverty-oppressed multitudes in India. Why, of all places, would things come to a head in the Middle East? Today, after considering the source of the world's oil and all the global hands reaching out to grasp it, we don't ask that question nearly as often!

Here's an interesting sidelight about world oil reserves. My friend Robert Morgan flew into New Orleans several years ago, and the man who met him at the airport was a geophysicist for a major oil company. Driving to the hotel, he explained to Robert that oil deposits result from the decomposition of plant and animal life now buried by eons of time. Oil is found all over the world, he said, even under the ice of the Arctic and Antarctic. That means forests and abundant vegetation once covered the world until destroyed in a vast global cataclysm (such as a worldwide flood).

The geophysicist went on to say that the earth's richest, deepest, and largest deposits of petroleum lie under the sands of countries just to the east of Israel, in the location pinpointed in the Bible as the garden of Eden. Eden was a teeming expanse of forests, foliage, and gardens with rich fertility unparalleled in human history.[9]

Barren sand and blazing desert now exist where once grew a garden flourishing with dense, lush flora, the likes of which the world has not seen since. It was destroyed in some disastrous upheaval and has decayed into the largest deposits of oil in the world. I had never before imagined that the gasoline I pump into my car might be the ruined remains of the rich, vast foliage of the garden of Eden.

It's ironic to think that Satan may finance the Battle of Armageddon at the end of human history with revenues generated from the garden he spoiled at the beginning of human history.

The Consumers of the World's Oil Supply

The vast majority of the world's oil is consumed by four entities. Russia ranks fourth with 2.92 million barrels used per day. Japan is third, consuming 5.16 million barrels per day. China, the world's largest country in terms of population, is now number two in oil consumption at 7.27 million barrels per day. At a rate of 20.7 million barrels per day, the United States ranks first in oil consumption.[10]

China continues to increase her thirst for oil. In 2005, China had a total of twenty million cars on the road.[11] One well-known investment firm now estimates that China will have 1.1 billion cars on the road by 2050.

The European Union, once the number-two consumer of oil, now burns 1.83 million barrels per day and has fallen to thirteenth place among the top oil-consuming nations, an overall usage reduction despite growth in the number of member nations.[12] Last year when we visited London, our hosts told us how Brits had handled the oil situation in their country. Responding to the energy crisis in 1973, they reduced consumption and imposed taxes on gasoline to raise significant revenue to import high-priced oil. By 2007, conservation had become a way of life in England, even as the price per gallon of gas more than doubled its cost in the United States. I later discovered that the same thing had happened all over Europe.

It probably comes as no surprise to anyone that the world's number-one consumer of oil is America, guzzling almost 21 million barrels of crude oil per day, or 25 percent of all the oil produced in the world. If present trends continue, US consumption will rise to 27 million barrels a day by 2020, and demand will expand to 34 percent by 2030. Added to this is the fact that the United States consumes 43 percent of the world's motor gasoline, and no new gasoline refinery has been built in the United States since 1976. Stop for a moment and ponder the meaning of all this: the United States is number eleven in oil reserves and number one in oil consumption, with the demand growing by leaps and bounds. It doesn't take a rocket scientist to see that a crisis is looming in our future.

Many forward-looking statesmen worldwide, aware of the coming crisis, have mandated the development and use of alternative energy sources such as solar and wind power and alternative fuels for motor vehicles. However, recent studies have shown that despite such mandates for biofuels use, the "law of unintended consequences" is at work. Rather than saving the planet from oil dependence and global warming, biofuels are raising food prices, endangering the hungry, and only slightly reducing the need for oil. Even if all the corn and soybean crops produced in the United States were converted for fuel, it would only be enough to meet 20 percent of consumption demands.[13]

At this point in time, no alternative energy source shows promise of solving the problem. And until that solution surfaces, the United States will continue to be heavily dependent on foreign sources to maintain its vital influx of oil.

The Conflicts over the World's Oil Supply

In 1973 a group of Arab nations launched an attack on Israel, initiating the Yom Kippur War. One result of this war was the uniting of Arab nations in a common cause as never before. This new show of unity was manifest partly in the military conflict and partly in a less obvious way. On October 17, 1973, the Arab nations conspired to reduce their oil production below the previous norm and attempted to embargo nations that favored Israel, principally the United States and the Netherlands. This hostile act made it increasingly evident that the Arab world would use their control of major oil reserves to leverage their bid for world power.

Some US citizens will remember the effect of that Arab embargo. The price of oil quadrupled to twelve dollars a barrel. Cars formed long, winding lines at gas stations. Conservation measures were put into effect, including a national highway speed limit of 55 mph. We were being attacked in a new kind of war—an economic war with ominous implications. The price of oil did not go down after the Arab oil blackmail of 1973–74, and that crisis precipitated the fastest transfer of money in history, sucking dollars out of the United States and stashing them in swelling Arab treasuries. The ultimate price of the war, however, would not be exacted in money alone, but in the political and economic reshaping of the world. For the first time in centuries, the Middle East became a major consideration in every international event.

The first acknowledgment of this new political reality came from President Jimmy Carter in his State of the Union address on January 23, 1980. In that address Carter announced an important policy change concerning the Middle East:

> Let our position be absolutely clear: An attempt by any outside force to gain control of the Persian Gulf region will be regarded as an assault on the vital interests of the United States of America, and such an assault will be repelled by any means necessary including military force.[14]

This became known as the Carter Doctrine: the determination to protect the Persian Gulf even at the expense of our own troops. This paradigm shift in foreign policy would soon be tested.

In August 1990, Iraqi dictator Saddam Hussein sent troops into Kuwait to take over that nation's oil fields. President George H. W. Bush and his defense secretary, Dick Cheney, put the Carter Doctrine into action, sending US troops to Kuwait to repel the Iraqi invasion. President Bush defended his action to the nation, saying, "Our country now imports nearly half the oil it consumes and could face a major threat to its economic independence . . . The sovereign independence of Saudi Arabia is of vital interest to the United States."[15]

While other justifications for the war were given, experts agree that the Gulf War in 1990–91 was the first in world history fought almost entirely over oil. And make no mistake: while the war in Iraq is about terrorism, it is also about oil—oil that is sold to finance the Muslim terrorist regime and oil that is necessary for the West to function economically.

The Concerns About the World's Oil Supply

Are We Running Out of Oil?

It was Saturday morning, and I was on my way to my office to put the final touches on the message for the weekend. I was scheduled to preach on the importance of oil in the prophetic program of the end times. When I stopped to get a cup of coffee, I spotted the weekend edition of the *Wall Street Journal*. The headline read, "Where Has All The Oil Gone?" The article, written by Ann Davis, was about the huge oil tanks in Cushing, Oklahoma, where many of our reserves are stored. According to the article, a run on oil futures has depleted the tanks to their lowest level ever.[16]

So where *has* all the oil gone? Do these near-empty tanks mean we are running out of it? This is a difficult question to answer. According to the CEO and president of the Saudi Aramco, we have tapped "only 18 percent of [global] conventional and non-conventional producible potential." In his words, "we are looking at more than 4.5 trillion barrels of potentially recoverable oil"—enough to power the globe at current levels of consumption for "more than 140 years."[17] On the other hand, we do not have access to all of that oil, nor do we have the present-day capacity to harvest it all if we knew where it was.

The rate of oil discovery has been falling ever since the 1960s when 47 billion barrels a year were discovered, mostly in the Middle East. In the '70s the rate dropped to about 35 billion barrels while the industry concentrated on the North Sea. In the '80s it was Russia's turn, and the discovery rate dropped to 24 billion. It dropped even further in the '90s as the industry concentrated on West Africa but only found some 14 billion barrels.[18]

To say that we are running out of oil might be untrue but to say that we are consuming at the level of our current ability to produce oil is true. The oil shortage is real and will continue to have an enormous effect upon our culture. According to the official energy statistics posted by the U.S. government, last updated in July of 2007, the total world oil supply in 2006 was exceeded by the total world petroleum consumption in 2005.[19]

Did you catch the sobering point in this quote? Let me repeat it: in 2005 the world used more oil than was even produced in the following year. And there is one energy rule that even I can understand: energy use cannot exceed available supply.

Can We Protect Our Sources of Oil?

Our dependence on foreign oil has become a major concern—especially since the oil lies under the control of nations with which we have tenuous or hostile relationships. Paul Roberts addressed this concern in his book, *The End of Oil: On the Edge of a Perilous New World*. Perhaps the greatest casualty of the Iraq war may be the very idea of energy security:

But with the continuing fiasco in Iraq, it is now clear that even the most powerful military entity in world history cannot stabilize a country at will or "make it" produce oil simply by sending in soldiers and tanks. In other words, since the Iraqi invasion, the oil market now understands that the United States cannot guarantee the security of oil supplies—for itself or for anyone else. That new and chilling knowledge, as much as anything else, explains the high price of oil.[20]

According to Roberts, our ability to protect our foreign oil inflow is limited at best. Even if we commit to using brute military force, as the Carter Doctrine says we are ready to do, we cannot ensure an endless supply of oil from hostile countries.

Is There Any Oil in Israel?

It would help, of course, if we could depend on oil from our one staunch Middle Eastern ally, Israel. But as former prime minister Golda Meir ruefully quipped, "Let me tell you something we Israelis have against Moses. He took us forty years into the desert in order to bring us to the one place in the Middle East that has no oil."[21]

While little oil has ever been discovered in Israel, today there is a growing belief that there may be significant oil deposits under its surface. Two major oil companies have been formed to explore oblique references to oil found in the Bible. Ezekiel speaks of a time when God would do better for Israel than at her beginnings (36:11). How could Israel ever be more prosperous than she was in the days of King Solomon? During his reign the wealth of Israel was the wonder and envy of the known world. Yet here is God telling Israel that at some time in the future she will be wealthier still.

In his book *The Coming Peace in the Middle East*, Dr. Tim LaHaye suggests one way that this coming wealth could be explained:

Suppose that a pool of oil, greater than anything in Arabia . . . were discovered by the Jews . . . This would change the course of history. Before long, Israel would be able independently to solve its economic woes, finance the resettlement of the Palestinians, and supply housing for Jews and Arabs in the West Bank, East Bank, or anywhere else they might choose to live.[22]

In an article written for WorldNet Daily, Aaron Klein asked this question: "Is Israel sitting on an enormous oil reserve mapped out in the Old Testament that when found will immediately change the geopolitical structure of the Middle East and confirm the validity of the Bible to people around the world?"[23] John Brown, an evangelical Christian and founder and chairman of Zion Oil and Gas, believes that there is indeed oil in Israel. He is certain that several biblical passages indicate where rich deposits might be found. As examples, he cites two passages: "Let Asher be blessed . . . and let him dip his foot in oil" (Deuteronomy 33:24 KJV). "Joseph is . . . a fruitful bough by a well . . . Blessings of heaven above, blessings of the deep that lies beneath . . . shall be on the head of Joseph, and on the crown of the head." (Genesis 49:22–26 NKJV).

Brown's explanation of why these passages indicate the presence of oil is fascinating. He says that maps of the territory allotted to the twelve tribes when they entered Palestine show that the shape of Asher's area resembles a giant foot. That foot is "dipped" into the top, or "crown" area belonging to the land given to the tribe of Joseph's son Manasseh. "The oil is there," Brown asserts, "where Joseph's head is met by Asher's foot."[24] And Brown is willing to put his money where his mouth is. In 2007, his company was granted two extended licenses for approximately 162,100 acres that include the Joseph and Asher-Menashe areas, which Brown believes contain oil.[25]

The discovery of oil on Israeli soil would greatly reduce the threat against Israel from her hostile allies, taking the oil weapon out of their hands. "Finding oil will give Israel a huge strategic advantage" over its Arab enemies, Brown said. "It will change the political and economic structure of the region overnight."[26]

But in spite of the tantalizing possibilities of oil in Israel, it has not yet been found. This means we must continue to deal with the reality of a world in which oil remains in the control of countries essentially hostile to us or at best only tenuously allied.

How Does the Oil Situation Affect Our Future?

The Emergence of Prophetic Alliances

Ezekiel foretold a time when Russia would attack Israel. In detailing how the military aggression would take place, the prophet listed a coalition of some of the nations that would join with Russia in the attack. "I will turn you around, put hooks into your jaws, and lead you out, with all your army, horses, and horsemen, all splendidly clothed, a great company with bucklers and shields, all of them handling swords. Persia, Ethiopia, and Libya are with them, all of them with shield and helmet" (38: 4–5).

Until March 21, 1935, Persia was the official name of the country we now call Iran. Not once in the past twenty-five hundred years has Russia formed a military connection with Persia/Iran, until now.[27] But now these two nations have formed a military alliance that continues to be strengthened by the political situation in our world. Russia recently signed a billion-dollar deal to sell missiles and other weaponry to Iran. And the connection is even broader, as Joel C. Rosenberg, former aid to Israeli prime minister Benjamin Netanyahu, points out: "Over 1000 Iranian nuclear scientists have been trained in Russia by senior Russian scientists."[28] Here is an end-time alliance that was prophesied twenty-five hundred years ago, and in the last five years it has become a reality. Obviously, the stage is being set!

The Emergence of Petroleum Alliances

Omer Selah, with Israel's Fuel Authority, was recently quoted in the *Jerusalem Post*:

The issue of oil becomes more and more critical with each passing year, for Western democracies in general, and for Israel in particular. What we are seeing is a confluence of several negative factors and processes in this region . . . A huge percentage of the world's oil reserves . . . is found in the possession of powers not friendly to the West or to Israel.[29]

And the wealth of these few oil-producing nations is growing at such an exponential rate that they are struggling to find ways to invest their exploding resources. The magnitude of their investment "problem" was reported in a *New York Times* article. Between 2000 and 2007, oil revenues for the OPEC nations went from $243 billion to $688 billion, not including the price spikes that occurred in November and December of 2007. It's estimated that these countries have $4 trillion invested around the world from the money earned in oil exports.[30]

Our enemies consider this kind of wealth to be a gigantic weapon with the blessing of Allah. As author Don Richardson puts it: "Muslim strategists ask their followers, *Why do we find in these modern times that Allah has entrusted most of the world's oil wealth primarily to Muslim nations?* Their answer: Allah foresaw Islam's need for funds to finance a final politico-religious victory over what Islam perceives as its ultimate enemy: Christianized Euro-American civilization."[31]

Another *New York Times* article headlined in the spring of 2002, "Iranian Urges Muslims to Use Oil as a Weapon." In this article, Ayatollah Ali Khamenei is quoted as having said:

The oil belongs to the people and can be used as a weapon against the West and those who support the savage regime of Israel . . . If Islamic and Arab countries . . . for only one month suspend the export of oil to Israel and its supporter, the world would be shaken.[32]

It should be clear to us that America's ride on the crest of wealth and power faces unprecedented threats from newly rich, newly united Middle Eastern countries that have no love for us. Indeed, many of them would love to see us reduced to the ashes of history. And it should be just as clear that they are feeling the newfound power that control of most of the world's oil has given them. These factors do not bode well for the United States, Israel, and their Western allies.

What Are We to Do?

So far this chapter has given you very little good news and little reason to be optimistic—that is, if your outlook is entirely earthly. As we look back on where we have been as a nation and where we find ourselves today, we could easily become discouraged. The secret, however, is to look beyond both the past and the present and focus on the future. We are, in fact, unusually blessed. We are being given the opportunity to be firsthand observers to the staging of events that will precede the ultimate coming of Christ to this earth. Events written about centuries ago are now unfolding right before our eyes and are telling us that our patient anticipation will soon be rewarded. In the meantime, we must . . .

Keep on Waiting

Jesus told His disciples that just as you can tell that summer is near when the fig tree puts forth leaves, you can also tell that the Son of Man is returning by recognizing the signs given by the prophets

(Matthew 24:32). As we see these signs appearing, our question is, what shall we do?

First of all, we wait. There is nothing we can do to hasten His coming, so we have been called to be patient. "Therefore be patient, brethren, until the coming of the Lord. The farmer waits for the precious produce of the soil, being patient about it, until it gets the early and late rains. You too be patient; strengthen your hearts, for the coming of the Lord is near" (James 5:7–8 NASB). No man knows exactly when the Lord will return (Matthew 24:36), but by the signs we can discern the season of His coming. And I am not alone in believing we are in that season. We do not, however, know exactly how long that season will be, so our duty as faithful servants is to wait patiently.

Keep on Working

Some modern believers seem to have concluded that the coming of Christ is a call to passivity. Their attitude seems to be, *Well, since He's coming soon, there's no point in making any big plans or working to fulfill them. It's all about to come to an end anyway.* Over the years we've seen extreme examples of passive waiting. People who believed they had pinpointed the time of His coming to the day got rid of their earthly goods, gathered on a mountaintop or in a compound, and simply waited passively. That is emphatically not what is meant by waiting. The Lord Himself set the example while He was on this earth. He said, "I must work the works of Him who sent Me while it is day; the night is coming when no one can work" (John 9:4 NKJV). In one of His parables, He also said, "Blessed is that servant whom his master, when he comes, will find so doing [serving]" (Matthew 24:46 NKJV).

That is the key to pleasing the Lord in these last days—continue to work diligently at what God has called you to do. Believing in the imminent return of Jesus involves more than simply waiting, as important as that may be. It is rather a matter of *working* while we wait. Working hard. Working faithfully. Working in the power and joy and filling of the Holy Spirit.

Someone once asked me what I would like to be doing when the Lord comes back. That's easy. I would like to be standing behind my pulpit before my flock, declaring and explaining and applying the Word of God. For me there is nothing better. There is no greater joy.

What would you like to be doing when He returns? Where would you like to be when the trumpet sounds, when the archangel shouts, and when, in the twinkling of an eye, we are changed and rise into the clouds to meet Him?

Keep on Watching

On numerous occasions Jesus told His followers to watch. He exhorted them to be full of anticipation, to look up and lift their heads up and realize that their redemption was drawing near (Luke 21:28). The apostle Paul continued the theme of watchfulness, telling the Roman believers to awake out of their sleep, for their salvation was nearer than when they first believed (Romans 13:11).

Wait, work, and watch: these are the three things Christians are exhorted to do when they see the signs of Christ's imminent coming. What does this look like for Christians today? How can we gear up our wills and our emotions to keep on going in this era of church history when the future looks so ominous?

C. S. Lewis answered that question almost seventy years ago in another time when extreme danger loomed on the horizon. In an address to

Oxford University students shortly after the English declared war with Germany, Lewis stated well the attitude Christians should have in times like his and ours:

> This impending war has taught us some important things. Life is short. The world is fragile. All of us are vulnerable, but we are here because this is our calling. Our lives are rooted not only in time, but also in eternity, and the life of learning, humbly offered to God, is its own reward.[33]

In his speech, Lewis asserted that an impending crisis makes no difference to the nature of our duty and our calling. The truth is that danger is always part of our environment in this fallen world; the presence of an obvious and immediate danger merely intensifies our awareness of this reality that we tend to ignore. Any one of us could meet death at any moment through an accident, an invisible blood clot, or by an act of a deranged gunman. An impending war such as that which Lewis and his students faced, or an impending battle that may be in our own future changes nothing. Our task as faithful stewards to God's calling is to keep to our duty—to be patient and watch, but also to keep on working.

We need not despair. As children of the living God, we live with continual hope. We work, we love, and we laugh and find joy because we always know that an end is coming. Whether the battle does or doesn't come in our lifetime changes nothing about the way we should live. Our own "end time" will come, and it could arrive at any moment. So our task is to keep on plugging along, faithfully fitting into the place where God put us as productive members of society.

I am convinced that God puts each one of us exactly where He wants us and gives each of us a task that advances His eternal plan in a particular way. Remember the words of Queen Esther's guardian Mordecai when she was afraid to face the deadly danger of appearing uninvited before the king to plead for her people: ". . . If you remain silent at this time, relief and deliverance will arise for the Jews from another place . . . And who knows whether you have not attained royalty for such a time as this?" (Esther 4:14 NASB). God raised up Esther at a particular time for a particular purpose. Today is the time God has ordained for you and me to be alive, and we are placed in our time and place with no less purpose than Esther. Your task may not be as grandiose as hers; you may not be called on to save your nation. But as Lewis said elsewhere in his speech to the Oxford undergraduates, "The work of a Beethoven and the work of a charwoman become spiritual on precisely the same condition, that of being offered to God, of being done humbly 'as to the Lord.'"[34]

You may wonder, *What's the point in keeping on doing my little insignificant job when such doom hangs over the world?* The point is that you are filling your role as an agent of God in this particular time, and your work may have a greater effect than you imagine. Few of us see the ultimate result of our actions. But by the power of the ripple effect, what you do either as a CEO or a salesclerk may join the current of God's intent and bring about His will in enormous ways you would never dream of. So it is vital that each of us takes our God-given tasks seriously. We must stick to our work, remain watchful, and patiently wait on the timing of the Lord.

Southern evangelist Vance Havner gives us the real key to keeping to our task and finding joy in the face of impending doom: "We are not just looking for something to happen, we are looking for Someone to come! And when these things begin to come to pass, we are not to drop our heads in discouragement, or shake our heads in despair, but we are to lift our heads in delight."[35]

THREE

Modern Europe . . . Ancient Rome

THE RED, STAMPED WORDS *TOP SECRET* GLARED OMINOUSLY from the manila envelope on the president's desk. The top government officials had been ordered to the Oval Office promptly at 8:00 a.m. Security was at its highest level; word must not leak out that the president of the United States, the vice president, the joint chiefs of staff, the National Security Council, congressional leaders, and selected members of the cabinet had been called for this executive briefing.

The president had never looked more serious. As the high officials and advisors assembled—men entrusted with decisions that could affect millions of lives—the president's face was ashen and grim. With his fingers pressed together under his chin, he looked as if he were praying. Considering the news he was about to share, his attitude was perfectly appropriate. When the group was assembled, he signaled to an armed guard, who opened a door to allow one more man to enter.

The man hesitated for a moment until the president pointed to a chair directly in front of the polished executive desk. The man took his seat before the leadership advisers of the most powerful nation on earth and awaited the president's signal.

"Gentlemen," the president said soberly, "prepare yourself to hear stunning news that will profoundly affect our nation and the future of the world as we know it. Listen carefully, for your very lives are at stake."[1]

This scene has not occurred exactly as described, yet it is not altogether fiction. It did occur at a different time in a different place with different players. And it may easily occur again in the near future. Let's begin by examining the time when it did occur—when one man, divinely moved to write the inspired words, accurately prophesied the rise and fall of empires and their rulers.

The Vision of the King

More than two thousand years ago, God gave His servant Daniel a vision of the future that we recognize as the most comprehensive prophetic insight ever given to man. While it was not uncommon for God to communicate to His own people through dreams and visions, it is astounding to realize that He gave this greatest vision of all time not only to Daniel, but also to a Babylonian king named Nebuchadnezzar, one of history's most wicked Gentile rulers.

Here is how that message came about. It was the second year of Nebuchadnezzar's rule over Babylon. Although the king was secure on his throne with all of his enemies subdued or in captivity, he nevertheless found himself in great anxiety about the future. His anxiety stemmed from a recurring dream sent to him by Almighty God—a vivid, nightmarish dream, and one he could not understand, though he sensed ominous implications within it. So the king called in his counselors. But since he had forgotten important details of the dream, he demanded that his brain trust not only interpret the nightmare, but that they also give him a vivid description of it.

The king's demand was unprecedented and, as you can imagine, his counselors thought it a bit unfair. When they could not meet his demand, Nebuchadnezzar, in a fit of pique, ordered the execution of all the wise men of Babylon (Daniel 2:12–13).

When the Jewish captive Daniel heard of the king's edict, he and his friends prayed to God for a vision of Nebuchadnezzar's dream and its interpretation. Then he went to the executioner and said, "Do not destroy the wise men of Babylon; take me before the king, and I will tell the king the interpretation" (v. 24).

Daniel soon found himself standing before Nebuchadnezzar, who asked him if he could reveal the meaning of his dream. Daniel explained that he could not, but he had connections with Someone who could: "The secret which the king has demanded, the wise men, the astrologers, the magicians, and the soothsayers cannot declare to the king. But there is a God in heaven who reveals secrets, and He has made known to King Nebuchadnezzar what will be in the latter days. Your dream, and the visions of your head upon your bed were these" (vv. 27–28).

As Daniel explained, just as God had sent the dream to Nebuchadnezzar, God had also revealed the dream and its interpretation to Daniel (v. 19). Then came the scene in Nebuchadnezzar's "oval office" as the Jewish prophet stood before the king and unfolded for him the future of his nation.

First Daniel described the king's vision:

"As for you, O king, thoughts came to your mind while on your bed, about what would come to pass after this; and He who reveals secrets has made known to you what will be . . . You, O king, were watching; and behold, a great image! This great image, whose splendor was excellent, stood before you; and its form was awesome. This image's head was of fine gold, its chest and arms of silver, its belly and thighs of bronze, its legs of iron, its feet partly of iron and partly of clay." (Daniel 2:29, 31–33)

The overarching purpose of this image was to teach Nebuchadnezzar, Daniel, and everyone else on the planet what happens when man puts himself in control. This vision gives us the history of human civilization, written not by Will Durant or Edward Gibbon, but by God Himself.

While the events Daniel unfolded may seem to come about by the power of kings and armies, he understood that the collapse and rise of empires is all God's doing: "*He* changes the times and the seasons; *He* removes kings and raises up kings; *He* gives wisdom to the wise and knowledge to those who have understanding" (Daniel 2:21, *emphasis added*).

Daniel then began to explain to Nebuchadnezzar that his dream was about the kingdoms of this world—his own kingdom and those that would succeed it. He told the king that the colossal metallic image represents four successive gentile world powers that would rule over Israel in the days ahead. The word *kingdom* is used ten times in these verses (vv. 36–45). Exactly what is a kingdom? It is the dominion that a king rules, or a "*king-dom*inion." It designates the people and territory under the rule of a single government. As Daniel was about to explain, the varied components of this statue represent the worldwide dominions that would follow and replace one another in the future.

The Four World Empires

Through Daniel, God gave King Nebuchadnezzar a composite history of the remaining days of the world. We know this because he spoke specifically of "days to come" and "things to come" (Daniel 2:28, 29 NIV).

He began to reveal the meaning of the dream of the statue in five sections: the head of gold, the breast and arms of silver, the belly and thighs of copper and brass, the legs of iron, and the feet . . . part iron, part clay.

The first world empire, represented by the statue's head of gold, was Nebuchadnezzar's own kingdom of Babylon. Daniel's words to the king are clear. "You, O king, are a king of kings. For the God of heaven has given you a kingdom, power, strength, and glory; and wherever the children of men dwell, or the beasts of the field and the birds of the heaven, He has given them into your hand, and has made you ruler over them all—you are this head of gold" (Daniel 2:37–38 NKJV).

Nebuchadnezzar would not have doubted that the head of gold referred to his kingdom since the chief deity of Babylon was Marduk, known as "the god of gold." The historian Herodotus described the image of Marduk as a dazzling sight—a golden statue seated upon a golden throne before a golden table and a golden altar. Pliny tells us that the robes of Marduk's priests were interlaced with gold.[2]

The second world empire revealed in the king's dream is represented by the image's chest of silver, from which two silver arms emerge (Daniel 2:32). This is the Medo-Persian Empire that conquered Babylon in 539 BC and remained in power for approximately two hundred years. We need feel no uncertainty about that interpretation because later, when Daniel reported the events surrounding the end of the Babylonian empire, he stated clearly that it would be the dual monarchy of the Medes and the Persians that would take control of Nebuchadnezzar's empire (Daniel 5:28). The two nations are again confirmed as Babylon's successor in Daniel 8:20.

The third world empire revealed within the image is represented by its belly and thighs of bronze. Daniel told the king it will be a "kingdom of bronze, which shall rule over all the earth" (Daniel 2:39). This is the empire of Greece, the kingdom of Phillip of Macedon and his famous son, Alexander the Great. Not only does history confirm Greece as the empire that succeeded the Medo-Persians, but Daniel himself affirmed it by naming Greece specifically in Daniel 8:21. Under Alexander, the Greek empire was unified and encompassed more territory than either of the previous empires. Alexander had such a lust for conquest that after subduing virtually all of the known world, he sat down and wept, fearing there were no more territories left to conquer. It is appropriate that this third kingdom is characterized by the bronze midsection of the massive image. Alexander's soldiers armored themselves in bronze and brass helmets and breastplates, and carried bronze and brass shields and swords.

The fourth empire displayed in the image is symbolized by its legs of iron. Daniel describes this empire as "strong as iron, inasmuch as iron breaks in pieces and shatters everything; and like iron that crushes, that kingdom will break in pieces and crush all the others" (2:40). History shows us clearly that Rome is the fourth kingdom. Not only was Rome the successor to the Greek empire, but the iron legs of the image provide a powerful symbol that characterizes the nature of the Romans. The word *iron* is used fourteen times in the text describing Rome in Daniel 2. Historians often use *iron* as an adjective when characterizing the Roman Empire: Rome's *iron hand*. Rome's *iron grip.* Rome's *iron rule.* Rome's *iron fist.* Rome's *iron heel.* Rome's *iron legions.*

History confirms the progression of Daniel's explanation of Nebuchadnezzar's dream. The Babylonians were overthrown by the Medo-Persians; the Medo-Persians were conquered by the Greeks; and when the Grecian empire was conquered by Rome, all of the lands and peoples of the previous kingdoms were assimilated into one kingdom known as the Roman Empire. This empire came into existence fifty years before Jesus was born, and it continued in power throughout the Lord's earthly ministry and beyond. It was Roman rule that put Jesus on the cross. It was the imperialistic Romans who ruled ruthlessly throughout the world during the early days of the church.

The fact that Rome is represented in the statue by its two iron legs is also significant, as the following quote explains:

> By A.D. 395 the Roman Empire had split into two political areas of rule: the [Latin-speaking] West with its capital in Rome, and the [Greek-speaking] East with its capital in Constantinople (modern Istanbul, Turkey), which included the land of Israel. This division of the empire is depicted in the statue's two legs.[3]

But this splitting of the mighty Roman Empire into two political units was not to be the last division that kingdom would suffer as Daniel explained to Nebuchadnezzar when he turned his attention to the statue's feet and toes. He noted that in the king's dream, the feet and toes were composed of a mixture of iron and clay. Though positioned at the bottom of the image, these extremities are apparently highly important, for Daniel said as much about the feet and toes as he had said about all the other parts of the image combined.

Here are Daniel's words as he explained to the king the meaning of the material composing the image's feet:

> "Whereas you saw the feet and toes, partly of potter's clay and partly of iron, the kingdom shall be divided; yet the strength of iron shall be in it, just as you saw the iron mixed with ceramic clay. And as the toes of the feet were partly of iron and partly of clay, so the kingdom shall be partly strong and partly fragile. As you saw iron mixed with ceramic clay, they will mingle with the seed of men; but they will not adhere to one another, just as iron does not mix with clay." (Daniel 2:41–43)

According to Daniel, there is to be yet another division in the Roman Empire. Not a division of two, as indicated by the image's two legs, but of ten, as symbolized by its ten toes. Daniel foretells a time when the Roman Empire will consist of ten kingdoms or leaders. Since the downward movement from one section of the statue to the next represents the passage of time, the "feet and toes" stage must follow the "legs" stage. But when we look back at the history that followed Daniel's prediction, we find nothing in history that even remotely corresponds to a tenfold Roman coalition. That shows us that this fifth and final feet-and-toes-stage kingdom is yet to come and is yet to perform its prescribed role in human history.

Daniel gives us one other piece of information that enables us to understand the timing of the events conveyed in Nebuchadnezzar's dream. He tells us that this final form of the Roman Empire will be on the earth when God sets up His earthly kingdom. "And in the days of these kings [the rulers of the ten segments of the Roman kingdom], the God of heaven will set up a kingdom which shall never be destroyed; and the kingdom shall not be left to other people; it shall break in pieces and consume all these kingdoms, and it shall stand forever" (Daniel 2:44).

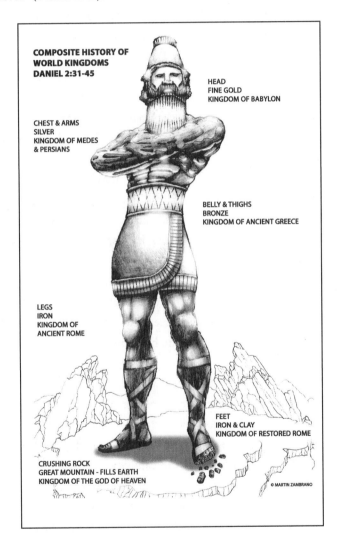

COMPOSITE HISTORY OF WORLD KINGDOMS DANIEL 2:31-45

HEAD
FINE GOLD
KINGDOM OF BABYLON

CHEST & ARMS
SILVER
KINGDOM OF MEDES
& PERSIANS

BELLY & THIGHS
BRONZE
KINGDOM OF ANCIENT GREECE

LEGS
IRON
KINGDOM OF
ANCIENT ROME

FEET
IRON & CLAY
KINGDOM OF RESTORED ROME

CRUSHING ROCK
GREAT MOUNTAIN - FILLS EARTH
KINGDOM OF THE GOD OF HEAVEN

© MARTIN ZAMBRANO

Daniel's Corroborating Dream

Years after Nebuchadnezzar's dream of the towering image and four-teen years before Babylon fell to the Medes and the Persians, Daniel had a vision of his own that confirms and expands our understanding of Nebuchadnezzar's dream. In Daniel's vision, a powerful wind stirred the ocean, and "four great beasts came up from the sea, each different from the other" (Daniel 7:3). These beasts represented the same gentile kingdoms as those depicted in the king's dream of the image of the man, but this time the character of those kingdoms was revealed. The first vision (Daniel 2) characterized the kingdoms of the world *as man assessed them*—majestic, massive, impressive, gigan-tic, and overwhelming. Man is impressed with his accomplishments. In the second vision (Daniel 7), the kingdoms were shown as savage beasts of the jungle, slashing and attacking one another and fighting to the death.

This second vision gives us *God's appraisal* of these gentile king-doms—destructive, divisive, angry, and cruel. While the two visions were radically different in their presentation, both were given for the same purpose—to show Daniel and his people what in the world was going on!

Why did God choose this particular time in history to reveal so great a prophecy? It was designed to assure His people in a desperate moment of their history. Assyria had taken the Northern Kingdom of Israel captive in 722 BC, and now, two hundred years later, the Southern Kingdom of Judah was in captivity in Babylon. If you had been a Jew during that time, you might well have wondered, *Is God finished with us? Are we to be put on the shelf forever?* Through these two visions, God assured His beleaguered people: *This isn't the end.*

There is a time in the future when I will once again be involved with you
as a nation. But I want you to know what is going to happen between
now and then.

Much of what was revealed to Daniel in these dreams has already
happened. But not all of it. The three prophesied kingdoms have
come and gone, and the fourth kingdom has also made its appearance
in history. But Daniel's later vision included additional information
about the future of the fourth kingdom not given to the Babylonian
monarch—information about events that are yet in the future. Let's
look at how Daniel describes it: "After this I saw in the night visions,
and behold, a fourth beast, dreadful and terrible, exceedingly strong.
It had huge iron teeth; it was devouring, breaking in pieces, and
trampling the residue with its feet. It was different from all the beasts
that were before it, and it had ten horns" (Daniel 7:7). Daniel is careful to explain that the ten horns are ten kings who shall arise from this
kingdom (v. 24).

We know that this ten-kingdom prophecy of Daniel's remains in the
future because not only has the ten-leader form of the Roman Empire
never existed in history, but neither has such a kingdom been suddenly
crushed as prophecy indicates it will be. According to Daniel 2, the
Roman Empire in its final form will experience sudden destruction.
The Roman Empire of Jesus' day did not end suddenly. It gradually
deteriorated and declined over many centuries until the western part,
the Holy Roman Empire, fell in AD 476, and the eastern part, the
Byzantine Empire, fell in AD 1453. You can hardly imagine a more
gradual slide from glory to oblivion! We must conclude, then, that
some form of the Roman Empire must emerge in the end times, and
according to Daniel, it will be in place prior to the coming of Christ to
rule and reign over the earth.

The Rebirth of the Roman Empire

The future manifestation of the Roman Empire that Daniel prophesied twenty-five hundred years ago will take the form of a coalition or confederation of ten world leaders and will encompass the same territory as the historic Roman Empire. And today we can see that coalition taking shape right before our eyes! It began as early as 1930, when the French statesman Aristide Briand attempted to enlist twenty-six nations in what he first called "the United States of Europe" and modified to "the European Union." In his proposal he said, "The nations of Europe today must unite in order to live and prosper." The European press gave Briand's novel idea little attention, and nothing came of it.[4]

That is, nothing came of it *at that time*. But Briand's call for European unity was merely one world war ahead of the curve. Fewer than twenty years later, one of the world's most respected leaders issued the same call:

> In 1946, following the devastation of Europe during the Second World War, Winston Churchill forcefully asserted that "the tragedy of Europe" could only be solved if the issues of ancient nationalism and sovereignty could give way to a sense of European "national grouping." He said that the path to European peace and prosperity on the world stage was clear: "We must build a United States of Europe."[5]

Churchill's call initiated a series of steps toward unification; some were faltering, but others gained traction. The Benelux Conference of 1948, held in Brussels, Belgium, would lay the foundation for a new organization "to unite European countries economically and politically to secure a lasting peace."[6] Only three tiny nations attended the meeting—the Netherlands, Luxembourg, and Belgium. These nations came together because they saw unity as their only hope of survival in the postwar world.

Another step was taken in April 1951, when these three nations signed the Treaty of Paris with three additional nations, Germany, France, and Italy, forming a common market for coal and steel in an environment of peace and equality.

March 25, 1957, saw a major step toward European unification when the Treaty of Rome was signed on Capitoline Hill, one of the famous Seven Hills of Rome. On this occasion, Italy, France, and Germany joined the Netherlands, Luxembourg, and Belgium, creating the European Economic Community—the Common Market.

In 1973, the United Kingdom, Ireland, and Denmark joined the EEC, and Greece was added in 1981, making it a ten-nation confederation. On January 1, 1986, Spain and Portugal came into the union, and the agenda expanded beyond economics when the EEC officially adopted the goal of a politically unified Europe. In 1987 the Single European Act was implemented. With the fall of the Berlin Wall in 1989, Germany was reunified, and East Germany was integrated into the membership. In December 1992, the economic borders between the nations of the European community were removed, and a common passport was issued to travelers. Study in universities within the nations was also permitted without any restrictions. Austria, Finland, and Sweden joined the Union in 1995.

In 2002, eighty billion coins were produced for use in the twelve participating nations of the Eurozone, thus introducing the new monetary unit, the euro. Despite expected fluctuations, the rise in euro value has been steady and observable. The dollar is declining against the euro, and many experts believe that within five years the euro may actually replace the US dollar as the standard world currency. As we learned in the previous chapter, the Iranians have recently refused to accept the American dollar as payment for oil, requiring payment to be made in euro.

The march toward European unification continued on May 1, 2004, when Cyprus, the Czech Republic, Estonia, Hungary, Latvia, Lithuania, Malta, Poland, Slovakia, and Slovenia were added, bringing the total to twenty-five nations. These nations brought 75 million people into the European Union, expanding its population to 450 million people and surpassing North America as the world's biggest economic zone. In January 2007, Romania and Bulgaria were admitted to the EU, bringing the total number of nations to twenty-seven.[7]

While Israel was part of the original Roman Empire, it is not currently a part of the European Union. The EU considers Israel ineligible for membership due to human rights violations, based on its occupation of the West Bank, Gaza Strip, Golan Heights, and East Jerusalem. It has been proposed, however, that if Israel would sign a peace treaty with its hostile neighbors, it would be offered membership in the EU.[8]

Gradually yet steadily, the nations of Europe have come together, creating a modern replica of the ancient Roman Empire. Europe is more integrated today than at any time since the days of ancient Rome. The United States of Europe is considered by many to be the second most powerful political force in our world.

ROMAN EMPIRE
THEN & NOW

Old Roman Empire Outlined in Black
European Union Nations in Gray

Consolidation of the European Government

Currently the EU government is organized into three bodies: a Parliament, the Council of European Union, and the European Commission. The Parliament is considered "the Voice of the People" because citizens of the EU directly elect its 785 members. The Parliament passes European laws in conjunction with the Council. Its president is elected to serve a five-year term.

The Council, "the Voice of the Member States," consists of twenty-seven members who are also the heads of their national governments. This body participates with Parliament in the passing of laws and also establishes common foreign policy and security policies. As I write this book, a Reform Treaty is currently in the ratification process. This treaty contains proposals for two major changes to the structure of the Council. First, it will reduce the membership of the Council from twenty-seven to seventeen and elect a full-time president for a two and a half-year extendable term, replacing the current rotating presidency, which changes every six months. These steps toward power consolidation may have very serious implications for the future.

The third body of EU government, the European Commission, consists of twenty-seven commissioners whose tasks are to draft new laws and implement policies and funding. Its president is nominated by the Council of European Union for a five-year term.[9]

Other EU governmental entities include: the Court of Justice, the Court of Auditors, the European Central Bank, and the European Investment Bank.[10]

Former British prime minister Tony Blair is rumored to be the likely candidate for Europe's first president of the Council. These rumors circulated as far back as 2002 and gained momentum in 2007 after Blair stepped down from his position as prime minister of Great Britain. French president Nicolas Sarkozy was the first leader to propose Blair for Europe's first president. In a speech given in January 2008, Sarkozy said this about Tony Blair:

He is intelligent, he is brave and he is a friend. We need him in Europe. How can we govern a continent of 450 million people if the President changes every six months and has to run his own country at the same time? I want a President chosen from the top—not a compromise candidate—who will serve for two-and-a-half years.[11]

As we track these developments toward ever-increasing unity and more centralized power among the European nations, we can see a new empire in the making—an empire that occupies the same territory as the ancient Roman Empire. Turning back to Daniel for further insight into the nature of this rising coalition, we are intrigued by his description of it as a mixture of two noncohering materials. We already know that iron represented the strength of the old Roman Empire. In the newly constituted empire, however, the prophecy tells us that iron will be mixed with ceramic clay. Clay is nothing like the other materials that composed the image of Nebuchadnezzar's dream. Clay speaks of weakness and instability.

The best interpretation of this unstable mix is that the combination of clay and iron represents the diverse racial, religious, and political elements that will comprise this final form of the Roman Empire. That is, in fact, what we see today in the early manifestation of the European coalition. While the EU has great economic and political clout, the cultures and languages of its various countries are so incredibly diverse that it cannot hold together any more than iron and clay unless unity is imposed and enforced by an extremely powerful leader. As the EU prepares to elect a strong president for a longer term, we can see how an uneasy unity could come about.

The Need for Renewed Vigilance

From this brief study of modern Europe and ancient Rome, we can begin to understand the meaning of what is going on in the world today. Three things in particular emerge from our study that should increase our vigilance.

The Consolidation of World Power

Since the time of the Roman Empire, there has been no nation or empire with the power to govern or dominate the known world. But it is coming. In the future there will be a short period of time when the world will be unified under one dominant leader.

We saw in Daniel's second vision that the fourth beast had ten horns growing from its head. We need not wonder at the meaning of the beast and the ten horns, for the meaning of Daniel's dream was given directly to him: "The fourth beast shall be a fourth kingdom on earth, which shall . . . devour the whole earth, trample it and break it in pieces. The ten horns are ten kings who shall arise from this kingdom" (Daniel 7:23–24). The fourth beast represents the fourth successive kingdom after Babylon, which history identifies as the Roman Empire. But since Rome was never ruled simultaneously by ten kings, we know that those kings are yet to arrive on the stage of world history to rule a newly formed empire that overlays the territory of the ancient Roman Empire. Today the concentration of power in the European Union signals the beginning of this new world order.

The Coming of One World Leader

According to Daniel's prophecy, a supreme leader will rise from among the ten-leader confederacy in Europe. "And another shall rise after them; he shall be different from the first ones, and shall subdue three kings. He shall speak pompous words against the Most High, shall persecute the saints of the Most High, and shall intend to change times and law. Then the saints shall be given into his hand for a time and times and half a time" (Daniel 7:24–25). This leader will emerge from the group of ten to take control of the new European Union. He will become the final world dictator. We know him as the Antichrist, and we will have more to say about him in chapter 7. But the point we must not miss now is this: the new European Union is one of the conditional preludes to the coming of the Antichrist. As Arno Froese, executive director of Midnight Call Ministries, wrote:

> The new European power structure will fulfill the prophetic predictions which tell us that a one world system will be implemented. When established, it will fall into the hands of the Antichrist.[12]

And we can have little doubt that such a thing could easily happen when we see how glibly statesmen and politicians can gravitate to power. Paul-Henri Spaak, the first president of the UN General Assembly, first president of the European Parliament, and onetime secretary general of NATO, is credited with making this stunning statement:

> We do not need another committee. We have too many already. What we want is a man of sufficient stature to hold the allegiance of all people, and to lift us out of the economic morass into which we are sinking. Send us such a man and be he god or devil, we will receive him.[13]

Statements such as this should chill us to the bone. It shows that the world as a whole in its ignorance will actually embrace the power that will seek to enslave it. The European Union is the kindling awaiting the spark of the Antichrist to inflame the world with unprecedented evil. It is certainly a time to be vigilant.

The Condition for the Treaty with Israel

In the ninth chapter of Daniel's prophecy, he tells us of a treaty that will be signed between his people and the world leader who will head the realigned Roman Empire: "Then he shall confirm a covenant with many for one week; but in the middle of the week he shall bring an end to sacrifice and offering" (Daniel 9:27). Daniel tells us here that Israel will sign a treaty with the Antichrist, and that this treaty will be forged to last for a "week," literally in prophetic language, a "week of years," or seven years. This treaty will be an attempt to settle the Arab-Israeli controversy that today focuses the world's attention on the Middle East. After three and one-half years, that treaty will be broken, and the countdown to Armageddon will begin.

Heeding the Warning

The stage is now set in Europe for these events to occur. Israel is back in her land, oil is concentrating world focus on the Middle East, and the nations of the ancient Roman Empire are reunifying. Prophecies of events long predicted are coming to pass. I think any honest person must admit that something big is going on in the world. The prophecies of Daniel show us what it is: the hands on the prophetic clock are moving toward midnight. The warning has been sounded, and we will do well to heed it.

I live in San Diego, and these days the people of my area get a bit edgy as the end of October approaches. While most of the country is gathering frost on pumpkins, we are experiencing extreme heat, low humidity, and powerful winds—perfect conditions for devastating wildfires that devour everything in their path.

In 2003 we lived through the firestorm that consumed more than 390,000 acres of land, destroyed 2,430 homes, and inflicted $2.2 billion in property damage.[14] In October 2007, the National Weather Service issued a Red Flag Warning, indicating that conditions were ripe for another major wildfire. On Sunday, October 21, while we were worshipping in our first morning service, ominous billows of smoke began to rise from the backcountry, thirty-three miles away. When I walked out of church that morning, I could see the smoke, and the frightening images of 2003 returned to my mind.

The San Diego Fire Department, using a sophisticated new warning system called Reverse 9-1-1, sent phone messages to homes that were in harm's way. The messages were short and to the point: "This area, get out! This area, get out!" Thousands of San Diegans evacuated their homes, but as is always the case, some refused to leave.

In an attempt to protect their home, one father and his fifteen-year-old son chose to remain behind when the rest of their family evacuated. Two and a half hours into the fire, Capt. Ray Rapue of Cal Fire ordered them to evacuate the area immediately. The father got into his pickup truck, his son got on an ATV, and they started to leave their property. But for reasons unknown, when Fire Engine 3387 drove onto their property, both the father and his son turned around and went back to the house.

The captain again warned them to evacuate because of the dense smoke. The father jumped on the ATV with his son, but lack of oxygen caused the ATV to stall out. Then they both climbed into the fire engine and were warned to stay in the cab while the firefighters continued their work. Soon, depleted oxygen, intense heat, and choking smoke drove the firefighters to attempt their own escape. But the now-overloaded fire engine also stalled.

What happened next is called a *burnover*. Before the firefighters could deploy their tentlike emergency shelters inside the cab, the windows exploded from the heat of the fire advancing from the double-wide home. Fireman Brooke Linman was trying to comfort the panicked young man when voracious flames leapt into the cab. The boy let out a terrible scream as nearly half his body was severely burned. "He kept asking me if we were going to die," reported the fireman later. "I said, 'No, we're not going to die.'" The captain ordered the firefighters and the young man out of the burning cab, and they sought refuge behind large rocks on the property.

Overhead in a command airplane, CAL FIRE chief Ray Chaney reported hearing over his radio a primal scream from the ground below. "Ahhhh! Ahhhh! Ahhhh!" came the wrenching sound in plaintive, agonized spurts. Chief Chaney was able to guide a helicopter through the dense smoke to within a few feet of the trapped group. Two minutes later the helicopter lifted off with its cargo of the injured and quickly returned for the two others. All the rescued were then transported to a trauma center. The father died in that blaze. The son and four heroic fire personnel were severely burned. As I write this chapter five months later, the young man remains hospitalized.[15]

The Importance of Warnings

We will never know why this man and his son chose to disregard the repeated warnings, but the point came when all warnings were futile.

There was no longer any time to run. Living in the fire zone of Southern California has made me aware of the importance of warnings.

As I look at world events through the lens of God's prophetic Word, I have become acutely aware of the warning signs. But warnings are useful only if we heed them. As the prophetic clock moves toward its final strike, we must not wait until it's too late to move out of harm's way. The admonition of Paul to the Roman believers should spur us to action: "Knowing the time, that now it is high time to awake out of sleep: for now our salvation is nearer than when we first believed" (Romans 13:11).

Knowing the meaning behind the events we see in the daily news helps us to understand what is going on in the world. Today's headlines show the wisdom of Paul's warning—it is high time for us to awake out of sleep and realize that things will not continue to go on indefinitely as they are now. Indeed, as the signs from Daniel's prophecies show us, things are coming to a head. Events are moving us toward the moment when warnings will be too late, and we will be caught in the firestorm of a great evil that will trouble the world before Christ finally returns to set things right.

The question for you is, are you heeding the warnings? Are you prepared to stand before God? Have you accepted His offer of salvation? He is telling us by the events that surround us that the window of opportunity will soon be gone. Please do not wait until it is too late!

FOUR

Islamic Terrorism

GEORGES SADA WAS AN AIR FORCE GENERAL UNDER SADDAM Hussein. Though ethnically an Iraqi, he was not a Muslim but an Assyrian Christian. He refused to join the Baathist Party under Saddam, which blocked his ascent into the ranks of power. But he was a military hero, Iraq's top air force pilot, and the man Saddam called on to hear the truth about military matters because Saddam knew his yes-men would tell him only whatever he wanted to hear.

In his book, *Saddam's Secrets: How an Iraqi General Defied and Survived Saddam Hussein,* Sada speaks about the spreading impact of Islam around the world:

I'm often asked about militant Islam and the threat of global terrorism. More than once I've been asked about the meaning of the Arabic words *Fatah* and *Jihad*. What I normally tell them is that to followers of the militant brand of Islam, these doctrines express the belief that Allah has commanded them to conquer the nations of the world both by cultural invasion and by the sword. In some cases this means moving thousands of Muslim families into a foreign land—by building mosques and changing the culture from the inside out, and by refusing to assimilate or adopt the beliefs or values of that nation—to conquer the land for Islam. This is an invidious doctrine, but it's . . . being carried out in some places today by followers of this type of Islam.[1]

Sada went on to warn Americans not to think that the Islamic revolution is a Middle Eastern or European problem. Their ultimate goal is conquest of the West and America:

> [They] won't be stopped by appeasement. They are not interested in political solutions. They don't want welfare—their animosity is not caused by hunger or poverty or anything of the sort. They understand only one thing: total and complete conquest of the West and of any-one who does not bow to them and their dangerous and out-of-date ideology of hate and revenge.[2]

Americans do not seem to take the threat of Islam seriously. In fact, the Pew Research Center tells us that US citizens are essentially oblivious to the potential danger of radical Muslims. "According to poll results issued recently, 58 percent of Americans indicated that they knew either 'not very much' or 'nothing' about the Muslim religion, Islam . . . the fastest growing religion in America."[3]

According to Sada, Americans are particularly vulnerable to the spread of militant Islam because our enemies take advantage of traits that we consider socially positive:

> What I want to say next is not easy for me to say but I think I must say it anyway. One of the nicest things about the American people is

that you are generous and friendly people, and because of this you are sometimes naïve and overly trusting. You want to be friendly, so you open up to people and then you're surprised when they stab you in the back. Many brave young soldiers have died in Iraq for this reason, but I think this is also a big part of the problem with the State Department and others in government who fail to understand the true nature of this enemy.[4]

General Sada's book addresses a major phenomenon that is going on in our world today, and one that we all should want to know more about. The rise of radical Islam has changed the lives of everyone, especially since 9-11. We experience it every time we wait in an airport security line, every time we hear news reports of another terrorist bombing, and indeed, every time we turn on the news and hear reporters and commentators speak of how Islamic culture is growing in our own land. Most of us don't know how to respond. We hear on the one hand that Islam is a major threat to our world, and on the other that Muslims are greatly misunderstood and want nothing more than to be at peace with us. In this chapter I hope to show you what is going on in the world behind the headlines and give you information on how to understand and deal with the new rise of Islam.

Is Islam Militant or Peaceful?

Last year Fox News aired a special called "Radical Islam: Terror in Its Own Words," which revealed "the evil aims of radical Islam." The documentary included shocking clips from Islamic television, showing clerics and political leaders openly advocating attacks on the United States and Israel. The documentary also included programs shown on

Islamic TV in which young children sing of their desire to participate in violent *jihad* or to become suicide bombers. The program went on to show never-before-aired footage from a radical Islamic rally in California where the audience was told, "One day you will see the flag of Islam over the White House."[5]

More recently, al-Aqsa, the Hamas-owned television station in Gaza, aired a children's program in which a boy puppet sneaks into the White House, kills President George W. Bush with "the sword of Islam," and vows "the White House would be turned into a mosque."[6]

In the face of such reports as these, one of the most baffling and unsettling puzzles about Islam is the constant contention on the part of some Muslim leaders that they are a peace-loving people. Yet even as they make the claim, Islamic terrorists continue to brutally murder any person or group with whom they find fault. In his foreword to Don Richardson's book *The Secrets of the Koran*, former radical Shi'ite Muslim Reza F. Safa asked:

> If Islam is a peaceful religion, then why did Mohammed engage in 47 battles? Why, in every campaign the Muslim armies have fought throughout history, have they slaughtered men, women and children who did not bow their knees to the lordship of Islam? The reign of terror of men such as Saddam, Khomeini, Ghadafi, Idi Amin and many other Muslim dictators are modern examples. If Islam is so peaceful, why are there so many verses in the Koran about killing the infidels and those who resist Islam? If Islam is peaceful, why isn't there even one Muslim country that will allow freedom of religion and speech? Not one! If Islam is peaceful, who is imparting this awful violence to hundreds of Islamic groups throughout the world who kill innocent people in the name of Allah?

But since the statehood of Israel . . . men such as Ghadafi and Osama bin Laden have been blowing the dust off the sword of a forceful world-invading religion.[7]

To get a handle on these two contradictory sides of Islam, it will help us to delve briefly into the history of how the religion came to be and what beliefs it holds today.

The History of Islam

In his book *The Age of Faith*, Will Durant wrote:

In the year 565 Justinian died, master of a great empire. Five years later Mohammed was born into a poor family in a country three quarters desert, sparsely peopled by nomad tribes whose total wealth could hardly have furnished the sanctuary of St. Sophia. No one in those years would have dreamed that within a century these nomads would conquer half of Byzantine Asia, all of Persia and Egypt, most of North Africa, and be on their way to Spain. The explosion of the Arabian peninsula into the conquest and conversion of half the Mediterranean world is the most extraordinary phenomenon of medieval history.[8]

The name *Islam* literally means *submission*. A Muslim is "one who submits to God." According to conservative estimates, there are about 1.5 billion Muslims in our world today. Approximately 1.4 million live in the United States, which is about 6 percent of the US adult population. While we usually associate Islam with the Middle East, the largest Muslim populations are actually in Asia.[9]

According to Islamic tradition, the founder of Islam, Mohammad, was born in Mecca (in present-day Saudi Arabia) in AD 570. Mecca was a thriving center of religious pilgrimage, filled with numerous temples and statues dedicated to the many gods the Arabian people worshipped at the time.

Mohammad's father died before the prophet was born, and his mother died when he was six years old. He was raised by his paternal grandfather, grew up to become a camel driver and then a merchant, and at the age of twenty-six, married a wealthy caravan owner named Khadija. Khadija was forty years old and had been divorced four times. In spite of her age, she and Mohammad had six children together.

Durant further noted, "Mohammad's son-in-law, Ali, described his father-in-law as being "of middle stature, neither tall nor short. His complexion was rosy white; his eyes black; his hair, thick, brilliant, and beautiful, fell to his shoulders. His profuse beard fell to his breast . . . There was such sweetness in his visage that no one, once in his presence, could leave him. If I hungered, a single look at the Prophet's face dispelled the hunger. Before him, all forgot their griefs and pains."[10]

Mohammad worked in professions that brought him into contact with a number of Christians and Jews who caused him to question the religion of his own people. He was forty years old and meditating in a cave outside Mecca when he received his first revelation. From that moment on, according to his testimony, God occasionally revealed messages to him, which he declared to the people. These messages, which Muhammad received throughout his life, form the verses of the Qu'ran, which Muslims regard as the divine word of God.

In the seventh-century Arabian world of Mohammad, the people worshipped more than 360 different gods, one for each day of the lunar year. One of these was the moon god, the male counterpart to the female sun god. The moon god was called by various names, one of which was Allah, and it was the favorite god of Mohammad's family. As Dr. Robert Morey explains, "The literal Arabic name of Muhammad's father was Abd-Allah. His uncle's name was literally Obied-Allah. These names ... reveal the personal devotion that Muhammed's pagan family had to the worship of Allah, the moon god."[11]

As Mohammad began to promote his new religion, it was only natural that he would choose to elevate the moon god, Allah, and declare him to be the one true God. His devotion to Allah was single-minded and fierce, and in establishing and spreading his religion of Islam, Mohammad slaughtered thousands of people who resisted conversion. As his instructions to his followers show, there was no subtlety in his evangelistic technique. Abd El Schafi, an expert on ancient Muslim scholarship, informs us: "One of Muhammad's popular claims is that God commanded him to fight people until they became Muslims . . . All Muslim scholars without exception agree on this."[12]

Opposition in Mecca forced Mohammad and his followers to flee to Medina in AD 620, where he became the head of the first Muslim community. In AD 631 he returned to Mecca, where he died the following year. At his death, the Islamic community became bitterly divided over the question of who would be Mohammad's successor. Even today that division survives in the two Islamic sects, now known as Shi'ite and Sunni. Conflict between these sects is one of the major stress points in Iraq and throughout the Islamic world.

At the death of Mohammad, the group we know as the Sunni followed the leadership of Abu Bakr, Mohammad's personally chosen successor. The Sunni now comprise about 90 percent of the Islamic world. They believe that Muhammad's spiritual gifts died with him and that their only authority today is the Qu'ran. The Baath party of Saddam Hussein was part of the Sunni sect.

The Shi'ites maintained that Mohammad passed on a legacy of personal authority in addition to the Qu'ran, called the Hadith, as author Winfried Corduan explains:

> The Shi'ites, on the other hand, identified with Muhammad's son-in-law Ali, whom they saw as possessing a spiritual endowment directly from the prophet. The Shi'ites believe that their leaders, the imams, have authority on par with the Qu'ran. It is the Shi'ites that believe that the Twelfth Imam went into concealment hundreds of years ago and continues to live there until he returns as the Mahdi . . . the Muslim Messiah![13]

When Abu Bakr succeeded Mohammad, he and his successors launched *jihads* (or holy wars) that spread the religion of Islam from northern Spain to India and threatened Christian Europe. Christians resisted the threat, and a series of wars followed that drove the Islamic invaders back into the Middle Eastern countries, where they still dominate. Their zeal to have their religion dominate the world has not diminished, however, and it remains a threat to all who do not maintain vigilance.

The Habits of Islam

Sunni Muslims mandate five acts of worship, which are frequently referred to as the five pillars of Islam. Shi'ite Muslim worship comprises eight ritual practices, but these overlap and encompass the same five pillars of Islam as practiced by the Sunni. The five pillars are as follows:[14]

1. *To recite the* Shahadah: The *Shahadah* is the Islamic creed, "There is no god but Allah, and Muhammad is his messenger." Its recitation is the duty of every Muslim.

2. *To pray (salat)*: Muslims pray while bowing toward Mecca five times each day: in the early morning, in the early and late afternoon, at sunset, and an hour after sunset.

3. *To fast (sawm)*: Muslims refrain from food during the day-light hours throughout the lunar month of Ramadan. This month is to be given over to meditation and reflection, and it ends with a joyous celebration.

4. *To give alms (zakat)*: Muslims are required to give 2.5 percent (one-fortieth) of their income to the poor and those in need. They may give more as a means of gaining further divine reward, but the 2.5 percent is an obligatory minimum. The percentage is based on the amount of accumulated wealth or income held for a lunar year above a minimum of three ounces of gold.

5. *To make the pilgrimage (hajj)*: Those physically and finan-cially able must visit Mecca at least once during their lifetime. The journey usually takes at least a week and includes many stops at other holy sites along the way.

The Hatred of Islam

No doubt the most frightening word associated with Islam is *jihad*. Sometimes called the "sixth pillar" of Islam, *jihad* actually means "struggle." The "Greater Jihad" is the inner struggle of each Muslim to submit to Allah. The "Lesser Jihad" is the outward struggle to defend the Islamic community. This is the jihad that strikes fear in the hearts of any who reject radical Islam. These Muslims take jihad to mean violent defense of Islam; to them it authorizes the expansion of the Islamic religion even by means of deadly aggression.

The overt hatred for the West expressed in jihad has already spawned many mortal attacks, and the fanaticism that produced them has not diminished. In her book, completed days before her assassination, former prime minister of Pakistan Benazir Bhutto wrote that one of the primary aims of the militants is:

> . . . to provoke a clash of civilizations between the West and . . . Islam. The great hope of the militants is a collision, an explosion between the values of the West and what the extremists claim to be the values of Islam . . . The attacks on September 11, 2001, heralded the . . . dream of bloody confrontation . . . if the fanatics and extremists prevail . . . then a great *fitna* (disorder through schism or division) would sweep the world. Here lies their ultimate goal: chaos.[15]

The hatred that the Muslims have for the Jews needs no documentation. But the settlement of Israel into her homeland in 1948 took this hatred to a level of murderous fury. The militants and radicals refer to Israel as "little Satan," and the United States as "big Satan," and they are determined to wipe both countries off the map.

While the majority of the world's 1.5 billion Muslims want no part of this deadly violence and attempt to live in peace with their neighbors, the number of radicals who preach violence and terror is mushrooming around the world. Experts say that 15 to 20 percent of Muslims are radical enough to strap a bomb on their bodies in order to kill Christians and Jews. If this number is accurate, it means about three hundred million Muslims are willing to die in order to take you and me down.

To get a picture of how bitterly Islam hates Jews and Christians, one has only to listen to the speeches of their clerics and leaders. Recently, Sheikh Ibrahim Mdaires delivered a sermon at a mosque in the Gaza Strip that was broadcast live to the Arab world. The text of that sermon has circulated around the globe. It represents the alarming doctrines and attitudes being taught and preached in many mosques and Islamic schools.

With the establishment of the state of Israel, the entire Islamic nation was lost, because Israel is a cancer . . . The Jews are a virus resembling AIDS, from which the entire world suffers. You will find that the Jews were behind all the civil strife in this world. The Jews are behind the suffering of the nations . . . We [the Muslims] have ruled the world before, and by Allah, the day will come when we will rule the entire world again. The day will come when we will rule America. The day will come when we will rule Britain and the entire world—except the Jews. The Jews will not enjoy a life of tranquility under our rule, because they are treacherous by nature, as they have been throughout history. The day will come when everything will be relieved of the Jews . . . Listen to the Prophet Muhammad, who tells you about the evil that awaits the Jews. The stones and trees will want the Muslims to finish off every Jew.[16]

If this diatribe does not give you reason enough to believe that Islam is the enemy of America and Christianity, consider that today, as I write these words, there is not a single one of the fifty-five predominately Muslim nations on earth today where Christians are not persecuted. As General Sada warned, we cannot afford to relax our vigilance in the name of naïve tolerance and multiculturalism.

The Hopes of Islam

Speeches like that of Mdaires show us that radical Islam has a vision of its future that does not bode well for those who stand in the way. To get a better understanding of this vision, we will now look briefly at some of the goals the Islamic world hopes to achieve.

Islam Hopes to Rule the World

In his book *Secrets of the Koran,* Don Richardson tells the chilling story of Islam's plan to gain political and religious control of the entire world:

> The world needs to be warned. At least 40 million Muslim youth in the Muslim world's religious schools, called madrasas, are avidly memorizing the entire Koran plus a generally extremist body of related traditions—the hadiths . . . These schools are breeding grounds for potential terrorists . . . Hatred for Jews and Christians (largely synonymous with Israel and America) and general disdain for all non-Muslims . . . are deeply instilled . . . Simply put, 40 million trainees in Muslim madrasas are a societal nuclear bomb.
>
> Consider this from professor Mochtar Buchori, a member of the Indonesian Parliament: If we add all the universities, colleges, high schools, junior high schools, and elementary schools in the United States, we find that the total is about 24,000 institutions. Yet Buchori counts 37,362 Muslim madrassas in Indonesia, alone! Of these only 8 percent have any input from Indonesia's government. In 92 percent, the teaching agenda is controlled by Muslim clerics.[17]

Traditionally in the United States, Arabic language courses have been taught only at universities, mosques, and Islamic schools. But that has recently changed. In September 2006, Carver Elementary School, a publicly financed K–8 school in San Diego, absorbed into its enrollment about one hundred students from a defunct charter school serving mostly Somali Muslims. To accommodate the special religious customs of the Muslim children, the administration formed, in effect, an Islamic school within an American school. Accommodations included adding courses in the Arabic language, modifying the cafeteria menu in accordance with Islamic dietary restrictions, providing gender-separated classes, and establishing an afternoon recess allowing for the Islamic prayer specified for that time of the day—all at an additional cost to the school district of $450,000!

Just when Carver was becoming comfortable with this arrangement, a substitute teacher observed that the afternoon Muslim prayer was being led by an employee of the school district. The sub reported the apparent "indoctrination" of students to Islam at a public session of the school board. Investigations began into the accommodations and the apparent double standard that bans Christianity from public institutions and yet accommodates "an organized attempt to push public conformance with Islamic law."[18]

Here we see General Sada's warning played out in tangible form. We Americans want to be nice. We want to accommodate. We want to believe that if we are tolerant of others, they will reciprocate. We tend to forget the general's warning that militant Muslims don't think that way, and each inch we give in the name of accommodation, they will take in the name of conquest.

It is one thing to read about Muslim determination to take over the world; it is quite another to watch it happening right before our eyes, as it is in Europe. The most startling and underreported social migration of our age is the Islamification of Europe, which has great bearing on the territories of the old Roman Empire that we discussed in the previous chapter. Tony Blankley of the *Washington Times* devoted his book, *The West's Last Chance,* to sounding an alarm about this Islamic infiltration. This is how he sees this threat to Western culture:

> In much of the West, and particularly in Europe, there is blind denial that radical Islam is transforming the world. Most Europe elites and far too many American politicians and journalists believe that our challenges are business and politics as usual. They are sheep who cannot sense the wolf pack in the woods . . . The threat of the radical Islamists taking over Europe is every bit as great to the United States as was the threat of the Nazis taking over Europe in the 1940s. We cannot afford to lose Europe. We cannot afford to see Europe transformed into a launching pad for Islamist jihad . . .
>
> The moral threat we face comes not merely from Osama bin Laden and a few thousand terrorists. Rather, we are confronted with the Islamic world—a fifth of mankind—in turmoil, and insurgent as it has not been in at least five hundred years, if not fifteen hundred years. The magnitude of this cultural upheaval cannot yet be measured . . . To point out the obvious, the resurgence of a militant Islam drove America to fight two wars in Muslim countries in two years, disrupted America's alliance with Europe, caused the largest reorganization of the American government in half a century (with the creation of the Department of Homeland Security), changed election results in Europe, and threatened the stability of most of the governments in the Middle East.[19]

We can easily see and resist the effects of jihad in militant terrorism, but we have trouble seeing and resisting the more subtle strategy that the Muslims call *fatah*. *Fatah* is infiltration, moving into a country in numbers large enough to affect the culture. It means taking advantage of tolerant laws and accommodative policies to insert the influence of Islam. In places where a military invasion will not succeed, the slow, systematic, and unrelenting methods of *fatah* are conquering whole nations. Two illustrations are instructive, the first concerning France:

> What we're seeing in many places is a "demographic revolution." Some experts are projecting that by the year 2040, 80 percent of the population of France will be Muslim. At that point the Muslim majority will control commerce, industry, education, and religion in that country. They will also, of course, control the government, as well, and occupy all the key positions in the French Parliament. And a Muslim will be president.[20]

Islamification is also happening in England, but the Muslims there are not waiting for further population growth to institute *fatah*. They are advancing their goal of dominance by taking advantage of the British policy of pluralistic tolerance. An example occurred in September 2006 when the British home secretary, John Reid, gave a speech to Muslim parents in east London, encouraging them to protect their children from pressure to become suicide bombers. A robed and turbaned fundamentalist Muslim leader who had lavishly praised the suicide bombers of the horrific attack on London's transportation system was in the audience. He got up and shouted the speaker down. He ranted at the home secretary for five minutes, shouting, "How dare you come to a Muslim area? . . . I am furious. I am absolutely furious—John Reid should not come to a Muslim area." Muslims are not only immigrating massively to western countries but also claiming entitlement to keep their settlements off-limits to native citizens. The "ghettoization" of London into "non-Muslim no-go zones" is an ongoing controversy in the British press.[21]

Earlier this year in the city of Oxford—where Hugh Latimer, Nicholas Ridley, and Thomas Cranmer were martyred for their Christian faith and the famous Oxford Movement began—the seven hundred members of a mosque, which is valued at two million British pounds, petitioned "for their right as British citizens to practice their faith." What right did they demand? The right to broadcast a two-minute *adhan*—the Muslim call to prayer—from the mosque minaret three times a day. The amplified call would be heard a mile or more away, meaning the volume would disrupt the lives of countless non-Muslims. One Oxford University professor summed up the controversy in this way: "It's not a matter of people's right to religious freedom, it's about making Islam the religion of public space."[22]

In early 2008, England's archbishop of Canterbury, Rowan Williams, gave the world a stunning example of General Sada's claim of Western naiveté concerning Islamic intentions. Williams told a BBC correspondent that the growing Islamic population in Britain made it expedient to be accommodative. He said "the UK had to face up to the fact" that it "seems unavoidable" that Islam's legal system, *sharia* law, will be "incorporated into British law." His term for this blending of laws was "constructive accommodation."[23] *Sharia* law, derived from the Qu'ran and teachings of Muhammad, is the legal system by which Muslims are to live. In the West, the law is fairly benign and deals mainly with family and business. But in Muslim countries it can include such things as "honor killings" in cases of suspected immorality.

Some foresee the incorporation of *sharia* into English law as a fatal blow to the historic Christianity of England. A recent Church of England General Synod survey reported that "63 percent fear that the Church will be disestablished within a generation, breaking a bond that has existed between the Church and State since the Reformation."[24] The controversy is not merely about allowing religious freedom, but rather about how intrusive a tolerant nation should allow an immigrant religion to be.

You may hear other terms used to describe the Islamic goal of world domination. For example, "biological jihad" or "demographic jihad" describes the nonviolent strategy of Muslims moving into Europe and the West and having more babies than their hosts. Within several generations they hope to repopulate traditionally Christian cultures with their own people, and they are certainly on track to reach that goal. According to a Vatican report issued recently, the Roman Catholic Church understands this: "For the first time in history, we are no longer at the top: Muslims have overtaken us."[25]

Islam Hopes to Return Its Messiah

This Islamic hope surfaced in a speech by Iranian president Mahmoud Ahmadinejad, a disciple of Ayatollah Khomeini, the cleric who launched the successful 1979 revolution that turned Iran into a strict Islamic state. In 2005, Ahmadinejad was called before the United Nations Security Council to explain his continued determination to develop nuclear weapons. He began his speech by declaring: "In the Name of the God of Mercy, Compassion, Peace, Freedom and Justice . . ." and ended his speech with this prayer: "I pray to you to hasten the emergence of your last repository, the promised one, that perfect and pure human being, the one that will fill this world with justice and peace."[26] The "promised one" in Ahmadinejad's prayer was a reference to the Twelfth Imam, a figure in Shi'ite teaching that parallels the figure of Al-Mahdi in Sunni teaching. In essence, both of these titles refer to the Islamic messiah who is yet to come.

Shi'ia Islam believes that the Twelfth Imam can appear only during a time of worldwide chaos. This explains many of Ahmadinejad's defiant actions—why he presses forward with his nuclear program in spite of world censure and why he is adamant about destroying Israel. In an infamous speech in Tehran on October 25, 2005, he said, "Israel must be wiped off the map," and he warned leaders of Muslim nations who recognized the state of Israel that they would "face the wrath of their own people."[27] With these defiant and divisive actions, Ahmadinejad is fomenting the chaotic environment that he believes will induce the Islamic messiah to come. In a televised speech in January 2008, Ahmadinejad reiterated: "What we have right now is the last chapter . . . Accept that the life of Zionists will sooner or later come to an end."[28] On March 14, 2008, Ahmadinejad "swept the nationwide ballot with about 70 percent support."[29]

The world as a whole seems to be starting to take Ahmadinejad seriously, but the people of Israel are totally convinced. They understand that he is determined to destroy them. And the prophet Ezekiel backs up that understanding. He tells us that the hatred Iran bears (Iran being the current name of the biblical Persia) toward the Jewish nation will play an important role in a major end-time battle. John Walvoord summarizes the scenario:

> The rise of Islamic terror is setting the stage for the events in Ezekiel 38–39. These chapters prophesy an invasion of Israel in the end times by a vast coalition of nations, all of whom are Islamic today except Russia. Israel has said that a new "axis of terror"—Iran, Syria,

and the Hamas-run Palestinian government—is sowing the seeds of the first world war of the twenty-first century. The rise of Islam, and especially radical Islamic terrorism, strikingly foreshadows Ezekiel's great prophecy.[30]

Even though the hope for an Islamic messiah is surely futile, the chaos radical Islamic leaders are creating to bring about that hope is all too real and deadly. So deadly that much of the biblical prophecies concerning the end times will be brought about by the beliefs and actions of radical Islam. And we are beginning to feel the pressure of those impending events in the rise and rapid spread of Islamic radicalism in our own time.

Responding to the Islamic Threat

How are we responding to the rise of Islamic radicalism? Not too well, I fear. On the whole, those who shape our culture and policies seem to bear out General Sada's observation that we "fail to understand the true nature of this enemy." In our rush to be democratic, tolerant, and inclusive, we are inadvertently accommodating the radical agenda of Islamic conquest. We must stop being deceived about this threat. We must stand our ground and affirm truths that many seem all too willing to give up in the name of tolerance and accommodation. If you are looking for a beginning place, here are two truths on which I see much confusion today. It is critical that we affirm these truths to maintain a clear understanding of the vast chasm between Christianity and Islam.

"Allah" Is Not Another Name for the God of the Bible

In mid-August 2007, Fox News instigated a blogger's field day when it reported that seventy-one-year-old Dutch Catholic Bishop

Muskens of Breda "wants everyone to call God 'Allah.'" Fox quoted from Muskens's interview on a Dutch TV program in which he said, "Allah is a very beautiful word for God. Shouldn't we all say that from now on, we will call God 'Allah'?" The bishop further added, "What does God care what we call him?" Fox's Roman Catholic news analyst disagreed with the bishop, stating, "Words and names mean things. Referring to God as Allah means something."[31]

Indeed they do! As journalist Stan Goodenough reminded his *Jerusalem Newswire* readers, in the name of Allah, people hijack planes and use them to wreak unspeakable devastation, blow themselves up in crowded public venues to annihilate innocent people, and in the name of Allah, "millions of people pray for the destruction of Israel and the United States." Goodenough observed that when God introduced Himself to Moses, He gave His name as YHWH—Jehovah. He went on to say, "He also has many other names describing aspects of His nature and character. 'Allah' is not one of them."[32]

Bishop Muskens surely knows the biblical names for God, so what was he thinking when he urged Christians to call God Allah? As he explained, "If Muslims and Christians address God with the same name, this contributes to harmonious living between both religions."[33] When Islamic leaders heard this, their mosques must have rung with the slaps of high fives. Their policy of *fatah* was working beautifully. And they must have ascended into unspeakable ecstasies when the spokesman for the Council on American-Islamic Relations immediately embraced Muskens's proposal, saying, "It reinforces the fact that Muslims, Christians and Jews all worship the same God."[34]

We hear this appalling claim often these days, but nothing could be farther from the truth. Allah and God are emphatically not the same! To claim otherwise is nothing short of a slander against the one true God. As Hal Lindsey explains:

The doctrine of Satan is that all religions are equally valid, that all paths lead to God, that God is impersonal, unknowable, and it is therefore irrelevant to Him what we call Him or how we worship Him. If Allah and God are one and the same, then wouldn't the worship of the Hindu chief gods, Vishnu and Shiva, also be the worship of Allah and God, only by a different name? Pretty soon, everybody is God . . . Which is the same as saying that nobody is.[35]

The God of the Bible and the Allah of the Qu'ran are nothing alike. The differences are vast and allow no possibility of synthesis. The God of the Bible is knowable. According to the Qu'ran, Allah is so exalted that he cannot be known. The God of the Bible is a personal being with intellect, emotion, and will. Muslim theology tells us Allah is not to be understood as a person. The God of the Bible is a spirit. To Muslims, such a thought is blasphemous and demeaning to Allah. The God of the Bible is one God in three persons. The Qu'ran denies the Trinity and views it as a major heresy. The God of the Bible is a God of love. Allah does not have emotional feelings toward man. The God of the Bible is a God of grace. According to the Qu'ran, there is no savior or intercessor. Clearly the God of the Bible and Allah are not at all the same and should never be equated with one another![36]

The Qu'ran Is Not a Divine Book on Par with the Bible

Just as many say the God of the Bible and Allah are the same, many also say that we should consider the Qu'ran to be on the same level as the Bible. Actually, the Muslims believe the Qu'ran to be the mother of all books and the Bible as subservient to it. A comparison of the two books will show the absurdity of such a claim. The Bible is a masterpiece of cohesion, depth, literate quality, and consistency. God inspired more than 40 men over a period of 1,400 years to write the God-breathed words that carry His unified message from Genesis to Revelation (2 Timothy 3:16).

The Qu'ran, on the other hand, is a self-contradicting book supposedly given by the angel Gabriel to Mohammad. Since Mohammad could neither read nor write, the sayings were translated and collected from the memories of those who had heard him.

Objective readers who have read both the Bible and the Qu'ran are immediately able to tell the difference between the quality and comprehensibility of the two books. Historian Edward Gibbon (1737–1794) is an example of such a reader. He could hardly be accused of being a Christian, yet he described the Qu'ran as "an incoherent rhapsody of fable, and precept, and declamation, which sometimes crawls in the dust, and sometimes is lost in the clouds."[37]

Muslims Are Not Beyond the Reach of God's Grace

Recently I saw a bumper sticker that made me stop and consider. It read, "Have You Prayed for Osama Bin Laden Today." I must admit I had not. Yet Peter reminds us that "the Lord is . . . not willing that any should perish but that all should come to repentance" (2 Peter 3:9). I am absolutely certain that the "any" of this verse includes Muslims. We may find it hard to pray for avowed enemies who threaten our destruction, but one of the characteristics of Christlikeness given by Jesus Himself is to "love your enemies, bless those who curse you, do good to those who hate you, and pray for those who spitefully use you and persecute you" (Matthew 5:44). I believe that includes Osama bin Laden and his radical Islamic counterparts.

We have good evidence that such prayers are effective. Through the miracle of satellite delivery, our weekly television program, *Turning*

Point, is now available in almost every Arab country. We routinely get e-mail and letters from individuals who have come to Christ through the ministry of God's Word beamed into their lives via satellite TV. Recently we received a letter from an Arab country. The writer told us that he had accepted Christ into his heart and expressed great gratitude for the encouragement of God's truth. A note at the bottom of the letter pleaded with us not to send any materials to his address. That postscript made us vividly aware of the courage it takes for a Muslim in an Islamic country to confess Christ as Savior.

God is at work in the Islamic world. We have reports that many Muslims are being confronted with the gospel in their dreams. Here is the testimony of one Saudi Arabian who was born close to Mecca and grew up going to the mosque five times a day. For many nights he had a terrifying nightmare in which he was being taken down into hell. This dream, always vivid and horrifying, destroyed the man's peace night after night. Suddenly one evening, Jesus appeared in his dream and said, "Son, I am the way, the truth, and the life. And if you would give your life to Me, I would save you from the hell that you have seen."

This young man knew something of Jesus from the distorted teachings of the Qu'ran, but he didn't know the Jesus of the New Testament. So he began searching for a Christian who could help him. Since Christianity is banned in Saudi Arabia, and a Christian caught witnessing to a Muslim could be beheaded, the young man's search took time. But the Lord eventually led him to an Egyptian Christian who gave him a Bible. He began reading, and when he got into the New Testament, he was moved to give his life totally to Jesus Christ.

Soon afterward, an opponent of the young man discovered his conversion and accused him of being a Christian. The authorities arrested and imprisoned him. In jail, he was tortured and eventually sentenced to death by beheading. But on the morning of his scheduled execution, no one showed up to escort him from the cell. Two days later the authorities threw open his cell door and screamed at him: "You demon! Get out of this place!"[38]

The man learned later that his execution had not taken place because on the very day he was to be beheaded, the son of his accuser had mysteriously died. The new Christian is now quietly working to bring other Muslims to faith in Christ.

In this chapter we have explored one of the unsettling events that is going on in today's world—the rising threat of radical Islam. In the true story I related above, we have the key to the Christian response to this threat. As Abraham Lincoln said, "The best way to destroy an enemy is to make him a friend." The best way to counter the threat of Islam is to make Christians out of Muslims. I don't claim that this will turn away prophecies of events sure to come, but it does give you a role in the drama to be played. Our prayers, our testimonies, our love and care for our Islamic neighbors may not turn the inevitable tide for the world, but they can turn the tide for individuals and allow them to escape the wrath to come. And that is definitely worth doing.

FIVE

Vanished Without a Trace

ONE OF THE MORE POPULAR CBS TV SHOWS IS THE FICTIONAL drama *Without a Trace.* It is set in New York City's special FBI missing persons unit. Each episode is devoted to finding one missing person, and, usually, one of the agents assigned to the case develops a strong emotional interest that carries the story along. In reality, the FBI has no dedicated missing persons unit; investigations into disappearances are assigned to agents on a case-by-case basis. At the end of each episode, however, the show does touch on reality by providing public service information to help the FBI locate real-life missing persons.

Another TV show built on the theme of missing persons was the Fox Broadcasting drama *Vanished.* The plotline centered on a Georgia senator whose wife apparently vanished into thin air. That series failed to attract enough viewers to survive the season, provoking anger among those who had become hooked when the thirteen aired episodes never resolved the mystery.

And mystery is exactly what the word *vanished* implies. Headlines about people who vanish rivet our attention: "Relatives Wait for Word of Vanished Sailors"; "Man Vanishes After Concert"; "Search Continues for Woman Who Vanished"; "Police Say Man Vanished Without a Trace." We read such headlines with eerie wonder: *What could have happened to the missing person? How could he have simply been there one moment and not the next?*

According to the Bible, a time is coming when this very thing will happen on a massive, global scale. A day is coming when a billion people will suddenly vanish from the face of the earth without a trace! And when that event occurs, calling in the FBI will be of no use. A TV series based on the mystery would never have a conclusion, for these vanished people will never again be seen until the Lord Himself returns. What will this worldwide phenomenon be like? That is a question in the minds of many who—through popular novels, sermons, or religious writings—have heard of this event but don't understand it. They know that Christians call it the Rapture, yet they have little idea what it means or what in the world is going on that could bring it about. In this chapter I will seek to resolve this common confusion.

The Great Disappearance

Some of us are familiar with massive evacuations, which leave large areas empty and desolate, as if their inhabitants had simply vanished. As I mentioned in a previous chapter, I pastor a church located in the fire zone of Southern California. In October 2007, we witnessed the largest evacuation of homes in California history, and the largest evacuation for fire in United States history. Emergency personnel evacuated 350,000 homes, displacing 1 million Californians as sixteen simultaneous fires swept through our community.[1]

Imagine a person who missed the call to evacuate, waking up after everyone was gone and stumbling through the acrid smoke and empty streets, confused and amazed, wondering why he had been left behind. That person's reaction would be nothing compared to the shock of those who witness the coming worldwide evacuation.

The Bible tells us that on that day, millions of people will disappear from the face of the earth in less than a millisecond. And the purpose of that evacuation is similar to that of the emergency evacuation of Southern Californians: to avoid horrific devastation. This evacuation will remove God's people from the disastrous effects of coming earthquakes, fire, and global chaos. As Bruce Bickel and Stan Jantz explain, the evacuation itself will create considerable chaos and destruction:

> Jumbo jets plummet to earth as they no longer have a pilot at the controls. Driverless buses, trains, subways, and cars will cause unimaginable disaster. Classrooms will suddenly be without teachers . . . Doctors and nurses seem to abandon their patients in the middle of surgical operations, and patients will vanish from operating tables. Children disappear from their beds. People run through the streets looking for missing family members who were there just moments ago. Panic grips every household, city and country.[2]

Attempting to put realism into this event for my first youth group as a fledgling pastor, I utilized the idea of an imaginary newspaper covering the recent Rapture. The lead article read:

> At 12:05 last night a telephone operator reported three frantic calls regarding missing relatives. Within fifteen minutes all communications were jammed with similar inquiries. A spot check around the

nation found the same situation in every city. Sobbing husbands sought information about the mysterious disappearance of wives. One husband reported, "I turned on the light to ask my wife if she remembered to set the clock, but she was gone. Her bedclothes were there, her watch was on the floor . . . she had vanished!" An alarmed woman calling from Brooklyn tearfully reported, "My husband just returned from the late shift . . . I kissed him . . . he just disappeared in my arms."

These two descriptions of the coming disappearance are quite disturbing. Considering the devastation, loss, grief, and confusion the event will cause, it may seem strange that it is called the Rapture. According to my online dictionary, the word *rapture* means "an expression or manifestation of ecstasy or passion," and "being carried away by overwhelming emotion."[3] Everyone wants that kind of euphoric delight, which is why marketing experts have made *rapture* a popular term in today's culture.

There's a perfume called Rapture, and also a well-known New York City-based rock band. Many novels and movies carry the word *rapture* in their titles. A concert-promoting agency calls itself Planet Rapture. One sporting goods company even sells a set of golf clubs called Rapture! The world is looking for rapture, so marketers offer it everywhere.

So why would Christians use *Rapture*, of all terms, to denote a chaotic event when a billion people will suddenly disappear from the earth? The word *Rapture* is the Latin version of a phrase the Bible uses to describe the catching away of all Christians before the end times.

The focus is on looking at the event not from the viewpoint of those who remain, but from that of those who are evacuated. All true Christians will be caught up from the earth and raptured into the presence of the Lord before the seven-year period of evil, the Tribulation, breaks throughout the earth. This will fulfill the promise He made to His disciples in John 14:1–3:

> Let not your heart be troubled; you believe in God, believe also in Me. In My Father's house are many mansions; if it were not so, I would have told you. I go to prepare a place for you. And if I go and prepare a place for you, I will come again and receive you to Myself; that where I am, there you may be also.

Followers of Christ who are raptured will be spared the trauma of death and the coming disasters that will occur when the Tribulation breaks out upon the earth. That is indeed a cause for true rapture on the part of those who love the Lord and long to be with Him.

One morning recently I spoke about the Rapture during a series of messages on prophecy. Later I was told that on the way out of church, a girl expressed confusion to her mother about something I had said. "Dr. Jeremiah keeps talking about all the signs that are developing concerning the Lord's return. And then in the next breath he says that nothing needs to happen before Jesus comes back to take us home to be with Him. I don't understand!" It seemed to this girl that I had contradicted myself. First, I seemed to say that certain prophesied signs would occur before the coming of Christ; then I seemed to say that nothing needed to occur before Jesus comes to claim His own. The girl's honest confusion deserves to be addressed because I believe she speaks for many who are similarly puzzled about events relating to the Rapture.

Most of the misunderstanding comes from confusing two events: the Rapture and the Second Coming. When we talk about the signs that signal the return of Christ, we speak not of the Rapture but of the Lord's ultimate return to the earth with all His saints. According to the book of Revelation, this coming of Christ occurs after the Rapture and differs from it in at least two ways: First, the Rapture will be a "stealth event" in which Christ will be witnessed by believers only. His second coming, on the other hand, will be a public event. Everyone will see Him. "Behold, He is coming with clouds, and every eye will see Him, even they who pierced Him. And all the tribes of the earth will mourn because of Him" (Revelation 1:7; see also Zechariah 14:1, 3–5; Revelation 19:11–21).

Second, all believers are raptured. He will immediately take them back into heaven with Him. But when Christ returns to earth seven years later in the Second Coming, He is coming to stay. This return, usually referred to as "the Second Advent," will take place at the end of the Tribulation period and usher in the Millennium—a thousand-year reign of Christ on this earth. So, first, the Rapture will occur seven years before the Second Advent. At that time Christ will take us to be with Him in heaven, immediately before the seven-year tribulation period. Then second, we will return to earth with Him at His Second Advent.

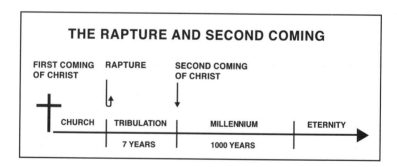

There is another important difference. There are no events that must take place before the Rapture occurs. It's all a matter of God's perfect timing. When I preached that signs are developing concerning the Lord's return, I referred to events that must yet occur before the return of Christ in the Second Advent.

The prophecies I spoke of concern the Second Advent, but that does not mean that the Rapture doesn't figure into prophecy. Future events cast shadows that are precursors to their coming. Since the Rapture takes place seven years before the Second Advent, the signs that point to the Second Advent cast shadows that clue us in to the imminent Rapture. The fact that the Rapture precedes the Second Advent makes the signs portending the Advent all the more immediate and ominous. For those who are left behind, the Rapture will give irrefutable confirmation of end-time events, seven years before they come to pass.

The New Testament indicates that the Rapture of those who have put their trust in Christ is the next major event on the prophetic calendar. In other words, the Rapture awaits us on the horizon—it could happen at any moment. This is the clear message of the Bible, and it is a truth I have taught consistently for more than thirty years.

Unraveling the Rapture

The apostle Paul was the first to reveal the details of the Rapture. He wrote of it in his first letter to the Corinthians, but it was in his first letter to the church in Thessalonica that he presented his most concise teaching on the subject.

Like many today, the Christians in that city were confused about the events that would take place in the future. They, too, wondered what in the world was going on. While they believed that Jesus was coming back someday, they could not figure out what would happen to their Christian parents and loved ones who had already died. So Paul wrote to instruct them concerning God's plan for both the living and the dead in the Rapture. In this writing, he explained in detail exactly what the Rapture is all about.

> But I do not want you to be ignorant, brethren, concerning those who have fallen asleep, lest you sorrow as others who have no hope. For if we believe that Jesus died and rose again, even so God will bring with Him those who sleep in Jesus.
>
> For this we say to you by the word of the Lord, that we who are alive and remain until the coming of the Lord will by no means precede those who are asleep. For the Lord Himself will descend from heaven with a shout, with the voice of an archangel, and with the trumpet of God. And the dead in Christ will rise first. Then we who are alive and remain shall be caught up together with them in the clouds to meet the Lord in the air. And thus we shall always be with the Lord. Therefore comfort one another with these words. (1 Thessalonians 4:13–18)

This passage tells us all we need to know about the Rapture. Let's look more deeply into what Paul said, point by point. First, he wrote: "But I do not want you to be ignorant, brethren, concerning those who have fallen asleep, lest you sorrow as others who have no hope" (1 Thessalonians 4:13). In this statement, the apostle addressed the ignorance of the Thessalonians concerning the state of those who had died believing in Christ. The word he used to describe that state has great significance for every believer today. Paul said that they had fallen asleep. For the word translated *asleep*, he used the Greek word *koimao*, which has as one of its meanings, "to sleep in death." The same word is used to describe the deaths of Lazarus, Stephen, David, and Jesus Christ (*emphasis added in the following examples*):

Lazarus: "These things He said, and after that He said to them,
'Our friend Lazarus *sleeps*, but I go that I may wake him
up.'" (John 11:11)

Stephen: "Then he [Stephen] knelt down and cried out with a
loud voice, 'Lord, do not charge them with this sin.' And
when he had said this, he *fell asleep*." (Acts 7:60)

David: "For David, after he had served his own generation by
the will of God, *fell asleep*, was buried with his fathers, and
saw corruption." (Acts 13:36)

Jesus Christ: "But now Christ is risen from the dead, and has
become the firstfruits of those who have *fallen asleep*."
(1 Corinthians 15:20)

This concept of death is emphasized in the wonderful word early
Christians adopted for the burying places of their loved ones. It was
the Greek word *koimeterion*, which means "a rest house for strangers,
a sleeping place." It is the word from which we get our English word
cemetery. In Paul's day, this word was used for inns or what we would
call a hotel or motel. We check in at a Hilton Hotel or a Ramada Inn,
expecting to spend the night in sleep before we wake up in the morning refreshed and raring to go. That is exactly the thought Paul
expressed in words such as *koimao* and *koimeterion*. When Christians
die, it's as if they are slumbering peacefully in a place of rest, ready to
be awakened at the return of the Lord. The words have great import,
for they convey the Christian concept of death, not as a tragic finality,
but as a temporary sleep.

In the next part of the Thessalonian passage, we find Paul affirm-
ing their hopes that their loved ones will live again. He did this by
tying that hope to the Resurrection and the Rapture: "lest you sorrow

as others who have no hope. For if we believe that Jesus died and rose again, even so God will bring with Him those who sleep in Jesus" (1 Thessalonians 4:13c–14). Here Paul tells the Thessalonians (and us) that God's plan for our future gives us such a new perspective on death that when someone we love dies, we are not overcome with sorrow and despair, for on that day when those who are alive in Christ are raptured, those who died in Christ will be raised to be with Him.

Paul reasoned that Christians can believe this promise of resurrection because it is backed up by the resurrection of Christ Himself. The logic is simple: if we believe that Jesus died and rose again, is it hard to believe His promise that He can perform the same miracle for us and those we love?

Paul did not forbid us to grieve; it is natural to feel sorrow when a loved one passes away, even when that loved one is a Christian. We miss the person terribly, and as Tennyson put it, we long for "the touch of a vanished hand and the sound of a voice that is still."[4] Jesus Himself wept by the tomb of Lazarus. But because of our Lord's promise of resurrection, we are not to grieve the way non-Christians do—as people to whom death is the ultimate tragedy—for they have no grounds for hope.

Tim LaHaye is the coauthor of the famous Left Behind series, which at last count had sold more than sixty-five million books. He became fascinated with the doctrine of the Rapture as a nine-year-old boy at his father's grave. He wrote:

> My love for second-coming teachings, particularly the Rapture of the church, was sparked as I stood at my father's grave at the age of nine. His sudden death of a heart attack left me devastated. My pastor, who

also was my uncle, pointed his finger toward heaven and proclaimed, "This is not the last of Frank LaHaye. Because of his personal faith in Christ, one day he will be resurrected by the shout of the Lord; we will be translated to meet him and our other loved ones in the clouds and be with them and our Lord forever." That promise from Scripture was the only hope for my broken heart that day. And that same promise has comforted millions of others through the years.[5]

As Dr. LaHaye said, the promise of the Rapture has comforted millions, and it is right that it should, for it is a promise we can depend on to be utterly sound.

The Chronological Program of the Rapture

As Paul continued in his letter to the Thessalonians, he wrote: "For this we say to you by the word of the Lord" (1 Thessalonians 4:15a).

Here Paul affirms that what he is about to say is by divine authority. He is authorized to say it "by the word of the Lord." This bold assertion suggests that what followed was not to be taken lightly because it was a revelation given directly to the apostle by God himself. In 1 Corinthians, Paul referred to the Rapture as a "mystery" (15:51). And the biblical definition of a mystery is "a truth that has not been revealed before."

Having established his authority to reveal what had formerly been a mystery, Paul went on to explain the first of the sequence of events that make up the Rapture.

There Will Be an Order of Priority

Paul then told the Thessalonians, "we who are alive and remain until the coming of the Lord will by no means precede those who are asleep" (1 Thessalonians 4:15b). Here Paul was saying that not only will those who have died in Christ be present at the return of the Lord, but they will actually have a place of priority. He said that those who are alive at the Rapture will not be taken up to Christ ahead of "those who are asleep," which means all believers who have died prior to the Rapture.

There is a linguistic root we need to examine here. The Greek word *phthano* in this verse means "come before, precede." When the Greek was translated into the English of the King James era, the word "prevent" was used because it then carried the meaning "to go or arrive before." Over many years, *prevent* has come to mean "to keep from happening." The emphatic point of this verse is that we will "by no means precede those who are asleep" in Christ. Those who have died believing in Christ will take precedence over us in the Rapture.

There Will Be a Return

Paul continued by saying, "For the Lord Himself will descend from heaven with a shout, with the voice of an archangel, and with the trumpet of God" (1 Thessalonians 4:16a).

As you read these words, the Lord Jesus Christ is seated in the heavens at the right hand of the Almighty Father. But when the right moment comes, He will initiate the Rapture by literally and physically rising from the throne, stepping into the corridors of light, and actually descending into the atmosphere of planet Earth from which He rose into the heavens over the Mount of Olives two thousand years ago. It is not the angels or the Holy Spirit but the Lord Himself who is coming to draw believers into the heavens in the Rapture.

The details of this passage paint an amazingly complete sensory picture of the Rapture. Paul even gave the sounds that will be heard—a shout, the voice of an archangel, and the trumpet of God. The purpose and relationship of these three sounds have generated considerable discussion. Some have claimed that the shout is for the church, the archangel's voice is for the Jews, and the trumpet is for all gentile believers. But these claims are mistaken. The three allusions to sounds are not to be taken as coordinate but rather as subordinate. Paul was not describing three separate sounds; he was describing only one sound in three different ways.

This sound will be like a shout, ringing with command authority like the voice of an archangel. It will also be like the blare of a trumpet in its volume and clarity. And the sound will be exclusively directed— heard only by those who have placed their trust in Christ. When Jesus raised Lazarus from the dead, he shouted "Lazarus, come forth!" (John 11:43). I've heard Bible students speculate as to what might have happened had Jesus forgotten to mention Lazarus's name. Would all the dead within the range of His voice have emerged from their graves? At the Rapture that is exactly what will happen. His shout of "Come forth!" will not name a single individual, but it will be heard by every believer in every grave around the world. All those tombs will empty, and the resurrected believers will fly skyward.

This arising from the grave was the hope that Winston Churchill movingly expressed in the planning of his own funeral. Following the prayer by the archbishop of Canterbury and the singing of "God Save the Queen," a trumpeter perched in the highest reaches of the dome of St. Paul's Cathedral sounded "The Last Post" (or "Taps" as we know it). As the last sorrowful note faded, "high in another gallery, sounded the stronger blaring 'Reveille.'"[6] The call to sleep was followed by a call to arise.

There Will Be a Resurrection

As Paul continued his writing to the Thessalonians, he asserted that the expectation expressed by believers such as Churchill is not vain. The coming resurrection is a reality. Paul wrote, "And the dead in Christ will rise first" (1 Thessalonians 4:16*b*). As he indicates here, the call to resurrection at the Rapture will not summon all the dead, but believers only. A time will come much later when *all* the dead will be raised to stand before the white throne in judgment. But at this first call, our believing loved ones who have already died will arise to take first place in the program of the Rapture.

There Will Be a Rapture

Paul explained the next event in the Rapture sequence: "Then we who are alive and remain shall be caught up" (1 Thessalonians 4:17*a*). The words *caught up* are translated from a Greek word that has as one of its meanings "to snatch out or away speedily." This word emphasizes the sudden nature of the Rapture. Paul described this suddenness in his letter to the Corinthians: ". . . in a moment, in the twinkling of an eye, at the last trumpet. For the trumpet will sound, and the dead will be raised incorruptible, and we shall be changed" (1 Corinthians 15:52).

In a split second the Lord will call all believers to Himself to share in His glory; not one will remain behind. It is hard to imagine just what that will be like, but I read a paragraph recently that created this vivid picture:

> Millions of people from all parts of the earth feel a tingling sensation pulsating throughout their bodies. They are all suddenly energized. Those with physical deformities are healed. The blind suddenly see.

Wrinkles disappear on the elderly as their youth is restored. As these people marvel at their physical transformation, they are lifted skyward. Those in buildings pass right through the ceiling and roof without pain or damage. Their flesh and bones seem to dematerialize, defying all known laws of physics and biology. As they travel heavenward, some of them see and greet those who have risen from their graves. After a brief mystical union . . . they all vanish from sight.[7]

Lest such pictures as this lead us to think the Rapture is a fanciful, futuristic dream, we find such experiences validated historically. Throughout the Bible, we have records of several people who had actual experiences very similar to the Rapture:

Enoch: "By faith Enoch was taken away so that he did not see death, 'and was not found, because God had taken him'; for before he was taken he had this testimony, that he pleased God." (Hebrews 11:5)

Elijah: "Then it happened, as they continued on and talked, that suddenly a chariot of fire appeared with horses of fire, and separated the two of them; and Elijah went up by a whirlwind into heaven." (2 Kings 2:11)

Paul: "I know a man in Christ who fourteen years ago—whether in the body I do not know, or whether out of the body I do not know, God knows—such a one, was *caught up* to the third heaven. And I know such a man—whether in the body or out of the body I do not know, God knows—how he was *caught up* into Paradise and heard inexpressible words, which it is not lawful for a man to utter." (2 Corinthians 12:2–4, *emphasis added*)

I find it significant that twice in this passage Paul used the words *caught up*, which are translated from the word meaning "rapture" in the Greek language.

> Jesus Christ: "And while they looked steadfastly toward heaven as He went up, behold, two men stood by them in white apparel, who also said, 'Men of Galilee, why do you stand gazing up into heaven? This same Jesus, who was taken up from you into heaven, will so come in like manner as you saw Him go into heaven.'" (Acts 1:10–11)

These records affirm the utter reality of the Rapture by providing us with prototypes of sorts to show that God can accomplish this coming event He promises to His people.

There Will Be a Reunion

Paul continued his explanation of the Rapture: "Then we who are alive and remain shall be caught up together with them [the believing dead who have arisen] in the clouds to meet the Lord in the air. And thus we shall always be with the Lord" (1 Thessalonians 4:17). Note that Paul began here with the word *then*, which is an adverb indicating sequence. It connects the previous events of the Rapture that we have already considered with this final event in a definite order of sequential reunions as follows:

1. Dead bodies reunited with their spirits

2. Resurrected believers reunited with living believers

3. Resurrected believers and raptured believers meet the Lord

As Paul pointed out, the ultimate consequence of this reunion with the Lord is that there will be no subsequent parting. After His return, our union and communion with Him will be uninterrupted and eternal. This glorious fact alone shows us why the word *rapture* is an altogether appropriate term for this event.

The Comforting Purpose of the Rapture

After completing his description of the Rapture to the Thessalonians, Paul wrapped up the passage with this practical admonition: "Therefore comfort one another with these words" (1 Thessalonians 4:18).

Here the apostle was telling both the Thessalonians and believers today that it's not enough simply to passively understand what was just explained about the Rapture, Christian death, and the Resurrection. Our understanding should spur us toward a certain action—to "comfort one another." And in the preceding verses he gave exactly the kind of information that makes true comfort possible. When believers suffer the loss of family members or dearly loved friends, we have in Paul's descriptions of Christian death and resurrection all that is needed to comfort each other in these losses. Christian death is not permanent; it is merely a sleep. A time is coming when we and our loved ones will be reunited in a rapturous meeting, when Christ Himself calls us out of this world or out of our graves to be with Him forever in an ecstatic relationship of eternal love. Nineteenth-century Bible teacher A. T. Pierson made this interesting observation about these things:

It is a remarkable fact that in the New Testament, so far as I remember, it is never once said, after Christ's resurrection, that a disciple died—that is, without some qualification: Stephen *fell asleep*. David, after he had served his own generation by the will of God *fell asleep and was laid with his father*. Peter says, "Knowing that I must shortly *put off this my tabernacle* as the Lord showed me." Paul says, "*the time of my departure is at hand."* (The figure here is taken from a vessel that, as she leaves a dock, throws the cables off the fastenings, and opens her sails to the wind to depart for the haven) . . . The only time where the word "dead" is used, it is with qualification: "the *dead in Christ,*" "the *dead which die in the Lord.*"[8]

As Pierson implies, Christ abolished death so completely that even the term *death* is no longer appropriate for believers. That is why Paul wrote that we should comfort one another with reminders that for Christians, what we call death is nothing more than a temporary sleep before we are called into our uninterrupted relationship with Christ forever.

Today as never before, we are beginning to see the signs of our Lord's impending return. Some of these signs we have already covered—the rebirth of Israel as a nation, the growing crises over oil, the reformation of Europe in accordance with Daniel's prophecy, and the growth of militant, radical Islam. All these developments point toward that day when our Lord will come to rapture His followers out of this world.

I believe it is the Rapture that will trigger the cataclysmic upheavals that will ravage the earth for the seven years that follow it. The Tribulation will come about by the law of natural consequences. According to Jesus, Christians are the salt and light of the world (Matthew 5:13–14). Salt prevents decay; light proclaims truth. When all the Christians in the entire world are removed from the earth in one day, all the salt and all the light will suddenly be gone. The result is predictable. You may think the world today is degenerating into rampant greed and immorality, and indeed it is. But as bad as things are becoming, we can hardly overstate the horror that will occur when society loses the tempering influence of Christians.

As the Bible teaches, every believer in Christ is indwelt by the Holy Spirit. This means the Holy Spirit ministers to today's world through followers of Christ. When all Christians are removed from the earth, the restraining ministry of the Holy Spirit will be completely absent. No salt! No light! No indwelling Spirit of God! The result will be horrific. Jesus himself described what will happen next: "For then there will be great tribulation, such as has not been since the beginning of the world until this time, no, nor ever shall be. And unless those days were shortened, no flesh would be saved" (Matthew 24:21–22).

As these dire words are being fulfilled during the Tribulation period, we who are followers of Christ will have already been raptured to heaven. This is another source of great comfort for Christians. No promise has been more precious to believers than the one made to the church of Philadelphia in Revelation: "Because you have kept My command to persevere, I also will keep you from the hour of trial which shall come upon the whole world, to test those who dwell on the earth" (Revelation 3:10).

Please note that our Lord's promise is not merely to keep us *in* the hour of trial, but rather *from* the hour of trial. As Paul wrote, "God did not appoint us to wrath, but to obtain salvation through our Lord Jesus Christ" (1 Thessalonians 5:9). The promise is that we who are believers will not experience the horrors of the Tribulation, and this is an enormous source of comfort.

How Shall We then Live?

We have been given two directives as to how we should live as we anticipate Christ's return. We should be looking for Him and living for Him.

We Should Be Looking for the Lord

Paul warned us in three of his letters to be alert and watchful for the Lord's return:

Looking for the blessed hope and glorious appearing of our great God and Savior Jesus Christ. (Titus 2:13)

For our citizenship is in heaven, from which we also eagerly wait for the Savior, the Lord Jesus Christ. (Philippians 3:20)

And to wait for His Son from heaven, whom He raised from the dead, even Jesus who delivers us from the wrath to come. (1 Thessalonians 1:10)

Wayne Grudem suggests that the degree to which we are actually longing for Christ's return is a measure of our spiritual condition. As he explains:

The more Christians are caught up in enjoying the good things of this life, and the more they neglect genuine Christian fellowship and their personal relationship with Christ, the less they will long for His return. On the other hand, many Christians who are experiencing suffering or persecution, or who are more elderly and infirm, and those whose daily walk with Christ is vital and deep, will have a more intense longing for His return.[9]

As Dr. Grudem suggests, the idea is not merely to watch for Jesus' coming as we might watch for a storm in a black cloud, but rather to anticipate it as something we look forward to and long for.

We Should Be Living for the Lord

The three great apostles, Paul, Peter, and John, all had something to say about how we should live in the face of Christ's impending return:

For the grace of God that brings salvation has appeared to all men, teaching us that, denying ungodliness and worldly lusts, we should live soberly, righteously, and godly in the present age, looking for the blessed hope and glorious appearing of our great God and Savior Jesus Christ, who gave Himself for us, that He might redeem us from every lawless deed and purify for Himself His own special people, zealous for good works. (Titus 2:11–14)

Therefore, since all these things will be dissolved, what manner of persons ought you to be in holy conduct and godliness. (2 Peter 3:11)

Beloved, now are we children of God; and it has not yet been revealed what we shall be, but we know that when He is revealed, we shall be like Him, for we shall see Him as He is. And everyone who has this hope in Him purifies himself, just as He is pure. (1 John 3:2–3)

You would think it obvious that since signs tell us that Christ is coming soon, people would take extra care to live as God would have them live—lives of purity and holiness. If you know that guests are coming soon to your home but you don't know exactly when they will arrive, you will keep your house swept, picked up, and dusted in anticipation. You don't want them ringing your doorbell with your dishes piled in the sink, beds unmade, and mud prints tracking the carpet. The admonitions of Paul, Peter, and John to stay ready by living pure and holy lives are hardly more than just plain common sense. But common sense does not always prevail in the lives of fallen humans, and that is why these apostles felt it worthwhile to admonish us to live as if Jesus could come at any moment. The fact is He can.

Two years after the wildfires of 2003, San Diego regional authorities installed Reverse 9-1-1. The early warning system was first used to warn residents of the approaching wildfires of 2007. Some home owners, however, did not receive a call or had phone systems that screened out the warning call as an unrecognized number. Others received the call but chose to ignore it. Some of those who did not hear the warning did not vacate their homes and, as a result, lost their lives.[10]

God has sounded the warnings loudly and clearly. They have come through His prophets in the Old Testament, through New Testament writers, and even through Jesus Himself. The firestorm is coming in the form of the seven years of tribulation, when no Christian influence will temper the evil that will plunge the earth into a cauldron of misery and devastation. But you can avoid the destruction and be evacuated. You can enter your name on the list of those who will hear the trumpet call of the Rapture by turning to Christ and beginning to live the pure and holy life that characterizes those who will enter heaven. As the apostle John wrote: "But there shall by no means enter it [the heavenly city of God] anything that defiles, or causes an abomination or a lie, but only those who are written in the Lamb's Book of Life" (Revelation 21:27).

If your name is not in that book, when the Rapture occurs you will be left behind to experience horrors worse than anything the world has yet seen. I hope you will not wait another day; turn to Jesus Christ now, before it is too late, and become one of those who will hear His call on that great and terrible day.

SIX

Does America Have a Role in Prophecy?

EVERY DAY WHEN THE SUN RISES OVER WASHINGTON DC, ITS first rays fall on the eastern side of the city's tallest structure, the 555-foot Washington Monument. The first part of that monument to reflect the rising sun is the eastern side of its aluminum capstone, where these words are inscribed: *Laus Deo*, Latin for "Praise be to God." This compact prayer of praise, visible to the eyes of heaven alone, is tacit recognition of our nation's unique acknowledgment of the place of God in its founding and its continuance.[1]

Were these words merely a grandiose but empty claim to national piety, or do they reflect a true reality? In the introduction to the book *The Light and the Glory,* authors Peter Marshall and David Manuel ask a very profound question:

> What if Columbus' discovering of America had not been accidental at all? What if it were merely the opening curtain of an extraordinary

drama? Did God have a special plan for America? . . . What if He dealt with whole nations like He dealt with individuals? What if in particular He had a plan for those He would bring to America, a plan which saw this continent as a stage for a new era in the drama of mankind's redemption?[2]

President Ronald Reagan believed that God did have a plan for our nation. He wrote, "I have always believed that this anointed land was set apart in an uncommon way, that a divine plan placed this great continent here between the oceans to be found by people from every corner of the earth who had a special love of faith and freedom."[3]

The Sovereignty of God in the Founding of America

I am convinced that references such as the preceding three are not in vain. It seems clear that God *does* have a plan for America. It is true that we have no direct reference to that plan in the Old or New Testament, but that does not discount the evident fact that God has a sovereign purpose for America in His redemptive plan.

As authors Marshall and Manuel suggest, God's hand on America began with its discoverer. In the rotunda of the Capitol Building is a great painting entitled *The Landing of Columbus,* depicting his arrival on the shores of America. As Marshall asserts, the great explorer discovered the New World "by accident," but yet *not* by accident. God had His hand upon the wheel of the ship and brought it here.

Columbus was not oblivious to God's providence in his discovery. In his journal, Columbus expressed his literal belief that "his voyages were ushering in a millennial age . . . and initiat[ing] a messianic period." He was firmly convinced that Isaiah's words, "so shall they fear the name of the LORD from the west" (Isaiah 59:19), referred to the lands west of Europe that had not yet been discovered. The journal from his first voyage shows that the primary purpose of his explorations was to take the message of salvation through Jesus Christ to the people in this unknown land.[4]

Throughout our nation's history we see America's leaders turning to God for guidance. We see Washington kneeling in the snow of Valley Forge. We see our Founding Fathers on their knees at the first Continental Congress. We see the gaunt Lincoln praying in the hour of national crisis. We see Woodrow Wilson reading his Bible late at night by the White House lights. Washington summarized this national dependence on God, which was evident before his time and continued after him, when he said, "No people can be bound to acknowledge and adore the invisible hand which conducts the affairs of man more than those of the United States."[5]

Clearly America did not become the land of the free and the home of the brave by blind fate or a happy set of coincidences. A benevolent God was hovering over this nation from her very conception so that today, although America has only 5 percent of the world's population, she has more than 50 percent of the modern luxuries that characterize civilization.

Why has God blessed this nation above all other lands? Why has America in her short history outstripped the wealth, power, and influence of all ancient and modern civilizations? Can God have blessed a nation so richly without having for her a pivotal purpose? What is God's plan for America? What is its place in end-time prophecy? These are questions many people are asking today as they watch events coalesce toward world crises. They wonder how America fits into what is going on in the world.

In order to understand America's place in end-time prophecy, we must first answer the question we raised in the previous paragraph: Why has America been blessed above all other lands? Let's explore the reasons for God's favor on America, and then we will show what this means in terms of coming events.

America Has Been the Force Behind World Missions

"To the United States belongs the distinction of providing three-fourths of the missionaries of the last century and approximately the same amount of money and material aid."[6] This means that 75 percent of all missionaries have come from a country boasting only 5 percent of the total world population. God blesses those who make His priorities their priorities. The church I pastor in California is a case in point. More than fifteen years ago that church committed to give to world missions the first 20 percent of every dollar received in offerings. When we started that program back in the early '90s, our missions budget was not quite $250,000 per year. Today it is well over ten times that figure. God loves the world. He loves the people who are yet to hear the gospel. When we love whom He loves, He blesses us. And I believe that principle applies to our nation as well as to our church.

God has blessed America because we have been the launching pad of the world's great missionary movement. In the aftermath of World War II, Americans started 1,800 missions agencies and sent out more than 350,000 missionaries.[7] And as a result, "today, 95 percent of the world's population have access, not only to some portion of Scripture in their language, but also to Christian radio broadcasts, audio recordings, and the *Jesus* film."[8] That achievement is due largely to the missionary zeal of churches in the United States.

America Has Been a Friend to the Jewish People

Ever since the turn of the twentieth century, Jews have made up 3 percent of the total population of the United States, where they have been protected from harassment and anti-Semitism. America has given Jews opportunity for economic, educational, and cultural advancement without fear of losing their religious freedom.

America's historic support of Israel is based not so much on efforts by Jewish lobbyists in Washington or the presence of Jewish groups in our society, but on the Judeo-Christian heritage of our nation. President Truman's determination to recognize Israel as a modern state was fueled by his lifelong belief that in the book of Deuteronomy, God had given the land of Israel to the Jewish people for all time.

At the founding of the modern state of Israel, surrounding Arab nations immediately declared war on the new nation. Few felt Israel could survive, and western nations did not want to become embroiled in the conflict. Truman was under pressure not to intervene. In a dramatic speech to seek support before the United Nations, the Jewish statesman Abba Eban said:

> Israel is the product of the most sustained historic tenacity which the ages recall. The Jewish people have not striven toward this goal for twenty centuries in order that, having once achieved it, it will surrender it in response to an illegitimate and unsuccessful aggression. Whatever else changes, this will not. The state of Israel is an immutable part of the international landscape. To plan the future without it is to build delusions on the sand.[9]

In spite of Eban's eloquent plea, the young nation was in great danger. Both US and UN recognition of Israel were in serious doubt.

Following his speech, Eban flew to Paris to meet with an American delegation regarding recognition. Secretary of State George Marshall, whose support of Israel was tepid at best, had to return home for medical treatment. His deputy, John Foster Dulles, assumed leadership of the delegation.

Eban later wrote that Dulles held the key to the success of the talks. "Behind a dry manner, redolent of oak-paneled courtrooms in the United States, there *was a curious strain of Protestant mysticism* which led him to give the Israel questions a larger importance that its geopolitical weight would indicate"[10] (*emphasis added*).

What Eban called "a curious strain of Protestant mysticism" is actually the historic love that Christians have for the land and people of Israel, based upon their shared religious heritage and scriptures. This, more than anything else, has cemented the friendship between America and Israel for more than sixty years.

As we discovered in the first chapter of this book, God has promised to bless those who bless Israel (Genesis 12:1–3). He has amply fulfilled that promise. America has been abundantly blessed as a nation because we have blessed the Jews.

America Has Been a Free Nation

In my studies of both the Old and New Testaments, I have observed that the principles of freedom are united with the tenets of Christianity. America today is the laboratory where those blended principles can grow and develop and become an example to all the world. The Bible says, "You shall know the truth, and the truth shall make you free" (John 8:32).

Freedom can never be taken for granted in our world. In early 2007, Freedom House released its annual survey, *Freedom in the World*, which stated that 3 billion people—46 percent of the world's population—live in a free to partly free country. Conversely, 54 percent—or more than half the population of the world—do not live in freedom.[11] In fact, the tendency in a fallen world is always away from freedom and toward despotism and tyranny.

In his 1981 inaugural address, President Ronald Reagan spoke of our freedom in these stirring words: "Above all, we must realize that no arsenal or no weapon in the arsenals of the world is so formidable as the will and moral courage of free men and women. It is a weapon our adversaries in today's world do not have. It is a weapon that we as Americans do have. Let that be understood by those who practice terrorism and prey upon their neighbors."[12]

America has learned what our repressive and terrorist adversaries do not understand: that liberty without law is anarchy, liberty to defy law is rebellion, but liberty limited by law is the cornerstone of civilization. We Americans have tried to share what we have learned by exporting freedom wherever we have gone in the world. We have tried to help people understand that freedom is what creates the life God intended us to have from the very beginning.

America has become the paradise of human liberty—a great oasis in a global desert of trouble, suffering, repression, and tyranny. Our nation is a dramatic exclamation point to the assertion that freedom works!

Today our precious heritage of freedom is being challenged internally by the erosion of our culture. As long-held freedoms come under fire, some Americans, especially those with wealth, are deciding that the United States is no longer the best place to live. According to the book *Getting Out: Your Guide to Leaving America,* some three hundred thousand Americans a year are choosing to leave the country. This is the first time in history that the number of people exiting this nation has become large enough to be significant, and the emergence of such a trend calls our attention to the degenerating character of America. If our culture continues to jettison the principles that made our nation great, we can hardly expect the blessing of Almighty God to continue.

America Has Been Founded on God and His Word

It is no mystery why America's founders insisted on the principle of freedom. Their dependence on the God of the Bible led them to subject themselves to Him as the ultimate authority for law rather than set themselves up as autocrats with the audacity to control the lives of their subjects. And because they submitted to God's authority, He has blessed this nation as none has ever been blessed. The Psalmist wrote, "Blessed is the nation whose God is the LORD, the people He has chosen as His own inheritance" (Psalm 33:12). The book of Proverbs adds, "Righteousness exalts a nation, but sin is a reproach to any people" (14:34).

I opened this chapter with a brief look at how America's founders and early leaders exhibited humble reliance on Almighty God. Now I want to show how that godly dependence characterized our governmental philosophy through several generations and resulted in God's blessings on our nation. Our leaders stabilized government with a lifeline between their country and their God, with authority and blessing flowing downward as dependence and thanksgiving flowed upward.

George Washington set the tone for the nation's governmental authority when he said, "It is impossible to rightly govern the world without God and the Bible."[13] That philosophy remained intact through the time of Abraham Lincoln, who is quoted as saying, "God is my witness that it is my constant anxiety and prayer that both myself and this nation should be on the Lord's side."[14]

Benjamin Franklin explained why he requested that each day of the Constitutional Convention be opened in prayer, saying: "The longer I live, the more convincing proofs I see of the truth—that God governs in the affairs of Men. And," he continued, "without His aid, we shall succeed in this political building no better than the builders of Babel."[15]

Henry Wilson (1812–1875) was a US senator and vice president under Ulysses S. Grant from 1873 to 1875. On December 23, 1866, he spoke to a YMCA gathering in Natick, Massachusetts, where he said:

> Remember ever, and always, that your country was founded, not by the "most superficial, the lightest, the most irreflective of all European races," but by the stern old Puritans who made the deck of the *Mayflower* an altar of the living God, and whose first act on touching the soil of the new world was to offer on bended knees thanksgiving to Almighty God.[16]

In 1911, President Woodrow Wilson said:

> The Bible . . . is the one supreme source of revelation of the meaning of life, the nature of God and spiritual nature and needs of men. It is the only guide of life which really leads the spirit in the way of peace and salvation. America was born a Christian nation. America was born to exemplify that devotion to the elements of righteousness which are derived from the revelations of Holy Scripture.[17]

Today as I write these words, our heritage of national dependence on God is under fire. Forces within our nation threaten its divine lifeline. The attitude of many in our culture today seems symbolized by the powerful legal tides now trying to remove the words *under God* from the Pledge of Allegiance. Those two words were inserted into the pledge in 1954, partly to distinguish our nation from the atheistic communism of the Soviet Union. But while these words came late to the pledge, they certainly reflected what had been a part of America's heritage from the beginning.

For example, on July 2, 1776, General George Washington wrote in the general orders to his men that day, "The fate of unborn millions will now depend, *under God*, on the courage and conduct of this army."[18] Almost a hundred years later, Abraham Lincoln consecrated the military cemetery on the battlefield of Gettysburg, saying: "We here highly resolved that these dead shall not have died in vain; that this nation, *under God,* shall have a new birth of freedom; and that government of the people, by the people, for the people, shall not perish from the earth" (*emphasis added*).[19]

This recognition that our nation was founded on godly principles of freedom and divine authority continued to be the basic assumption of government through the middle of the twentieth century. Our leaders realized that once America failed to acknowledge that we were under God, our basis for freedom and equitable government would come crashing down. President Calvin Coolidge said it well: "The foundation of our society and our government rests so much on the teachings of the Bible that it would be difficult to support them if faith in these teachings would cease to be practically universal in our country."[20] In other words, when America turns from its position of being under God, we can no longer expect His blessings on this nation to continue. We will have broken our lifeline.

As I've been writing this book, two attempts to hack through that lifeline were exposed. At a Dallas-area elementary school, one parent complained that the national motto, "In God We Trust," was painted on a wall in the gym. The school board promptly had the offending words painted over. When several parents complained about its abrupt removal, Texas law and Texas Education Code prevailed, causing a school district representative to admit the district had "made a mistake" and announced, "'In God We Trust' will be repainted on the wall."[21]

Do you remember the capstone of the Washington Monument I wrote about at the beginning of this chapter? Since the actual inscription is not visible at its stately height, the National Park Service has maintained a replica capstone in an exhibit at the 490-foot level. Located near a wall detailing the construction of the monument, the capstone case was positioned such that the public could see the inscription. However, late last year, the display was changed. The case was repositioned against the wall and turned so the east side inscription *Laus Deo* was no longer viewable. A previous reference to that inscription was also omitted from the new description tag on the exhibit. When some citizens complained of the unacceptable modifications, an NPS official responded by saying, "We made a mistake and we are fixing it."[22]

More than a mistake, these removals are an assault. Almost routinely these days, attacks are made on any public reminder of our dependence on God's grace for our national existence. I fear our lifeline is fraying.

The Silence of the Bible on the Future of America

Dr. Tim LaHaye wrote, "One of the hardest things for American prophecy students to accept is that the United States is not clearly mentioned in Bible prophecy, yet our nation is the only superpower in the world today."[23] Indeed, no specific mention of the United States or any other country in North or South America can be found in the Bible. One reason may be that in the grand scheme of history, the United States is a new kid on the block. As a nation, it is less than 250 years old—much younger than the nations of Bible times that are featured in biblical prophecy. In fact, the Bible makes no mention of most nations in the modern world. The ancient prophets were primarily concerned with the Holy Land and its immediate neighbors. Areas remote from Israel do not figure in prophecy and are not mentioned in the Bible.

Dr. LaHaye went on to raise this question:

"Does the United States have a place in end time prophecy?" My first response is no, there is nothing about the U.S. in prophecy. At least nothing that is specific. There is an allusion to a group of nations in Ezekiel 38:13 that could apply, but even that is not specific. The question is why? Why would the God of prophecy not refer to the supreme superpower nation in the end times in preparation for the one-world government of the Antichrist?[24]

The question has no one, simple answer, but it will help us understand what is going on in the world today if we look at some of the best thinking that students of prophecy have given us on why America is absent from end-time prophecies.

America Will Be Incorporated into the European Coalition

Our first answer comes from noted prophecy expert John Walvoord, who wrote:

Although the Scriptures do not give any clear word concerning the role of the United States in relation to the revived Roman Empire, it is clear this will be a consolidation of the power of the West. Unlike the coalitions led by the United States, this coalition will be led by others—the Group of Ten . . . Most citizens of the United States of America have come from Europe, and their sympathies would more naturally be with a European alliance than with Russia, Asia, and Africa . . . Europe and America may be in formal alliance with Israel in opposition to the radical Islamic countries of the Middle East.[25]

According to this theory, though America is not mentioned by name in prophecy, it will be in the mix of the political realignments that foreshadow the end of time. And we can see signs of such realignments taking place today.

With the usual presidential fanfare, President Bush welcomed EU Commission president Jos Barroso and the serving president of the European Council, German chancellor Angela Merkel, in the Rose Garden of the White House in April 2007. The president thanked the two for their part in "the trans-Atlantic economic integration plan that the three of us signed today. It is a statement of the importance of trade. It is a commitment to eliminating barriers to trade. It is a recognition that the closer that the United States and the EU become, the better off our people become. So this is a substantial agreement and I appreciate it."[26] The president went on to say, "I believe it's in this country's interests that we reject isolationism and protectionism and encourage free trade."

The agreement these three leaders signed is called "Framework for Advancing Transatlantic Economic Integration between the United

States of America and the European Union"—an appropriately long title for what one would expect to be a long process. But things moved swiftly. In less than seven months the Transatlantic Economic Council held its first official meeting in Washington DC. In a joint statement it was announced, "Since April, the United States and the European Union have made substantial progress in removing barriers to trade and investment and in easing regulatory burdens."[27]

On the surface there seems to be nothing ominous about such an agreement; it appears to be simply about freeing up economic trade between nations. But a similar, less publicized meeting was held in March 2008 at the State Department, which focused on linking the United States, Mexico, and Canada in a "North American community with the European Union" in anticipation of the "creation of a 'Transatlantic Economic Union' between the European Union and North America."[28] One participant—whose identity is protected by the Chatham House Rule, which permits information to be disseminated without attribution to guarantee confidentiality—made this revealing statement:

> North America should be a premiere platform to establish continental institutions. That's why we need to move the security perimeters to include the whole continent, especially as we open the borders between North American countries for expanding free trade.[29]

Statements such as this reveal an intention toward union that has implications far beyond mere economic trade. And considering the speed at which leaders are pushing union between nations, it appears that it will not be long before we see such a union instituted. What does this mean for America?

America Will Be Invaded by Outside Forces

Perhaps the silence of Scripture on the future of America indicates that by the time the Tribulation period arrives, America will have lost her influence in the world and will no longer be a major player. As we have noted, America's thirst for oil and our inability to close the gap between supply and demand could cripple our ability to defend our borders and protect our nation. Once again John Walvoord addresses the issue:

> Some maintain that the total absence of any scriptural reference to America in the end time is evidence that the United States will have been crippled by a nuclear attack, weapons of mass destruction, or some other major catastrophe . . . In the post 9/11 world the detonation of a dirty bomb, nuclear device, or biological weapon on U.S. soil is a dreaded yet distinct possibility. Such an attack could kill millions of people and reduce the United States to a second rate power overnight.[30]

Since the deployment of the first atomic bomb on the city of Hiroshima in August 1945, America has enjoyed a certain fear-based aura of invincibility. We now had the big stick, and we were the king of the hill. Both friends and enemies knew that we would use any and all weapons in our formidable arsenal to protect our nation. Even today, according to Ed Timperlake, who served in the Office of the Defense Secretary under Ronald Reagan, "Air Force and Navy personnel continue to stand vigilant 24 hours a day, seven days a week inside the strategic triad of bombers, land-based ICBMs and submarine 'boomers.'"[31]

In today's world, however, such power and vigilance may no longer deter enemies determined to attack the United States. In a truly frightening column in *The Washington Times*, Timperlake went on to observe: "a totally new dimension has emerged regarding a nuclear attack on America. The great tragedy of the murder of Benazir Bhutto brought the world's attention to the possibility of loose nukes falling into the hands of fanatics who would use them." In other words, the political instability in Pakistan could lead to nuclear warheads falling into the hands of radical Islamic jihadists. "It is certain," continued Timperlake, "that a nuclear weapon in the hands of fanatical jihadists will be used. The only current deterrence against its use is a worldwide hunt for the device before Israel, London, New York, or D.C. disappears in a flash."[32]

Timperlake went on to say that jihadists are not our only threat from a rogue nation armed with nuclear weapons. "What about the criminal state of North Korea or the vitriolic anti-Semitic nation of Iran?" he asked. "Either country for many perverse reasons can slip a device to a terrorist group."[33] As if to underscore his point, in late March of 2008, North Korea "test-fired a battery of short-range missiles" only one day after they "expelled South Korean officials from a joint industrial complex north of the border." The three "ship-to-ship missiles [were] launched into the sea."[34]

These enemies have different agendas, but they share a common disregard for human life and a burning hatred for the United States. While we would like to close our ears to predictions of impending disaster, experts such as Timperlake and others see a major attack on our country in the near future as virtually inevitable.

America Will Be Infected with Moral Decay

The average lifespan of all the world's greatest civilizations from the beginning of history has been about two hundred years. During that two-century span, each of these nations progressed through the following sequence: from bondage to spiritual faith; from spiritual faith to great courage; from courage to liberty; from liberty to abundance; from abundance to complacency; from complacency to apathy; from apathy to dependence; and from dependence back into bondage.[35]

At what point is America in this cycle? Popular blogger La Shawn Barber answered this question in an article titled, "America on the Decline." She wrote:

> In *The Decline and Fall of the Roman Empire*, author Edward Gibbon discusses several reasons for the great civilization's demise, including the undermining of the dignity and sanctity of the home and the decay of religion. America has been compared to the Roman Empire in secular and religious ways. Regardless of its ultimate legacy, America is a civilization on the decline. A couple of centuries from now (or sooner), someone will lament the loss of a once-great civilization that brought prosperity to the world and tried to make it safe for democracy. The glory that was the United States will lay in ruins, brought down not by terrorists but its own debauchery and complacency.[36]

Barber's analysis is right on the money with one exception: given the present situation in our world, another "couple of centuries" for America is not in the equation. Nevertheless, her analysis is perceptive, and she continues it by referencing an expert from decades past. In 1947, forward-looking sociologist Dr. Carle Zimmerman wrote a text called *Family and Civilization*. He identified eleven "symptoms of final decay" observable in the fall of both the Greek and Roman civilizations. See how many characterize our society:

1. No-fault divorce
2. "Birth Dearth"; increased disrespect for parenthood and parents
3. Meaningless marriage rites/ceremonies
4. Defamation of past national heroes
5. Acceptance of alternative marriage forms
6. Widespread attitudes of feminism, narcissism, hedonism
7. Propagation of antifamily sentiment
8. Acceptance of most forms of adultery
9. Rebellious children
10. Increased juvenile delinquency
11. Common acceptance of all forms of sexual perversion[37]

One cannot read lists such as these and doubt that America is throwing away its treasured position as the most blessed nation ever on the face of the earth. Remember, as we noted earlier, God blessed this country for a reason: our nation was founded on submission to Him. But now as the reasons for His blessings upon America are eroding, we can expect the blessings themselves to fade as well. It's a simple matter of cause and effect: remove the cause, and the effect ceases. Once, we invited God into our nation. From the first moments of our existence, we opened our national doors to Him and made Him welcome as our most honored guest. But now our culture seems bent on shutting Him out, as author Mike Evans laments:

> Most can remember the classic painting of Jesus standing outside a door waiting to be allowed entry. That poignant portrayal of Christ on the

outside, wanting to fellowship with His creation, has never been more powerful than it is today. Prayer has been excised from schools, suits have been filed to force Congress to remove "under God" from the Pledge of Allegiance, displays of the Ten Commandments have been removed from public buildings, and the motto, "In God We Trust," is in danger of extinction. Teachers have been forbidden even to carry a personal Bible in view of students, Christian literature has been removed from library shelves, religious Christmas carols have been banned from school programs, and "spring break" has replaced Easter vacation.[38]

Almost six decades ago, former president Herbert Hoover wrote a warning that I fear America has not heeded. After calling attention to several new programs and concepts, including "New Freedom" and "New Religion," Hoover stated, "We have overworked the word 'new' . . . The practical thing we can do, if we want to make the world over, is to try out the word 'Old' for a while. There are some 'old' things that made this country . . . Some old things are slipping badly in American life and if they slip too far, the lights will go out of America!" Among the old things he listed: "Old Virtues of religious faith, integrity and whole truth . . . honor in public office, economy in government, individual liberty . . . willingness to sacrifice . . . Our greatest danger is not from invasion by foreign armies. Our dangers are that we may commit suicide from within by complaisance with evil."[39]

It saddens me to say it, but I believe the signs make it certain that America is now infected with the deadly disease of moral decay. And as that infection eats away at our foundations, we can expect the law of cause and effect to come into play. Scripture often warns us that even a long-suffering God will not forever strive with men. If we ignore divine directives, we cannot expect God's blessing. A limb that cuts itself off from the trunk will not continue to live.

America Will Be Impotent Because of the Rapture

If the Rapture were to happen today and all the true believers in Jesus Christ disappeared into heaven in a single moment, America as we know it could be obliterated. It is estimated that at the Rapture, America will lose millions of citizens—all its Christians and their small children.[40] This means that not only would the country lose a minimum of 25 percent of her population, but she would also lose the very best, the "salt" and "light" of the nation. Who can imagine the chaos in our country when all the godly people disappear—enough to populate many vast cities—leaving only those who have rejected God? It is not a pretty picture. We who love Christ will be blessed by the Rapture in more ways than one. We not only will know the joy of being with our beloved Lord but also will be spared the horrors that the world will suffer through the evil of people left in the wake of the Rapture. It's like a reverse surgical operation—one in which all the healthy cells are removed and only the cancerous ones are left to consume one another.

Yet as we look back at all we have been learning, we who will be rescued cannot help but feel a sense of tension in our hearts. Yes, God will save us, but things we've never experienced are about to happen, and changes such as we've never imagined loom on the horizon. It is important to realize that God understands this internal tension. We do not sin by feeling uneasy. Perhaps it's a little like getting married. We anticipate the event with joy but also with butterflies in the stomach. It's not a matter of dread or wanting to draw back; it's merely a matter of our natural discomfort when facing new experiences. But in spite of the uneasiness, we approach with confidence the events we are anticipating because we know they were put into play by the Creator of the universe. He knows the end from the beginning, and because we are His friends, He is letting us in on the eternal secrets of His determined will.

In an article about the United States in prophecy, Herman A. Hoyt made a fine statement that makes a fitting conclusion to this chapter. He wrote:

> Since the promise of Christ's coming for the Church has always been held out to His people as an event that could take place at any moment, surely the events of the present hour in relation to the United States ought to give new stimulus to watch momentarily for His coming. In these days of crisis, our trust should not rest in a nation that may shortly disappear, but in Him who works all things after the counsel of His own will.[41]

Dr. Hoyt is right; what do we have to worry about? Our trust has never been in governments, civilizations, or cultures. By the standards of eternity, these institutions last but a moment, crumbling into dust to be swept away by the winds of history. They are helpful while they are here, but they have never been worthy of our trust. We have always put our trust in the One who stands above institutions, above history, and even above time itself—the One by whose power and permission these things exist, and who knows their times and the ends of their days. Only He is worthy of our ultimate allegiance.

SEVEN

When One Man Rules the World

WHEN I FIRST BEGAN STUDYING PROPHECY NEARLY FORTY YEARS ago, I encountered the Bible's prediction that one man would eventually take control of the entire world. Frankly, I could not imagine how such a thing would ever happen. But since the Bible presented this as a major part of the end-time landscape, I believed it, and I preached it even though I could not comprehend it.

Today it is much easier to envision the possibility of such a world ruler. Technology has given us instant global communication. CNN is seen everywhere in the world. The Internet and satellite cell phones reach every country on the face of the earth. Air transportation has shrunk the planet to the point where we can set foot on the soil of any nation in a matter of hours. I am told that there are now missiles that can reach any part of the world in fewer than thirty minutes. Men and nations no longer live in isolation.

There are also other factors that make the ascendance of a global leader more plausible than ever before. The Bible predicts that worldwide chaos, instability, and disorder will increase as we approach the end of this age. Jesus Himself said that there would be wars, rumors of wars, famines, and earthquakes in various places (Matthew 24:6–7). Just before these tensions explode into world chaos, the Rapture of the church will depopulate much of the planet. As many as seventy million people could suddenly disappear from our nation alone.

The devastation wrought by these disasters will spur a worldwide outcry for relief and order at almost any cost. That will set the stage for the emergence of a new world leader who will, like a pied piper, promise a solution to all problems. He will negotiate world peace and promise order and security. This leader, who will emerge out of the newly formed European Union, is commonly referred to in the Bible as the Antichrist.

The very word *antichrist* sends a shudder through the hearts of Christians. All have heard or read of him, and the fear that some feel at the mention of his name comes largely from misunderstandings and confusion about who he is, when he will appear, and what powers he can exercise over God's people. In this chapter I want to dispel those fears and clear up the confusion. I want to show you what is going on in the world as it relates to the biblical predictions and descriptions of the Antichrist and his work.

The word *antichrist* is used four times in the New Testament, each time by the apostle John, and it is found only in his epistles (1 John 2:18, 22; 4:3; and 2 John 7). As the word suggests, the Antichrist is a person who is against Christ. The prefix *anti* can also mean "instead of," and both meanings will apply to this coming world leader. He will overtly oppose Christ and at the same time pass himself off as Christ.

The Antichrist will aggressively live up to his terrible name. He will be Satan's superman, who persecutes, tortures, and kills the people of God and leads the armies of the world into the climactic Battle of Armageddon. He will be the most powerful dictator the world has ever seen, making Caesar, Hitler, Mao, and Saddam seem weak and tame by comparison.

Even though the Antichrist is identified by that name only four times in the Bible, he appears many more times under various aliases. He is also called:

- "the prince who is to come" (Daniel 9:26 NKJV)
- a "fierce" king (Daniel 8:23 NKJV)
- "a master of intrigue" (Daniel 8:23 NIV)
- "a despicable man" (Daniel 11:21 NLT)
- a "worthless shepherd" (Zechariah 11:16–17 NLT)
- "the one who brings destruction" (2 Thessalonians 2:3 NLT)
- "the lawless one" (2 Thessalonians 2:8 NKJV)
- "the evil man" (2 Thessalonians 2:9 NLT)
- the "beast" (Revelation 13:1 NKJV)

As a study of these references shows, the Antichrist is introduced and described in great detail in the Bible, yet his identity is not revealed. That lack of specific identification, however, has not stopped speculation on who he might be and even the outright naming of certain individuals. Many names have been suggested. When you google "Who is Antichrist?" you get about 1.5 million hits. Some of the Web sites post incredibly long and detailed articles—a sign of the extreme fascination generated by this sensational subject.

In the late 1930s and early 1940s, when Hitler was moving through Europe and swallowing up whole nations, many believed that he was the coming Antichrist.

> Hitler offered himself as a messiah with a divine mission to save Germany. On one occasion he displayed the whip he often carried to demonstrate that "in driving out the Jews I remind myself of Jesus in the temple." He declared, "Just like Christ, I have a duty to my own people." He even boasted that just as Christ's birth had changed the calendar, so his victory over the Jews would be the beginning of a new age. "What Christ began," he said, "I will complete." . . . At one of the Nuremberg rallies, a giant photo of Hitler carried the caption, "In the beginning was the Word."[1]

I have a pamphlet in my file called *The Beast: The False Prophet and Hitler*. It was published in 1941, the year I was born. This pamphlet presented the formula for identifying Hitler as the Antichrist by showing how the letters in the word *Hitler* link him numerologically with the "number of the beast" given in Revelation 13:16–18:

> He causes all, both small and great, rich and poor, free and slave, to receive a mark on their right hand or on their foreheads, and that no one may buy or sell except one who has the mark or the name of the beast, or the number of his name. Here is wisdom. Let him who has understanding calculate the number of the beast, for it is the number of a man: His number is 666.

The pamphlet bases its conclusion on a numerologic formula. Numerologists believe that meaning can be assigned to numbers.

Some biblical numerologists tell us that the number 666, when worked out through a transposition of number assignments to alphabetical letters, will identify the name of a certain man. In the Revelation passage we have only three numerals—666—but according to numerology, through these numbers we can find the man's name. The first step is to numeralize the alphabet: you let 100 stand for A, 101 for B, 102 for C, and so on through the rest of the letters. Then you take Hitler's name and give each letter its numerical value: H=107, I=108, T=119, L=111, E=104, R=117. Now, add up these six numbers, and voilà! The total is 666! So obviously Hitler must be the Antichrist.

Now, to get the most fun out of the game of "Who is the Antichrist?" you must play by these three rules: If the proper name does not reach the necessary total, add a title. If the sum cannot be found in English, try Hebrew, Greek, or Latin. Don't be too particular about the spelling.

And above all, be persistent. If you keep working at it, you can make anybody the Antichrist!

If numerology doesn't work for you, don't despair. There are other ways to identify the Antichrist, as we see by looking at another favorite candidate for the role: President John F. Kennedy. What signs pointed to him? He went through "death" and "resurrection" as a PT boat commander in the South Pacific during World War II. At the Democratic convention in 1956, he received 666 votes. He was also elected president and shot through the head, which is what the Bible says will happen to this future dictator. There were some who expected that as President Kennedy lay in state in the rotunda of the Capitol, he would come out of his casket and assert himself as the ruler of the world . . . which, of course, he failed to do. So, in spite of the elaborate and contrived reasons for believing that these two men and several others in history were to have been the Antichrist, all efforts to identify him have failed.

And they will continue to fail. As I noted above, the Bible does not tell us who the Antichrist will be. In fact, Paul tells us in the second chapter of Thessalonians that this coming world ruler will not be revealed until after the Rapture of the church. "So if you ever reach the point where you think you know who he is, that must mean you have been left behind."[2]

Yet while it is not possible to know the identity of the future world ruler, it is possible to know what kind of a man he will be, for the Bible gives us a wealth of information about him. Let's explore some of that information and learn a little more about the Antichrist.

The Personality of the Coming World Ruler

He Will Be a Charismatic Leader

The prophet Daniel described the Antichrist in these graphic terms: "After this I saw in the night visions, and behold, a fourth beast . . . And there . . . were eyes like the eyes of a man, and a mouth speaking pompous words. . . . He shall speak pompous words against the Most High" (Daniel 7:7–8, 25).

In these passages Daniel gives us one of the characteristics of the coming world ruler—his charismatic personality enhanced by his speaking ability, which he will use to sway the masses with spellbinding words of power and promise. We little realize the power of good speaking ability. An actor who is not classically handsome, such as James Earl Jones, can land great parts and charm audiences simply by the power of his resonant and articulate voice. Often Americans are swayed by political candidates who have little to offer, but they offer it in the beautiful package of their smooth intonation and syntax. As Daniel says, the coming world leader will be renowned for this kind of eloquence, which will capture the attention and admiration of the world.

Daniel goes on to tell us that this golden-tongued orator not only will speak in high-blown terms but also will utter pompous words against God. The apostle John described him in a similar fashion in the book of Revelation: "And he was given a mouth speaking great things and blasphemies" (Revelation 13:5).

Considering these and other prophecies, it's not hard to understand why Hitler has often been pegged as the prototype of the Antichrist. Hitler was a man of charisma, great oratory, and pomp. In his now classic book, *Kingdoms in Conflict*, Charles Colson described the well-orchestrated events that were played out in countless crowded halls as Hitler manipulated the German people:

> Solemn symphonic music began the set-up. The music then stopped, a hush prevailed, and a patriotic anthem began and "from the back, walking slowly down the wide central aisle," strutted Hitler. Finally, the Fuhrer himself rises to speak. Beginning in a low, velvet voice, which makes the audience unconsciously lean forward to hear, he speaks his love for Germany . . . and gradually his pitch increases until he reaches a screaming crescendo. But his audience does not think his rasping shouts excessive. They are screaming with him.[3]

Hitler's pomp and charisma were not the only parallels between him and biblical prophecy.

The Bible predicts that a world ruler will arise in Europe who will promise peace while preparing for war. He will mesmerize the world, demanding the worship of the masses in exchange for the right to buy bread. He, like Hitler, will be indwelt by demonic forces, most likely by Satan himself. The parallels are so striking that Robert Van Kampen in his book *The Sign* says that he believes the Antichrist will actually be Hitler raised from the dead. Though this supposition is unlikely, Hitler does provide us a sneak preview showing in miniscule format the kind of man the Antichrist is likely to be.[4]

Daniel continued his description of the Antichrist by telling us he is a man "whose appearance was greater than his fellows" (Daniel 7:20). In terms of his outward appearance, this man will be a strikingly attractive person. The combination of magnetic personality, speaking ability, and extreme good looks will make him virtually irresistible to the masses. When he comes on the scene, people will flock to him like flies to honey, and they will fall over themselves to do anything he asks.

He Will Be a Cunning Leader

Daniel was given a picture of this world leader in his famous dream recorded in the seventh chapter of his book. Here is what he reported: "I was considering the horns, and there was another horn, a little one, coming up among them, before whom three of the first horns were plucked out by the roots" (Daniel 7:8).

If we read carefully and understand the prophetic symbol of the horns, we learn from this verse that the coming world leader subdues three other kings by plucking them out by their roots. This man will squeeze out the old to make room for the new. He will take over three kingdoms, one by one, not by making war but by clever political manipulation. He begins as the little horn, but then he succeeds in uprooting three of the first horns and thus abrogates their power to himself. Daniel reiterated this event in the eleventh chapter of his prophecy, telling us that this future world leader "shall come in peaceably, and seize the kingdom by intrigue" (Daniel 11:21). The Antichrist will be a political genius, a masterful diplomat, and a clever leader. Arthur W. Pink wrote of him:

> Satan has had full opportunity afforded him to study fallen human nature . . . The devil knows full well how to dazzle people by the attraction of power . . . He knows how to gratify the craving for knowledge . . . He can delight the ear with music and the eye with entrancing beauty . . . He knows how to exalt people to dizzying heights of worldly greatness and fame, and how to control the greatness so that it may be employed against God and His people.[5]

In today's world, every leader wants to be the one who solves the perpetual crisis in the Middle East. American presidents dream of adding that distinction to their legacy. Jimmy Carter thought he had achieved it at Camp David. Bill Clinton tried frantically to eke out a settlement during the final months of his administration. Today, in a renewal of that shuttle diplomacy, President Bush also seeks to broker such a peace agreement. If this attempt fails, and if campaign speeches are any indication, the next US president appears likely to join the pursuit to complete the "road map to world peace."

Perhaps no diplomat worked harder at this goal than secretary of state Henry Kissinger during the Nixon and Ford years. Kissinger was himself a Jew whose family had escaped Germany during the Nazi years and who negotiated the end of the Yom Kippur War. In September 1970, Kissinger managed a Middle Eastern crisis between

Israel, Jordan, and Syria, during which he virtually lived in the White House Situation Room. One top US official who was involved in the sessions was asked if Dr. Kissinger enjoyed the manipulation of American power. "'Enjoy?' exclaimed the official. 'Henry adores power, absolutely adores it. To Henry, diplomacy is nothing without it.'" A Pentagon aid related how Kissinger leaned over large maps, moving toy battleships and aircraft carriers from one end of the Mediterranean to the other, arguing with admirals, expounding on military tactics and then picking up the phone to order the Joint Chiefs of Staff to change the deployment of the Sixth Fleet. The World War II sergeant had become all at once a general and an admiral and, during that crisis, a kind of deputy commander in chief.[6]

Because Kissinger was a European-born Jew of great brilliance who became the most powerful voice in world politics in the 1970s, some people speculated that he might be the Antichrist. He wasn't, of course, nor was he able to resolve the Israeli-Arab conflict. But Kissinger's love for power gives us a snapshot of one characteristic of the coming world ruler. One day a cunning superleader—a man who adores power—will arise and use his manipulative ability to succeed where all other diplomats have failed. He will resolve the Israeli-Arab conflict.

He Will Be a Cruel Leader

Once again we turn to the writings of Daniel to understand the personality of this coming tyrant.

Thus he said: "The fourth beast shall be a fourth kingdom on earth, which shall be different from all other kingdoms, and shall devour the whole earth, trample it and break it in pieces . . . He shall speak pompous words against the Most High, shall persecute the saints of the Most High, and shall intend to change times and law. Then the saints shall be given into his hand for a time and times and half a time." (Daniel 7:23, 25)

Here Daniel tells us that the Antichrist is going to devour the whole world; he will tread the world down. He will break it in pieces. These words hint at something utterly horrific. What will happen to agitate the Antichrist to unleash this immense cruelty? Although all the believers of the present age will be taken to heaven before the reign of this man, new converts will come to Christ during the years of tribulation. This will infuriate the Antichrist, and he will take out his wrath on those new Christians. Many followers of Christ will be martyred for their faith.

The word *persecute* in Daniel 7:25 literally means to "wear out." The same word is used to describe the wearing out of garments. The use of the word here indicates a slow, painful wearing down of the people of God—a torturous, cruel persecution reminiscent of the horrors Nero inflicted on Christians in ancient Rome, but even worse. It would be easier for the saints during the Tribulation if they were simply killed outright, but instead they will be "worn out"—mercilessly tortured by this unthinkably cruel man.

Again, we find a prototype of what is to come in the regime of Hitler. Charles Colson gives us a chilling description of what went on in Nazi concentration camps:

The first Nazi concentration camp opened in 1933. In one camp, hundreds of Jewish prisoners survived in disease-infested barracks on little food and gruesome, backbreaking work. Each day the prisoners were marched to the compound's giant factory, where tons of human waste and garbage were distilled into alcohol to be used as a fuel additive. Even worse than the nauseating smell was the realization that they were fueling the Nazi war machine.[7]

Colson goes on to say that as the result of the humiliation and drudgery of their lives, "dozens of the prisoners went mad and ran from their work, only to be shot by the guards or electrocuted by the fence."[8]

Hitler and the Nazis did not annihilate the Jews all at once; they deliberately and systematically wore down their souls. And that gives us a picture of what will happen in the Tribulation when the Antichrist is in power. He will be a cruel, blood-shedding leader, taking out his wrath on the saints who come to Christ under his regime.

The Profile of the Coming World Ruler

In the twelfth chapter of Revelation we read of the dragon, or Satan, being thrown out of heaven in a great war. Then in the thirteenth chapter we discover that the dragon comes to earth to begin his program by embodying his agent, the Antichrist. When we link this chapter with verses from Daniel, we get a good profile of this leader by looking at how he comes to power from several different viewpoints. Each of these viewpoints—the political, the national, the spiritual, and the providential—give us a good picture of what he will be like. So let's briefly explore what the Bible tells us about how the Antichrist comes to power.

He Will Be Politically Inconspicuous

Daniel 7 tells us that the Antichrist will not make a big splash when he arrives on the political scene. He will not enter with a fanfare, announcing, "I am here! I will now take over!" Instead, he will squeeze his way in, little by little, beginning as one among many minor political leaders. In prophetic imagery, he is the little horn who grows to be the big horn. He will attract little attention as he methodically begins to grasp more and more power.

John the apostle emphasized this fact when he wrote that this ominous personality will arise from among the mass of ordinary people. "Then I stood on the sand of the sea. And I saw a beast rising up out of the sea, having seven heads and ten horns, and on his horns ten crowns, and on his heads a blasphemous name" (Revelation 13:1). The *sea* in biblical imagery stands for the general mass of humanity or, more specifically, the gentile nations. We find confirmation of that meaning for the sea in Revelation 17: "Then he said to me, 'The waters which you saw, where the harlot sits, are peoples, multitudes, nations, and tongues'" (v. 15).

What we learn in these passages is that at first the Antichrist will not be obvious. He will not burst onto the scene in all his power and glory, but rather he will rise out of the sea of common humanity, or emerge inauspiciously from among ordinary people, as did Napoleon and Hitler.

He Will Emerge from a Gentile Nation

From what nation will the coming world ruler emerge? Often we hear that he must come from the Jewish nation. Since he will make a covenant with the nation of Israel, many people reason that perhaps he will be the Jew that Israel anticipates as her messiah. But the Bible gives us no evidence for determining that the Antichrist is a Jew. In fact, we have strong evidence for believing the opposite. Dr. Thomas Ice weighed in on the ethnicity of the Antichrist and concluded:

A widely held belief throughout the history of the church has been the notion that Antichrist will be of Jewish origin. This view is still somewhat popular in our day. However, upon closer examination we find no real Scriptural basis for such a view. In fact, the Bible teaches just the opposite . . . that Antichrist will be of Gentile descent.[9]

As we saw in an earlier chapter, some form of the Roman Empire must be revived before the end times, and this appears to be coming about through the formation of the European Union. The Antichrist will emerge from one of the unified European nations. John's revelation affirms that the world ruler will arise from the masses within a gentile nation.

He Will Be Spiritually Blasphemous

Daniel said of this world leader, "He shall speak *pompous* words against the Most High, shall persecute the saints of the Most High, and shall intend to change times and law" (Daniel 7:25, *emphasis added*). In his second letter to the Thessalonians, Paul described him as one "who opposes and exalts himself above all that is called God or that is worshiped, so that he sits as God in the temple of God, showing himself that he is God" (2 Thessalonians 2:4).

As Paul wrote in Romans 1, and as the history of ancient Israel warns us over and over, it is a terrible thing to worship a *creature* instead of the *Creator*. Yet as Daniel warned, this man will defy God and demand to be worshipped instead of Him. And his demand will be met. As John wrote, "All who dwell on the earth will worship him, whose names have not been written in the Book of Life of the Lamb slain from the foundation of the world" (Revelation 13:8).

As if declaring himself to be God gives him power over nature and human nature, this ruler will also attempt to change the moral and natural laws of the universe. In the early days of the French Revolution, the new leaders tried to get control of the masses by changing everything that grew out of Christianity or Christian tradition. They set up a new calendar by which years were numbered, not from the birth of Christ but from the date of the revolution. They issued decrees to change all Christian churches to "temples of reason" and to melt down church bells for the metal. They actually tried to replace the seven-day week established by God with a ten-day week.[10] Such extreme actions showing hostility to everything related to God will characterize the coming world leader. No doubt he would even change the length of a year if he could somehow gain control of the earth's rotation!

While the Antichrist is pictured as "the beast rising up out of the *sea,*" John wrote that the beast, "that ascends out of the bottomless *pit,*" the one who will again be remanded to the bottomless pit until the end of the Millennium, is none other than Satan himself (Revelation 9:11; 11:7; 20:1–3, *emphasis added*). The Antichrist, with his seven heads, ten horns with their ten crowns, and his blasphemous mouth . . . whom all the world marveled at and followed, was given his power by Satan (Revelation 13:1–4).

He Will Be Limited Providentially

As both Daniel and John show us, the Antichrist is a terrifying person. He is the epitome of evil, the ultimate negation of everything good, the avowed enemy and despiser of God. Every follower of Christ ought to bow before God at this moment and give thanks that he or she will not be on this earth during the reign of the Antichrist. At the same time, we must not forget that this satanic creature is not equal to God. He does not have absolute power or anything close to it. God has him on a chain. In fact, in Revelation 13, we are reminded repeatedly that the Antichrist can only do what he is allowed to do.

Twice in this chapter, we find the little phrase, *and he was given*. "And he was given a mouth speaking great things and blasphemies, and he was given authority to continue for forty-two months" (v. 5). We also find in this chapter, "It was granted to him to make war with the saints and to overcome them. And authority was given him over every tribe, tongue, and nation" (v. 7). As in the story of Job, Satan (and his puppet, the Antichrist) will be able to do only that which God allows. The Antichrist will be able to create terrible havoc and chaos, but ultimately God is still God, and no enemy of His will go beyond the boundaries He sets.

He Will Have an Intimidating Presence

The four major kingdoms depicted in Daniel's other prophetic vision were likened to certain animals: Babylon was like a lion, Medo-Persia was like a bear, Greece was like a leopard, and Rome was like the ten-horned beast (Daniel 7). In the descriptions of the beast in Revelation, we have all of these characteristics combined into one horrific creature (Revelation 13:2). This likeness of the Antichrist to ferocious beasts is meant to show us the intimidating presence of this satanic creature. He combines in his person all of the threatening characteristics of the kingdoms which have gone before him. Dr. W. A. Criswell wrote:

Think of the golden majesty of Babylon. Of the mighty ponderous massiveness of Cyrus the Persian. Think of the beauty and the elegance and the intellect of the ancient Greek world. Think of the

Roman with his laws and his order and his idea of justice. All of these glories will be summed up in the majesty of this one eventual *Antichrist* who will be like Nebuchadnezzar, like Cyrus, like Tiglath Pileser, like Shalmanezer, like Julius Caesar, like Caesar Augustus, like Alexander the Great, like Napoleon Bonaparte, like Frederick the Great and Charlemagne, all bound up into one.[11]

It's no wonder that people will follow this man and even fall down and worship him. We see in our own political campaigns how quickly people gravitate to charisma and power. Give us a fine-looking candidate with a golden voice, a powerful presence, and the ability to enthrall people with vague rhetoric about an undefined better future, and we follow like sheep as the media bleats the candidate's praises. Completely overlooked is the substance of the man's program. The presence and charisma of the Antichrist will be similar, making his rise to power inevitable.

The Program of the Coming World Ruler

One of the first acts of this world leader will be to make peace with Israel. And he will keep this covenant during the first three and a half years of his rule. At that point, however, he will change his tactics. He will drop all pretensions of peace and adopt a program of crushing power. He will break his covenant with Israel and subject the Jews to great persecution (Daniel 9:27; Isaiah 28:18).

Then will come the leader's most sensational moment. The Antichrist will actually be killed, but to the astonishment of all the world, he will be raised back to life by the power of Satan in a grotesque counterfeit of the Resurrection of Jesus Christ (Revelation 13:3–4).

After his death and satanic resurrection, the Antichrist will assassinate the leaders of three countries in the European Union, and all other nations will immediately relinquish their power to him. It is then that he will set himself up to be worshipped by all the people of the world. Through his associate, the false prophet, the mark of the beast will be placed upon all those who will follow him. Anyone who does not bear this mark will be unable to buy or sell in the world's economy.

In times past, the idea of a mark that would individually identify everyone in the world for governmental control seemed a far-fetched fantasy possible only in science fiction. No one today, however, questions the possibility of such an identification process. New methods of identification are being invented every day. Recently I became acquainted with RFID, or Radio Frequency Identification. RFID is on the crest of the current wave of technology. The system involves the implantation of a tiny chip (0.05 by 0.05 millimeters) into retail items to thwart shoplifters. They have also been implanted into pets to track them should they stray, and more recently into Alzheimer's patients. These microchips can also be used as personal identity markers surgically implanted under your skin and loaded with tons of recorded information about you.[12] The Antichrist will have available to him this technology and many other options when it comes to implementing the mark of the beast.

In a final act of rebellion against God, this vile person will set himself up in Jerusalem and desecrate the rebuilt temple in what is called the "abomination of desolation." He will then attempt to annihilate every Jew on earth, thus sounding the first ominous note in the prelude to the Battle of Armageddon.

This despot of all despots will be ultimately destroyed when Jesus Christ comes to battle against the Antichrist and his armies. In that climactic war the Antichrist will be killed, and his forces will be destroyed. The victorious Christ will assume His throne as rightful king and ruler of the universe.

More important than speculating about the identity of the Antichrist is remembering that his power broker, Satan, is not the equal opposite of Almighty God. Only God knows the day, the hour, the millisecond that will usher in Satan's reign on earth as Christ raptures the church. Like us, Satan can only look for the signs and wait. Throughout the millennia of his waiting, it is likely that he has been reading scouting reports and evaluating some choice candidates and maybe even issuing a few letters of intent so he will be ready when his hour does come.

Is the Antichrist lurking somewhere out there in the masses of humanity right now? Is his darkened mind already plotting the evils that he will inflict in the last days? I believe it is entirely possible, if not highly probable.

Gary Frazier gives us a possible scenario:

Somewhere at this moment there may be a young man growing to maturity. He is in all likelihood a brooding, thoughtful young man. Inside his heart, however, there is a hellish rage. It boils like a caldron of molten lead. He hates God. He despises Jesus Christ. He detests the Church. In his mind there is taking shape the form of a dream of conquest. He will disingenuously present himself as a friend of Christ and the Church. Yet . . . He will, once empowered, pour out hell itself onto this world. Can the world produce such a prodigy? Hitler was once a little boy. Stalin was a lad. Nero was a child. The tenderness of childhood will be shaped by the devil into the terror of the *antichrist*.[13]

I realize that the picture of the future I've presented in this chapter is not a pretty one. Yet I am so often questioned about the identity of the Antichrist, and there is so much spurious and false information about him floating around, that I felt compelled to address the question. Christians need to know what is going on in the world concerning this dreaded person. But of much greater importance than looking for the Antichrist, we are to be "looking for the blessed hope and glorious appearing of our great God and Savior Jesus Christ" (Titus 2:13).

Jesus told us what to do during this time of waiting. We are to keep our hearts from being unnecessarily troubled. If we believe in Him, He will one day take us to that home He has been preparing for us, and we will be with Him! There is only one way to have that assurance. Jesus said, "I am the way, the truth, and the life. No one comes to the Father except through Me" (John 14:6).

Giving your life to Christ is the only absolute and certain guarantee that when He comes, you will be saved from personally experiencing the evil of the Antichrist by that daring air rescue called the Rapture. You will be taken out of the world into His glorious presence, never to experience the horrors Daniel and John described in their prophecies.

Keep looking up!

EIGHT

The New Axis of Evil

ON JANUARY 29, 2002, IN HIS STATE OF THE UNION ADDRESS, President George W. Bush used the term *Axis of Evil* for the first time. He identified Iran, Iraq, and North Korea as "states . . . [who are] arming to threaten the peace of the world . . . These regimes," he said, "pose a grave threat and growing danger. They could provide these arms to terrorists, giving them the means to match their hatred."[1] President Bush was roundly criticized for calling these nations *evil*, but as we will see in this chapter, his description was more than accurate.

On May 6, 2002, US ambassador to the United Nations John Bolton gave a speech titled "Beyond the Axis of Evil," in which he added three more rogue states to the axis: Libya, Syria, and Cuba. Today the term *Axis of Evil* includes all six states.

One nation on this Axis of Evil list is of special interest to us because we find that it is also on God's list. That nation and that list are found in the thirty-eighth and thirty-ninth chapters of Ezekiel. These chapters, written some twenty-six hundred years ago, give us one of the most important and dramatic prophecies in all Scripture.

It is commonly referred to as the prophecy against Gog and Magog, and it is the most detailed prophecy concerning war in the entire Bible. The prophecy predicts an invasion of Israel in the last days—an invasion comprised of enormous masses of troops from a coalition of nations led by Russia and Iran.

It is likely that this invasion will occur shortly after Israel signs a covenant with the new leader of the European Union. Because of this agreement, Israel will be at peace with her Islamic neighbors. The people of Israel will believe that the European powers will protect them from any outside aggressor or invader ... especially from Russia, which will have joined forces with Iran to develop weapons for the purpose of utterly destroying Israel.

The Identity of the Nations

Now the word of the LORD came to me, saying, "Son of man, set your face against Gog, of the land of Magog, the prince of Rosh, Meshech, and Tubal, and prophesy against him, and say, 'Thus says the Lord GOD: "Behold, I am against you, O Gog, the prince of Rosh, Meshech, and Tubal. I will turn you around, put hooks into your jaws, and lead you out, with all your army, horses, and horse-men, all splendidly clothed, a great company with bucklers and shields, all of them handling swords. Persia, Ethiopia, and Libya are with them, all of them with shield and helmet; Gomer and all its troops; the house of Togarmah from the far north and all its troops—many people are with you. Prepare yourself and be ready, you and all your companies that are gathered about you; and be a guard for them."'" (Ezekiel 38:1–7)

Here we see that Ezekiel's prophecy begins with a list of proper names. Many of these names identify certain grandchildren and great-grandchildren of Noah who were the fathers of nations that for a time bore their names (Genesis 10). These nations, which today no longer have those original names, will ultimately form a coalition that will march against Israel. As we identify these nations by their present names and locate them on today's world map, we can see how the stage is being set for this predicted Russian/Islamic invasion of Israel.

Gog is an exception on Ezekiel's list. Gog is not one of the descendants of Noah listed in Genesis 10. This name, however, is found twelve times in Ezekiel 38–39. It is not the name of a nation, but rather the title of a ruler. In fact, the word means "ruler," or "the man on top." It is clear that Gog is an individual rather than a nation because God addresses him as such in this prophecy (Ezekiel 38:14; 39:1). Furthermore, Gog is explicitly called "the prince" in Ezekiel 38:2 and 39:1.

The next name in Ezekiel's prophecy is Magog. In his book, *The Nations in Prophecy,* John F. Walvoord wrote, "Magog is best identified with the Scythians . . . The ancient historian Josephus makes that identification and we have no reason to question it. The Scythians apparently lived immediately to the north of . . . Israel, then some of them emigrated north, going all the way to the Asiatic Circle."[2] Interestingly, Herodotus records that these Scythians were of Indo-Aryan heritage and spoke an Iranian language related to Persian.[3] Using these clues, we can identify Magog today as being made up of nations that were formerly parts of the Soviet Union: Kazakhstan, Kyrgyzstan, Uzbekistan, Turkmenistan, Tajikistan, Azerbaijan, Georgia, and possibly Afghanistan.

The next name on Ezekiel's list is Rosh, which is found in the Old Testament more than six hundred times. During Ezekiel's time, the word *Rosh* identified a nation that included people living north of the Black Sea. In the prophecies of Ezekiel, we are told three times (38:6, 15; 39:2) that part of the force that invades Israel will come from the "distant north," or "the remotest parts of the north." The land that is most distantly north and remote to Israel is Russia.

John F. Walvoord wrote:

> If one takes any map of the world and draws a line north of the land of Israel he will inevitably come to the nation of Russia. As soon as the line is drawn to the far north beyond Asia Minor and the Black Sea it is in Russia and continues to be Russia for many hundreds of miles all the way to the Arctic Circle . . . On the basis of geography alone, it seems quite clear that the only nation which could possibly be referred to as coming from the far north would the nation of Russia.[4]

When the Soviet Union collapsed in the 1990s, many thought that Russia's days of prominence and power were over. But fewer than two decades later we find a resurgent Russia seeking to reclaim the strategic ground she lost. Someone has said that since the days of the collapse of the Soviet Union, the great Russian bear has been like a mother bear robbed of her cubs.[5] If Magog includes the countries of the collapsed Soviet Union, Rosh specifically identifies the nation of Russia, which is presently trying to reassemble its lost empire.

Edward Lucas, a journalist who has covered Eastern Europe for the *Economist* for more than twenty years, has recently written a frightening book titled *The New Cold War*. He warns that Russia is rising again as a hostile power. It is reasserting its military muscle, intensely pursuing global energy markets, coercing neighboring nations back into the old Soviet orbit, silencing journalists and dissidents, and laying the groundwork with modernized weaponry for reestablishing its former power and influence. The West, wrote Lucas, is asleep to the growing danger and is losing the New Cold War. I would have to agree.

His Web site gives some very insightful examples:

Russia's vengeful, xenophobic, and ruthless rulers have turned the sick man of Europe into a menacing bully. The rise to power of Vladimir Putin and his ex-KGB colleagues coincided with a tenfold rise in world oil prices. Though its incompetent authoritarian rule is a tragic missed opportunity for the Russian people, Kremlin, Inc. has paid off the state's crippling debts and is restoring its clout at home and abroad. Inside Russia it has crushed every constraint, muzzling the media, brushing aside political opposition, castrating the courts and closing down critical pressure groups.[6]

So successful is Russia's return to the world stage that *Time* magazine chose Russian president Vladimir Putin as its 2007 Person of the Year for "taking Russia from chaos to a position of importance in the world today."[7] Although the Russian leader appears to have quelled chaos within his own country by use of autocratic power, he seems intent on fomenting chaos on the world stage by advancing a new cold war. He "accused the West of encroaching on Russia's borders and starting a new arms race,"[8] and "the United States of trying to impose its will on the world by military force."[9]

Attempting to justify his hostility toward the West, Putin said, "We [Russians] are striving to create a fairer world based on the principles of equality . . . Time has shown our views find support in Arab and other Muslim states."[10] In fact, "Russia is determined to further enhance its relations with Muslim countries . . . We are all allies of the kingdom in working to meet the world's need for energy."[11]

In October 2007, during Putin's first ever visit to Iran, an Iranian newspaper reported that he "reassured Iran that the Bushehr nuclear reactor, a billion-dollar energy project being built by Russia and dogged by delays, would be completed." The report went on to suggest, "Maybe the most important result of Putin's trip is to show the independence of Russia toward America and the West."[12] Putin made other first-time-ever visits of a Russian leader to the Muslim nations of Saudi Arabia, Qatar, Jordan, United Arab Emirates, Indonesia, and most currently, Libya. By all reports, his visits were successful financially, resulting in lucrative agreements and contracts for further joint efforts in the production of oil and the exploration of natural gas reserves.

Apparently the Russian president was successful politically as well. In Libya, President Gadhafi and Putin agreed that the United Nations "needs to be reformed in order to face an 'imbalance of forces' internationally," and especially "the Security Council with which we can work together to resolve problems."[13]

Europe is not blind to what is going on in Russia. European leaders have taken note of Russia's resurgence with growing alarm and dismay. According to a former German foreign minister, "Today, it is the Kremlin that sets the agenda for EU–Russia relations, and it does so in a manner that increasingly defies the rules of the game."[14] According to one source, "Russia appears to be winning the energy dominance game, signing individual deals with EU member states and moving forward with . . . pipelines."[15] Among these EU member states are several of Russia's former cubs. As the mother bear regains her strength, she is actively seeking to draw her brood back into her den.

Meshech and Tubal, the next names on Ezekiel's list, are usually mentioned together when they appear in the Bible. In the past, it has been widely assumed that these were ancient names for the modern cities of Moscow and Tobolsk. But very few scholars today identify Meshech and Tubal as Russian cities. One reason is Ezekiel's assertion that they were trading partners with ancient Tyre: "Javan, Tubal, and Meshech were your traders. They bartered human lives and vessels of bronze for your merchandise" (Ezekiel 27:13). It is highly unlikely that ancient Tyre (modern Lebanon) would be trading with Moscow and the Siberian city of Tobolsk. The more probable identification of Meshech and Tubal is as part of the present nation of Turkey.

The next country Ezekiel names is Persia, a name that appears thirty-five times in the Old Testament. Persia is easy for us to identify because it retained the name it had held since ancient times until March 1935, when it became the nation of Iran. Nearly four and a half decades later, Iran officially changed its name to the Islamic Republic of Iran. Today, with its population of 70 million people, Iran has become the hotbed of militant Islam and anti-Semitic hatred.

Iran's government is officially a theocratic republic whose ultimate political authority resides in the supreme leader, currently Ayatollah Ali Khamenei. This fact surprises many people who assume that the persistently vocal and visible president Mahmoud Ahmadinejad is the top man in Iran. But despite his virulent verbalizing, threats, and saber rattling, Ahmadinejad is only a figurehead under Khamenei. Iran's geographical location on the Persian Gulf and the vital Strait of Hormuz gives her great power. According to CIA reports in 2007, vast oil reserves and the upwardly spiraling price of crude oil gave Iran sixty billion dollars in foreign exchange reserves. Yet her people continue to live with high unemployment and inflation. Iran is identified as a prime player in the human trafficking trade. It is also a "key transshipment point" for heroin into Europe and has the "highest percentage of the populations in the world using opiates."[16] Additionally, the United States has identified Iran as a state sponsor of terrorism.

In a cat-and-mouse game that's been going on since August 2002, world governments have been in a continual on-again, off-again confrontation with Iran over its uranium enrichment capabilities. But world opinion seems to have no more effect on Iran than water on the back of a duck. As a US State Department spokesman recently commented, "the Iranian regime is continuing on a path of defiance of the international community."[17] Despite two rounds of sanctions and the possibility of a third, in February 2008 a defiant Ahmadinejad thumbed his nose at the UN Security Council's demand that Iran suspend uranium enrichment. He said, "With the help of Allah, the Iranian nation with its unity, faith, and determination stood and defeated the world powers and brought them to their knees."[18]

In a surprising reversal, the United States announced in early December 2007 that while Iran did have a secret nuclear weapons program at one time, the program had been abandoned, and Iran was no longer pursuing nuclear capabilities. Perhaps emboldened by the US announcement, in January 2008, five armed Iranian boats menaced three US Navy vessels in the Strait of Hormuz. The tense confrontation prompted a White House warning: "We urge the Iranians to refrain from such provocative actions that could lead to a dangerous incident in the future."[19]

The Iranian regime is well known for its hatred of Israel and its desire to eliminate her. In October 2005, the newly elected president Ahmadinejad declared to the World Without Zionism audience, "As the imam said, Israel must be wiped off the map . . . Anybody who recognizes Israel will burn in the fire of the Islamic nation's fury." He went on to say that any Islamic leader "who recognizes the Zionist regime means he is acknowledging the surrender and defeat of the Islamic world."[20]

Iran's militant influence extends beyond her own borders. In March 2008, Hezbollah chief Hassan Nasrallah railed, "The presence of Israel is but temporary and cannot go on in the region. We will see you killed in the fields, we will kill you in the cities, we will fight you like you have never seen before."[21] Hezbollah leaders do not have the authority to make such threats on their own. Hezbollah is an Islamic fundamentalist group, and though its base of operations is Lebanon, its authority comes from a source higher in the Islamic hierarchy. As Hezbollah's deputy chief, Sheikh Naim Qassem has said, "Even when it comes to firing rockets on Israeli civilians, that decision requires an in-principle permission from [the ruling jurisprudent]."[22] In this case the ruling jurisprudent would be the supreme leader of Iran—Ayatollah Ali Khamenei. "We ask, receive answers, and then apply. This is even true for acts of suicide for the sake of Allah—no one may kill himself without a jurisprudence permission [from Khamenei]."[23] Thus we can see that the aggressive and threatening influence of Iran infects and controls other Islamic terrorist organizations.

In reply to the Iranian-Hezbollah verbal bullying, UN secretary-general Ban Ki-Moon stated, "I am concerned by the threats of open war against Israel by the secretary general of Hezbollah."[24] Such deadly threats and utter disdain for world opinion is pretty convincing evidence that our national leaders are right on target in including Iran as a member of the Axis of Evil.

The next nation Ezekiel lists is Ethiopia. Some Bible translations render this nation as Cush, who is identified as a grandson of Noah, the first of Ham's four sons. "The sons of Ham were Cush, Mizraim, Put, and Canaan" (Genesis 10:6). In the verses that follow, we learn that the descendants of Cush settled in Arabia, Mesopotamia, and Assyria. The Cushites themselves, however, were established in Africa where they occupied a territory much larger than the modern Ethiopia, for the Ethiopia of ancient times included the present-day Sudan. This fact is significant to us, as Sudan is hardly a friend to the West. Sudan supported Iraq in the Gulf War and also harbored Osama bin Laden.

The next nation identified by Ezekiel is Libya. Some Bible translations render this nation as Put, which we find in Genesis 10 to be the name of another grandson of Noah. There is no ambiguity about the present identity of this nation, for ancient maps show that the territory occupied in Ezekiel's time by the nation of Put is now the modern nation of Libya. Since 1969, Libya has been under the dictatorial control of Colonel Mu'ammar al Gadhafi. It is an Islamic nation seething with a great hatred for Israel and, ominously, has recently formed a new alliance with Russia.

Gomer is next on Ezekiel's list. Gomer is mentioned in Genesis 10 as one of Japheth's sons. Genesis 10:3 helps us identify Gomer further by telling us that one of Gomer's relatives is Ashkenaz. Today, Israelis describe Jews from Germany, Austria, and Poland as *Ashkenazim.* This gives us a clue to Gomer's present-day identity, as this term associated with Gomer has likely been passed down through generations, retaining the identify of the people even as the name of the country has changed. Gibbon, in *The Decline and Fall of the Roman Empire,* said, "Gomer is modern Germany."[25] The modern nation identified as the ancient land of Gomer is usually thought to be either Germany or Turkey.

Ezekiel 38:6 refers to Gomer with "all its troops" (NKJV), or "all his bands" (KJV), or "all its hordes" (ASV), indicating that this nation will provide a powerful army in the assault on Israel. If ancient Gomer is part of the modern Turkey, as I believe it to be, it is a country with a growing allegiance to Russia. If we listen to the nightly news, we know that this nation has a strong military presence on the northern border of Iraq—quite possibly the "hordes" that Ezekiel refers to—and is already involved in the conflict over the control of the Middle East.

At the end of his list, Ezekiel added the house of Togarmah or, as it is rendered in some translations, Beth Togarmah (which is the same thing since the word *beth* is the Hebrew word for *house*). Secular historians usually place Beth Togarmah in the geographic location of Phrygia, a western kingdom in Asia Minor. Like Meshech, Tubal, and Gomer, Beth Togarmah was a part of the geographical area we currently call Turkey.

Thus Ezekiel completed his list of specifically identified nations that will come against Israel in the last days. And what a formidable list it is! Yet as if those nations were not enough, Ezekiel added that many more nations will also join the coalition to crush Israel: "many people are with you," he wrote. This is a reference to many smaller countries that have become allied with the more significant nations that Ezekiel specifically identifies. Nearly all of these nations are either Islamic or pro-Islamic. When this formidable mass of armies comes against Israel, there will be no possible human defense for the Israelis.

In a verse that follows this prophecy, Ezekiel spoke of some nations that will not be involved in the invasion of Israel: "Sheba, Dedan, the merchants of Tarshish, and all their young lions will say to you, 'Have you come to take plunder? Have you gathered your army to take booty, to carry away silver and gold, to take away livestock and goods, to take great plunder?'" (v. 13). Most Bible scholars believe that Sheba and Dedan refer to the peoples of the Arabian Peninsula, including modern-day Saudi Arabia, Yemen, Oman, and the Gulf countries of Kuwait and the United Arab Emirates.

Tarshish was a term that in ancient times described the western-most part of human civilization. Many scholars believe that "the merchants of Tarshish" and its "villages" and "young lions" refer to the market-based economies of Western Europe. Some scholars have even dared to be more specific. Dr. David L. Cooper wrote, "When all the historical statements are examined thoroughly, it seems that the evidence is in favor of identifying Tarshish as England."[26] Another scholar, Theodore Epp, agrees with this identification. He points out that the lion is a symbol for Britain and suggests that Britain's colonies, many of which have spun off to become nations of their own, are the cubs, or "young lions" in Ezekiel's prophecy. He said, "Great Britain's young lions, such as Canada, Australia, New Zealand, the African colonies, and the United States are strong enough to make an exhibit of disfavor in that day."[27]

If Theodore Epp and Dr. Cooper are right, it seems that the West in general will not participate in the invasion of Israel. What interests us in this study is that Ezekiel's prophecy of the alignment of nations, showing which ones will and which will not rise to crush Israel, squares very closely with the alignment of nations we see shaping up in the world right now. Thus we find that Ezekiel's ancient prophecy, written some twenty-six hundred years ago, informs us as to what is going on in the world today right before our very eyes.

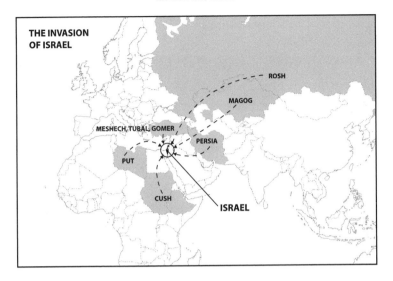

THE INVASION OF ISRAEL

ROSH

MAGOG

MESHECH, TUBAL, GOMER

PERSIA

PUT

CUSH

ISRAEL

The Invasion of Israel

The Place of the Invasion

Ezekiel clearly identifies Israel as the land that will be invaded by the nations named on the map above. He stresses this fact at least five times in chapter 38—sometimes obliquely, giving us some characteristic of the people to be invaded, and sometimes explicitly, identifying the land by name: "you will come into the land of those brought back from the sword and gathered from many people on the mountains of Israel, which had long been desolate; they were brought out of the nations, and now all of them dwell safely" (v. 8); "a land of unwalled villages; I will go to a peaceful people, who dwell safely, all of them dwelling without walls, and having neither bars nor gates" (v. 11); "a people gathered from the nations" (v. 12); "'On that day when My people Israel dwell safely'" (v. 14); "'You will come up against my people Israel'" (v. 16). There can be no question about what nation these amassed armies will invade. It will be the land of Israel.

When you look at Ezekiel's list of attacking nations and compare them to the one nation to be invaded, you see a case of overkill like nothing ever witnessed in world history. Israel is one of the smallest nations on earth. It is one-nineteenth the size of California and roughly the size of our third smallest state, New Jersey. Israel is 260 miles at its longest, 60 miles at its widest, and between 3 and 9 miles at its narrowest. The nation of Israel is a democratic republic surrounded by twenty-two hostile Arab/Islamic dictatorships that are 640 times her size and 60 times her population.[28]

The Period of the Invasion

Ezekiel does not give a specific date for the invasion, but he does give us ways to identify the time when it will occur: "'After many days . . . in the latter years . . .'" (Ezekiel 38: 8); "'On that day when My people Israel dwell safely . . .'" (v. 14); "'It will be in the latter days that I will bring you against My land'" (v.16).

The prophet tells us that the invasion of Israel will take place sometime in the future (latter years). It will happen at a time when Israel is dwelling in peace and safety and not involved in conflict with other nations.

Has there ever been such a time in Israel's history? No, there has not! Is today such a time? No! When will there be such a time? The only period in Israel's life likely to meet this requirement comes immediately following the Rapture of the church when the Antichrist and the European Union make a treaty with Israel to guarantee her peace and security. When this treaty is signed, the people of Israel will relax the diligence they have been forced to maintain since the founding of their nation in 1948. They will rely on the treaty and turn their attention away from defense to concentrate on increasing their wealth. Israel will truly be a land of unwalled villages. Her defenses will be down, and she will be woefully unprepared for the invasion by the armies of Russia and the coalition.

The Purpose of the Invasion

The nations in the battle of Gog and Magog will come down on the nation of Israel, pursuing three primary goals. The first goal will be to seize her land. As Ezekiel puts it, "to stretch out your hand against the waste places which are again inhabited" (Ezekiel 38:12). The second goal of the invaders will be to steal Israel's wealth: "To take plunder and to take booty, to stretch out your hand . . . against a people gathered from the nations, who have acquired livestock and goods, who dwell in the midst of the land . . . to carry away silver and gold, to take away livestock and goods, to take great plunder" (vv. 12–13).

And there is plenty of wealth to be plundered in modern Israel, as we can see by the following quote from a recent article in the *Jerusalem Post*: "Despite a population of only slightly more than 7 million people . . . Israel is now home to more than 7,200 millionaires . . . Of the 500 wealthiest people in the world, six are now Israeli, and all told, Israel's rich had assets in 2007 of more than 35 billion dollars . . . Israel's GDP is almost double that of any other Middle East country."[29]

Success and wealth in the high-tech industry has replaced earlier agricultural kibbutzim and started her on "the extraordinary road . . . from the socialist experiment of defiant European Jews to the high-tech revolution that has created a Silicon Valley in the Middle East, second only to the United States in start-ups.[30] In 2007, venture capitalists invested 1.76 billion dollars in start-up companies in developing "advanced telecom equipment" in Israel's "Silicon Wadi."[31]

According to one prosperity index, Israel exported goods and services of more than $70 billion last year, including $34.2 billion from the technology sector alone. "Israel is the highest-ranking Middle Eastern country in the index."[32] In 2007, she had a per capita gross domestic product index of $28,800, which compared favorably with the much larger European Union at $32,900.[33] Any way you measure it, Israel has become prosperous, and despite a recent recession and military conflict, her economy has continued to grow.

Finally, the invading nations have as their ultimate goal the wholesale slaughter of Israel's people: "I will go to a peaceful people, who dwell safely, all of them dwelling without walls, and having neither bars nor gates . . . to stretch out your hand . . . against a people gathered from the nations . . . You will come up against My people Israel like a cloud, to cover the land" (vv. 11–12, 16). The historical accumulated hatred for the Jews will drive these armies forward with the assurance that this time, the people of Israel will not escape death.

The Particulars of the Invasion

"You will ascend, coming like a storm, covering the land like a cloud, you and all your troops and many peoples with you . . . Then you will come from your place out of the far north, you and many peoples with you, all of them riding on horses, a great company and a mighty army. You will come up against My people Israel like a cloud, to cover the land." (Ezekiel 38:9, 15–16)

In these passages Ezekiel tells us that the coalition of massive armies will gather from all the attacking nations and assemble on the mountains of Israel. One writer helps us understand the strategy of invading from these mountains:

> The mountains of Israel are mainly located on the country's northern borders with modern-day Syria, Lebanon, and northern Jordan (notably the strategically important Golan Heights). Since the Russian-Iranian coalition is described by the prophet as coming primarily from the north, it is reasonable to conclude that Syria and Lebanon are participants in the coalition. Jordan maybe as well, though this is not entirely clear.[34]

Now that we have set the stage for the invasion of the assembled armies against Israel by identifying the place, the timing, the purpose, and some of the particulars, let's look next at what will happen when this invasion actually begins.

The Intervention of God

When the massive Russian-Islamic armies assemble on the northern mountains of Israel, ready to come against that tiny country, it will appear to be the most grossly mismatched contest in military history. The Israelis will be so outnumbered that there will be no human way they can win this war. Only intervention by God himself could possibly save them. And that is exactly what will happen. As Ezekiel tells us: "'And it will come to pass at the same time, when Gog comes against the land of Israel,' says the Lord GOD, 'that My fury will show in My face. For in My jealousy, and in the fire of My wrath I have spoken'" (Ezekiel 38:18–19a).

How will God accomplish this miraculous feat? What will be the results of His intervention? These are questions we can answer by continuing to explore Ezekiel's prophecy, and the answers will enable us to understand how today's events will play out to fulfill God's purposes in the near future.

The Arsenal of Weapons

When God goes to war, He uses weapons unique to Him—weapons that render the arsenals of men as ineffective as a water pistol against a nuclear bomb. God will save His people Israel by employing four of these weapons simultaneously. First, he will rout the armies of Israel's attackers with massive convulsions in the earth. As Ezekiel explains:

> "For in My jealousy and in the fire of My wrath I have spoken: 'Surely in that day there shall be a great earthquake in the land of Israel, so that the fish of the sea, the birds of the heavens, the beasts of the field, all creeping things that creep on the earth, and all men who are on the face of the earth shall shake at My presence. The mountains shall be thrown down, the steep places shall fall, and every wall shall fall to the ground.'" (38:19–20)

God will follow these convulsions of the earth with His second weapon, which will be to create such confusion among the attacking troops that they will panic and begin killing one another: "'I will call for a sword against Gog throughout all My mountains,' says the Lord GOD. 'Every man's sword shall be against his brother'" (Ezekiel 38:21).

In the seventh and eighth chapters of Judges, we see a similar event reported. We are told that 135,000 Midianites had gathered against Israel. Gideon and his little band of three hundred men, under the direction of God and through the power of God, threw the enemy into total confusion, and the Lord set every man's sword against his brother. As a result, 120,000 Midianite soldiers died, largely by what today we would call "friendly fire."

In Ezekiel we can see how God's first two weapons work together in a one-two punch. A sudden earthquake in the mountains of Israel would certainly panic an army. With the ground moving like sea waves, the upheaval of the earth generating dense clouds of dust, it would be impossible for warriors to distinguish an enemy from an ally, and in their blind terror they would kill anything that moved.

The third divine weapon will be the contagion of disease: "And I will bring him to judgment with pestilence and bloodshed," asserts the Lord (38:22a). He will infect the invading troops with some debilitating disease that will render them incapable of carrying out an effective attack. God will follow this contagion with his fourth and final weapon: calamities from the sky. "I will rain down on him, on his troops, and on the many peoples who are with him, flooding rain, great hailstones, fire, and brimstone" (v. 22b).

We find the prototype for this strategy in God's judgment upon Sodom and Gomorrah, where the two decadent cities were forever buried under the briny waters of the Dead Sea by a storm of fire and brimstone. One man has written: "Every force of nature is a servant of the Living God, and in a moment can be made a soldier, armed to the teeth. Men are slowly discovering that God's forces stored in nature are mightier than the brawn of the human arm."[35] When God goes to war, no army on earth can stand against His formidable arsenal. The armies that come against Israel in the last days will learn that truth the hard way.

The Aftermath of War

First, there will be a feast. There is strong irony in using the term *feast* for what will happen immediately following the destruction of Israel's enemies. It will not be a feast of victory for the rescued Israelis; it will be a feast for vultures and predators feeding on the incredible masses of bodies strewn across the battlefield. Here is how Ezekiel described the grisly banquet:

> "You shall fall upon the mountains of Israel, you and all of your troops and the peoples who are with you; I will give you to birds of prey of every sort and to the beasts of the field to be devoured. You shall fall on the open field; for I have spoken," says the Lord God . . . "And as for you, son of man, thus says the Lord God, 'Speak to every sort of bird and to every beast of the field:
>
> > "Assemble yourselves and come;
> > Gather together from all sides to My sacrificial meal
> > Which I am sacrificing for you,
> > A great sacrificial meal on the mountains of Israel,
> > That you may eat flesh and drink blood.
> > You shall eat the flesh of the mighty,
> > Drink the blood of the princes of earth,
> > Of rams and lambs,
> > Of goats and bulls,
> > All of them fatlings of Bashan.
> > You shall eat fat till you are full,

And drink blood till you are drunk,

At My sacrificial meal

Which I am sacrificing for you.

You shall be filled at My table

With horses and riders,

With mighty men

And with all the men of war,'" says the Lord GOD. (Ezekiel 39:4–5,

17–20)

This chilling prophecy uses the language of a feast—what God calls His "sacrificial feast"—to show how the intervention of God will result in a gruesome spectacle of uncountable bodies littering the landscape like debris from a tornado, creating a bountiful banquet for His guests, the birds of the air and the beasts of the field.

The second event that will occur after the destruction of Israel's enemies is a great funeral. Ezekiel described it:

It will come to pass in that day that I will give Gog a burial place there in Israel, the valley of those who pass by east of the sea; and it will obstruct travelers, because there they will bury Gog and all his multitude. Therefore they will call it the valley of Hamon Gog. For seven months the house of Israel will be burying them, in order to cleanse the land . . . They will set apart men regularly employed, with the help of a search party, to pass through the land and bury those bodies remaining on the ground, in order to cleanse it. At the end of seven months they will make a search. The search party will pass through the land; and when anyone sees a man's bone, he shall set up a marker by it, till the buriers have buried it in the Valley of Hamon Gog. (Ezekiel 39:11–12, 14–16)

Here Ezekiel painted another chilling and macabre picture of the horrendous death and destruction inflicted on Israel's invaders. This war will produce so many casualties that it will take seven months to bury all the bodies. In fact, the task will be so enormous that a special detachment of soldiers will be assigned to carry it out. According to the Old Testament, an unburied corpse is a reproach to God and causes a land to be defiled (Deuteronomy 21:23). Thus the Israelis will feel compelled to clean up the bloody battlefield and bury all the dead.

The third aftermath of the war against Israel will be a great and long-burning fire. Here's how Ezekiel explained the fire and its purpose:

> "Then those who dwell in the cities of Israel will go out and set on fire and burn the weapons, both the shields and bucklers, the bows and arrows, the javelins and spears; and they will make fires with them for seven years . . . They will not take wood from the field nor cut down any from the forests, because they will make fires with the weapons; and they will plunder those who plundered them, and pillage those who pillaged them," says the Lord God. (Ezekiel 39:9–10)

This passage indicates that the arsenal of weaponry and military equipment brought against Israel by the coalition of nations will be utterly staggering. While it will take seven months to bury the bodies, which is astonishing enough, it will take *seven years* to burn the weapons.

Some readers of Ezekiel are troubled that the prophet described these as weapons of ancient origin, whereas a battle that is yet to occur in the future will surely employ modern weaponry and highly sophisticated military equipment—guns, tanks, planes, bombs, missiles, and possibly even nuclear weapons. But we must allow common sense to prevail in our reading of Ezekiel. He did what all prophets have done: he spoke of the future using terms and descriptions that he and the people of his day would understand. If he had written of tanks and missiles and bombs, those living in his time would have been utterly mystified, and his message would have had no meaning to them.

The burial of the bodies and the burning of the weapons comprise what Ezekiel calls the "cleansing of the land" from the defilement of death and destruction wrought upon it by the enemies of God's people. These massive cleanup operations in the aftermath of the war give us an eye-opening picture of the enormity of the destruction predicted in Ezekiel's end-time prophecy. As we try to comprehend these cataclysmic events, we can only shake our heads in wonder and ask, "What in the world is going on?" I believe Ezekiel helps us to answer that question as we look further into his prophecy.

The Sovereignty of God's Plan

The Inevitable Accomplishment of God's Purpose

To understand what is going on in the war and destruction described in Ezekiel's prophecy, we must first consider the sovereignty of God's plan. Throughout this book we have observed that even in the most devastating of times, God is still in control. In fact, He often orchestrates events to bring about His purposes. He tells us what He will do to Israel's enemies in no uncertain terms: "I will turn you around, put hooks into your jaws, and lead you out, with all your army, horses, and horsemen" (Ezekiel 38:4); "It will be in the latter days that I will bring you against My land" (v. 16); "and I will turn you around and lead you on, bringing you up from the far north, and bring you against the mountains of Israel" (39:2).

Passages such as these confuse many people because of the seeming implication that God leads men to be evil or to do evil things. But the Bible never says that God instills evil in the hearts of men. Some would attempt to refute this claim by pointing out that during the Exodus, the Bible explicitly says that God hardened Pharaoh's heart. It does say that, of course, but the statement speaks about the nature of Pharaoh's heart, not about God overriding man's free will. Some hearts are like clay; the sun's heat will harden them. Others are like wax; the sun will cause them to melt. It's not the sun's fault that it hardens one substance and melts the other; it all depends on the nature of the material. Pharaoh's heart was the sort that would harden when exposed to God's light. It had nothing to do with God coercing him to do evil.

The Old Testament, especially, is intended to show that God is the sovereign ruler over all. Even though men try to thwart His plan and wreak great destruction, God's purpose will always win out. When Ezekiel wrote that God will bring the enemy against His land, he was simply saying that God will bring these nations to the doom that their wickedness inevitably demands. Everyone accomplishes God's will in the end. Those who conform to His will accomplish it willingly; those who do not conform accomplish it inadvertently as an unwitting tool in His hands.

The Simplicity of God's Purpose

Secondly, let's look at the simplicity of God's purpose. As you read the following verses from Ezekiel's prophecy, you will have no difficulty picking out the defining purpose clauses:

I will bring you against My land, so that the nations may know Me, when I am hallowed in you, O Gog, before their eyes. (38:16)

Thus I will magnify Myself and sanctify Myself, and I will be known in the eyes of many nations. Then they shall know that I am the LORD. (38:23)

Then they shall know that I am the LORD. (39:6)

So I will make My holy name known in the midst of My people Israel, and I will not let them profane My holy name anymore. Then the nations shall know that I am the LORD. (39:7)

I will set My glory among the nations; all the nations shall see My judgment which I have executed, and My hand which I have laid on them. So the house of Israel shall know that I am the LORD their God from that day forward. (39:21–22)

It doesn't take a rocket scientist to figure out God's purpose in the cataclysmic battle of the last days. It is very clear and very simple. God intends for people to recognize Him as the Lord God of heaven, whose name is holy, whose glory fills the universe, and whom men must recognize as sovereign if they are to find the peace and joy He desires for His people.

The Salvation of God's People

Finally, note the sovereignty of God's plan in rescuing His people. Ezekiel tells us that the ultimate outcome of the battle of Gog and Magog will be the salvation of the Jewish people:

Therefore thus says the Lord GOD: "Now I will bring back the captives of Jacob, and have mercy on the whole house of Israel; and I will be jealous for My holy name—after they have borne their shame, and all their unfaithfulness in which they were unfaithful to Me, when they dwelt safely in their own land, and no one made them afraid. When I have brought them back from the peoples and gathered them out of their enemies' lands, and I am hallowed in them in the sight of many nations, then they shall know that I am the LORD their God, who sent them into captivity among the nations, but also brought them back to their land, and left none of them captive any longer. And I will not hide My face from them anymore; for I shall have poured out My Spirit on the house of Israel," says the Lord GOD. (39:25–29)

Thus Ezekiel ends his monumental prophecy on a high note, extolling God's tender love and compassion toward His people. No matter how great the evil in men's hearts, no matter how much destruction and death that evil brings about, God's ultimate purpose in confronting that evil, in revealing His glory among the nations, and in bringing His own from the lands of the enemy is always to accomplish the salvation of His people.

As Ezekiel shows us so vividly, God's destruction of the Axis of Evil in the last days will accomplish the salvation of his people, the nation of Israel. By identifying this Axis of Evil as modern nations who are unwittingly bent on fulfilling this devastating prophecy, we have answered another question about what is going on in the world today. We have shown how present events will lead to the ultimate accomplishment of God's purposes.

As I close this chapter, I think it is important to point out that there is, in a sense, the potential for an axis of evil within the heart of every one of us. As the apostle Paul tells us, each of us has in our heart that "sinful nature" we inherited from Adam—a propensity for selfish evil that, if not controlled by the presence of God's Spirit, can run rampant and produce destruction in our own lives and in the lives of those about us.

But thanks be to God, His salvation is not for Israel only. All men and women today can choose to be among God's people. You don't have to be a Jew to receive salvation, nor does being a Russian or an Iranian force one to be a part of the Axis of Evil. God in His infinite love pours out His Spirit on all who believe and turn to Him. With that wonderful transaction, and as His Spirit is poured out on the redeemed, the axis of evil in our hearts is transformed by God's love.

I will conclude this chapter by passing on to you a fine and touching example of this principle, which I recently found in a true incident reported by Robert Morgan:

Daniel Christiansen tells about a relative, a Romanian soldier in World War II, named Ana Gheorghe. It was 1941, and troops had overrun the Romanian region of Bessarabia and entered Moldavia. Ana and his comrades were badly frightened. Bullets whizzed around them, and mortar shells shook the earth. By day, Ana sought relief reading his Bible, but at night he could only crouch close to the earth and recall verses memorized in childhood.

One day during a spray of enemy fire, Ana was separated from his company. In a panic, he bolted deeper and deeper into the woods until, huddling at the base of a large tree, he fell asleep from exhaustion. The next day, trying to find his comrades, he moved cautiously toward the front, staying in the shadows of the trees, nibbling a crust of bread, drinking from streams. Hearing the battle closing in, he unslung his rifle, pulled the bolt, and watched for the enemy, his nerves near the breaking point. Twenty yards away, a Russian soldier suddenly appeared.

All my mental rehearsals of bravery served me nothing. I dropped my gun and fell to my knees, then buried my face in my sweating palms and began to pray. While praying, I waited for the cold touch of the Russian's rifle barrel against my head.

I felt a slight pressure on my shoulder close to my neck. I opened my eyes slowly. There was my enemy kneeling in front of me, his gun lying next to mine among the wildflowers. His eyes were closed in prayer. We did not understand a single word of the other's language, but we could pray. We ended our prayer with two words that need no translation: "Alleluia . . . Amen!"

Then, after a tearful embrace, we walked quickly to opposite sides of the clearing and disappeared beneath the trees.[36]

NINE

Arming for Armageddon

GENERAL DOUGLAS MACARTHUR STOOD TALL ON THE DECK OF the USS *Missouri* in Tokyo harbor. It was September 2, 1945, and this man who had engineered America's hard-fought victory in the Pacific had just witnessed the signatures of Japan's leaders ending the bloody global struggle known as World War II. On that day, this authentic American hero uttered a profound warning, which he later repeated in his famous farewell address before the United States Congress: "We have had our last chance," he said. "If we do not now devise some greater and more equitable system, Armageddon will be at our door."[1]

Shortly after he was inaugurated as the fortieth president of the United States, Ronald Reagan was astounded by the complexities of the Middle East. Israel, on its thin strip of land, was surrounded by well-armed Arab enemies who were splintered like broken glass into countless factions and divisions impossible to reconcile. On Friday, May 15, 1981, scribbling in his diary, Reagan noted the intractable problems involving Lebanon, Syria, Saudi Arabia, the Soviet Union, and Israel. "Sometimes I wonder," he wrote, "if we are destined to witness Armageddon."

Only three weeks later, on Sunday, June 7, he received news that Israel had bombed the Iraqi nuclear reactor. That afternoon, Reagan wrote in his diary: "Got word of Israel bombing of Iraq—nuclear reactor. I swear I believe Armageddon is near."[2]

Armageddon. The very word chills the soul. Probably there are few adults who are not familiar with that word and what it implies. Why have our national leaders, in the twentieth and twenty-first centuries, begun to use that doomsday word in their speaking and writing? I believe it is because they can see how modern weaponry and international tensions are showing how quickly global equilibrium could get out of control, leading to a cataclysmic war such as the world has never seen before.

Our nation is no stranger to war. According to the US Army Military Institute, the United States has been involved in twenty-nine wars or military conflicts. This averages out to one war for every eight years of America's history. This number includes not only the major conflicts, but also lesser-known engagements, such as the Seminole wars, America's involvement in the Boxer rebellion, and the invasion of Panama. Approximately 1,314,971 troops have died for their country in these wars. This includes 25,000 who died in the War of Independence; 623,026 in the Civil War; more than 400,000 in World War II; more than 58,000 in Vietnam; and nearly 4,000 in the current conflicts in Iraq and Afghanistan. (That number has increased to more than 4,000 since the report was published.)[3]

The Bible tells us that there is yet another war to be fought on this earth. This war, called Armageddon, makes all the wars America has fought to date look like minor skirmishes. This war will draw the final curtain on modern civilization. In this chapter we will lift the biblical veil to show what is going on in the world that will lead to Armageddon. In fact, preparations for that war are underway right now throughout the world. The only thing holding back its rapid approach is the yet-to-occur disappearance of all true believers in Jesus Christ, the event we know as the Rapture of the church.

The Preparation for the Battle of Armageddon

In the twelfth chapter of Revelation, the apostle John revealed how this conflagration will come about. "So the great dragon was cast out, that serpent of old, called the Devil and Satan, who deceives the whole world; he was cast to the earth, and his angels were cast out with him . . . Now when the dragon saw that he had been cast to the earth, he persecuted the woman who gave birth to the male Child" (vv. 9, 13).

These verses tell us that during the Tribulation, when Satan is cast out of heaven to the earth, he will begin immediately to persecute the woman who brought forth the male child. The "woman" is an obvious metaphor for Israel, through whom the child Jesus was born. Satan's first attempt at persecution will be the battle of Gog and Magog. As we learned in the previous chapter, this battle, which precedes the Battle of Armageddon, will be a massive, Russian-led coalition of nations coming against Israel like swarms of hornets against a defenseless child. As Revelation tells us, Satan will be the motivating force behind this invasion. But before he accomplishes his intended annihilation of Israel, she will be rescued by Almighty God.

The thwarting of the battle of Gog and Magog will be a setback to Satan, but he will not give up; he is relentless in his persecution of the

Jews. His purpose, beginning in the middle of the Tribulation period, is to destroy the Jewish people before Christ can set up His kingdom, thus wrecking God's prophesied rule over the earth. According to Revelation 16, Satan will employ two fearful personalities in these plans: "And I saw three unclean spirits like frogs coming out of the mouth of the dragon, out of the mouth of the *beast,* and out of the mouth of the *false prophet*" (v. 13, *emphasis added*).

Here John tells us that Satan will empower the beast, who is the head of the reestablished Roman Empire, and the false prophet, the head of the new world religious system. Thus Satan (the dragon), the Beast (the Antichrist), and the false prophet become the unholy trinity committed to the destruction of Israel. When the church of Jesus Christ is taken safely into heaven and the Tribulation period begins, the unrestrained satanic persecution of Israel will propel the entire world toward the Battle of Armageddon.

The Place of the Battle of Armageddon

"And they gathered them together to the place called in Hebrew, Armageddon" (Revelation 16:16).

As we noted previously, the word *Armageddon* is much bandied about these days. It has become a synonym for every kind of doomsday scenario. We hear talk of an impending *financial* Armageddon, an *ecological* Armageddon, an e*nvironmental* Armageddon, and a *nuclear* Armageddon for which physicist Stephen Hawking tells us we should prepare by relocating ourselves "somewhere else in another solar system."[4] Obviously the popular imagination has captured the essence of the type of event that will occur at Armageddon, but people have missed the inherent meaning of the word by a country mile. Armageddon is not actually a battle; it is a place.

Given the enormous attention this word receives, it may surprise you that *Armageddon* is mentioned only once in the Bible—right here in the sixteenth chapter of Revelation. The Hebrew word *harmageddon* means "the mount of Megiddo." *Har* means mount, and *megiddo* means slaughter; so the meaning of *Armageddon* is "Mount of Slaughter." The mountain of Megiddo is an actual geographical feature located in northern Israel. It includes an extended plain that reaches from the Mediterranean Sea to the northern part of the land of Israel. Megiddo is about eighteen miles southeast of Haifa, fifty-five miles north of Jerusalem, and a little more than ten miles from Nazareth, the town where Jesus grew up.

While the word *Armageddon* is mentioned only once in the Bible, the mountain of Megiddo has a rich biblical history. It was at Megiddo that Deborah and Barak defeated the Canaanites (Judges 4–5). It was also there that: Gideon defeated the Midianites (Judges 7); Saul was slain during a war with the Philistines (1 Samuel 31); Ahaziah was slain by Jehu (2 Kings 9); and Josiah was slain by the invading Egyptians (2 Kings 23).

These are not by any means the only battles that have been fought on this bloody ground. Last year I stood at the top of Megiddo, overlooking the plain of Armageddon. If I could have watched past centuries fast-forward before my eyes, I would have seen a long succession of waged battles as great armies marched across the field one after the other—the Crusaders, the Egyptians, the Persians, the Druze, the Greeks, the Turks, and the Arabs. During World War I, British general Edmund Allenby led his army against the Turks in a fierce battle on the plain of Armageddon. According to scholar Alan Johnson, "More than 200 battles have been fought at or near there."[5] As you can see, Megiddo has earned its awful name: it is indeed a Mount of Slaughter.

Why Megiddo? Why will this be the location of the world's final conflict? One of the world's greatest military figures gives us the answer. In 1799, Napoleon stood at Megiddo before the battle that ended his quest to conquer the East and rebuild the Roman Empire. Considering the enormous plain of Armageddon, he declared: "All the armies of the world could maneuver their forces on this vast plain . . . There is no place in the whole world more suited for war than this . . . [It is] the most natural battleground on the whole earth."[6]

While it is no mystery why the earth's final battle will be fought at Armageddon, it is important to understand that the battle will be centralized on that field but not contained there. All the ancient prophets agree that this war will be fought throughout the entire land of Israel. In the book he edited on Armageddon, A. Sims wrote:

> It appears from Scripture that this last great battle of that great day of God Almighty will reach far beyond Armageddon, or the Valley of Megiddo. Armageddon appears to be mainly the place where the troops will gather together from the four corners of the earth, and from Armageddon the Battle will spread out over the entire [country of Israel]. Joel speaks of the last battle being fought in the Valley of Jehoshaphat, which is close by Jerusalem and Isaiah shows Christ coming with blood-stained garments "from Edom," [present day Jordan]. So the battle of Armageddon, it seems, will stretch from the Valley of Megiddo in the north . . . through the Valley of Jehoshaphat, near Jerusalem, [and down to Jordan, south of Israel]. And to this agree the words of the prophet Ezekiel that the armies of this great battle will "cover the land" . . . But Jerusalem will no doubt be the center of interest during the battle of Armageddon, for God's Word says: "I will gather all nations against Jerusalem to battle."[7]

The words of the prophet Zechariah support Sims's view of Jerusalem as the center of conflict in the Armageddon war. "Behold, I will make Jerusalem a cup of drunkenness to all the surrounding peoples, when they lay siege against Judah and Jerusalem. And it shall happen in that day that I will make Jerusalem a very heavy stone for all peoples; all who would heave it away will surely be cut in pieces, though all nations of the earth are gathered against it" (Zechariah 12:2–3). So while we use the term *Armageddon* and localize the war to the plain of Megiddo, Scripture teaches that the battle will literally fill the whole land of Israel with war and bloodshed.

This war will be so horrific that the Bible says blood will flow in staggering torrents. "And the winepress was trampled outside the city, and blood came out of the winepress, up to the horses' bridles, for one thousand six hundred furlongs" (Revelation 14:20). If you translate these ancient measurements into the terminology of today, sixteen hundred furlongs is almost exactly two hundred miles—the distance from the northern to the southern tip of the land of Israel.

While that image may be hard for us to visualize, it is not unknown in human experience. Ancient historians Plutarch and Herodotus describe similar scenes during vicious battles of their days. Of the siege of Athens in 405–404 BC, Plutarch wrote:

About midnight Sylla entered the breach, with all terrors of trumpets and coronets sounding, with the triumphant shout and cry of an army let loose to spoil and slaughter, and scouring through the streets with sword drawn. There was no numbering the slain; the amount is to this day conjectured only from the space of ground overflowed with blood. For without mentioning the execution done in the other quarters of the city, the blood that was shed about the marketplace spread over the whole [public square] . . . and passed through the gate and overflowed the suburb.[8]

Similarly, writing of the fall of Jerusalem to the Roman hordes in AD 70, Josephus wrote:

When they [Romans] went in numbers into the lanes of the city, with their swords drawn, they slew those whom they overtook, without mercy, and set fire to the houses wither the Jews fled . . . they ran every one through whom they met with, and obstructed the very lanes with their dead bodies, and made the whole city run down with blood, to such a degree indeed that the fire of many of the houses was quenched with these men's blood.[9]

We would actually be more accurate to refer to this conflict as the "*Campaign* of Armageddon." The word translated as *battle* in Revelation 16:14 is the Greek word *polemos*, which signifies a war or campaign. Armageddon will involve many battles fought throughout the entire land of Israel over a three-and-one-half-year period of time.

The Purpose of the Battle of Armageddon

Our sensibilities revolt when we read of the carnage the Bible pictures when describing the Battle of Armageddon. And the horrible scene raises all kinds of questions that many people find difficult to answer. We wonder what is going on, not only in the world but also in the mind of God. What is the purpose of this war in the plan of God? Let's address these questions in order to show God's purpose, plan, and intent in allowing the Battle of Armageddon to occur. Just what are His purposes?

To Finish His Judgment upon Israel

The Tribulation period is a time of divine indignation against the people of Israel, the people who rejected their Messiah and—time and time again after given the chance to return—failed to heed the corrective and punitive judgment of God. It is no accident that this future period of time is often referred to as "the time of Jacob's trouble" (Jeremiah 30:7).

To Finalize His Judgment upon the Nations that Have Persecuted Israel

Those nations that have persecuted the Jewish people are finally gathered together in the Battle of Armageddon, in the Valley of Jehoshaphat, giving God the perfect opportunity to deal with them finally and decisively.

> I will also gather all nations,
> And bring them down to the Valley of Jehoshaphat;
> And I will enter into judgment with them there
> On account of My people, My heritage Israel,
> Whom they have scattered among the nations;
> They have also divided up My land. (Joel 3:2)

To Formally Judge All the Nations that Have Rejected Him

"Now out of His mouth goes a sharp sword, that with it He should strike the nations. And He Himself will rule them with a rod of iron. He Himself treads the winepress of the fierceness and wrath of Almighty God" (Revelation 19:15).

This verse gives us another of God's purposes in bringing about Armageddon. Notice particularly that last phrase: "He Himself treads the winepress of the fierceness and wrath of Almighty God." To our time-bound senses, God's activity often seems so slow and ponderous that people pursuing ungodly goals tend to dismiss His judgment as a factor to be taken seriously. Thus the nations do not believe that a time is coming when God's judgment will inevitably descend. But be assured, He is storing up judgment against a day to come. The Bible is clear: one of these days God will have had enough, and His judgment will pour down like consuming fire against the world's wicked nations. "And men were scorched with great heat, and they blasphemed the name of God who has power over these plagues; and they did not repent and give Him glory" (Revelation 16:9).

This verse tells us just how incredibly wicked the nations will have become when God's judgment descends. Even when these men are writhing and screaming with the excruciating pain God inflicts upon them, they will continue to curse Him to His face. They will be so far gone, so given over to evil, that in their prideful defiance they will refuse to repent, even in the grip of fatal judgment.

The Particularities of the Battle of Armageddon

Just to be sure there is no confusion about the wars in the Tribulation period, I want to make it clear that we have identified two separate battles. In the previous chapter we learned about the first battle, the one that will occur at the beginning of the Tribulation period when Gog (Russia) assembles a mass of nations against Israel that are thwarted by God's intervention. In this chapter we are learning about a second battle, one that will end the Tribulation period. It is easy to confuse the two, but the Bible presents them as two distinct events. The battle of Gog and the Battle of Armageddon are separated by several years and involve different participants. Here are some of the differences that will help us keep the two battles separate in our minds:

- In the battle of Gog, Russia and at least five other nations are involved (Ezekiel 38:2–6). In the Battle of Armageddon, all the nations of the world are involved (Joel 3:2; Zechariah 14:2).

- In the battle of Gog, the invaders will attack from the north (Ezekiel 38:6, 15; 39:2). In the Battle of Armageddon, the armies come from the north, south, east, and west (Daniel 11:40–45; Zechariah 14:2; Revelation 16:12–16).

- In the battle of Gog, the purpose of the armies is to "take a spoil, and to take a prey" (Ezekiel 38:12 KJV). In the Battle of Armageddon, the purpose is to annihilate the Jews and to fight Christ and His army (Zechariah 12:2–3, 9; 14:2; Revelation 19:19).

- In the battle of Gog, Russia will be the leader of the nations (Ezekiel 38:13). In the Battle of Armageddon, the Antichrist will be the leader (Revelation 19:19).

- In the battle of Gog, God defeats the northern invaders with the convulsions of the earth, the confusion of the troops, the contagion of diseases, and calamities from the sky. In the Battle of Armageddon, the armies are defeated by the word of Christ—"a sharp sword" (Revelation 19:15; see also verse 21 NKJV).

- In the battle of Gog, Israel's enemies will perish upon the mountains of Israel and in the open field (Ezekiel 39:4–5). In the Battle of Armageddon, those slain by the Lord will lie where they fall, from one end of the earth to the other (Jeremiah 25:33).

- In the battle of Gog, the dead will be buried (Ezekiel 39:12–15). In the Battle of Armageddon, the dead will not be buried, but their carcasses will be totally consumed by the birds (Jeremiah 25:33; Revelation 19:17–18, 21).

- After the battle of Gog, war will continue among the nations involved (other than Israel) during the remainder of the Tribulation (Revelation 13:4–7). After the Battle of Armageddon, swords and spears will be beaten into plowshares and pruning hooks (Isaiah 2:4) and the nations will study war no more.[10]

The Participants in the Battle of Armageddon

As we have noted, all the nations of the world will be involved in the Battle of Armageddon, and they will be led by the Antichrist. But the Bible gives us many more details about the motives and actions of the participants in this battle. These are worth exploring, as they provide insights into the nature of the war and why it will be fought.

The Deal Between Israel and Antichrist

Referring specifically to the Antichrist, Daniel tells us that "he shall confirm a covenant with many for one week" (Daniel 9:27a). In prophetic language, this means a week of years, so the covenant will be made for seven years. Until recently I thought Israel would simply be duped into thinking this peace treaty would be a lasting agreement, because I couldn't imagine any national leader taking seriously a peace treaty that was openly proposed for a prescribed period of time. Until, that is, maverick peace broker and former president Jimmy Carter and the leadership of Hamas recently proposed a peace treaty, a *hudna*, to Israel with a ten-year time limit.[11] Apparently in the last days, Israel will be so wearied of continual threats of war that they will think any treaty, even one that gives them a short space of breathing room, will be better than no peace at all.

The Antichrist, who will at this time be the head of the European Union, will sign such a covenant with Israel, guaranteeing peace and security for seven years. Israel will view this man not as the evil Antichrist but as a beneficent and charismatic leader.

The Worship of the Antichrist

On the heels of the covenant with Israel, this self-appointed world ruler will begin to strengthen his power by performing amazing signs and wonders, including even a supposed resurrection from the dead (Revelation 13:3). Then with his grip on the world greatly enhanced, he will boldly take the next step in his arrogant defiance of God: "Then the king shall do according to his own will: he shall exalt and magnify himself above every god, shall speak blasphemies against the God of gods" (Daniel 11:36).

Daniel goes on to give us a further description of the Antichrist's insidious methods:

He shall regard neither the God of his fathers nor the desire of women, nor regard any god; for he shall exalt himself above them all. But in their place he shall honor a god of fortresses, and a god which his fathers did not know he shall honor with gold and silver, with precious stones and pleasant things. Thus he shall act against the strongest fortresses with a foreign god, which he shall acknowledge, and advance its glory; and he shall cause them to rule over many, and divide the land for gain. (Daniel 11:37–39)

The Antichrist will be the epitome of the man with a compulsion to extend his dominion over everything and everyone. To achieve this end, the Antichrist will bow to no god but the "god of fortresses." That is, he will build enormous military might and engage in extensive warfare to extend his power throughout the world.

Daniel then describes how the swollen megalomania of the Antichrist will drive him to take his next step in Daniel 11:36, quoted earlier. John expanded on Daniel's description of the Antichrist's blasphemous acts by telling us that every living person will be required to worship this man. "He was granted power to give breath to the image of the beast, that the image of the beast should both speak and cause as many as would not worship the image of the beast to be killed" (Revelation 13:15). Step by step, the Antichrist will promote himself from a European leader, to a world leader, to a tyrannical global dictator, and finally to a god.

The Decision to Fight Against the Antichrist

The Antichrist's grip on global power will not last long. The world will become increasingly discontented with the leadership of this global dictator, who has gone back on every promise he made. Major segments of the world will begin to assemble their own military forces and rebel against him.

The king of the south and his armies will be the first to come after the Antichrist, followed by the armies of the north. "At the time of the end the king of the South shall attack him; and the king of the North shall come against him like a whirlwind, with chariots, horseman, and with many ships" (Daniel 11:40). John Walvoord pinpoints the source of this army and describes the magnitude of the initial thrust against the Antichrist:

> Daniel's prophecy described a great army from Africa, including not only Egypt but other countries of that continent. This army, probably numbering in the millions, will attack the Middle East from the south. At the same time Russia and other armies to the north will mobilize another powerful military force to descend on the Holy Land and challenge the world dictator. Although Russia will have had a severe setback about four years earlier in the prophetic sequence of events, she apparently will have been able to recoup her losses enough to put another army in the field.[12]

The Antichrist will put down some of these first attempts at rebellion against him. But before he can celebrate and move on toward his goal of destroying Israel and Jerusalem, something will happen.

The Disturbing News from the East

"But news from the east and the north shall trouble him; therefore he shall go out with great fury" (Daniel 11:44). The Bible leaves no doubt as to the source of the news that so disturbs and enrages the Antichrist: "Then the sixth angel poured out his bowl on the great river Euphrates, and its water was dried up, so that the way of the kings from the east might be prepared" (Revelation 16:12).

The Euphrates is one of the greatest rivers in the world. It flows from the mountains of western Turkey, through Syria, and continues on right through the heart of Iraq, not far from Baghdad. It eventually unites with the Tigris to become the *Shatt el Arab*, and finally empties into the Persian Gulf. The entirety of the Euphrates flows through Muslim territory. In Genesis 15 and Deuteronomy 11, the Lord specified that the Euphrates would be the easternmost border of the promised land. It serves both as a border and a barrier between Israel and her enemies.

Is it possible that a river the size of the Euphrates could be dried up? According to author Alon Liel, it is not only possible, it has recently happened. He wrote:

> On one occasion recently, the Euphrates was cut off. The headwaters of both the Euphrates and Tigris Rivers, on which both Syria and Iraq so heavily depend, are located in Turkish Territory, which makes Turkey's relations with those nations all the more sensitive. Tensions mounted in early 1990 when Turkey stopped the flow of the Euphrates River for an entire month during the construction of the Ataturk Dam . . . Having already showed it can completely cut off this flow, Turkey has strengthened its bargaining position in its complex relationships with its southern neighbors.[13]

What is the significance of the drying up of the Euphrates River, and why will that event have such a disturbing effect on the Antichrist? For an explanation, let's turn once more to John Walvoord:

> The drying-up of the Euphrates is a prelude to the final act of the drama, not the act itself. We must conclude then, that the most probable interpretation of the drying-up of the Euphrates is that by an act of God its flow will be interrupted even as were the waters of the Red Sea and of Jordan. This time the way will open not for Israel but for

those who are referred to as the Kings of the East . . . The evidence points, then, to a literal interpretation of Revelation 16:12 in relation to the Euphrates.[14]

It's no wonder the world dictator is disturbed and frustrated. He has just put down rebellions by defeating armies from the south and the north, and just when it appears that he is about to gain control of everything, he gets word that the Euphrates River has dried up and massive armies of the east are crossing it to come against him. He had thought himself safe, as no army could cross this barrier and come into the Israeli arena where he fought. But now that barrier is down, and an army of unprecedented numbers is marching toward him.

Just how large is that army? Listen to what John tells us: "Now the number of the army of the horsemen was two hundred million; I heard the number of them" (Revelation 9:16). Suddenly the Antichrist must divert the major portion of his attention to defending himself against an amassed force the size of which the world has never seen.

Is an army of two hundred million soldiers really believable? Dr. Larry Wortzel, a retired US Army colonel, is a leading authority on China and served as the director of the Strategic Studies Institute of the US Army War College. In October 1998, he filed the following report: "China's standing armed force of some 2.8 million active soldiers in uniform is the largest military force in the world. Approximately 1 million reservists and some 15 million militia back them up. With a population of over 1.2 billion people, China also has a potential manpower base of another 200 million males fit for military service available at any time."[15] So an army of that size is not only possible, the potential for it exists even at this moment.

When this unprecedented army crosses the bed of the Euphrates against the Antichrist, the greatest war of all history, involving hundreds of millions of people, will be set in motion. The major battleground for that war will be the land of Israel.

As if this news is not frightening enough, John tells us that all these events are inspired and directed by the demons of hell: "For they are spirits of demons, performing signs, which go out to the kings of the earth and of the whole world, to gather them to the battle of that great day of God Almighty" (Revelation 16:14).

> No doubt demonism in every shape and form will manifest itself more and more as the end draws near, until at last it all ends in Armageddon . . . But besides these hosts of human armies, there will also be present at Armageddon an innumerable host of supernatural beings . . . So Armageddon will truly be a battle of heaven and earth and hell.[16]

So just at the moment when the Antichrist is about to attack and destroy Israel and Jerusalem, a diversion occurs in the form of another massive army entering the field of conflict. Thus the stage is set for the last, stunning movement in the Battle of Armageddon.

The Descending Lord from the Heavens

If you are a follower of Christ, what happens next may instill an urge to stand up and shout like a football fan watching the star quarterback come onto the field.

> Now I saw heaven opened, and behold, a white horse. And He who sat on him was called Faithful and True, and in righteousness He judges

and makes war. His eyes were like a flame of fire, and on His head were many crowns. He had a name written that no one knew except Himself. He was clothed with a robe dipped in blood, and His name is called The Word of God. And the armies in heaven, clothed in fine linen, white and clean, followed Him on white horses. Now out of His mouth goes a sharp sword, that with it He should strike the nations. And He Himself will rule them with a rod of iron. He Himself treads the winepress of the fierceness and wrath of Almighty God. And He has on His robe and on His thigh a name written: KING OF KINGS AND LORD OF LORDS. (Revelation 19:11–16)

The great Lord Jesus, the captain of the Lord's hosts, the King over all kings will descend to defend and protect His chosen people and put a once-and-for-all end to the evil of the Antichrist.

Descending with His Saints

But the Lord Jesus, captain of the Lord's hosts, will not descend alone, as the following scriptures make abundantly clear:

Thus the LORD my God will come;
and all the saints with You. (Zechariah 14:5)

The coming of our Lord Jesus Christ with all His saints . . . (1 Thessalonians 3:13)

When he comes, in that Day, to be glorified in His saints and to be admired among all those who believe. (2 Thessalonians 1:10)

Behold, the Lord comes with ten thousands of His saints. (Jude 14)

All those who have died in the Lord, along with those who were raptured before the years of the Tribulation, will join with the Lord and participate in the battle to reclaim the world for the rule of Christ.

Descending with His Angels

The saints are not the only ones who will comprise the army of the Lord. Both Matthew and Paul tell us that the angels will also descend with Christ. "When the Son of Man comes in His glory, and all the holy angels with Him, then He will sit on the throne of His glory" (Matthew 25:31); "and to give you who are troubled rest with us when the Lord Jesus is revealed from heaven with His mighty angels" (2 Thessalonians 1:7).

How many angels are available for conscription into this army? The Bible shows their numbers to be staggering. In Matthew 26:52–53, Jesus told Peter in the Garden of Gethsemane, "Put your sword in its place . . . Do you think that I cannot call on My Father, and He will provide Me more than twelve legions of angels?" A Roman legion numbered about six thousand soldiers, so Jesus claimed instant access to the protection of seventy-two thousand angelic soldiers who would have rushed to His rescue had He but said the word. Revelation 5:11, at the very least, supports that number, saying, "I heard the voice of many angels around the throne, the living creatures, and the elders; and the number of them was ten thousand times ten thousand, and thousands of thousands." The Greek says literally, "numbering myriads of myriads and thousands of thousands." The *New Living Transaltion* renders the passage as "thousands and millions of angels."

Hebrews 12:22 sums it up by talking about innumerable angels in "joyful assembly" (NIV). Angels as far as the eye can see and the mind can imagine.[17]

This admixture of saints and angels calls to mind scenes from great fantasies such as *The Chronicles of Narnia* and *The Lord of the Rings,* where humans fight alongside other-worldly creatures to defeat the forces of evil. It's a thrilling picture to think of human saints side-by-side with God's angels doing battle.

The inception of the Battle of Armageddon has something of a historical precedent in miniature. Author Randall Price recounts the event:

The Yom Kippur War began at 2 P.M. on October 6, 1973. It was a surprise attack on Israel from the Arab nations of Egypt and Syria, which were intent on the destruction of the Jewish State. Overwhelming evidence of large-scale Arab military preparations on the morning of October 6 had compelled Chief of Staff David Elazar to ask the United States to help restrain the Arabs. U.S. Secretary of State Henry Kissinger urged Prime Minister Golda Meir to not issue a preemptive strike, but to trust international guarantees for Israel's security. To which Mrs. Meir, in her characteristic up-front manner, retorted, "By the time they come to save Israel, there won't be an Israel!"

When international intervention finally came in calling for cease-fire negotiations, Israel's casualties had mounted to 2,552 dead and over 3000 wounded. And it would have been much worse if Israel hadn't realized that if nobody was going to fight for them, they were going to have to fight for themselves. For that reason, Israel has come to rely upon their own defenses for their security. That attack is just a foretaste of what Israel can expect in the future, when the worst attack in its history will come and will be centered on Jerusalem. In that day there will be no allies, not even reluctant ones . . . But Scripture has prophesied otherwise. At the right time, Jerusalem's Savior will return.[18]

As Price tells us, Israel in this last war will be forced to rely on herself and not depend on assistance from allies. That is the similarity between the inception of the Battle of Armageddon and the Yom Kippur War, its miniature historical precedent. But what about the outcome? Will the end of the final war be anything like the end of Israel's Yom Kippur War? We will answer that question by telling the full story of the event in the next chapter.

We will close this chapter on a high note, (or perhaps on an acoustic guitar chord) by giving you the lyrics of an old country music song written by Roy Acuff and Odell McLeod and recorded by Hank Williams. The title is "The Battle of Armageddon":

There's a mighty battle coming and it's well now on its way.
It'll be fought at Armageddon, it shall be a sad, sad day.
In the book of Revelation, words in chapter sixteen say:
There'll be gathered there great armies for that battle on that day.

Refrain:
All the way from the gates of Eden to the battle of Armageddon
There's been troubles and tribulation, there'll be sorrow and despair.
He has said "ye not be troubled for these things shall come to pass."
Then your life will be eternal when you dwell with him at last.

Turn the pages of your Bible, in St. Matthew you will see,
Start with chapter twenty-four and read from one to thirty-three.
In our Savior's blessed words he said on earth, he prophesied,
For he spoke of this great battle that is coming by and by.

Refrain

There'll be nation against nation, there'll be war and rumor of war.

There'll be great signs in heaven, in the sun, the moon, the stars.

Oh, the hearts of men shall fail them, there'll be gnashing of the teeth.

Those who seek it will receive it, mercy at the Savior's feet.

Terrible and terrifying as the events we've discussed in this chapter may be, the last line of this old country song gives us the good news. We may be disturbed by the signs we see of coming catastrophic events. We may feel uneasy due to the continual reports of wars and wanton terrorism. We may quail at reports of nature turning against us. But the last line of this song is our bottom line: we who trust the Lord as our Savior need have no fear. He loves and protects His own, and whatever comes, if we seek Him and His will for our lives, we will be among those whom He saves from the wrath to come.

TEN

The Return of the King

IN A ROOM DECORATED FOR AN ALBANIAN FUNERAL, OUR missionary to Albania, Ian Loring, delivered a powerful Good Friday message about Christ's great sacrificial death. Afterward, he invited everyone to come back on Sunday to observe the "third day ritual." In Albanian culture, friends return three days after a funeral to sit with the family, drink bitter coffee, and remember the one who has died. More than three hundred people filled the room that Easter Sunday. Ian preached about the "not quite empty tomb," observing that Christ's empty grave clothes still bore His shape, but the napkin, which had been wrapped around His head, was placed away from the other grave clothes, folded. To Ian's congregation, that minor detail held great meaning and promise. In Albania, when a person has finished a meal and prepares to leave the table, he crumples up his napkin to indicate that he is finished. But if, instead, he leaves his napkin folded, it is a sign that he plans to come back. The application was obvious to the Albanians. Jesus is coming back!

The second coming of Christ is a central theme of much of the Bible, and it is one of the best-attested promises in all of Scripture. Christians can rest in the sure conviction that just as Jesus came to earth the first time, so He will return at the conclusion of the Great Tribulation.

As Christians, we are quite familiar with our Lord's first coming to earth because we accept the record of the four Gospels. It is history. The Bible clearly tells us that He is coming to earth again. Though the exact expression "the second coming of Christ" is not found in the Bible, it makes the assertion in many places. For example, the writer of Hebrews said: "And as it is appointed for men to die once, but after this the judgment, so Christ was offered once to bear the sins of many. To those who eagerly wait for Him *He will appear a second time,* apart from sin, for salvation" (9:27–28, *emphasis added*).

The Old Testament prophecies of Christ's first and second advents are so mingled that Jewish scholars did not clearly see them as separate events. Their perception of these prophecies was like viewing a mountain range from a distance. They saw what appeared to be one mountain, failing to see that there was another equally high mountain behind it, obscured from their sight through the perspective of distance. The prophets saw both comings of Christ either as one event or as very closely related in time. One Bible scholar has written: "Words spoken in one breath, and written in one sentence, may contain prophetic events millennia apart in their fulfillments."[1]

This mixing of two prophetic events into one may partially explain why the Jews as a whole rejected Christ. The prophecies speak of the Messiah both enduring great suffering and accomplishing a great conquest. They thought the suffering savior would become the conquering savior in one advent. They did not realize He would come a first time to suffer and then a second time to conquer.

It is evident that even Jesus' followers expected Him to fulfill the glorious promises relating to His second coming when He came the first time. Only after He ascended to heaven did they realize that they were living in the time period between His two appearances, as if on a plain between two mountains. Theologian John F. Walvoord explains:

> From the present day vantage point . . . since the first coming is history and Second Coming is prophecy, it is comparatively easy to go back into the Old Testament and separate the doctrine of Jesus' two comings. In His first coming He came as a man, lived among people, performed miracles, ministered as a prophet as the Old Testament predicted, and died on the cross and rose again. All these events clearly relate to His first coming. On the other hand, the passages that speak of His coming to reign, judging the earth, rescuing the righteous from the wicked, and installing His kingdom on earth relate to His second coming. They are prophecy, not history.[2]

Nothing could be more dramatic than the contrast between our Lord's first and second comings:

- In His first coming He was wrapped in swaddling clothes. In His second coming He will be clothed royally in a robe dipped in blood.

- In His first coming He was surrounded by cattle and common people. In His second coming He will be accompanied by the massive armies of heaven.

- In His first coming the door of the inn was closed to Him. In His second coming the door of the heavens will be opened to Him.

- In His first coming His voice was the tiny cry of a baby. In His second coming His voice will thunder as the sound of many waters.

- In His first coming, He was the Lamb of God who came bringing salvation. In His second coming, He will be the Lion of the tribe of Judah who comes bringing judgment.

Rapture / Translation	Second Coming/ Established Kingdom
1. Translation of all believers	1. No translation at all
2. Translated saints go to heaven	2. Translated saints return to earth
3. Earth not judged	3. Earth judged and righteousness established
4. Imminent, any moment, signless	4. Follows definite predicted signs, including the Tribulation
5. Not in Old Testament	5. Predicted often in Old Testament
6. Believers only	6. Affects all humanity
7. Before the day of wrath	7. Concluding the day of wrath
8. No references to Satan	8. Satan bound
9. Christ comes *for* His own	9. Christ comes *with* His own
10. He comes in the *air*	10. He comes to the *earth*
11. He claims His bride	11. He comes with His bride
12. Only His own see Him	12. Every eye shall see Him
13. Tribulation begins	

Courtesy of Thomas Ice and Timothy Demy

The Anticipation of Christ

Although Christians are most familiar with the first coming of Christ, it is the second coming that gets the most ink in the Bible. References to the Second Coming outnumber references to the first by a factor of eight to one. Scholars count 1,845 biblical references to the Second Coming, including 318 in the New Testament. His return is emphasized in no less than seventeen Old Testament books and seven out of every ten chapters in the New Testament. The Lord Himself referred to His return twenty-one times. The Second Coming is second only to faith as the most dominant subject in the New Testament. Let's look briefly at some of the most significant of these references.

The Prophets Foretold the Second Coming of Christ

While many of the Old Testament prophets wrote concerning the second coming of Christ, it is Zechariah who has given us the clearest and most concise prediction of it:

> Then the LORD will go forth
> And fight against those nations,
> As He fights in the day of battle.
> And in that day His feet will stand on the Mount of Olives,
> Which faces Jerusalem on the east.
> And the Mount of Olives shall be split in two,
> From east to west,
> Making a very large valley;
> Half of the mountain shall move toward the north
> And half of it toward the south. (Zechariah 14:3–4)

Notice how Zechariah deals in specifics, even pinpointing the geographic location to which Christ will return: "In that day His feet will stand on the Mount of Olives" (14:4). Like Armageddon, the Mount of Olives is an explicitly identifiable place that retains its ancient name even today. Recently I visited a Jewish cemetery that has been on this site since biblical times. The prophet's specificity gives us confidence that his prophecy is true and accurate. Unlike vague fortune-tellers and prophetic charlatans, this prophet dared to be explicit and specific so that the truth of his prophecy cannot be missed when the event occurs.

Jesus Himself Announced His Second Coming

Jesus, speaking from the Mount of Olives, affirmed His second coming to His disciples in dramatic and cataclysmic terms:

"For as the lightning comes from the east and flashes to the west, so also will the coming of the Son of Man be . . . Immediately after the tribulation of those days the sun will be darkened, and the moon will not give its light; the stars will fall from heaven, and the powers of the heavens will be shaken. Then the sign of the Son of Man will appear in heaven, and then all the tribes of the earth will mourn, and they will see the Son of Man coming on the clouds of heaven with power and great glory." (Matthew 24:27, 29–30)

The Angels Announced that Jesus Would Return

Immediately following Christ's ascension into heaven, two angels appeared to the stunned disciples and spoke words of comfort to them. "Men of Galilee," they said, "why do you stand gazing up into heaven? This same Jesus, who was taken from you into heaven, will so come in like manner as you saw Him go into heaven" (Acts 1:11). The next verse tells us "they returned to Jerusalem from the mount called Olivet" (v. 12). Did you catch that? Jesus ascended to heaven from the Mount of Olives. According to the angels, Christ will return to that very same spot—the Mount of Olives. The words of the angels conveyed both consolation for the disciples' present loss of Jesus and confirmation of His future return.

John the Apostle Foretold Jesus' Second Coming

The prophecies of Christ's return are like bookends to John's Revelation. In the first chapter he wrote: "Behold, He is coming with clouds, and every eye will see Him, even they who pierced Him. And all the tribes of the earth will mourn because of Him" (v. 7). And in the last pages of the last chapter—indeed, almost the last words of the New Testament—our Lord emphatically affirms His second coming: "He who testifies to these things says, 'Surely I am coming quickly.' Amen. Even so, come, Lord Jesus!" (22:20).

Obviously we have excellent reason to anticipate the return of Christ. The Bible affirms it throughout as a certainty, describing it in specific terms and with ample corroboration.

The Advent of Christ

Twice in the book of Revelation we are told that the door to heaven will be opened. It is first opened to receive the church into heaven at the time of the Rapture: "After these things I looked, and behold, a door standing open in heaven. And the first voice which I heard was like a trumpet speaking with me, saying, 'Come up here, and I will show you things which must take place after this'" (4:1). The door swings open a second time for Christ and His church to proceed from heaven on their militant march back to earth (19:11,14). The first opening is for the Rapture of the saints; the second is for the return of Christ!

When Jesus arrives on earth the second time, His landing will dramatically herald the purpose of His coming. The moment His feet touch the Mount of Olives, the mountain will split apart, creating a broad passageway from Jerusalem to Jericho. As you can imagine, this will be an unprecedented geological cataclysm. In describing it, Dr. Tim LaHaye wrote: "There will be a Stellar Event. Celestial. Cosmic. Greater than earth. Greater than the heavens. And it will suck the air out of humanity's lungs and send men and women and kings and presidents and tyrants to their knees. It will have no need of spotlights, fog machines, amplified music, synthesizers, or special effects. It will be real."[3]

Thus Christ's return will be amplified by a devastating spectacle that will make Hollywood disaster movies look like Saturday morning child's fare. The world will see and recognize its rightful Lord and King. Whereas He came the first time in humility and simplicity, this time His glory and majesty will be spectacularly displayed for all to see.

Let's look briefly at the Bible's description of the glory and majesty Christ will display at His second coming.

His Designation

In Revelation 19, the descending Lord is given three meaningful titles.

> Now I saw heaven opened, and behold, a white horse. And He who sat on him was called Faithful and True, and in righteousness He judges and makes war . . . He had a name written that no one knew except Himself . . . and His name is called The Word of God . . . And He has on His robe and on His thigh a name written: KING OF KINGS AND LORD OF LORDS. (vv. 11–13, 16)

These three names are not merely rhetorical embellishments or empty titles. Prophecy scholar Harry Ironside gives us insight into their significance:

> In these three names we have set forth first, our Lord's dignity as the Eternal Son; second, His incarnation—the Word became Flesh; and last, His second advent to reign as King of Kings and Lord of Lords.[4]

These three names encompass the entire ministry of the Lord Jesus Christ. The first name, the one known only to God, indicates His intimacy and oneness with the Father and thus His eternal existence, including His role in the Trinity as creator and sustainer of the world. The second name, the Word of God, harks back to the first chapter of John's gospel and indicates His incarnation when "the Word became flesh," walked as a man upon this earth, and revealed God to us. The third name, the majestic and towering syllables, King of kings and Lord of lords, is the title He will wear at His second coming, designating His role as the sovereign ruler over all the earth.

His Description

The eyes of the returning Christ are described as burning like a flame of fire, signifying His ability as a judge to see deeply into the hearts of men and ferret out all injustice (Revelation 1:14; 2:18; 19:12). His eyes will pierce through the motives of nations and individuals and judge them for what they really are . . . not for how they hope their masks of hypocrisy will make them appear!

The head of the returning Christ is crowned with many crowns (Revelation 19:12), testifying to His status as the absolute sovereign King of kings and Lord of lords—the undisputed monarch of the entire earth. Famed nineteenth-century London preacher Charles

Haddon Spurgeon described the comfort and security that we derive from the sovereignty of Christ:

> I am sure there is no more delightful doctrine to a Christian, than that of Christ's absolute sovereignty. I am glad there is no such thing as chance, that nothing is left to itself, but that Christ everywhere hath sway. If I thought that there was a devil in hell that Christ did not govern, I should be afraid that devil would destroy me. If I thought there was a circumstance on earth, which Christ did not over-rule, I should fear that that circumstance would ruin me. Nay, if there were an angel in heaven that was not one of Jehovah's subjects, I should tremble even at him. But since Christ is King of kings, and I am his poor brother, one whom he loves, I give all my cares to him, for he careth for me; and leaning on his breast, my soul hath full repose, confidence, and security.[5]

The robe of the returning Christ is dipped in blood, reminding us that He is the sacrificial Lamb of God. Earlier in Revelation, John described Him as "the Lamb slain from the foundation of the world" (13:8). In fact, Jesus will be represented to us as the Lamb of God throughout eternity. In a sense, eternity will be an extended Communion service as we remember forever with love and gratitude the sacrifice of Jesus Christ that united us with God and gave us an eternity of joy with Him.

The Armies of Christ

When Jesus returns to this earth to put down the world's ultimate rebellion, the armies of heaven will accompany him. John described these armies as "clothed in fine linen, white and clean, [following] Him on white horses" (Revelation 19:14).

In the short epistle that immediately precedes the book of Revelation, Jude described this epic event in verses 14 and 15:

> Now Enoch, the seventh from Adam, prophesied about these men also, saying, "Behold, the Lord comes with ten thousands of His saints, to execute judgment on all, to convict all who are ungodly among them of all their ungodly deeds which they have committed in an ungodly way, and of all the harsh things which ungodly sinners have spoken against Him."

In one short verse, Jude used the word *ungodly* four times. This repetition is not accidental. Jude was emphasizing the fact that when Christ comes the second time, His long-suffering patience will have run its course. He will come to impose judgment upon those who have defied Him, and that judgment will be massive. At this point the people on the earth will have rejected the ministry of the 144,000 preachers and the two witnesses that God sent to them for their salvation, just as the prophet Jonah was sent to the Ninevites. In His loving mercy, God endeavored to turn them away from their fatal rebellion. But unlike the Ninevites, the people in the last days will have hardened their hearts beyond repentance.

In his second letter to the Thessalonians, Paul wrote in chilling terms of the judgment that will descend on these rebels:

> The Lord Jesus is revealed from heaven with His mighty angels, in flaming fire taking vengeance on those who do not know God, and those who do not obey the gospel of our Lord Jesus Christ. These shall

be punished with everlasting destruction from the presence of the Lord and from the glory of His power, when He comes, in that Day, to be glorified in His saints and to be admired among all those who believe, because our testimony among you was believed. (1:7–10)

As we learned in the previous chapter, the armies of heaven that accompany Christ in His second coming will be made up of saints and angels—people like you and me standing side-by-side with heavenly beings of immense power. These legions are dressed not in military fatigues but in dazzling white. Yet they need not worry about their pristine uniforms getting soiled because their role is largely ceremonial and honorary; they will not fight. Jesus Himself will slay the rebels with the deadly sword darting out of His mouth.

The Authority of Christ

When the Lord returns to earth at the end of the Tribulation, the men and nations who have defied Him will no more be able to stand against Him than a spiderweb could stand against an eagle. His victory will be assured and His authority undisputed. Here is how John described the finality of His judgment and the firmness of His rule: "And he Himself will rule them with a rod of iron. He Himself treads the winepress of the fierceness and wrath of Almighty God. And He has on His robe and on His thigh a name written: KING OF KINGS AND LORD OF LORDS" (Revelation 19:15–16).

This grand title, King of kings and Lord of lords, identifies our Lord at His second coming. It speaks of His unassailable authority. At this name every king on earth will bow, and every lord will kneel. Don't be confused about the sword proceeding from Christ's mouth; it is not "the sword of the Spirit, which is the word of God" (Ephesians 6:17). This is an altogether different and fearful sword—the sword of judgment—a sharp instrument of war with which Christ will smite the nations into utter submission and establish His absolute rule.

When Christ returns the second time, He will finally fulfill the prophecy of Isaiah that we often quote and hear choirs sing to Handel's lofty music at Christmastime: "For unto us a Child is born, unto us a Son is given; and the government will be upon His shoulder. And His name will be called Wonderful, Counselor, Mighty God, Everlasting Father, Prince of Peace" (Isaiah 9:6). At His first coming, Jesus fulfilled the first part of Isaiah's prophecy, the heartwarming Christmas part. At His second coming, He will fulfill the second part—the part that reveals His iron-hard power and authority over all the nations. The government of the world will at last be upon His shoulder!

The Avenging of Christ

The book of Revelation is divided into three sections. At the beginning of the book we are introduced to the world ruined by Man. As we move to the latter half of the Tribulation period, we witness the world ruled by Satan. But now as we come to Christ's return at the end of the Tribulation period, we see the world reclaimed by Christ.

Reclaiming the earth, however, is not merely a simple matter of Christ's stepping in and planting His flag. Before the earth can be reclaimed, it must be cleansed. You wouldn't move back into a house infested with rats without first exterminating and cleaning it up. That is what Christ must do before He reclaims the earth. All rebellion must be rooted out. He must avenge the damage done to His perfect creation by wiping the rebels from the face of the earth. The last verses of Revelation 19 give us an account of this purging and cleansing, and each step in the process is a dramatic story within itself. Let's briefly examine these avenging acts that will cleanse and reclaim the earth.

The Fowls of Heaven

In the classic Alfred Hitchcock film *The Birds*, a coastal California town is terrorized by the escalating attacks of vicious birds. Throughout the film the terror increases to the point that birds merely sitting in rows on highline wires look ominous and foreboding. Instead of closing the film with his typical "The End," Hitchcock simply fades the screen to black, leaving the viewer with a lingering sense of terror as he drives from the theater and sees birds sitting on the high wires in his neighborhood. As horrifying as that story is, it pales in comparison to the grisly bird scene that John unveils.

> Then I saw an angel standing in the sun; and he cried with a loud voice, saying to all the birds that fly in the midst of heaven, "Come and gather together for the supper of the great God, that you may eat the flesh of kings, the flesh of captains, the flesh of mighty men, the flesh of horses and of those who sit on them, and the flesh of all people, free and slave, both small and great" . . . And all the birds were filled with their flesh. (Revelation 19:17–18, 21)

Words are hardly adequate to describe the horror of this appalling scene. The fowl of the earth's air all gather at Armageddon to feast upon the massive piles of human flesh that will litter the battlefield for miles upon miles. The word translated *fowl* or *birds* is found only three times in the Bible: twice here in Revelation 19 (verses 17 and 21), and once more in Revelation 18:2. It is the Greek word *arnin*, which designates a scavenger bird that is best translated into English as *vulture*.

In John's vision the angel is calling the vultures of the earth to Armageddon to "the supper of the Great God," where they will feast on the fallen carcasses of the enemies of the Lord. The text says that these corpses include both great and small, kings and generals, bond and free. As Harry Ironside wrote, "It is an awful picture—the climax of man's audacious resistance to God."[6]

The book of Revelation tells of another supper, one altogether different from that of the vultures on the field of Armageddon. In Revelation 19:7 we read, "Let us be glad and rejoice and give Him glory, for the marriage of the Lamb has come, and His wife has made herself ready." In verse 9, we read of the feast that will follow the wedding: "Then he said to me, 'Write: "Blessed are those who are called to the marriage supper of the Lamb!"'"

The marriage supper of the Lamb is a time of great joy, celebrating the wedding between the bridegroom Christ and His bride, the church. I am glad that I have a confirmed reservation for the marriage supper of the Lamb where I will feast at the table of heaven, for at the other supper—the supper of the Great God on the fields of Armageddon— the human participants will *be* the food.

I pause here to ask a few important questions: Which supper will you be attending? Have you made your reservation for the marriage supper of the Lamb? Have you accepted the saving work of the Lamb of God in your behalf? Have you confessed your sin and surrendered your will to the authority of the Lamb? I sincerely hope you have, for doing so secures your invitation to a celebration you don't want to miss.

Strangely, as W. A. Criswell pointed out, as glorious as this feast is, it is never described explicitly:

Concerning the marriage itself, is it not a strange narrative that God should omit to describe it? Nothing is said about it, no word is used to describe it. The Greek word here says, "*elthen* [aorist], the marriage is come . . ." and that is all. Just the fact of it. John just hears the Hallelujah chorus announcing it. He has a word to say about the wife, the bride of Christ, who has made herself ready. He describes the robe of our righteousness that shall be our reward at the Bema of Christ. But He never recounts the actual wedding itself. The event just happens and all heaven bursts into Hallelujahs concerning it.[7]

Yet in spite of the lack of description, John made it clear that this feast will be glorious through a writer's technique known as *indirection*. When an event is too wonderful for words, it is sometimes more effective to show the wonder through reactions to the event rather than through the event itself. Instead of describing the feast directly, John used the reactions of others to show its character indirectly. Thus, we are told of the glorious robe we'll wear, the loveliness of the bride, and finally of the hallelujahs that will spring from heaven expressing the pure joy of the occasion. Through these indirect impressions we can see that the marriage supper will be a celebration beyond anything we can imagine. I strongly urge you to RSVP immediately.

The Foes of Heaven

"And I saw the beast, the kings of the earth, and their armies, gathered together to make war against Him who sat on the horse and against His army" (Revelation 19:19). Could there be anything more futile than creatures fighting against their Creator? Than little men stuck on one tiny planet, floating in the immeasurable cosmos, striking back at the Creator of the universe? Yet futility is not beyond hearts turned away from God. John warned that the beast and the false prophet will persuade the armies of the earth to go to war against Christ and the armies of heaven. It's like persuading mice to declare war against lions. This final war will be the culmination of all of the rebellion that men have leveled against Almighty God from the beginning of time! And there's not one iota of doubt about the outcome.

The Fatality of the Beast and False Prophet

The Bible tells us that God simply snatches up the Antichrist beast and the false prophet and flings them into the fiery lake. "Then the beast was captured, and with him the false prophet who worked signs in his presence, by which he deceived those who received the mark of the beast and those who worshiped his image. These two were cast alive into the lake of fire burning with brimstone" (Revelation 19:20).

These two evil creatures have the unwanted honor of actually getting to that awful place before Satan, whose confinement occurs much later: "The devil, who deceived them, was cast into the lake of fire and brimstone where the beast and false prophet are. And they will be tormented day and night forever and ever" (Revelation 20:10). Satan does not join the beast and the false prophet there until the end of the Millennium, one thousand years later.

Once again I turn to Harry Ironside for an interesting sidelight concerning the nature of the punishment these two men experience: "'Note that two men, are taken alive' . . . These two men are 'cast alive into [the lake burning with fire and brimstone]' where a thousand years later, they are still said to be 'suffering the vengeance of eternal fire' (Jude 7)." He focuses our attention on two important truths from God's Word; the men are alive when they arrive, and they are still alive a thousand years later—and still experiencing suffering. He draws a profound conclusion: "the lake of fire is neither annihilation nor purgatorial because it neither annihilates nor purifies these two fallen foes of God and man after a thousand years under judgment."[8]

Hell has become an unpopular subject these days. As church historian Martin Marty noted, "Hell disappeared. And no one noticed."[9] There have been many attempts of late to soften the impact of this thoroughly biblical doctrine in favor of what C. S. Lewis called a grandfatherly God of indulgent kindness who would never consign anyone to hell, but says of anything we happen to like doing, "What does it matter so long as they are contended?"[10]

As God's judgment in Revelation clearly shows, God is not that soft. He intends to remake us in His own image, which is often a painful and self-denying process. If we refuse to be remade, we must endure the hellish consequence that choice brings. As John's vision shows us, hell is frightfully real. And it shows how deadly it is to be an enemy of the Almighty God. His power is infinite, and His justice is certain. No rebellion can stand against Him, and the consequences of such rebellion are terrible and eternal.

The Finality of Christ's Victory over Rebellion

"And the rest were killed with the sword which proceeded from the mouth of Him who sat on the horse" (Revelation 19:21). Here is how John F. Walvoord describes the victory:

> When Christ returns at the end of the tribulation period, the armies that have been fighting with each other for power will have invaded

the city of Jerusalem and will have been engaged in house-to-house fighting. When the glory of the second coming of Christ appears in the heavens, however, these soldiers will forget their contest for power on earth and will turn to fight the army from heaven (16:16; 19:19). Yet their best efforts will be futile because Christ will smite them with the sword in His mouth (19:15, 21), and they will all be killed, along with their horses.[11]

Again we see the utter futility of fighting against God. Not only will the leaders of the rebellion be flung into hell, but also all the armies that joined them will be slaughtered by the mighty strokes of Christ's deadly sword.

The Application of Christ's Second Coming

Throughout my years of ministry as a pastor and Bible teacher, I have talked to more than a few pastors and Christian leaders who expressed doubts concerning the relevance of Bible prophecy. They usually say something like this: "I don't preach on prophecy because it has nothing to do with the needs of my people today. I try to preach on more relevant topics. I leave prophecy to people like you, Dr. Jeremiah."

My response is that today there are few subjects more relevant than biblical prophecy. In fact, as we move into times that are so clearly depicted in the prophetic scriptures, some of my critics are beginning to get questions from their own congregants who are looking at today's headlines and asking, "What in the world is going on?" When I preached to my own church the messages that became the basis for this book, we recorded some of the highest attendance figures in the history of our congregation. I suspect that many had come to hear these messages because they were not getting meaningful answers from their own pastors. I cannot imagine being a pastor in today's cataclysmic world and not using the Word of God to give people God's perspective on world events.

In spite of the high value I place on understanding future events, I find that studying prophecy has an even higher and more practical value. It provides a compelling motivation for living the Christian life. The immediacy of prophetic events shows the need to live each moment in Christlike readiness. As revered Southern Baptist evangelist Vance Havner has put it, "The devil has chloroformed the atmosphere of this age." Therefore, in view of the sure promises of Christ's return, as believers, we are to do more than merely be ready; we are to be expectant. In our day of "anarchy, apostasy, and apathy," Havner suggests that expectant living means: "We need to take down our 'Do Not Disturb' signs . . . snap out of our stupor and come out of our coma and awake from our apathy."[12] Havner reminds us that God's Word calls to us to awake out of our sleep, and to walk in righteousness, in the light Christ gives us (Romans 13:11; 1 Corinthians 15:34; Ephesians 5:14).

Prophecy can provide the wake-up call that Dr. Havner calls for. When we have heard and understood the truth of Christ's promised return, we cannot just keep living our lives in the same old way. Future events have present implications that we cannot ignore. When we know that Christ is coming again to this earth, we cannot go on being the same people. From the New Testament epistles, I have gleaned ten ways in which we should be different as a result of our prophetic knowledge. For emphasis in each scripture quotation, I have italicized the words connecting the admonition with the promise of Christ's return.

1. *Refrain from judging others:* "Therefore judge nothing before the time, *until the Lord comes,* who will both bring

to light the hidden things of darkness and reveal the counsels of the hearts. Then each one's praise will come from God" (1 Corinthians 4:5).

2. *Remember the Lord's table:* "For as often as you eat this bread and drink this cup, you proclaim the Lord's death *till He comes*" (1 Corinthians 11:26).

3. *Respond to life spiritually:* "If then you were raised with Christ, seek those things which are above, where Christ is, sitting at the right hand of God. Set your mind on things above, not on things on the earth. For you died, and your life is hidden with Christ in God. *When Christ who is our life appears*, then you also will appear with Him in glory" (Colossians 3:1–4).

4. *Relate to one another in love:* "And may the Lord make you increase and abound in love to one another and to all, just as we do to you, so that He may establish your hearts blameless in holiness before our God and Father at *the coming of our Lord Jesus Christ* with all His saints" (1 Thessalonians 3:12–13).

5. *Restore the bereaved:* "But I do not want you to be ignorant, brethren, concerning those who have fallen asleep, lest you sorrow as others who have no hope. For if we believe that Jesus died and rose again, even so God will bring with Him those who sleep in Jesus. For this we say to you by the word of the Lord, that we who are alive and remain *until the coming of the Lord* will by no means precede those who are asleep. For the Lord Himself will descend from heaven with a shout, with the voice of an archangel, and with the trumpet of God. And the dead in Christ will rise first. Then we who are alive and remain shall be caught up together with them

in the clouds to meet the Lord in the air. And thus we shall always be with the Lord. Therefore comfort one another with these words" (1 Thessalonians 4:13–18).

6. *Recommit ourselves to the ministry:* "I charge you therefore before God and the Lord Jesus Christ, who will judge the living and the dead *at His appearing* and His kingdom: Preach the word! Be ready in season and out of season. Convince, rebuke, exhort, with all longsuffering and teaching" (2 Timothy 4:1–2).

7. *Refuse to neglect church:* "And let us consider one another in order to stir up love and good works, not forsaking the assembling of ourselves together, as is the manner of some, but exhorting one another, and so much the more *as you see the Day approaching*" (Hebrews 10:24–25).

8. *Remain steadfast:* "Therefore be patient, brethren, until the coming of the Lord. See how the farmer waits for the precious fruit of the earth, waiting patiently for it until it receives the early and latter rain. You also be patient. Establish your hearts, for *the coming of the Lord is at hand*" (James 5:7–8).

9. *Renounce sin in our lives:* "And now, little children, abide in Him, that *when He appears*, we may have confidence and not be ashamed before Him *at His coming*. If you know that He is righteous, you know that everyone who practices righteousness is born of Him" (1 John 2:28–29).

10. *Reach the lost:* "Keep yourselves in the love of God, *looking for the mercy of our Lord Jesus Christ* unto eternal life. And on some have compassion, making a distinction; but others save with fear, pulling them out of the fire, hating even the garment defiled by the flesh" (Jude 21–23).

Hoping and Longing for Christ's Return

One of the finest stories I've heard about men longing for their leader's return is that of explorer/adventurer Sir Ernest Shackleton. On Saturday, August 8, 1914, one week after Germany declared war on Russia, twenty-nine men set sail in a three-masted wooden ship from Plymouth, England, to Antarctica on a quest to become the first adventurers to cross the Antarctic continent on foot. Sir Ernest Shackleton had recruited the men through an advertisement: "Men wanted for hazardous journey. Small wages. Bitter cold. Long months of complete darkness. Constant danger. Safe return doubtful. Honour and recognition in case of success."

Not only was Shackleton an honest man, for the men did experience all that his handbill promised, but he was also an able leader and a certified hero. His men came to refer to him as "the Boss," although he never thought of himself that way. He worked as hard as any crew member and built solid team unity aboard the ship, aptly named *Endurance*. In January 1915, the ship became entrapped in an ice pack and ultimately sank, leaving the men to set up camp on an ice floe—a flat, free-floating slice of sea ice. Shackleton kept the men busy by day and entertained by night. They played ice soccer, had nightly songfests, and held regular sled-dog competitions. It was in the ice floe camp that Shackleton proved his greatness as a leader. He willingly sacrificed his right to a warmer, fur-lined sleeping bag so that one of his men might have it, and he personally served hot milk to his men in their tents every morning.

In April 1916, their thinning ice floe threatened to break apart, forcing the men to seek refuge on nearby Elephant Island. Knowing that a rescue from such a desolate island was unlikely, Shackleton and five others left to cross eight hundred miles of open Antarctic sea in a 22.5-foot lifeboat with more of a hope than a promise of a return with rescuers. Finally, on August 30, after an arduous 105-day trip and three earlier attempts, Shackleton returned to rescue his stranded crew, becoming their hero.

But perhaps the real hero in this story is Frank Wild. Second in command, Wild was left in charge of the camp in Shackleton's absence. He maintained the routine the Boss had established. He assigned daily duties, served meals, held sing-alongs, planned athletic competitions, and generally kept up morale. Because "the camp was in constant danger of being buried in snow . . . and become completely invisible from the sea, so that a rescue party might look for it in vain," Wild kept the men busy shoveling away drifts.

The firing of a gun was to be the prearranged signal that the rescue ship was near the island, but as Wild reported, "Many times when the glaciers were 'calving' and chunks fell off with a report like a gun, we thought that it was the real thing, and after a time we got to distrust these signals." But he never lost hope in the return of the Boss. Confidently, Wild kept the last tin of kerosene and a supply of dry combustibles ready to ignite instantly for use as a locator signal when the "day of wonders" would arrive.

Barely four days' worth of rations remained in the camp when Shackleton finally arrived on a Chilean icebreaker. He personally made several trips through the icy waters in a small lifeboat in order to ferry his crew to safety. Miraculously, the leaden fog lifted long enough for all the men to make it to the icebreaker in one hour.

Shackleton later learned from the men how they were prepared to break camp so quickly and reported: "From a fortnight after I had left, Wild would roll up his sleeping bag each day with the remark,

'Get your things ready, boys, the Boss may come today.' And sure enough, one day the mist opened and revealed the ship for which they had been waiting and longing and hoping for over four months." Wild's "cheerful anticipation proved infectious," and all were prepared when the evacuation day came.[13]

Shackleton's stranded crew desperately hoped that their leader would come back to them, and they longed for his return. But as diligent and dedicated as Shackleton was, they could not be certain he would return. He was, after all, a mere man battling elements he could not control, so they knew he might not make it back. Unlike that desperate crew, we have a certain promise that the Lord will return. Ours is not a mere longing or a desperate hope, as theirs was, for our Lord is the Creator and Master of all, and His promise is as sure as His very existence.

The prophets, the angels, and the apostle John all echo the words of promise from Jesus Himself that He will return. God's Word further amplifies the promise by giving us clues in prophecy to help us identify the signs that His return is close at hand. The signs that tell us the second coming of the Lord is drawing near should motivate us as never before to live in readiness. As we noted in chapter 5, the Rapture, which is the next event on the prophetic calendar, will take place seven years before the events we have discussed in this final chapter. Future events cast their shadows before them. As we anticipate His return, we are not to foolishly set dates and leave our jobs and homes to wait for Him on some mountain. We are to remain busy doing the work set before us, living in love and serving in ministry, even when the days grow dark and the nights long. Be encouraged! Be anticipating! We are secure; we belong to Christ. And as the old gospel song says, "Soon and very soon, we are going to see the King!"

Jewish Population Statistics

Country	1970	2007	Projected 2020
World	12,633,000	13,155,000	13,558,000*
Israel	2,582,000	5,393,000	6,228,000*
United States	5,400,000	5,275,000	5,200,000
France	530,000	490,000	482,000
Canada	286,000	374,000	381,000*
United Kingdom	390,000	295,000	238,000
Russia	808,000	225,000	130,000
Argentina	282,000	184,000	162,000
Germany	30,000	120,000	108,000

* indicates anticipated Jewish population growth

Source: Jewish People Policy Planning Institute, *Annual Assessment 2007* (Jerusalem, Israel: Gefen Publishing House LTD, 2007)

Conventional Oil Reserves by Country
June 2007

Rank	Country	Proved reserves (billion barrels) June 2007	Percentage world oil reserves
1	Saudi Arabia	264.3	21.9%
2	Iran	137.5	11.4%
3	Iraq	115.0	9.5%
4	Kuwait	101.5	8.4%
5	United Arab Emirates	97.8	8.1%
6	Venezuela	80.0	6.6%
6	Russia	79.5	6.6%

Rank	Country	Proved reserves (billion barrels) June 2007	Percentage world oil reserves
8	Libya	41.5	3.4%
9	Kazakhstan	39.8	3.3%
10	Nigeria	36.2	3.0%
11	United States	29.9	2.5%
12	Canada *	17.1	1.4%
13	China Qatar	16.3 15.2	1.3% 1.3%
	Total World Reserves	1,208,200,000,000	

* When oil sands are included, Canada ranks second with 178.8 billion barrels of proved reserve. Currently oil sands are excluded from classification as reserves by the US Securities and Exchange Commission and are not included in BP statistics.

NOTES

Introduction: Knowing the Signs

1. "Speech by Dmitri A. Medvedev," *The New York Times* online, 11 December 2007, www.nytimes.com/2007/12/11/world/europe/medvedev-speech.html (accessed 2 June 2008).

2. "UN warns of more unrest over food shortages," EuroNews, 23 April 2008, www.euronews.net/index.php?page=info&article=482404&lng=1 (accessed 2 June 2008).

3. Pascale Bonnefoy, "Evacuation Ordered as Chilean Volcano Begins to Spew Ash," 7 May 2008, http://www.nytimes.com/2008/05/07/world/americas/07chile.html?ref=world (accessed 7 May 2008).

4. Adam Entous, "Gaza headmaster was Islamic 'rocket maker,'" Reuters wire service, 5 May 2008; available at www.thestar.com.my/news/story.asp?file=/2008/5/5/worldupdates/2008-05-05T203555Z_01_NOOTR_RTRMDNC_0_-334136-1&sec=Worldupdates (accessed 2 June 2008).

5. Skip Heitzig, *How to Study the Bible and Enjoy It* (Carol Stream, IL: Tyndale House Publishers, 2002), 96.

6. Tim LaHaye, *The Rapture* (Eugene, OR: Harvest House Publishers, 2002), 88.

7. William Zinsser, *Writing About Your Life* (New York: Marlowe & Company, 2004), 155–156.

Chapter One: The Israel Connection

1. Romesg Ratnesae, "May 14, 1948," *Time*, http://www.time.com/time/magazine/article/0,9171,1004510,00.html (accessed 27 February 2008).

2. The Declaration of Independence (Israel), 14 May 1948, Israel Ministry of Foreign Affairs, "The Signatories of the Declaration of the Establishment of the State of Israel," http://www.mfa.gov.il/mfa/history/modern%20history/israel%20at%2050/the%20signatories%20of%20the%20declaration%20of%20the%20establis (accessed 25 February 2008).

3. Rabbi Binyamin Elon, *God's Covenant with Israel* (Green Forest, AR: Balfour Books, 2005), 12.

4. Mark Twain, "Concerning the Jews," *Harper's*, September 1899, 535.

5. "Jewish Nobel Prize Winners," Jewish Virtual Library, http://www.jewishvirtuallibrary. org/jsource/Judaism/nobels.html (accessed 26 February 2008); "Nobel Laureate Facts," Nobelprize.org, http://nobelprize.org/nobel_prizes/nobelprize_facts.html (accessed 27 February 2008); and "Jewish Nobel Prize Winners," The Jewish Contribution to World Civilization (JINFO), www.jinfo.org/Nobel_Prizes.html (accessed 27 February 2008).

6. Jewish People Policy Planning Institute, *Annual Assessment 2007* (Jerusalem, Israel: Gefen Publishing House LTD, 2007), 15.

7. David Jeremiah, *Before It's Too Late* (Nashville, TN: Thomas Nelson, Inc., 1982), 126.

8. Hal Lindsey, "I will bless them that bless thee," WorldNetDaily, 18 January 2008, www. wnd.com/index.php?pageId=45604 (accessed 27 June 2008).

9. Elon, *God's Covenant with Israel,* 17.

10. Ibid.

11. Abraham Joshua Heschel, *Israel: An Echo of Eternity* (Woodstock, VT: Jewish Lights Publishing, 1997), 57.

12. John Walvoord, "Will Israel Possess the Promised Land?" *Jesus the King Is Coming,* Charles Lee Feinberg, ed. (Chicago: Moody Press, 1975), 128.

13. Quoted by Josephus, *Antiquities* xiv. 7.2, Leob edition, cited in A. F. Walls, "The Dispersion," *The New Bible Dictionary* (Grand Rapids: Wm. B. Eerdmans Pub. Co., 1962), 313–319.

14. Joseph Stein, *Fiddler on the Roof* screenplay, 1971.

15. Joel C. Rosenberg, from the audio track of the DVD *Epicenter* (Carol Stream, IL: Tyndale House Publishers, Inc., 2007). Used with permission.

16. Rabbi Leo Baeck, "A Minority Religion," *The Dynamics of Emancipation: The Jew in the Modern Age,* compiled by Nahum Norbert Glatzer (Boston: Beacon Press, 1965), 61. Reprinted by permission of Beacon Press.

17. David McCullough, *Truman* (New York: Simon & Schuster, 1992), 619.

18. Gary Frazier, *Signs of the Coming of Christ* (Arlington, TX; Discovery Ministries, 1998), 67.

19. Chaim Weizmann, *Trial and Error* (New York: Harper & Brothers, 1949), 141–194.

20. Israel Ministry of Foreign Affairs, "The Balfour Declaration," http://www.mfa.gov.il/ MFA/Peace+Process/Guide+to+the+Peace+Process/The+Balfour+Declaration.htm (accessed 27 February 2008); see also http://www.president.gov.il/chapters/chap_3/ file_3_3_1_en.asp.

21. Quoted in Gustav Niebuhr, "Religion Journal: Political Expressions of Personal Piety Increase, as Bush and Gore Showed," *The New York Times,* 16 December 2000, http:// query.nytimes.com/gst/fullpage.html?res=990DEED61539F935A25751C1A9669C8B63 (accessed 27 February 2008).

22. Yossi Beilin, *His Brother's Keeper: Israel and Diaspora Jews in the Twenty-first Century* (New York: Schocken Books, 2000), 99.

23. *The Jewish People Policy Planning Institute: Annual Assessment 2007* (Jerusalem, Israel: Gefen Publishing House LTD, 2007), 15.

24. Milton B. Lindberg, *The Jew and Modern Israel* (Chicago: Moody Press, 1969), 7.

25. Clark Clifford, *Counsel to the President* (New York: Random House, 1991), 3.

26. Ibid., 4.

27. Ibid., 7–8.

28. Ibid., 13.

29. Ibid., 22.

30. McCullough, *Truman*, 620.

Chapter Two: The Crude Awakening

1. "The Story of Oil in Pennsylvania," Paleontological Research Institution, www.priweb. org/ed/pgws/history/pennsylvania/pennsylvania.html (accessed 1 October 2007).

2. Fareed Zakaria,"Why We Can't Quit," *Newsweek*, http://www.newsweek.com/id/123482 (accessed 25 February 2008).

3. Ibid.

4. Ronald Bailey, "Oil Price Bubble?" Reason Online, 26 March 2008, www.reason.com/ news/printer/125414.html (accessed 3 June 2008).

5. "This Week in Petroleum," Energy Information Administration, 19 March 2008, www. tonto.eia.gov/oog/info/twip.html (accessed 26 March 2008); and International Business Times: Commodities & Futures, "This Week in Petroleum", 19 March 2008, http://www. ibtimes.com/articles/20080319/this-week-in-petroleum-mar-19.htm (accessed 17 June 2008).

6. Dilip Hiro, "The Power of Oil," Yale Center for the Study of Globilization, 10 January 2006, http://yaleglobal.yale.edu/display.article?id=6761.

7. Oil-Proved Reserves, "BP Statistical Review of World Energy June 2007," BP Global, http://www.bp.com/liveassets/bp_internet/globalbp/globalbp_uk_english/reports_and_ publications/statistical_energy_review_2007/STAGING/local_assets/downloads/pdf/ statistical_review_of_world_energy_full_report_2007.pdf (accessed 4 March 2008). (Note: a complete chart with an explanation of Canadian reserves can be found in appendix B.)

8. Daniel P. Erikson, "Ahmadinejad finds it warmer in Latin America" (editorial), *Los Angeles Times*, 3 October 2007, www.latimes.com/news/opinion/sunday/ commentary/la-oe-erikson3oct03,0,5434188.story (accessed 3 October 2007).

9. Robert J. Morgan, *My All in All* (Nashville, TN: B&H Publishing, 2008), entry for April 22.

10. "Country Energy Profiles," Energy Information Administration, http://tonto.eia.doe. gov/country/index.cfm (accessed 26 March 2008). (Note: this information is accessible under the "Consumption" tab in the "Top World Oil Consumers, 2006" table.)

11. Zakaria, "Why We Can't Quit."

12. Sara Nunnally and Bryan Bottarelli, "Oil Consumption Statistics: the European Union's Oil Consumption Growth," *Wavestrength Options Weekly*, 3 March 2007, www. wavestrength.com/wavestrength/marketreport/20070307_Oil_Consumption_Statistics_ and_Global_Markets_Market_Report.html (accessed 3 June 2008).

13. Michael Grunwald, "The Clean Energy Scam," *Time*, 7 April 2008, 40–45.

14. "Jimmy Carter State of the Union Address 1980," 23 January 1980, Jimmy Carter Library & Museum, www.jimmycarterlibrary.org/documents/speeches/su80jec.phtml (accessed 3 June 2008).

15. "Confrontation in the Gulf: Excerpts from Bush's Statement on the U.S. Defense of Saudis," *The New York Times*, 9 August 1990, http://query.nytimes.com/gst/fullpage.htm l?res=9C0CE0DC1F3FF93AA3575BC0A966958260&sec=&spon=&pagewanted=all (accessed 26 March 2008).

16. Ann Davis, "Where Has All the Oil Gone?" *Wall Street Journal*, 6 October 2007, http:// www.energyinvestmentstrategies.com/infoFiles/articlePDFs/100607SpeculatorsOilPrice s.pdf (accessed 17 June 2008).

17. Remarks by Abdallah S. Jum'ah, "The Impact of Upstream Technological Advances on Future Oil Supply," speech transcript, Third OPEC International Seminar, 12–13 September 2006, http://www.opec.org/opecna/Speeches/2006/OPEC_Seminar/PDF/ Abdallah%20Jumah.pdf (accessed 21 August 2007).

18. "Oil War," Global Policy Forum, Security Council, 26 March 2003, http://www. globalpolicy.org/security/oil/2003/0326oilwar.htm (accessed 26 June 2008).

19. Paul Roberts, *The End of Oil: On the Edge of a Perilous New World* (Boston: Mariner Books, 2005), 337. Reprinted by permission of Houghton Mifflin Harcourt Publishing Company. All rights reserved.

20. Ibid.

21. "Mrs. Meir Says Moses Made Israel Oil-Poor," *The New York Times*, 11 June 1973.

22. Tim LaHaye, *The Coming Peace in the Middle East* (Grand Rapids, MI: Zondervan, 1984), 105.

23. Aaron Klein, "Is Israel sitting on enormous oil reserve?" WorldNetDaily, 21 September 2005, www.worldnetdaily.com/news/article.asp?ARTICLE_ID=46428 (accessed 27 August 2007).

24. Ibid.

25. Zion Facts, "What are the terms of the Joseph License?" and "What are the terms of the Asher-Menashe License?" http://www.zionoil.com/investor-center/zion-faqs.html (accessed 31 March 2008).

26. Dan Ephron, "Israel: A Vision of Oil in the Holy Land," *Newsweek*, 13 June 2007, http://www.newsweek.com/id/50060 (accessed 2 October 2007).

27. Paul Crespo, "Author: 'Something Is Going On Between Russia and Iran,'" Newsmax, 30 January 2007, http://archive.newsmax.com/archives/articles/2007/1/29/212432. shtml?s=1h (accessed 26 March 2008).

28. Joel C. Rosenberg, *Epicenter* (Carol Stream, IL: Tyndale House Publishers, 2006), 113.

29. Amir Mizroch, "Israel launches new push to reduce its oil dependency," *Jerusalem Post*, 27 September 2007, posted at Forecast Highs, http://forecasthighs.wordpress.com/2007/ 09/27/ Israel-launches-new-push-to-reduce-its-oil-dependency (accessed 2 October 2007).

30. Steven R. Weisman, "Oil Producers See the World and Buy It Up," *The New York Times*, 28 November 2007.

31. Don Richardson, *The Secrets of the Koran* (Ventura, CA: Regal Books, 2003), 161.

32. Nazila Fathi, "Mideast Turmoil: Tehran; Iranian Urges Muslims to Use Oil as a Weapon," *The New York Times*, 6 April 2002, http://query.nytimes.com/gst/fullpage.htm l?res=9A05E5D6173DF935A35757C0A9649C8B63&scp=3&sq=Nazila+Fathi&st=nyt (accessed 25 June 2008).

33. Paraphrased by Timothy George, "Theology in an Age of Terror," *Christianity Today*, September 2006; from C. S. Lewis, "Learning in Wartime," *The Weight of Glory and Other Addresses* (New York: Macmillan, 1949), 41–52.

34. C. S. Lewis, "Learning in Wartime," *The Weight of Glory and Other Addresses* (New York: Macmillan, 1949), 26.

35. Vance Havner, *In Times Like These* (Old Tappan, NJ: Fleming H. Revell, 1969), 21.

Chapter Three: Modern Europe . . . Ancient Rome

1. Adapted from David Jeremiah, *The Handwriting on the Wall* (Nashville, TN: Thomas Nelson, Inc., 1992), 15–16.

2. "The Mists of Time," Amazing Discoveries, http://amazingdiscoveries.org/the-mists-of-time.html (accessed 21 March 2008).

3. Tim LaHaye, Ed Hindson, eds., *The Bible Prophecy Commentary* (Eugene, OR: Harvest House Publishers, 2006), 226.

4. "The European Union," *Time*, 26 May 1930, http://www.time.com/time/magazine/article/0,9171,739314,00.html (accessed 8 October 2007).

5. William R. Clark, *Petrodollar Warfare: Oil, Iraq and the Future of the Dollar* (New Society Publishers, 2005), 198; see also W. S. Churchill, *Collected Essays of Winston Churchill, Vol. II* (London: Library of Imperial History, 1976), 176–186.

6. "The History of the European Union," Europa, http://europa.eu./abc/history (accessed 8 October 2007).

7. Compiled from "The EU at a glance—Ten historic steps," Europa, http://europa.eu (accessed 8 October 2007).

8. Michael Shtender-Auberbach, "Israel and the EU: A Path to Peace," The Century Foundation, 3 November 2005, http://www.tcf.org/list.asp?type=NC&pubid=1129 (accessed 10 October 2007).

9. Council of the European Union Presidency Conclusions, http://www.consilium.europa.eu/ueDocs/cms_Data/docs/pressData/en/ec/94932.pdf (accessed 17 June 2008).

10. "How are we organized?" Europa, http://europa.eu/abc/panorama/howorganised/index_en.htm (accessed 5 March 2008).

11. Alex Duval Smith, "Blair kicks off campaign to become EU President," *The Guardian*, 13 January 2008, http://www.guardian.co.uk/uk/2008/jan/13/politics.world (accessed 5 March 2008); see also Dan Bilefsky, "2 Leaders Back Blair as European Union President," *The New York Times*, 20 October 2007, http://www.nytimes.com/2007/10/20/world/europe/20europe.html?_r=1&oref=slogin (accessed 5 March 2007).

12. Arno Froese, *How Democracy Will Elect the Antichrist* (Columbia, SC: Olive Press, 1997), 165.

13. Quoted in David L. Larsen, *Telling the Old, Old Story: The Art of Narrative Preaching* (Grand Rapids, MI: Kregel, 1995), 214.

14. Jim Madaffer, "The Firestorm—Two Weeks Later," City of San Diego, www.sandiego. gov/citycouncil/cd7/pdf/enews/2003/the_firestorm.pdf (accessed 5 March 2008).

15. "Burned Firefighter Describes Cheating Death," NBC San Diego, 14 November 2007, www.nbcsandiego.com/news/14598732/detail.html (accessed 15 November 2007); Tony Manolatos, "Cal fire report recounts tragic incident, rescue," *Union Tribune* (San Diego), 9 November 2007, http://www.signonsandiego.com/news/metro/20071109-9999-1n9report.htm (accessed 5 March 2008); Tony Manolatos, "Pilot who rescued fire crew didn't feel like a hero," *Union Tribune* (San Diego), 30 October 2007, http://www.signonsandiego.com/news/metro/20071030-1400-bn30pilot.html (accessed 31 October 2007); and Tony Manolatos, "During rescue effort that turned tragic, an act of heroism," *Union Tribune* (San Diego), 23 October 2007, http://www.signonsandiego.com/news/metro/20071023-9999-bn23firedead.html (accessed 26 October 2007).

Chapter Four: Islamic Terrorism

1. Georges Sada, *Saddam's Secrets: How an Iraqi General Defied and Survived Saddam Hussein* (Brentwood, TN: Integrity Publishers, 2006), 285–286.

2. Ibid., 289.

3. "Public Expresses Mixed Views of Islam, Mormonism," Pew Research Center Publications, 25 September 2007, http://pewresearch.org/pubs/602/public-expresses-mixed-views-of-islam-mormonism (accessed 1 October 2007).

4. Sada, *Saddam's Secrets*, 289–290.

5. Adapted from "New Poll Shows Worry over Islamic Terror Threat, to Be Detailed in Special Fox News Network Report," Fox News, 3 February 2007, www.foxnews.com/story/0,2933,249521,00.html (accessed 16 October 2007).

6. "Hamas TV puppet 'kills' Bush for helping Israel," Reuters wire service, 1 April 2008, http://www.reuters.com/article/worldNews/idUSL0146737420080401 (accessed 1 April 2008).

7. Reza F. Safa, Foreword to Don Richardson, *The Secrets of the Koran* (Ventura, CA: Regal Books, 2003), 10.

8. Will Durant, *The Age of Faith* (New York: Simon & Schuster, 1950), 155.

9. Statistics compiled from "Major Religions of the World Ranked by Adherents," Adherents.com. http://pewresearch.org/pubs/483/muslim-americans (accessed 17 October 2007); and "Muslim Americans: Middle Class and Mostly Mainstream," Pew Research Center, www.adherents.com/Religions_By_Adherents.html (accessed 17 October 2007).

10. Durant, *Age of Faith*, 163.

11. Robert A. Morey, *Islam Unveiled: The True Desert Storm* (Sherman's Dale, PA: The Scholar's Press, 1991), 49.

12. Abd El Schafi, *Behind the Veil* (Caney, KS: Pioneer Book Company, 1996), 32.

13. Winfried Corduan, *Pocket Guide to World Religions* (Downers Grove, IL: InterVarsity Press, 2006), 80–85.

14. Information on the five pillars adapted from Norman L. Geisler and Abdul Saleeb, *Answering Islam*, 2nd ed. (Grand Rapids, MI: Baker Books, 2006), 301.

15. Benazir Bhutto, *Reconciliation: Islam, Democracy, and the West* (New York: HarperCollins, 2008), 2–3, 20.

16. "Text of Ibrahim Mdaires's Sermon," *The Jerusalem Post*, 19 May 2005.

17. Richardson, *Secrets of the Koran*, 69–71.

18. Oren Dorell, "Some say schools giving Muslim special treatment," *USA Today*, 25 July 2007, http://www.usatoday.com/news/nation/2007-07-25-muslim-special-treatment-from-schools_N.htm (accessed 16 October 2007); see also Helen Gao, "Arabic program offered at school," (San Diego) *Union Tribune*, 12 April 2007, http://www.signonsandiego.com/news/education/20070412-9999-1m12carver.html (accessed 16 October 2007).

19. Tony Blankley, *The West's Last Chance* (Washington, DC: Regnery Publishing, Inc., 2005), 21–23, 39.

20. Sada, *Saddam's Secrets*, 287.

21. Philip Johnston, "Reid meets the furious face of Islam," (London) *Telegraph*, 21 September 2006, http://www.telegraph.co.uk/news/uknews/1529415/Reid-meets-the-furious-face-of-Islam.html (accessed 13 March 2008).

22. Nick Britten, "Religions collide under the dreaming spires," (London) *Telegraph*, 4 February 2008, http://www.telegraph.co.uk/news/uknews/1577340/Religions-collide-under-the-dreaming-spires.html (accessed 13 March 2008).

23. "Sharia law in UK is 'unavoidable'," BBC News, 7 February 2008, http://news.bbc.co.uk/2/hi/uk_news/7232661.stm (accessed 13 March 2008).

24. Jonathan Wynne-Jones, "Bishop warns of no-go zones for non-Muslims," (London) *Telegraph*, 5 January 2008, http://www.telegraph.co.uk/news/uknews/1574694/Bishop-warns-of-no-go-zones-for-non-Muslims.html (accessed 13 March 2008).

25. "Vatican: Muslims now outnumber Catholics," *USA Today*, 30 March 2008, http://www.usatoday.com/news/religion/2008-03-30-muslims-catholics_N.htm (accessed 2 April 2008).

26. "Ahmadinejad's 2005 address to the United Nations," Wikisource: United Nations, http://en.wikisource.org/wiki/Ahmadinejad's_2005_address_to_the_United-Nations.

27. "Ahmadinejad: Wipe Israel off map," Aljazeera News, 28 October 2005, http://english.aljazeera.net/English/archive/archive?ArchiveId=15816 (accessed 4 June 2008).

28. Stan Goodenough, "Ahmadinejad: Israel has reached its 'final' stage,'" *Jerusalem Newswire*, 30 January 2008, www.jnewswire.com/article/2314 (accessed 4 June 2008).

29. Mark Bentley and Ladane Nasseri, "Ahmadinejad's Nuclear Mandate Strengthened After Iran Election," Bloomberg News, 16 March 2008, www.bloomberg.com/apps/news?pid=20601087&sid=aGUPH1VLn.7c&refer=home (accessed 4 June 2008).

30. John F. Walvoord and Mark Hitchcock, *Armageddon, Oil and Terror* (Carol Stream, IL: Tyndale House Publishers, 2007), 44.

31. "Roman Catholic Bishop Wants Everyone to Call God 'Allah,'" Fox News, 16 August 2007, http://www.foxnews.com/story/0,2933,293394,00.html (accessed 14 March 2008).

32. Stan Goodenough, "Let's Call Him Allah," *Jerusalem Newswire*, 21 August 2007, http://www.foxnews.com/story/0,2933,293394,00.html (accessed 14 March 2008).

33. "Roman Catholic Bishop," Fox News.

34. Ibid.

35. Hal Lindsey, "Does God care what He's called?" WorldNetDaily, 17 August 2007, www. wnd.com/index.php?pageId=43089 (accessed 27 June 2008).

36. Adapted from Dr. Robert A. Morey, *Islam Unveiled,* (Shermandale, PA: The Scholar's Press, 1991), 60.

37. Edward Gibbon, *The Decline and Fall of the Roman Empire* (London: Milman Co., n.d.), 1:365.

38. "A Testimony from a Saudi Believer," Answering Islam: A Christian-Muslim Dialog and Apologetic, http://answering-islam.org./Testimonies/saudi.html (accessed 20 April 2006).

Chapter Five: Vanished Without a Trace

1. "Firefighters Gain Ground as Santa Ana Winds Decrease," KNBC Los Angeles, 24 October 2007, http://www.knbc.com/news/14401132/detail.html (accessed 26 October 2007).

2. Bruce Bickel and Stan Jantz, *Bible Prophecy 101* (Eugene, OR: Harvest House Publishers, 1999), 124.

3. *Merriam-Webster Online*, s. v. "rapture," www.merriam-webster.com/dictionary/rapture (accessed 5 June 2008).

4. Alfred Tennyson, "Break, Break, Break," *Poems, Vol. II* (Boston: Ticknor, Reed and Fields, 1851), 144.

5. Tim LaHaye, *The Rapture* (Eugene, OR: Harvest House Publishers, 2002), 69.

6. "100 Nations' Leaders Attend Churchill Funeral," Churchill Centre, www. winstonchurchill.org/i4a/pages/index.cfm?pageid=801 (accessed 4 March 2008).

7. Bickel and Jantz, *Bible Prophecy*, 123.

8. Arthur T. Pierson, *The Gospel, Vol. 3* (Grand Rapids, MI: Baker Book House, 1978), 136.

9. Wayne Grudem, *Systematic Theology* (Grand Rapids, MI: Zondervan, 1994), 1093.

10. Gig Conaughton, "County Buys Reverse 911 System," *North County Times*, 11 August 2005, http://www.nctimes.com/articles/2005/08/12/news/top_stories/21_13_388_11_05. txt (accessed 4 March 2008); see also "Mayor Sanders Unveils New Reverse 911 System," KGTV, 6 September 2007, http://www.10news.com/news/14061100/detail.html (accessed 4 March 2008); Gig Conaughton, "Officials Laud High-Speed Alert System," North County Times, 27 October 2007, http://www.nctimes.com/articles/2007/10/26/ news/top_stories/21_36_2110_25_07.txt (accessed 18 March 2008); Scott Glover, Jack Leonard, and Matt Lait, "Two Homes, Two Couples, Two Fates," Los Angeles Times, 26 October 2007, http://www.latimes.com/news/local/la-me-pool26oct26,0,3755059.story (accessed 26 October 2007).

Chapter Six: Does America Have a Role in Prophecy?

1. Adapted from Newt Gingrich, *Rediscovering God in America* (Nashville, TN: Integrity, 2006), 130.

2. Peter Marshall and David Manuel, *The Light and the Glory* (Old Tappan, NJ: Revell, 1977), 17, 18.

3. "President's Proclamation," *The New York Times*, 21 November 1982, http://select. nytimes.com/search/restricted/article?res=F30611FB395DOC728EDDA80994 (accessed 15 April 2008).

4. "The Journal of Christopher Columbus (1492)," The History Guide: Lectures on Early Modern European History, www.historyguide.org/earlymod/columbus.html (accessed 2 November 2007).

5. "Washington's First Inauguration Address, April 30, 1789," Library of Congress, www. loc.gov/exhibits/treasures/trt051.html (accessed 5 June 2008).

6. John F. Walvoord, "America and the Cause of World Missions," *America in History and Bible Prophecy*, Thomas McCall, ed. (Chicago: Moody Press, 1976), 21.

7. Gordon Robertson, "Into All the World," Christian Broadcasting Network, http://www. cbn.com/spirituallife/churchandministry/churchhistory/Gordon_Into_World.aspx (accessed 1 November 2007).

8. Luis Bush, "Where Are We Now?" Mission Frontiers, 2003, http://www. missionfrontiers.org/2000/03/bts20003.htm (accessed 1 November 2007).

9. Abba Eban, *An Autobiography* (New York: Random House, 1977), 126.

10. Ibid., 134.

11. "The Worst of the Worst: The World's Most Repressive Societies," Freedom House, April 2007, http://www.freedomhouse.org/template.cfm?page=383&report=58 (accessed 1 November 2007).

12. Ronald Reagan, "Inaugural Address, January 20, 1981," Ronald Reagan Presidential Library Archives, National Archives and Records Administration, www.reagan.utexas. edu/archives/speeches/1981/12081a.htm (accessed 5 June 2008).

13. Quoted in Newt Gingrich, *Winning the Future: A 21st Century Contract with America* (Washington, DC: Regnery Publishing, Inc., 2005), 200.

14. John Gilmary Shea, *The Lincoln Memorial: A Record of the Life, Assassination, and Obsequies of Abraham Lincoln* (New York: Bunce and Huntington Publishers, 1865), 237.

15. Benjamin Franklin, "Speech to the Constitutional Convention, June 28, 1787," Library of Congress, http://www.loc.gov/exhibits/religion/rel06.html (accessed 18 June 2008).

16. William J. Federer, ed., *America's God and Country—Encyclopedia of Quotations*, (St. Louis: Amerisearch, Inc., 2000), 696.

17. Ibid., 697–698.

18. Jared Sparks, ed., *The Writings of George Washington*, 12 vols. (Boston: Little, Brown and Company, 1837), vol. III, 449.

19. "The Gettysburg Address," http://www.loc.gov/exhibits/gadd/gadrft.html (accessed 18 June 2008).

20. Charles Fadiman, ed., *The American Treasury* (New York: Harper & Brothers, 1955), 127.

21. Jay Gormley, "LISD to Repaint 'In God We Trust' on Gym Wall," CBS11TV.com, 1 April 2008, http://cbs11tv.com/business/education/LISD.Repaints.motto.2.689875.html (accessed 7 April 2008).

22. "Laus Deo," Snopes Urban Legends Reference Pages, www.snopes.com/politics/religion/lausdeo.asp (accessed 7 April 2008); see also "Washington Monument," www.snopes.com/politics/religion/monument.asp (accessed 7 April 2008).

23. Tim LaHaye, as cited by Dr. Thomas Ice, "Is America in Bible Prophecy?" Pre-Trib Research Center, http://www.pre-trib.org/article-view.php?id=14 (accessed 18 June 2008).

24. Tim LaHaye, "The Role of the U.S.A. in End Times Prophecy," *Tim LaHaye's Perspective*, August 1999, http://209.85.173.104/search?q=cache:ZEQ46V4CQRYJ:www.yodelingfrog.com/Misc%2520Items/(doc)%2520-%2520Tim%2520LaHaye%2520-%2520The%2520Role%2520of%2520the%2520USA%2520in%2520End%2520Times%2520Prophecy.pdf+%22Does+the+United+States+have+a+place+in+end+time+prophecy%3F%22&hl=en&ct=clnk&cd=1&gl=us&lr=lang_en (accessed 18 June 2008).

25. John Walvoord and Mark Hitchcock, *Armageddon, Oil and Terror,* (Carol Stream, IL: Tyndale House Publishers, 2007), 67.

26. "President Bush Meets with EU Leaders, Chancellor Merkel of the Federal Republic of Germany and President Barroso of the European Council and President of the European Commission," press release dated 30 April 2007, The White House, http://www.whitehouse.gov/news/releases/2007/04/20070430-2.html (accessed 28 March 2008).

27. "Transatlantic Economic Council," European Commission, http://ec.europa.eu/enterprise/enterprise_policy/inter_rel/tec/index_en.htm (accessed 28 March 2008).

28. Jerome R. Cossi, "Premeditated Merger: Inside the hush-hush North American Union confab," WorldNetDaily, 13 March 2008, http://www.worldnetdaily.com/index.php?fa=PAGE.view&pageId=58788 (accessed 28 March 2008).

29. Ibid.

30. Walvoord and Hitchcock, *Armageddon*, 68.

31. Ed Timperlake, "Explosive missing debate item," *The Washington Times*, 5 March 2008, http://www.washingtontimes.com/news/2008/mar/05/explosive-missing-debate-item (accessed 28 March 2008).

32. Ed Timperlake, "Explosive missing debate item," *The Washington Times*, 5 March 2008, http://www.washingtontimes.com/news/2008/mar/05/explosive-missing-debate-item (accessed 28 March 2008).

33. Ed Timperlake, "Explosive missing debate item," *The Washington Times*, 5 March 2008, http://www.washingtontimes.com/news/2008/mar/05/explosive-missing-debate-item (accessed 28 March 2008).

34. "U.S. says N. Korea missile tests 'not constructive,'" Reuters, 28 March 2008, http://www.reuters.com/article/idUSWAT00920520080328 (accessed 28 March 2008).

35. Walvoord and Hitchcock, *Armageddon*, 65.

36. La Shawn Barber, "America on the Decline," La Shawn Barber's Corner, 25 February 2004, http://lashawnbarber.com/archives/2004/02/25/brstronglatest-column-america-on-the-declinestrong/ (accessed 28 March 2008).

37. Adapted from Carle C. Zimmerman, *Family and Civilization* (Wilmington, DE: ISI Books, 2008), 255.

38. Mike Evans, *The Final Move Beyond Iraq* (Lake Mary, FL: Front Line, 2007), 168.

39. Herbert C. Hoover, *Addresses upon the American Road 1950–1955* (Palo Alto, CA: Stanford University Press, 1955), 111–113,117.

40. Mark Hitchcock, *America in the End Times*, newsletter, The Left Behind Prophecy Club.

41. Herman A. Hoyt, *Is the United States in Prophecy?* (Winona Lake, ID: BMH Books, 1977), 16.

Chapter Seven: When One Man Rules the World

1. Erwin Lutzer, *Hitler's Cross* (Chicago: Moody Press, 1995), 62–63.

2. Tim LaHaye and Ed Hinson, *Global Warning* (Eugene, OR: Harvest House, 2007), 195.

3. Charles Colson, *Kingdoms in Conflict* (Grand Rapids, MI: Zondervan, 1987), 129–130.

4. Lutzer, *Hitler's Cross*, 73.

5. Arthur W. Pink, *The Antichrist* (Minneapolis: Klich & Klich, 1979), 77.

6. Marvin Kalb and Bernard Kalb, *Kissinger* (New York: Little, Brown and Company, 1974), 201–202.

7. Colson, *Kingdoms in Conflict*, 68.

8. Ibid.

9. Thomas Ice, "The Ethnicity of the Antichrist," Pre-Trib Research Center, www.pre-trib.org/article-view.php?id=230 (accessed 5 June 2008).

10. *Conservapedia*, French Revolution, http://www.conservapedia.com/French_Revolution (accessed 18 June 2008).

11. W. A. Criswell, *Expository Sermons on Revelation*, vol. IV (Dallas: Criswell Publishing, 1995), 109.

12. David E. Gumpert, "Animal Tags for People?" *Business Week*, 11 January 2007, www.businessweek.com/smallbiz/content/jan2007/sb20070111_186325.htm?chan=smallbiz_smallbiz+index+page_today's+top+stories (accessed 11 April 2008).

13. Gary Frazier, *Signs of the Coming of Christ* (Arlington, TX: Discovery Ministries, 1998), 149.

Chapter Eight: The New Axis of Evil

1. "President Delivers State of the Union Address," press release dated 29 January 2002, The White House, http://www.whitehouse.gov/news/releases/2002/01/20020129-11.html (accessed 10 March 2008).

2. John F. Walvoord, *The Nations in Prophecy* (Grand Rapids, MI: Zondervan, 1978), 107.

3. Erik Hildinger, *Warriors of the Steppe: A Military History of Central Asia, 500 B.C. to 1700* (New York: DaCapo Press, 2001), 33.

4. Walvoord, *Nations in Prophecy*, 106.

5. Ibid.,101.

6. Edward Lucas, "The New Cold War," www.edwardlucas.com (accessed 6 June 2008).

7. Mike Celizic, "*Time*'s Person of the Year Is Vladimir Putin," *Today*: People-msnbc.com, 19 December 2007, http://www.msnbc.msn.com/id/22323855 (accessed 17 April 2008).

8. Nabi Abdullaev, "Speech Suggest Best Is Yet to Come," *Moscow Times*, 11 February 2008, http://www.moscowtimes.ru/article/1010/42/302320.htm (accessed 11 February 2008).

9. Oleg Shchedrov, "Putin in Jordan to demonstrate regional ambitions," Reuters AlertNet, 12 February 2007, www.alertnet.org/thenews/newsdesk/L12935084.htm (accessed 6 June 2008).

10. Ibid.

11. Hassan M. Fattah, "Putin Visits Qatar for Talks on Natural Gas and Trade," *The New York Times*, 13 February 2007, www.nytimes.com/2007/02/13/world/middleeast/13putin.html (accessed 17 April 2008).

12. Scott Peterson, "Russia, Iran Harden Against West," *Christian Science Monitor*, 18 October 2007, http://www.csmonitor.com/2007/1018/p06s02-woeu.html (accessed 18 June 2008).

13. "Russia scraps Libya's debts as Putin visits Tripoli," AFP (Agence France-Presse), April 2008, BNET Business Network, http://findarticles.com/p/articles/mi_kmafp/is_200804/ai_n25344293 (accessed 17 April 2008).

14. "EU should unite behind new Russia strategy: study," ViewNews.net, 7 November 2007, http://viewnews.net/news/world/eu-should-unite-behind-new-russia-strategy-study.html (accessed 18 June 2008).

15. Andris Piebalgs, "Gas warms EU-Russian ties," repost of *New Europe*, 7 April 2008, http://www.mgimo.ru/alleurope/2006/21/bez-perevoda1.html (accessed 21 July 2008).

16. "Iran," CIA-The World Factbook, https://www.cia.gov/library/publications/the-world-factbook/geos/ir.html (accessed 26 June 2008).

17. Borzou Daragahi, "Tehran sharing more nuclear data, agency says," *Los Angeles Times*, 31 August 2007, http://articles.latimes.com/2007/aug/31/world/fg-irannukes31 (accessed 31 August 2007).

18. "Ahmadinejad in new attack on 'savage animal,'" AFP news wire, 20 February 2008, http://afp.google.com/article/ALeqM5g_nrxYSrTbp_LIZcVU4VGCBpQ0hQ (accessed 6 June 2008).

19. Thom Shanker and Brandan Knowlton, "U.S. Describes Confrontation with Iranian Boats," *The New York Times*, 8 January 2008, http://www.nytimes.com/2008/01/08/washington/08military.html?scp=2&sq=U.S.+Describes+Confrontation+With+Iranian+Boats&st=nyt (accessed 26 June 2008).

20. Nazila Fathi, "Iran's President Says 'Israel Must Be Wiped Off the Map,'" *The New York Times*, 26 October 2007, http://www.nytimes.com/2005/10/26/international/middleeast/26cnd-iran.html (accessed 18 April 2008).

21. "UN boss alarmed by Hezbollah's threat against Israel," Agence France-Presse, 3 March 2008, http://findarticles.com/p/articles/mi_kmafp/is_200803/ai_n24365391 (accessed 3 March 2008).

22. Aaron Klein, "Hezbollah: Rockets fired into Israel directed by Iran," WorldNetDaily, 7 May 2007, http://www.worldnetdaily.com/news/article.asp?ARTICLE_ID=55572 (accessed 5 September 2007).

23. Ibid.

24. "UN boss alarmed by Hezbollah's threat against Israel," Agence France-Presse, 3 March 2008.

25. Edward Gibbon, *The Decline and Fall of the Roman Empire* (London: Milman Co., London, n.d.), 1:204.

26. David L. Cooper, *When Gog's Armies Meet the Almighty* (Los Angeles: The Biblical Research Society, 1958), 17.

27. Theodore Epp, *Russia's Doom Prophesied* (Lincoln, NE: Good News Broadcasting, 1954), 40–42.

28. Barry L. Brumfield, "Israel; Politically and Geographically," Israel's Messiah.com, www.israelsmessiah.com/palestinian_refugees/israel_vs_arabs.htm (accessed 6 June 2008).

29. Matthew Kreiger, "7,200 Israeli millionaires today, up 13%," *Jerusalem Post,* 28 June 2007, http://www.jpost.com/servlet/Satellite?pagename=JPost%2FJPArticle%2FShowFull&cid=1182951032508 (accessed 17 April 2008).

30. Serge Schmemann, "Israel Redefines Its Dream, Finding Wealth in High Tech," *The New York Times*, 18 April 1998, http://query.nytimes.com/gst/fullpage.html?res=9502EED7123CF93BA25757C0A96E958260&sec=travel (accessed 6 June 2008).

31. "Land of milk and start-ups," *Economist*, 19 March 2008, www.economist.com/business/displaystory.cfm?story_id=10881264 (accessed 29 April 2008).

32. "Israel," Legatum Prosperity Index 2007, Legatum Institute, http://www.prosperity.org/profile.aspx?id=IS (accessed 29 April 2008).

33. "Israel," CIA-The World Factbook, https://www.cia.gov/library/publications/the-world-factbook/geos/is.html (accessed 26 June 2008).

34. Joel C. Rosenberg, *Epicenter* (Carol Stream, IL: Tyndale House Publishers, 2006), 131.

35. H. D. M. Spence and Joseph Excell, eds., *The Pulpit Commentary*, vol. 28 (New York: Funk & Wagnalls, 1880–93), 298.

36. Robert J. Morgan, *From This Verse* (Nashville, TN: Thomas Nelson, Inc., 1998), entry for December 29.

Chapter Nine: Arming for Armageddon

1. Douglas MacArthur, "Farewell Address to Congress," delivered 19 April 1951, American Rhetoric, www.americanrhetoric.com/speeches/douglasmacarthurfarewelladdress.htm (accessed 6 June 2008).

2. Douglas Brinkley, ed., *The Reagan Diaries,* (New York: HarperCollins, 2007), 19, 24.

3. "American War Deaths Through History," Military Factory.com, www.militaryfactory.com/american_war_deaths.asp (accessed 6 June 2008).

4. Sylvie Barak, "Stephen Hawking says NASA should budget for interstellar travel: rising for the moon," The Inquirer (blog), 22 April 2008, www.theinquirer.net/gb/inquirer/news/2008/04/22/stephen-hawking-argues-nasa (accessed 6 June 2008).

5. Alan Johnson, *The Expositor's Bible Commentary* (Grand Rapids: Zondervan, 1981), 12:551.

6. Vernon J. McGee, *Through the Bible*, vol. 3 (Nashville, TN: Thomas Nelson, Inc., 1982), 513.

7. A. Sims, ed., *The Coming Great War*, (Toronto: A. Sims, Publisher, 1932), 7–8.

8. John Dryden, trans., *Plutarch's Life of Sylla*. Public domain.

9. Josephus, *The Wars of the Jews, Book 6* from *The Works of Josephus*, translated by William Whiston (Peabody, MA: Hendrickson Publishers, 1987); available online: "Josephus Describes the Roman's Sack of Jerusalem," Frontline, http://www.pbs.org/wgbh/pages/frontline/shows/religion/maps/primary/josephussack.html (accessed 26 June 2008).

10. J. Dwight Pentecost, *Things to Come—A Study in Biblical Eschatology* (Findlay, OH: Dunham Publishing Company, 1958), 347–48.

11. "Hamas offers truce in return for 1967 borders," Associated Press, 21 April 2008, www.msnbc.msn.com/id/24235665/ (accessed 6 June 2008).

12. John Walvoord and Mark Hitchcock, *Armageddon, Oil and Terror* (Carol Stream, IL: Tyndale House Publishers, 2007), 174.

13. Alon Liel, *Turkey in the Middle East: Oil, Islam, and Politics* (Boulder, CO: Lynne Rienner Publishers, 2001), 20–21.

14. John F. Walvoord, "The Way of the Kings of the East," *Light for the World's Darkness,* John W. Bradbury, ed. (New York: Loizeaux Brothers, 1944), 164.

15. Larry M. Wortzel, "China's Military Potential," US Army Strategic Studies Institute, 2 October 1998, www.fas.org/nuke/guide/china/doctrine/chinamil.htm (accessed 6 June 2008).

16. Sims, *The Coming Great War*, 12–13.

17. Robert J. Morgan, *My All in All* (Nashville: B&H Publishers, 2008), entry for July 16.

18. Randall Price, *Jerusalem in Prophecy* (Eugene, OR: Harvest House Publishers, 1998), 1179–1180.

Chapter Ten: The Return of the King

1. Lehman Strauss, "Bible Prophecy" Bible.org, http://www.bible.org/page.php?page_id=412 (accessed 27 November 2007).

2. John F. Walvoord, *End Times* (Nashville, TN: Word Publishing, 1998), 143.

3. Tim LaHaye, *The Rapture* (Eugene, OR: Harvest House Publishers, 2002), 89.

4. Harry A. Ironside, *Revelation* (Grand Rapids, MI: Kregel, 2004), 187–188.

5. Charles Spurgeon, "The Saviour's Many Crowns," a sermon (no. 281) delivered 30 October 1859, The Spurgeon Archive, www.spurgeon.org/sermons/0281.htm (accessed 7 June 2008).

6. Ironside, *Revelation*, 189.

7. W. A. Criswell, *Expository Sermons on Revelation*, vol. 5 (Grand Rapids, MI: Zondervan, 1966), 31.

8. Ironside, *Revelation*; 189–190.

9. Kenneth Woodward, "Heaven," *Newsweek*, 27 March 1989, 54.

10. C. S. Lewis, *The Problem of Pain* (New York: Macmillan, 1940, 1973), 28.

11. Walvoord, *End Times*, 171.

12. Vance Havner, *In Times Like These* (Old Tappan, NJ: Fleming H. Revell Company, 1969), 29.

13. Based on Sir Ernest Henry Shackleton, *South! The Story of Shackleton's 1914–1917 Expedition*, public domain, available at Project Gutenberg, www.gutenberg.org/files/5199/5199-h/5199-h.htm (accessed 7 June 2008).

Appendix B: Conventional Oil Reserves by Country, June 2007

1. Oil-Proved Reserves, "BP Statistical Review of World Energy June 2007," BP Global, http://www.bp.com/liveassets/bp_internet/globalbp/globalbp_uk_english/reports_and_publications/statistical_energy_review_2007/STAGING/local_assets/downloads/pdf/statistical_review_of_world_energy_full_report_2007.pdf (accessed 4 March 2008).

About the Author

DR. DAVID JEREMIAH IS THE SENIOR PASTOR OF SHADOW Mountain Community Church in El Cajon, California. He is the author of several best-selling books, and his popular syndicated radio and television Bible-teaching program, *Turning Point*, is broadcast internationally. David and his wife, Donna, have four children and ten grandchildren.

Steps to Peace With God

1. God's Purpose: Peace and Life

God loves you and wants you to experience peace and life—abundant and eternal.

The Bible says ...

"We have peace with God through our Lord Jesus Christ." *Romans 5:1, NIV*

"For God so loved the world that He gave His only begotten Son, that whoever believes in Him should not perish but have everlasting life." *John 3:16, NKJV*

"I have come that they may have life, and that they may have it more abundantly." *John 10:10, NKJV*

Since God planned for us to have peace and the abundant life right now, why are most people not having this experience?

2. Our Problem: Separation From God

God created us in His own image to have an abundant life. He did not make us as robots to automatically love and obey Him, but gave us a will and a freedom of choice.

We chose to disobey God and go our own willful way. We still make this choice today. This results in separation from God.

The Bible says ...

"For all have sinned and fall short of the glory of God." *Romans 3:23, NIV*

"For the wages of sin is death, but the gift of God is eternal life in Christ Jesus our Lord." *Romans 6:23, NIV*

Our choice results in separation from God.

People (Sinful)   God (Holy)

Our Attempts

Through the ages, individuals have tried in many ways to bridge this gap ... without success ...

The Bible says ...

"There is a way that seems right to a man, but in the end it leads to death."
Proverbs 14:12, NIV

"But your iniquities have separated you from your God; and your sins have hidden His face from you, so that He will not hear."
Isaiah 59:2, NKJV

There is only one remedy for this problem of separation.

3. God's Remedy: The Cross

Jesus Christ is the only answer to this problem. He died on the cross and rose from the grave, paying the penalty for our sin and bridging the gap between God and people.

The Bible says ...

"For there is one God and one mediator between God and men, the man Christ Jesus."
1 Timothy 2:5, NIV

"For Christ also suffered once for sins, the just for the unjust, that He might bring us to God."
1 Peter 3:18, NKJV

"But God demonstrates His own love toward us, in that while we were still sinners, Christ died for us." *Romans 5:8, NKJV*

God has provided the only way ... we must make the choice ...

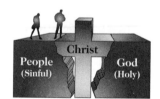

4. OUR RESPONSE: RECEIVE CHRIST

We must trust Jesus Christ and receive Him as Lord and Savior.

THE BIBLE SAYS ...

"Behold, I stand at the door and knock. If anyone hears My voice and opens the door, I will come in to him and dine with him, and he with Me." *Revelation 3:20, NKJV*

"But as many as received Him, to them He gave the right to become children of God, to those who believe in His name." *John 1:12, NKJV*

"If you confess with your mouth the Lord Jesus and believe in your heart that God has raised Him from the dead, you will be saved." *Romans 10:9, NKJV*

Are you here ... or here?

Is there any good reason why you cannot receive Jesus Christ right now?

HOW TO RECEIVE CHRIST:

1. Admit your need (say, "I am a sinner").
2. Be willing to turn from your sins (repent) and ask for God's forgiveness.
3. Believe that Jesus Christ died for you on the cross and rose from the grave.
4. Through prayer, invite Jesus Christ to come in and control your life through the Holy Spirit (receive Jesus as Lord and Savior).

WHAT TO PRAY:

> Dear Lord Jesus,
>   I know that I am a sinner, and I ask for Your forgiveness. I believe You died for my sins and rose from the dead. I turn from my sins and invite You to come into my heart and life. I want to trust and follow You as my Lord and Savior.
>
> In Your Name, Amen.
>
> _____   _____
> Date   Signature

God's Assurance: His Word

If you prayed this prayer,

the Bible says ...

"Everyone who calls on the name of the Lord will be saved."
Romans 10:13, NIV

Did you sincerely ask Jesus Christ to come into your life?
Where is He right now? What has He given you?

"For it is by grace you have been saved, through faith—and this not
from yourselves, it is the gift of God—not by works, so that no one
can boast." *Ephesians 2:8–9, NIV*

the Bible says ...

"He who has the Son has life; he who does not have the Son of God does not
have life. These things I have written to you who believe in the name of the
Son of God, that you may know that you have eternal life, and that you may
continue to believe in the name of the Son of God."
1 John 5:12–13, NKJV

Receiving Christ, we are born into God's family through the
supernatural work of the Holy Spirit who indwells every believer.
This is called regeneration or the "new birth."

This is just the beginning of a wonderful new life in Christ. To deepen
this relationship you should:

1. Read your Bible every day to know Christ better.
2. Talk to God in prayer every day.
3. Tell others about Christ.
4. Worship, fellowship, and serve with other Christians in a church where
   Christ is preached.
5. As Christ's representative in a needy world, demonstrate your new life
   by your love and concern for others.

God bless you as you do.

Billy Graham

If you are committing your life to Christ, please let us know!
Billy Graham Evangelistic Association
1 Billy Graham Parkway, Charlotte, NC 28201-0001
1-877-2GRAHAM (1-877-247-2426)
billygraham.org